The Vocation of a Teacher

OTHER BOOKS BY WAYNE C. BOOTH

The Rhetoric of Fiction (1961, 1983)

Now Don't Try to Reason With Me: Essays and Ironies for a Credulous Age (1970)

A Rhetoric of Irony (1974)

Modern Dogma and the Rhetoric of Assent (1974)

Critical Understanding: The Powers and Limits of Pluralism (1979)

The Harper & Row Rhetoric (with Marshall Gregory, 1987)

The Company We Keep: An Ethics of Fiction (1988)

EDITIONS

The Knowledge Most Worth Having (1967)

The Harper & Row Reader (with Marshall Gregory, 1984, 1988)

The VOCATION of a TEACHER

RHETORICAL OCCASIONS
1967–1988

Wayne C. Booth

THE UNIVERSITY OF CHICAGO PRESS

Chicago and London

WAYNE C. BOOTH is the George M. Pullman Distinguished
Service Professor in the Department of English Language and
Literature, the Committee on the Analysis of Ideas and Study of
Methods, and the College, University of Chicago.

The University of Chicago Press, Chicago 60637
The University of Chicago Press, Ltd., London

97 96 95 94 93 92 91 90 89 88   5 4 3 2 1

Library of Congress Cataloging-in-Publication Data
Booth, Wayne C.
    The vocation of a teacher : rhetorical occasions, 1967–1988 /
Wayne C. Booth.
        p.   cm.
    Includes index.
    ISBN 0-226-06581-2.   ISBN 0-226-06582-0 (pbk.)
    1. English philology—Study and teaching (Higher)—United States.
2. English language—Rhetoric—Study and teaching—United States.
3. English teachers—United States.   4. Teaching.   I. Title.
PE68.U5B66   1988
428'.007'1173—dc 19   88-14297
                                                                CIP

FOR ELEVEN BELOVED TEACHERS:

Miss Alice Parker,

> who in the first grade worried about how long it took a lumpish six-year-old to learn to read;

Miss Walker (first name unknown),

> who in the second grade suggested that this non-reader take home *The Wizard of Oz* "because it might not be too hard for you";

Mrs. Tuttle (first name unknown),

> who often read aloud to us in her fourth-grade class—*Tom Sawyer, Penrod and Sam*, and many a bouncing, silly poem;

Miss Jane McPherson,

> who insisted, tired as she was in her final years of teaching fifth and sixth grades, that we revise every one of our little essays; and who somehow led us to compose and perform wonderful dramas based on our reading;

Mr. Wadley (first name unknown),

> the only man in our school, who taught penmanship, poetic scansion, solfeggio, and three-part sight-reading—to sixth graders;

Miss Bessie Newman,

> who, though in her final illness, induced us reluctant ninth graders to perform *Julius Caesar;*

Miss Gene Clark,

> who in grade eleven flattered me into reading *Anthony Adverse* and *Brave New World;*

Mr. Luther Giddings,

> who in his chemistry class taught the liberal arts;

Mr. Karl Young,

> who in Freshman English unwittingly seduced me from chemistry to "LITCOMP";

Mr. "P. A." Christensen,

> who mocked my brilliantly ironic sophomore compositions because they lacked "unity, coherence, and emphasis";

Mr. Ronald Crane,

> who found so many genuine faults in my first *Tristram Shandy* chapter that I almost gave up on the doctoral program.

Human history becomes more and more a race between education and catastrophe.

H. G. Wells

Education has for its object the formation of character.

Herbert Spencer

Why, Hal, 'tis my vocation, Hal. 'Tis no sin for a man to labour in his vocation.

Falstaff, in *Henry IV, Part 1*.

By being so long in the lowest form [at Harrow] I gained an immense advantage over the cleverer boys. . . . I got into my bones the essential structure of the normal British sentence—which is a noble thing. Naturally I am biased in favor of boys learning English; and then I would let the clever ones learn Latin as an honour, and Greek as a treat.

Winston Churchill

Contents

Contents

Contents

ix

Preface

My title may seem to promise a bifurcated book: the calling of a teacher /
the calling of a "rhetorician." But of course I see the two as overlapping—
indeed as almost identical. To become a teacher of any subject is already to
aspire to skill in at least one kind of rhetoric, the kind that changes the
minds and possibly even the lives of students. And *English* teachers[1] are
enmeshed even more inextricably than other teachers in the problems that
were traditionally treated by rhetorical theorists—or so I shall try to show.
My hope is thus to present not two clashing perspectives but a kind of ste-
reoscopic, shifting image: through one lens, a forty-year vocation teaching
students who continue to be far more rewarding and responsive than our
recent popular exposés of national ignorance and educational disaster would
suggest; through the other, one possible view, a rhetorician's, of what our
job really is and how we might do it better.

A preliminary word, then, about my two overlapping lifetime projects:

Teaching English

"I assume you would agree that the profession of 'English' is in total,
shameful disarray?" My challenger, whom I have just met in the cocktail
hour before a banquet at which Secretary of Education William Bennett will
be the main speaker, is Joseph Epstein, editor of *The American Scholar* and
of a fine compilation of tributes to great teachers.[2]

What do you answer to a charge like that? Do you say, "Oh, yes, in-
deedy, we are in total, shameful disarray. You members of the wiser public
are quite right; we teachers have all sold out, we are all timeservers and
deadbeats; none of us knows what's what, not in the way you laymen, you
editors and bureaucrats do"?

I don't say that. Instead I say: "Well, we have our problems, but I think
we are obviously clearer about what we're doing than you magazine editors

---

1. I had taught English for a decade or so before I learned that some of my colleagues
considered the very phrase "English teacher" a solecism. "We are not 'English'—that is 'British'—teachers; we are teachers *of* English." I belong to the National Council of Teachers *of*
English, not the National Council of English Teachers; I teach in a Department *of* English, not
in one of those benighted English Departments. But I prefer now to think of myself as what I
started out to be (see Occasion 1): an English teacher.

2. *Masters: Portraits of Great Teachers* (New York, 1981).

are about *your* roles." Not a brilliant reply. He quite rightly ignores it and continues his charge.

"Well, everyone knows that most of you have simply bought into the latest fads—deconstruction, feminism, Marxism, God-knows-what. So far as I can tell, nobody is teaching students how to think critically, or how to read and write at a literate level. All of the studies show . . ."[3]

I assume, in my annoyance, that he has been doing some uncritical reading of the report of the National Assessment of Educational Progress, and of books like E. D. Hirsch's *Cultural Literacy*, Allan Bloom's *The Closing of the American Mind*, William Bennett's *To Reclaim a Legacy*, Diane Ravitch and Chester E. Finn's *What Do Our 17-Year-Olds Know?*, and Lynn Cheney's *American Memory*.[4] So I interrupt him to say that he ought to do a bit more hard thinking and actual observing before he . . .

But we are called to table and we part without my having a chance to set him straight. I could have told him, for example, about the excitement of the three-week "Coalition conference" I attended in July, along with fifty-nine other English teachers—elementary, secondary, and "higher"—a wonderfully challenging bunch who would shatter any observer's easy diagnoses and prescriptions about America's educational ills.[5] But it would have done no good, I can be sure. How can one hope to mediate between that group of devoted, articulate, energetic, and by-no-means despairing English

3. I must confess that, like Thucydides, like Herodotus, like Gibbon, like *Time* magazine, I report from memory speeches that must in fact have been somewhat different. Thucydides describes his own solution to the problem of historical accuracy: "My habit has been to make the speakers say what was in my opinion demanded of them by the various occasions, of course adhering as closely as possible to the general sense of what they really said." Our newspapers and weeklies don't seem to try even that hard. I aim for more literal accuracy than Thucydides claims, but I know from painful experience (checking diaries, comparing accounts of my past with hard data) that my capacity for literal verbal memory is no better than— yours?

4. National Assessment of Educational Progress, *Literature and U.S. History: The Instructional Experience and Factual Knowledge of High-School Juniors* (Princeton, 1987); E. D. Hirsch, Jr., *Cultural Literacy: What Every American Needs to Know* (Boston, 1987); Allan Bloom, *The Closing of the American Mind: Education and the Crisis of Reason* (New York, 1987); William Bennett, *To Reclaim a Legacy* (Washington, 1984); Diane Ravitch and Chester E. Finn, Jr., *What Do Our Seventeen-year-olds Know? A Report on the First National Assessment of History and Literature* (New York, 1987); Lynn Cheney, *American Memory: A Report on the Humanities in the Nation's Public Schools* (Washington, 1987).

5. The "Coalition conference" was sponsored by an "English Coalition" representing the following eight organizations: the Association of Departments of English, the College Language Association, the Conference for Secondary School English Department Chairpersons, the National Council of Teachers of English, the College English Association, the Conference on College Composition and Communication, the Conference on English Education, and the Modern Language Association. I offer a few pages about it at the end of Occasion 13.

teachers, and critics like Epstein with their easy indictments? In a way this book is an attempt at that impossible task, though I cannot, with the manuscript already in press, insert a full account of the Coalition's many ways of throwing doubt upon the superficialities and dogmatisms of those well-meaning popular critics. In any case, the book might be thought of as a start on what I'd like to say the next time a critic offers me some simple nostrum that in my view is more likely to kill than cure.

What *is* the profession of English teaching? Where *are* we, and where should we go from here? I here gather together a few of my efforts to think in public about such questions. In speeches and essays addressed mainly to students and teachers, only rarely or indirectly to members of "the public" like Epstein, I have tried both to uncover what we are up to in this puzzling profession, still only about a century old,[6] and to dramatize its importance. To be an English teacher—what is that? I turn to this vexing question in the introduction to Part One.

Practicing Rhetoric

"Occasional pieces" of the kind collected here are by definition not offerings of truths for the ages: each one is bound to its time and place. To some readers that may seem to condemn them, but any rhetorician will want to take that condemnation as a further occasion for thought: Just what *are* my time and my place? Today, addressing these readers? This decade, in Chicago? This century, in America? This bi-millennium, in Western Civilization? Our few million years' sojourn, on a troubled and perhaps lone planet? Some of my arguments seem placed in a time as old as Adam, while others will seem dated before the reviewers move in on me. None has a tone of permanence; I cannot claim, as some philosophers and scientists and poets do, that I am above the battle—whatever the battle turns out really to have been.

Those who pursue truth and beauty in pure forms, untainted by occasion, unconcerned for audiences, are never as different from the rhetorician as they sometimes claim. Human beings are by definition "occasional"—or what philosophers used to call "contingent"; we are part of the ever-fading, ever-renewing world. I have no doubt, unlike some of my fellow rhetoricians, that there are such things as eternal truths and beauties and "goods" (truth and beauty perhaps even the supreme goods); whatever they are, let us pursue them, let us even worship them. But let us not delude ourselves

---

6. See Gerald Graff, *Professing Literature: An Institutional History* (Chicago, 1987), for the best account I know of how we got to where we are today.

about the permanence of any one account of their splendors. Though philosophers, mathematicians, physicists, and even poets may try to ignore the restraints of occasions and address only eternal truths, everything they say can later be easily placed: nobody speaking in any other time or place would speak in quite *that* way. Even the aesthete who envies Euclid for looking on beauty bare and who writes with no thought about readers, even the purest poet must write from some unique here and now. Future academic examiners may legitimately ask students to place any author's special embrace of the eternal into its country and century, or even into its province and decade.

Still, there is something *more* occasional about these pieces of mine than about many an academic collection. Here the historical moment, with its peculiar rhetorical demands, is brought on the scene, often becoming a large part of the subject itself. Most of the pieces were "commissioned" (though often without fee). Almost all were composed with a quite precise picture of a specific occasion in mind: hall, podium, mike, and audience. Indeed, as I wrote them—and they were all written and revised many times before I arrived at a more or less "spontaneous" delivery—I heard myself speaking them (usually trying them out, aloud), and I always wrote with some kind of imaginary picture of listeners responding with smiles, scowls, or furrowed brows. Such prophecies often proved to be wildly awry: an imagined audience of thirty teachers who would have read the materials I sent them in advance turned out, in the reality faced a week or so later, to be ten teachers, along with two hundred captive freshmen reluctantly attending as part of their "reading" assignment; the audience for a "public lecture" was discovered to contain nobody from the public, only teachers. But such surprises don't really matter; the pictures have done their work. They have required me to put what I have to say into a language and form that I think best suited to get it heard, *here and now.*

That kind of attention to audience is part of what a committed rhetorician is committed to. It is by no means all, as I hope my discussions of rhetoric in Occasions 2, 6, and 19 will show. The study of rhetoric leads us into locations and stances that will surprise anyone who thinks of it only in the contemptuous definition implied whenever it appears in a newspaper headline. Most strikingly, students of rhetoric—in contrast to most students of linguistics, say—usually dwell on ways to improve it; we claim that some uses of rhetoric are better than others, and even that some occasional utterances turn out to be "for the ages." We devote our lives—and our occasional discourses—to discovering what makes for good rhetoric on a good rhetorical occasion.

The quest is naturally a bit imperialistic. Again and again throughout history, rhetoric has claimed for itself what I claim for it in Occasion 19:

entire dominion over all verbal pursuits. Logic, dialectic, grammar, philosophy, history, poetry—*all* are rhetoric. Even the graphic and musical arts have sometimes been claimed. But though the notion that "everything is rhetoric" is not a modern invention, this century, with its emphasis on language as the center of all inquiry, has perhaps exhibited more than its share of us empire-builders. Even the recent fashion in "deconstructing" all inquiries into their rhetorical tropes can be seen as just one further manifestation of the age-old claim with which I began: every writer or speaker addresses an occasion—and hence is a rhetorician.

It is hardly surprising, then, that when I became an "English teacher" I soon found myself viewing more and more of that confused stack of subjects called "English" as simply branches of rhetoric. And when I later on began to talk publicly about the profession and how to improve it, I naturally put my own rhetoric into the language of traditional rhetoricians. Soon I was declaring myself as not just an English teacher but a professor of rhetoric.

In doing so again now, I obviously risk attracting to my enterprise all of the pejorative overtones that the term "rhetoric" has accumulated since the time of Plato. "You'll say anything that will produce an effect, regardless of the truth." "You don't care about substance, only about surface." "Why should I believe you, when you implicitly claim to have been trained, as a sophist, to make the worse appear the better cause? The speaker I want to believe is the one who speaks spontaneously, from the heart, pursuing truth unstintingly, uncorrupted by the artifices and trickeries of mere rhetoric."

I can't do much about such charges here (though I face them in several of the following pieces), except to give the boy scout's salute and swear that, while in every case I have of course done what I could to "accommodate to the audience," as the tradition has it, I have tried never to sacrifice whatever truth even the most disinterested inquiry would lead an inquirer to say about the subject—whatever seemed to me, in that time and place, to be *the* truth. Pursuing what I have hoped will become a *shared* truth, I have always tried to discover, not only in the situation, but in my subject and its solid resistance to manipulation, what Aristotle calls "all the available means of persuasion"—including the means of persuading myself. I think of the results less as models for "how to do it" than as invitations to consider the most important of all professions as a vocation—a calling to improve our innumerable rhetorical occasions.

If my personal fusion of "English" and "rhetoric" is in a sense a kind of historical accident, I consider it a happy one, since I would not have met at least some of those to whom I dedicate the book if "English" as a field had been less ambiguously defined.

Still, the vocation is obviously not confined to anybody's definition of "English." I might well have discovered the profession of teacher-as-rhetorician (and what I later will rather timidly call "rhetorologist") if I had begun my studies under quite a different label. I have colleagues in this newly flourishing grand old field who are officially teachers of "speech" or "communications" or even political science; some are classicists, medieval historians, philosophers, lawyers, sociologists, cultural anthropologists. At least one is an economist, and I know two who teach accounting. But "English" departments are (at least in America) the home of a large majority of those who do serious rhetorical research and teaching, with or without the label. English departments have in this century carried the major responsibility for general education in the arts that classically were assigned to rhetoric: the arts of reading (or interpretation), of writing and speaking, and of the thinking that is inseparable from good writing and speaking. Every college that has any requirements at all requires some kind of freshman course in what I early learned to call "LITCOMP": a fusion of serious encounters with powerful writing and instruction in how to write well. Throughout my lifetime that course has generally been staffed by those of us who call ourselves English teachers. This marriage of rhetoric with something called English may prove quite temporary, as is suggested by the founding in the last decade or so of an increasing number of independent composition staffs and rhetoric departments. The marriage has never been free of tensions and charges of abuse and neglect. But for me, ever since that glorious freshman year in the LITCOMP class taught by an "English teacher," Karl Young, the marriage has seemed almost as natural as breathing.

To turn miscellaneous occasions into a genuine book requires some tough decisions, even when, as is true here, the various subjects addressed really belong together. For one thing, just how much of the repetition that was inevitable as the speaker moved from occasion to occasion will readers of a *book* tolerate or enjoy? As linguists insist, every act of communication depends on a good deal of "redundancy": what looks like "the same thing" must be said many times if it is to be heard at all. Every author must thus decide, consciously or unconsciously, just how much repetition will be found useful or tolerable—by some imagined, ideal reader. But collections are a special problem: the book may say to the collector, "Cut that anecdote, that allusion: you already used it back on page 35"—only to hear the original occasion reply, in wounded tones, "You can't cut *that*: it's essential to my argument here." Often I've listened to the book, even when it has ruled out many a favorite speech or essay. But sometimes I've had to honor the occasion.

xvi

The fuzzy borderline is what makes the trouble. Should I, for example, cut my reference to Malcolm X in one essay just because I have referred to him, though much more briefly, in another? To cut him from either would distort the case I wanted to make for *that* audience. (Indeed, Malcolm X appeared in four talks that I do not reprint; for some time there in the sixties I found him pertinent to almost every occasion.) Or again, should I cut my notion of courses in "Curiosity" from the speech to undergraduates in 1968, because I developed it further in a utopian spoof addressed to beginning scholars in 1981 and in my speech to the entire University of Chicago community in 1987? My hope is that there are no repetitions not justified by altered occasions and emphases.

A second editing problem was raised by readers who advised me to cut all allusions and examples that "date" these pieces. Should I bring each early essay up to date, by changing references to fit 1988? To do so would be to weaken the very embeddedness in occasion that I have wanted to emphasize. I have thus confined my revisions mostly to clarifying what I said *then*, not to making each piece say exactly what I would say *now*.

To hold to that decision has been especially difficult as I have faced the abundant instances of "critic . . . *he*" and "teacher . . . *his*" in the earlier pieces. These days I do not let myself say, "Every teacher must face his own choices," even though the various stylistic dodges that this choice forces me into are sometimes cumbersome (see Occasion 3, note 1). Many of my colleagues, male and female, resent the fussing of us feminists, female and male, about a usage that is "built into the language and that everyone understands as covering both sexes." I think that *they* are wrong, for reasons that Occasion 11 only partially makes clear. In any case, I've kept the pronouns pretty much as originally spoken or published because that's a fair record of how I (one? men?) wrote and spoke then. Only on Occasion 9 have I tried to clean things up and thus in a sense lied about my past.

Except for Occasions 3 and 13, these pieces were originally spoken; I was armed with a complete typescript but improvised frequently and sometimes relied heavily on physical signs of humor, sincerity, and passion. Written and spoken English differ more than most people realize; what has been spoken to good effect may prove puzzling or ineffective or even embarrassing when read cold. I've had to cut many of the jokes, corny when read cold, and I've revised some sentences to provide written equivalents for what in delivery was sometimes repaired on the spur of the moment and sometimes papered over with a confident smile. But to have removed all signs of oral delivery would have violated the entire project.

It would be absurd to try to acknowledge all of those who have contributed, as listeners and readers, to the final form of this volume. But it would be even more absurd not to thank two of them: Phyllis Booth, not only for reading various drafts but for frequently saving me from panic, a week or so before delivery, by suggesting possible rhetorical maneuvers; and Winifred Horner, for a reading that taught me what the book is really about.

PART I · TO STUDENTS AND TEACHERS UNDER SIEGE

You should never be polite to an English teacher. They don't deserve it. As a group, they are the most persistent and petty nitpickers in our entire society.

Mike Royko

He who can, does. He who cannot, teaches.

Attributed to many, including G. B. Shaw. Quoted by nine out of ten parents whose children consider teaching as a career.

C-l-e-a-n, clean, verb active, to make bright, to scour. W-i-n, win, d-e-r, winder, a casement. When the boy knows this out of the book, he goes and does it.

Mr. Squeers, in *Nicholas Nickleby*

It is safer to have a whole people respectably enlightened than a few in a high state of science and the many in ignorance.

Thomas Jefferson

To be an educator is quite obviously *not* a noble thing to be. But it is surely one of the best remaining ways to combat an ignoble world.

Anonymous

INTRODUCTION · *The Occasions*

What kind of "occasion," exactly, is faced by anyone choosing to become an English teacher in these late, threatening decades of a most puzzling and threatening century?

I

January, 1984

"How did your interview go?"

"Oh, it was awful, just awful."

Because she hadn't phoned me to talk about it after the MLA meetings at Christmas, I had expected something like her reply. But it feels to me like a personal blow anyway. It was her only interview—one response to twenty-nine letters to twenty-nine departments that had advertised positions.

"I'm sorry. Tell me what happened."

"Well, I went in and they mumbled introductions, and I sat down. And the first thing they said was, 'We've not had time to read your dossier, so why don't you begin by telling us about your dissertation?' So that was all right, in a way, because you and I had practiced that, but I didn't get far before Professor T——, whose work I didn't know, interrupted to ask me about various influences on the poems. I tried to explain that I'm not doing an influence study, but there was more interruption to ask about my theories of influence, and about what I thought had influenced the later work of Hardy. And I tried to explain that my study was entirely of the poems and the early novels, but by this time I was scared, and they were beginning to seem hostile. And then I began to feel mad, especially after Professor T—— began tapping with his pencil in a nervous way, and then stood up and began to thumb the pages of a book, as I tried to talk.

"At the end, Professor T—— said, 'Well, goodbye, Miss—or should I call you Mrs. or Ms., ah . . . ,' and then he got my name wrong. Oh, I know that it was all hopeless—and I couldn't even use it as a 'learning experience,' because I had no other interviews to turn to."

Her dissertation will be completed this month. After seven years of graduate study, she has been given one interview, by six men who had not read her dossier, had not read the chapter she sent them, had no knowledge of why she stood before them as an "older" woman, and insisted on fitting her work into a pattern of influence studies that she explicitly disclaims.

3

I try to console her a bit—but with what topics? I go to my library study, where I will work—once I have completed this note—on an article that is overdue. I usually enjoy working on that article, and I'll no doubt enjoy it this morning; I'm getting into that final phase when I discover what it is I've been trying to say, and that is usually fun. But at the moment I'm depressed, about the student's prospects, about my inability to help her, and about the quality of the men who conducted that interview. Even if I discount something from her picture of how they behaved, they behaved badly, rudely, stupidly, unprofessionally.

In effect they said to her, "We have invited you to travel a thousand miles for this one interview, but we have not troubled to find out whether we're interested in you or not. We are the buyers in a buyers' market. Tell us whether you are interesting." I feel like writing a protest letter, but of course I will not, because I may have to appeal to them about some other student another year. . . .

And so now, years later, I try to comfort myself with the forlorn hope that Professor T—— may stumble upon the following indictment:

> You there, you at Parlous State, I want you to know that nobody told me, when I joined up, that there were master sergeants like you in the company. If I'd suspected, I'd've taken up politics, where I would expect to meet some people who will destroy others when they can. May you have many sleepless nights; may your dreams be guilty nightmares.
>
> Yours truly,
> Wayne Booth
>
> P.S. Your victim recovered; she now teaches and publishes—brilliantly, as you could have predicted if you had taken the trouble to *see* her.

II

Twenty minutes out, on a flight from Utah to Chicago, my seatmate on the aisle interrupts my reading of *Time* magazine.

"Do you have trouble reading that magazine?"

I think he is asking whether it ever makes me angry, and I answer, "Yes."

"Me, too. Sometimes in a single issue I'll find eight or ten words I don't know the meaning of. I'm a college graduate, too. Computer science."

He pauses, looks me in the eye. "You a teacher?"

I admit it.

"What field?"

"English."

"Why do *you* have trouble, then?"

"Well, my troubles usually come when I catch them distorting news, or making stuff up."

"Golly, do they *do* that?"

"Oh, yes. Especially the quotations."

"How do you tell when *that* happens? You teach journalism or something?"

Before we know it we are in a lively, sometimes heated discussion about how one might read *Time*. As we approach Chicago, he says, "You teach that kind of thing to your students?"

"I try to, though we usually don't spend any time discussing *Time*."

"How do you suppose it was that none of *my* teachers talked about that kind of thing? It just makes me wish I could start my education over. Oh, I shouldn't say that, should I—talking with an English teacher and ending a sentence with a preposition! . . . Still, I *would* like to start over. But of course it's too late."

III

Four colleagues meet to plan a new course in criticism, for senior students.

"To me it would be disastrous," the full professor says, "to give a course in criticism that did not include a great deal of practical criticism. It's true that these days our students need a good strong dose of philosophically oriented theory; they've always needed that, and around here we've usually tried to give it to them. But they also need to know what the theory is *for*, and they learn that only by trying to apply various critical positions to novels, plays, or poems. So what I suggest . . ."

An assistant professor interrupts.

"Why do you think that critical theory is not a discipline worth studying in its own right?"

"What do you mean?"

"Why shouldn't they study the important theories of meaning and interpretation just in order to learn those theories?"

"Well, because none of those theories I can think of are as important, *as human achievements*, and thus as permanent possessions for the students, as the great works of literature. Don't you see . . ."

"According to what theory of literature do you make that claim? A wonderfully revealing word you use: 'possessions.' Don't you think that students should be made aware that every such claim is theory-ridden, and that the best minds of this century have thematized the problematics of what that theory-embeddedness means for us all?"

The discussion warms into a near-quarrel, and an associate professor (tenured) intervenes.

"Well, we don't have to decide this issue for certain at the beginning. Why don't we begin by trying out two versions, one with practical criticism included, the other with pure theory. Let's see what theory we would teach, if we *did* decide to study theory for its own sake."

They all agree, with seeming good grace.

The assistant professor takes the lead.

"In this century, literary studies have undergone the most important revolution ever. This is the golden age of criticism and theory. In my view it is a crying shame if our students graduate without knowing about the revolution from the inside. So I propose that we make up a list of the major figures, starting with Wittgenstein, or maybe Saussure, even, and ending with Derrida. Offhand, I would suggest . . ."

The senior professor interrupts.

"You're suggesting that we teach a course in literary criticism and theory and not even *mention* Aristotle or Plato or Johnson or Coleridge or Arnold or . . ."

"That's exactly what I am suggesting. Anybody who has understood anything about where we are now knows that the underpinnings of all that crowd have been permanently knocked out. Of course if you want to teach a *history* of *criticism*, those guys would have to be in it, but I thought we were trying to teach criticism and theory as something to be taken *seriously*, and what is serious is . . ."

Now the fourth teacher interrupts, a woman in her second year as an assistant professor.

"All you guys seem to me to be missing the boat. None of you has even mentioned Marx, let alone women's studies. If you're going to talk about revolution, why not talk about the liveliest criticism going on, and that is surely feminist criticism. Wayne Booth has said so; Jonathan Culler has said so; Jean Hagstrum has said so. I think that you're right [turning to the senior professor] that we should have a lot of practical criticism, but it should be genuinely practical, not that old I. A. Richards and New Critical shit; it should be the kind that . . ."

And on they go. No agreement is reached, except that at the end they all agree to meet again, this time to talk at greater length about the "grounds" of their enterprise, and possibly to plan a jointly-taught course that would pursue, with students, what those grounds might be.

IV

"What do you do?"

"I teach English."

Sometimes the response will be a groan, sometimes an apology ("Oh, dear, I must watch my grammar!"), and once in a while it will be another question.

"What does an English teacher teach?" If the questioner knows anything about today's academy, I will hear an added ominous phrase: "—*these* days?"

My answer usually includes, as it does in many of the pieces reprinted here, some sort of attempt to talk about "the humanities" or "liberal education."

"I teach how to read and write about literature and ideas—you know, how to *think* about . . ."

About what? I can't say "about rhetoric," though that's close to what I mean; my new companion will surely believe that rhetoric is what we use when we want to cover up our bad thinking and worse intentions. I can't say "about life," because that sounds pretentious, and besides, it's misleading. Surely I don't teach *life*, exactly.

What is the profession of English teaching? Where are we, and where should we go from here? Are we indeed, as many say, in a state of crisis more critical than the many crises announced by earlier members of our profession?

Like teachers in other disciplines—sociology, history, anthropology, philosophy—we tell each other these days that our profession is in disarray, that we suffer a crisis of confidence, that we cannot define what we are doing and why. Our anxieties may be justified, but we should not forget that our profession, the profession of scholar-teachers whose "stuff" is the English language and its literature, has always been a dubious, threatened enterprise. Departments of English have always been unfocused, controversial assemblages of many disciplines.[1] It is true that part of the time each of us teaches English in the narrower sense of teaching the elements of one particular language: we correct spelling errors, we object to unidiomatic expressions, we write "gr" for "grammatical error" in the margins of papers. But we soon reach the borderline between teaching the English language and teaching something else.

---

1. Gerald Graff, *Professing Literature: An Institutional History* (Chicago, 1987), esp. chaps. 4–7.

When I point out to a student that she probably does not want to write, "I could care less," or "Novelists are writing more of those kind of books," I am presumably teaching "English." But that's only a tiny fraction of my vocation. What am I teaching when I work with students on the ironies in *Oedipus Rex*, Herodotus's *Histories*, or "A Modest Proposal"? On the difficulties met in trying to read Thucydides, the American Constitution, *Newsweek*, or William James's *Pragmatism*? On the way in which most logical "fallacies" turn out to be indispensable rhetorical resources, not fallacies at all? On the skillful organization of Edmund Burke's overtly "disorganized" *Reflections on the Revolution in France*? On the reasons for thinking Ross MacDonald superior to Agatha Christie, and both of them worth more, for many readers on many occasions, than many an author touted by the worried defenders of our precious western heritage? On how to criticize one's own generalizations about "the Greeks" or about America today? It would be misleading to call all of this "the humanities" or "liberal education" or "critical thinking" or "the new rhetoric" or "hermeneutics," yet none of these labels would be as misleading, to most people, as calling it "English."

"English" began as a catch-all inheritance from the collapse of classical studies. Those studies, because of the richness of classical literature, were an equally ill-defined assemblage of history, archeology, philology, grammar, logic, rhetoric, literary theory and criticism (poetics), and dialectic. When "English" took over as the "discipline" charged with the major responsibility for liberal education, it initially took over some remnants of all of these except archeology. But most of the disciplines were quickly dropped or watered down, leaving philology and history for the specialists, and grammar and fragments of rhetoric for the teachers of non-majors.

In short, there has always been a controversy about where we should turn to find a respectable center—some subject matter a bit more imposing than grammar and spelling. Our founders in the late nineteenth century generally leaned on philology and literary history as their badge of respectability. Surely someone who had taken the trouble to master Old English, Old Norse, Icelandic, several varieties of Middle English, and the history of English literature from Beowulf to Charles Wolfe, was as true a scholar as those dying classicists. As Francis A. March joshed in 1892, a serious English teacher could now "make English as hard as Greek" (Graff, p. 74).

In the following decades our champions have offered a wide variety of purposes and techniques that would save us from being merely a police force charged with defending pure language. We were to employ literature for the grown-up task of building a progressive political movement (V. L. Parrington, Richard Ohmann, Fredric Jameson, Frank Lentricchia). We were to be the defenders of classical values (T. S. Eliot, T. E. Hulme). We

8

were to teach the arts of discerning just which literary works embody true intellectual and moral maturity (Yvor Winters, F. R. Leavis). We were to learn how to analyze and appreciate poetry as poetry, with full justice to its ironies and complexities (the "New Critics"). We were to discover the principles of formal construction that make great works *work* (the Chicago School, in which I was trained). We were to discover the architectonic vision that shows how all literary works belong together as alternative myths— metaphors for salvation and damnation (Northrop Frye). We were to redeem ourselves by developing and teaching this or that philosophy, sociology, anthropology, history, semantics, semiotics, or psychology. We were to discover and teach the truth about language: about a deeper grammar (the Chomsky craze); about the institution of writing (Derrida et al.); about metaphor (Legion). We were to develop and teach new disciplines—"communications studies," "popular culture," "narratology," "grammatology," "logology," "dialogics," women's studies, black studies, film studies, gay studies. Most recently we have been urged to make our center a theoretical study of our cultural placement: the study of "how we situate ourselves in reference to" the important texts of our tradition (James Kinkaid, Gerald Graff, Stephen Mailloux; see Graff, p. 262).

I have no interest in attacking any of these efforts at relocation. But I do want to underline the obvious point that each of them depends for its success on our learning to teach and practice the arts that this book places at the center—the arts of reading, thinking, writing, and speaking. These arts have been too often taken for granted by the partisans of substitute programs. It has been assumed that the secondary schools would somehow provide colleges with an endless supply of relatively literate students who could then study "literature," or some new improvement on it, as the capstone of their education.

The assumption was probably never justified, but in any case it is certainly not justified now. Nobody denies that most students entering most colleges write badly, read little, speak in puzzling fragments, and hence in effect *think* badly or not at all. They then enter "programs," most of which require little writing, scant reading (and then only of an undemanding kind, the predigested pablum of most textbooks), no disciplined speech, and "thinking" only of whatever kind is useful in practicing a given specialty.

The only required course in many colleges, and the only required reading-and-writing course in most, is something called "Freshman English," or "Freshman Composition," or "Communications Skills," or—rarely these days—"Composition and Rhetoric." The course, whatever its name, is usually taught by "English teachers" under the direction of the "English Department." (Some "composition staffs" have broken with Departments of

English, but even they are staffed predominantly by people trained in "English."[2]

This being so, is it an exaggeration to say that the future of our reading/writing/thinking/speaking culture is mainly in the hands of "English teachers"? That only if *we* serve and practice the arts that used to be called "liberal"—grammar, rhetoric, dialectic, logic—will they live? That if we abandon them, they will probably die?

A recent article in *The Chronicle of Higher Education* (October 23, 1985) claims that 40 percent of all teachers in higher education are considering, or have considered, leaving the profession, because they are so dissatisfied with their present position. My crystal ball—or should I say my computer modem?—does not reveal what the "job market" will be in five, ten, or fifteen years. But I do know that too many wonderfully promising teachers have been driven elsewhere by our current practices; two of the best teaching interns I've worked with (see "A Teacher's Journal," Occasion 13) have left for greener pastures. Would it be foolish to suggest to them or their kind that we will soon face an actual shortage of qualified teachers—and that well-trained teachers will soon once again face a seller's market?

Yes, it would be foolish—not only foolish but unfair to those who may find, after four to eight years of graduate study, that no one will offer any sort of position except that of "part-timer" at slave wages. On their behalf I want most to say to our various publics: "You are behaving in disastrously shortsighted ways, pinching pennies in this quarter while you spend public and private fortunes establishing dubious new programs and luring 'stars' who will teach no LITCOMP and perhaps no undergraduate courses at all. At the same time I would like to dare to say to all who have the slightest temptation to teach "English": "If you set out to become a teacher/scholar of English because you love the stuff we handle, and if you keep your mind on that stuff for however long it takes until you are ready to teach, you will almost certainly never regret it, whether you get a satisfactory job teaching English or not." I must say "almost," because "callings," vocations, are chancy; by their nature they can simply evaporate without a trace, boiled away by the fires of adverse circumstance. I must not hide the fact that at least two of my former graduate students now say that they regret their years of preparing to teach English. And that wonderful freshman English teacher of mine later confessed that he rather wished he had become—an anthropologist!

2. I note, in revising, the rash of expressions in quotation marks. I usually cut such evidences of a stylistic cowardice that I deplore. But I keep them here because they dramatize the problem of writing about such controversial and ill-defined matters.

OCCASION 1 · *To My Fellow Teacher/Scholars in the Modern Language Association*

The Credo of an English Teacher

I

In gathering here tonight, we tell each other a little sustaining story. Just by going through our traditional motions, we imply a narrative, one that might begin something like this:

Once upon a time there was a profession so important to a small portion of its members—shall we say one in a hundred?—that they wished to symbolize that importance with an annual ceremony. And so each year they gathered together at the winter solstice, gathered quietly, a bit shamefaced, with very little ritual and no prayer but with many other marks of a lingering piety. And what they told each other, hunkered down against the chill wind, in the twilight, was the story of how, in times long past, a small group of . . .

But as soon as we try to say precisely who we are and why we gather, our stories diverge. Though all of them have a similar setting, they portray different heroes, different beginnings and middles, and above all different ends, in two senses of the word. We do not agree about whether we enact a comedy, a tragedy, a farce, a morality play, or some horrifying, rough genre still slouching toward Los Angeles to be born.

Reading in our journals, we find various plausible myths:

—the story of a small number of true scholars, united in the service of truth above all other human values, especially to the truth about languages and literatures. These scholars banded together to share their conclusions and to defend themselves against an error-besotted world. For some decades they succeeded in keeping their organization pure, as a society of learned

Presidential address, Modern Language Association, Los Angeles, 1982. First published as "Arts and Scandals, 1982," *PMLA* 98 (May 1983): 312–22.

men, but as the organization expanded, its devotion to truth was polluted with other values, like concern for pedagogy—teaching the great unwashed public—and a host of silly, corrupting subjects like critical theory, research into how to teach writing, and women's studies. These nonsubjects threatened to destroy, by about the first of January 1983, all true scholarship. . . .

Or:

—the story of a pack of dry-as-dusts who hated teaching and who believed in only one value: publishing the results of a so-called pure and objective literary scholarship. Ignoring the problems of the world around them, including the problem of how to bring literacy to a great democratic public, determined to buttress their precarious perches as aristocrats of intellect, they founded an organization that spread evil doctrines in the world. More and more people were captured by the vicious ideal of a scholarship removed from all human values. But then, in the 1960s, a glorious revolution began, one that, despite setbacks in the seventies, promised to triumph by about the first of January 1984. . . .

Sometimes these primitive, militant, institutional myths imply even simpler personal myths, thinly disguised autobiographies that show how the MLA has frustrated what would otherwise have been glorious careers. Often they sound a bit like that "bully of humility," Dickens' Josiah Bounderby:

"I hadn't a shoe to my foot," says Mr. Bounderby to Mrs. Gradgrind, mythologizing a childhood that had actually been comfortably middle-class.

> As to a stocking, I didn't know such a thing by name. I passed the day in a ditch, and the night in a pigsty. . . . How I fought through it, *I* don't know. . . . I was determined, I suppose. I have been a determined character in later life, and I suppose I was then. Here I am, Mrs. Gradgrind, anyhow, and nobody to thank for my being here but myself. . . . I was to pull through it, I suppose, Mrs. Gradgrind. Whether I was to do it or not, ma'am, I did it. I pulled through it, though nobody threw me out a rope.

Well, here *we* are, Edmund Wilson and all ye other mockers of our enterprise; here we are, Walter Jackson Bate and Calvin Trillin. Here we are, James Sloan Allen, though *you* see our convention as "a circus of professional hokum." Here we are, all ye spreaders of obloquy, all ye satirists who depend for your Christmas cheer on what you take to be ridiculous titles from our annual program. Here we are, and nobody to thank but ourselves. We were to pull through, though nobody threw us out a rope.

The absurdity of many such accounts, whether for or against us, should not lead us to underestimate their importance. The life of any institution depends on the stories its members can bring themselves to tell each other. It seems to me a serious matter, then, to have to confess at the outset that I have no coherent story to tell about the MLA. I have tried, not only in preparing for tonight but through the years of working with the Commission on the Future of the Profession, tried again and again to write a short, intelligible account of who we are, of where we are, and of where we ought to go. But I must now confess that to the happily outgoing president of 1982, the Modern Language Association remains a monstrous, largely unintelligible growth. It serves, and has almost always served, many ends, some in obvious conflict with others. It leads a swarming, swirling, cacophonous life that nobody could ever want to defend lock, stock, and barrel. And yet all of us here have decided to continue in uneasy support of this monster, even while pursuing our more sharply defined goals in other, smaller organizations.

If we can't tell a single coherent story about ourselves, and if, as critics old and new tirelessly remind us, we are united by no single coherent theory of language or of literature, we might then well ask whether we really belong together at all. But if we consult not theory but experience; if we look at what we do when we are at our best, considering those arts all of us practice rather than what we *say* against each other; if we look not at the names we call each other but at the loves and fears that inform our daily work—then we may find, perhaps not exactly a unity, but enough of a center to shame us whenever we violate it.

Such a center, if it exists, will be found not in any one statement about it; rather it will be exhibited in our many arts, as we study and write and teach. And it will be best represented, for public sharing, not in any one conceptual summary but in a kind of collective narrative history—the sum of our individual myths about why we have chosen this profession from among all the other good ways to spend a life. Perhaps by going public with our private myths we can dramatize not just our inescapable plurality but the validity of our sense that we belong together, somehow working on common ground.

And so I turn tonight to that most risky of all rhetorical forms, the confession. Fortunately, the risk is all mine, because if my story turns out to be totally unlike yours, I'm the only one who will be worse off than when we began. You will simply have endured one more empty ceremony.

Turning to the confessional mode solves few problems. My ego offers still too many destructive myths.

My name is Wayne Booth. Born in the mid-nineteenth century, sir, the last of my kind. Raised in a cultural desert. How I fought through, *I* don't know. But here I am, with nobody to thank for my being here but myself. Attended American Fork High School, where they taught no history, no literature, no languages, and only a smattering of misinformation about chemistry. Often enough went hungry in order to buy books that nobody wanted me to take the time to read. Learned early how to cover irremediable ignorance with plausible style. Never succeeded in removing the ignorance but went on developing the plausibility. Because of a general decline in the standards of the profession, was elected to MLA presidency, a position that before my own time had *stood* for something. Know that if I had any remaining standards I would refuse to belong to any organization that would elect me president.

The stories I actually tell are often not as different from that one as I'd like. They often include something about deprived beginnings as compared with the silver spoons of all you *real* scholars, who took in Greek and bibliographical techniques at your family breakfast table. Too often they dwell on immense "gaps" papered over only by anxious, endless revision of every sentence and paragraph, always fearing the red pencil of *someone who knows.*

But there is one story perhaps close enough to our shared experience to justify the telling. It is a story of a man disappointed in love, and I hope that telling it may justify, at least partially, any bitter words about scandals that I speak before I am through.

II

The love story begins, as all modern stories should, toward the end, at a point long after its anti-hero has joined the MLA. It then moves through a sequence of fashionable flashbacks—what Gérard Genette would call "intradiagetic analepses"—interlaced with unfashionable omniscient commentary.

About four years ago I was invited to talk with a group of professors in Boston about my work in progress. They would read, the letter said, any pages I sent in advance, and then we could all discuss my project, in a spirit "irenic and open and informal."

Perhaps I should have predicted that none of those busy Bostonians would bother to read my manuscript pages with any care, but I could hardly have predicted how quickly our attempt at discussion turned into that ancient ritual: stoning the scapegoat for sins he had never even heard of. At the height of the bloody melee I heard a voice from my far left, snarling, "But where on earth did you get your *insane* love of literature?" The chairman intervened to allow as how the word "insane" seemed to him a *bit* strong. Later, as I was slinking off to catch my plane, the chairman said something like, "What we did to *you* was nothing! You should have seen what we did to Frank Kermode and Stanley Fish and . . . "

A moment like that burns in the mind long and sore. Where *did* I get my insane love, not just of literature but of critical discussion that cares more about the arts of inquiry than about drawing blood?

We flash back exactly one-half century to a Sunday afternoon in the parlor of my grandparents. My grandfather and his brothers and sisters have been telling stories to each other about the past, funny stories mostly. But there is one story that they always tell, a proud story about their father, my great-grandfather, Richard Thornton Booth, born in Lancashire in 1821. The story was told again and again throughout my childhood, and it was finally written down by my father's sister in her own *Autobiography* dictated to me when she was almost eighty.[1]

The son of working people, who in that age received meagre compensation for their labors, [Richard] was sent at the age of six years to work in the cotton and silk factories. Slowly he mastered the technique until he had a loom of his own. During this time he developed a strong desire to study, and having little time he figured out a way of working the loom with one hand [and] his legs and feet, leaving the other hand free to hold the book.

He worked so steadily at the loom in a crooked position in order to read that he became permanently crippled, one leg being shorter than the other. In his later life he was forced to use a cane to get around.

But he was not deterred in his search for knowledge. He read everything he could find. He learned the practical use of figures so he was able to do bookkeeping. He studied French until he could read and write the language though he could not speak it very well.

My aunt adds, as the family storytellers of the previous generations had always done, that the most important event of Richard Thornton Booth's life was his conversion to Mormonism, a conversion always described as resulting from a close reading of beloved books—*The Book of Mormon* and other sacred books that the Lord had given the world in my great-grandfather's own time.

Picture, now, a six-year-old boy who has heard many such stories about how salvation is to be found in books and who has just read his first book on his own. He marches proudly into his great-aunt Manda's hat shop to col-

1. Relva Booth Ross, *The Autobiography of Relva Booth Ross, with Lives of my Parents and Grandparents* (private printing, Provo, Utah, 1971).

lect the dollar she has promised him earlier for—*reading his first real book*. He will never forget the dollar, he will never forget the book, which happened to be *The Wizard of Oz*.

I must apologize now to those of you who are not in that strangely heterogeneous field called English. Personal stories do not cover all fields, and mine from here on cannot be fully representative of other languages and literatures, though it should easily "translate" without too much loss.

We now hear a voice-over:

Through a succession of junior high school English teachers who did not care much about anything but spelling and grammar, the boy had learned, by his junior year in high school, to detest English. But then Miss Gene Clark, in her first year of teaching, showed him his first glimpse of what it might mean to discuss a text with love and to write responses to it with critical attention. And Mr. Luther Giddings, chemistry teacher, showed him what it could mean to converse about books, in long leisurely sessions at the end of Saturdays spent in the chem lab. Giddings did not sharply distinguish what he did in that chem lab from what we did after hours. It was all critical yet loving talk. And since he was even more interesting than Gene Clark, and since even she called what she did "applying the scientific method to literature," the boy naturally decided to be a scientist, to major in chemistry and become a "chemical engineer," hoping to "learn to think" like those two heroes and the author implied by the books he read.

In the spring of 1940, I am standing one afternoon totally engrossed in conversation with a fellow college sophomore, Max Dalby, on Fifth North Street in Provo, Utah, breathing the lilac-scented air, feeling my oats, and ignoring as best I can the awful news from Europe. To me at the moment, the fall of nations is much less important than the rise of English.

"All right, then," I intone, pounding my points out on the roof of an old Ford, "I'll *be* an English teacher, even though it does mean that I'll always be poor. Let's go over it again: I want to work at something that I enjoy doing, something that will contribute to my continuing to grow. [Oh, yes, we talked like that, back then.] So that means I should be a teacher. But if I go into chemistry, that will mean teaching exactly the same stuff every year, the way my teachers have to. [How little I knew about the constant flux of science, as compared with the relative stability of literary experience!] But if I teach English I can do what Prof. Young was doing last year in LITCOMP, and Prof. Christensen has been doing this year in Advanced Comp; I can learn to read and write and think. I'll never think as well as they do, but I can try. And I can work with students on how to understand people, not just chemicals. Argal [we were by that time doing corny imitations of Shakespeare's comic characters], Argal, I must major in English."

Five years later we come to a graduate class in literary criticism, taught by Ronald Crane. Nothing happens here in a flash on any one day. The pace has been so seeming slow that many of us students think we are bored. We have spent too many days looking more and more closely at *Macbeth*, a play that has up to that time earned no love from me, sane or insane. "Why must we spend so much time on one work?" we students have complained to each other, not daring, of course, to put the question to Crane.

Crane goes on needling us about our inattention to what Shakespeare actually wrote. "Why do you suppose he dwells just this long and no longer on the Porter scene?" "Why would he place the banquet scene just here?" "What possible dramatic problem is he trying to solve by his choices of what to dramatize and what to narrate?" "What dangers did he face— Shakespeare, not Macbeth—in the fifth act?" And soon there emerges from the trudging a new and surprising love, a love that with all my previous reading I had not dreamed of: the love of skill, of craft, of getting clear in my mind, and then in my writing, what a great writer had *got right* in his work. Writing the paper for that course, on Shakespeare's dramatic skill in maintaining tragic sympathy for the criminal Macbeth, I realized with a flood of pleasure, late one night, that Shakespeare was, after all, not just a great poet but a great dramatist, and that now he was great for me not because the world said so, but for solid reasons, some of which I could articulate. It is important for the point of my little myth to emphasize that this new love had been produced by a form of prolonged and dry analysis that my younger self would have scorned as destructive professionalism.

A year later we are sitting in a seminar room, toward the end of a two-hour session run again by Crane. I have read a paper that I had thought might be a prospectus for an avant-garde critical dissertation on "the form of *Tristram Shandy*." The two hours have killed that dream. Crane has discovered fault after fault after fault. He and my fellow students have exposed my misquotations, my errors of fact, my non sequiturs. "And," Crane concludes, "what is finally the worst difficulty here is that you have not managed to construct an *argument*. What we have here is a collection of assertions that are at best interesting but quite unsupported by cogent reasoning."

That night I tell my wife that I am in the wrong profession. "I am simply not qualified to perform the kind of critical thinking Crane insists on. And besides, I went into this business in order to teach young students the way Karl Young taught them, not in order to become a dry-as-dust scholar. I'm quitting."

Somehow I did not quit graduate school, but I was a long way, believe me, from joining the Modern Language Association.

I was in fact deeply puzzled about how to connect what I was asked to do in most of my graduate courses to the vocation which, on the basis of those beginning English courses, I had announced in 1940. And I went on being puzzled through the years of the Ph.D. So far as I can remember, nobody ever addressed my problem. Nobody mentioned in my hearing that someday I would be teaching not the history of the self-conscious narrator in comic fiction before *Tristram Shandy*, to graduate students, but composition, to beginners. Though in my parallel work as an assistant instructor in the Chicago College I was learning to teach "LITCOMP," I saw no way to relate the excitement I felt in the staff meetings and classrooms of my courses there to my growing scholarly interests. Indeed, after completing the doctorate and getting a job teaching LITCOMP, I published a little pseudonymous attack on my graduate mentors for failing to prepare me for such teaching.

At the time I wrote that reductive piece, I had of course not joined the MLA, and I did not join it for many years to come. Instead, I joined the NCTE and CCCC—organizations that to me stood for what I cared for most in the profession: not scholarly publication, though I was beginning to try for some of that myself, but the effort to open the doors of understanding to those dwelling in the prison house of ignorance.

We now skip thirteen years of teaching mainly LITCOMP at Haverford and Earlham Colleges, and we move, in 1962, to the *scène à faire*. I am in the office of one of my former mentors at the University of Chicago. He is grilling me about my deepest professional beliefs, as he tries to decide whether to vote for an offer to any man who could have written that seditious pseudonymous attack on the supreme and exclusive value of advanced scholarship.

"I was wondering how you feel now, a decade later, about what you said in that piece about the irrelevance of your scholarly training to teaching beginners how to read and write. Do you still think of training in advanced scholarship as some kind of enemy?"

I can't remember what I said, but I think I lied to him. Certainly I did not tell him that the chance to teach beginning students again in the wonderful Chicago College attracted me at least as much as the chance to join a graduate faculty. I know for sure that I still could not, at that time, see any way to reconcile the aims of the learned professors and the aims of the frontline troops, the teachers of freshmen. I had decided to return to Chicago because I wanted to join both groups, but I had no conceptual way of uniting the two.

*

Twenty years later, opening my morning mail, I come to a letter from the chairman of a department that I happen to know cruelly neglects its freshmen and their underpaid instructors. They have recently cut two line positions, and they are hiring part-timers, who this year have a heavier student load than last. The letter goes like this:

We have succeeded in persuading our administration to take major steps in upgrading our department. As a result we are now expecting to make perhaps as many as three stellar appointments, of course at the senior level. The department agrees that at least one of these should be in critical theory, and we were wondering if you could suggest anyone who would be suitable. We intend to be competitive in salary, and the position offers a virtual carte blanche in teaching arrangements.

That is to say: no beginning students and few undergraduates.

The final scene is not my own, except as reading makes it my own. It is a reading of a section from *The Autobiography of Malcolm X*, the passage, by now famous, describing the course in LITCOMP that Malcolm Little gave to himself while in prison. It is all about how he learned not only to read words—which he could do when he entered prison—but to understand what he read and then to write about it. Frustrated by his inability to get his ideas across in his primitive efforts to write, Malcolm X decided to copy out the entire dictionary, memorizing definitions as he went. And suddenly he discovered that he could

> for the first time pick up a book and read and now begin to understand what the book was saying. Anyone who has read a great deal can imagine the new world that opened. Let me tell you something: from then until I left that prison, in every free moment I had, if I was not reading in the library, I was reading on my bunk. . . . [M]onths passed without my even thinking about being imprisoned. In fact, up to then, I never had been so truly free in my life.[2]

2. Malcolm X, *The Autobiography of Malcolm X*, ed. Alex Haley (New York, 1966), 172–73.

Perhaps when you think back now on my family's story about great-grandfather Booth, you will understand why reading about Malcolm X's awakening speaks to the question of where I got my "insane love."

III

I hope that these more or less True Moments from American Academic History will have suggested something a bit more important than why one man loves literature and the teaching of literature, or why he deplores that chairman's letter. I hope that they will spark memories of your own experiences with the liberating arts we share beneath our theoretical differences. But of course they cannot in their mere retelling demonstrate that we share a center. Certainly we appear almost torn apart by conflicts, both theoretical and practical. Our loves, sane or insane, seem to appear in far too many shapes and shades. There may be some professions that can declare simply and clearly a single love—of abstract truth, say, for one kind of philosopher or economist or mathematician; of beauty, say, for one kind of musician; of the past, for one kind of historian; of the cure of individual suffering persons, for one kind of psychotherapist; of moral and spiritual salvation, for one kind of clergyman or theologian. Most professions allow some simplification of choice, and all actual lives require it. No matter how much we talk of pluralism, each of us must to some degree choose from among the ultimate gods. Surely it is impossible to serve without limit more than one of these gods at a time—truth, beauty, salvation, political reform, preservation of standards, revision of the curriculum. . . . After all, I am not teaching undergraduates or reading beloved texts during the hours I spend working through successive drafts of a presidential address for the MLA.

Are we then incurably divided in our love of incompatibles? Do we as a profession, do I as a person with this complicated story to tell, simply stir a missionary stew of rival religions? Or is there something at our center that *deserves* a loving service and that can provide, when we appeal to it, a test of all that we do?

You will not be surprised to hear me say that I think there is a center of that kind. But I do not expect us ever to agree on any one verbal formula for it. As I see it now, my teachers and I, at every defensible stage of my story, were in the business of freeing ourselves into whatever was for us the next order of human awareness or understanding, the next step forward in our ability to join other minds, through language, and to join them in—well, in what? Shall we call it "rationality," as people used to do before our commitments and emotions were torn from the body of reason, leaving only its dried-out corpse, a synonym for logic? Shall we call it "critical intelligence"? That phrase again leaves out the loving, the passion. Shall we call it a "spiritual freeing," a "consciousness raising," a "revolution of mind and heart"? All the words are tainted. As an undergraduate I would have called it simply "LITCOMP."

My own present shorthand for our center is "critical understanding," a phrase that necessarily risks the oxymoronic in order to include both the thought and the passion. Today, whether working on my next book, or teaching an advanced graduate seminar in critical theory, or struggling with a beginning LITCOMP course or a survey course for majors, I should be trying at every point to increase the chances, always painfully low, that critical understanding will replace, on the one hand, sentimental and uncritical identifications that leave minds undisturbed and, on the other, hypercritical negations that freeze or alienate.

But I know better than to expect others to accept my proprietary name for the center. Perhaps, after this skirmishing with the impossible task of definition, I could for tonight just ask each of you to slot in, whenever I say "critical understanding," your own version of whatever central experience attracted you to this profession and keeps you here now. Call it "experience Q" if that will help. Whatever our terms for it, whatever out theories about how it happens or why it fails to happen more often, can we reasonably doubt the importance of that moment, at any level of study, when any of us—you, me, Malcolm X, my great-grandfather—succeeds in entering other minds, or "taking them in," as nourishment for our own? Can anyone claim that we have no rationale for what we do, when the hunger for critical understanding is so seldom aroused and satisfied in our world? And since nobody ever suffers from a surfeit of that mysterious food that is *not* "consumed with that which it was nourished by," how can we ever lack confidence in the importance of what we do, no matter how puzzled we are about how to explain it?

When I take seriously my own deficiencies in critical understanding, that earlier sharp divorce between my calling as teacher and my effort to meet the demands of so-called professionalism looks plain silly. I cannot now distinguish the aims of Karl Young when he helped me in my fumbling efforts to understand and write about Machiavelli and Cervantes and Wilbur Daniel Steele from the aims of Ronald Crane when he tortured me for misreading *Macbeth* and *Tristram Shandy* and miswriting about them. And with the collapse of that distinction between elementary and advanced, under the prodding of experience, a good many other distinctions that plague our profession reveal their absurdity. The distinction between theory and practice becomes problematic; in our profession, to state a theory is to practice our art, to practice it well or ill; it is an invitation to understand, critically.

A third distinction, between the objective and the subjective, gets blurred; all critical understanding will be *in* subjects, if anywhere, yet if it is understanding, it will be of some "other," not simply of some previously existing self, and if it is critical, it will include what we formerly sought in talking about "objectivity." A fourth sharp distinction, between literature as belles lettres, the preserve of aesthetic values, and literature that is didactic or rhetorical or "practical," loses most of its usefulness. That distinction is crucial in some intellectual enterprises; I cannot myself entirely reject it. Indeed, it can be illuminating in the hands of a great philosopher like Kant. But it can do great harm when it is employed hierarchically on the young, indoctrinating them into kinds of romantic nonsense about aesthetic purity that deserve full treatment by some powerful satirist. A fifth distinction, between language, or rhetoric, on the one hand, and reality, or action or "substance," on the other, simply disappears; the primary realities we know, in practicing this art, are made and remade in our rhetoric. Perhaps most important, the distinction between private pleasures and public goods becomes blurred, because there is no public good more important than the kind of shared life we lead when we pursue together the pleasures of critical understanding.

I have explored elsewhere each of these large claims about our theoretical structures, but I think it more important tonight to put them to one side and ask of each of our current institutional practices a single, simple question: "Will this practice, if pursued as we now pursue it, increase anyone's chances for critical understanding, for 'experience Q'?" When I ask that question, I find that a good deal of what we do not only makes little sense, it looks positively scandalous. And so I turn to a little list of scandals, unable to forgo my first and last chance to shout "*J'accuse*" at a whole profession.

IV

Our most obvious scandal is implicit in all that I have said. We are obviously failing to work as teacher/scholars who care as much for beginning students as for graduate seminars, and we are failing to build institutional structures that might make up for our individual deficiencies. This is the most threatening of all our failures, because if we do not face it squarely, everything else may be lost.

At what point does our profession have the best chance to serve critical understanding, to serve it in such a way as to ensure that the great world understands what we are up to, at all levels? Obviously in the beginning years, in the required courses, in LITCOMP and introductory language courses. That's where the public is, that's where the transformations will occur, if there are to be any. That's where most people in our society have their last chance to learn the joys and uses of critical understanding, unless later on they are very lucky indeed.

You may want to say that the even younger pupils are more important still. I agree. But our best service to those in the elementary and high school years is certainly indirect, as we teach or fail to teach their future teachers. That's where they meet us, if they are to meet us at all. Just like every congressman, every business leader, and every member of our White House gangs, all of our teachers have passed through our required courses. But where were we when they passed? Since most of them were not English majors, they met only those we delegated to teach college beginners— mainly our underpaid part-timers, our exploited TAs (many of them just out of college themselves), at best our assistant professors, who are told, sometimes without even an effort at euphemism, that the road to promotion is not to teach well but to get that book out, fast.

Why should the senators and governors who have passed through our offerings feel inclined to support us? Why should we expect them to understand the subtle issues of censorship or the silliness of the back-to-basics movement or the tragedy of fund cutting, if they have not encountered the real basics as taught by master teachers? Could our movers and shakers be the non-readers they are, could they talk and write the shallow nonsense they offer us, if they had encountered a succession of teachers who had led them into critical understanding? We cannot predict what would have been the consequences for their choice of political party if they had been baptized in critical understanding. But we can know that their present modes of addressing us would not have survived if we had taught them right—and if they knew that most Americans had not simply suffered through a beginning course but instead had been taught well there.

Scandal breeds scandal. Having abdicated from the position of greatest real power, we have inevitably developed scandalous methods for hiring our proxies. We have chosen—no one required it of us—to say to the world, almost in so many words, that we do not care *who* teaches the non-majors or under what conditions, so long as the troublesome hordes move on and out: forced in by requirements, forced out by discouragement, or by disgust, or by literal failure. The great public fears or despises us because we hire a vast army of underpaid flunkies to teach the so-called service courses, so that we can gladly teach, in our advanced courses, those precious souls who survive the gauntlet. Give us lovers and we will love them, but do not expect us to study courtship. If we had decided to run up a flag on the quad saying that we care not a whit whether our society consists of people who practice critical understanding, so long as we are left free to teach advanced courses, we could not have given a clearer message.

Each fall I keep a little tally of personal letters I receive alerting me to job openings. They never come from acquaintances at universities looking for outstanding teachers of LITCOMP. Sometimes they do seek an expert in rhetorical theory who might—apparently as a consequence of that expertise—be a good director of composition. I do receive a few from liberal arts colleges where teaching still counts. But most of them read like the letter I quoted earlier. Thus we seek luminous images of excellence, while the center is betrayed.

Not only are most of our beginning students taught by beginners who are given impossible teaching loads and paid one-half to one-third the already shamefully low salary paid to assistant professors. We have compounded the felony by providing for those beginners no orientation, little or no in-service supervision or exchange with experienced teachers, and no hope of any recognition for a job well done.[3] Whenever I voice this complaint I hear the claim that many of these green teachers do a fine job, a better job than many a ripe, gray professor would do. Granted, they do sometimes manage, miraculously, to frustrate our efforts to destroy them and their students. But we need no extensive market research to reveal that most of the students who pass through the courses taught by these vast staffs of hopeless hirelings are at best puzzled and bored. Often they are angry. They think of themselves as victims of a meaningless requirement. They are rightly determined to get the hurdle "out of the way," as their advisers obligingly put it to them. And they are doomed to resent and fear "English" for the rest of their lives.

Is there any wonder, then, that our top administrators, observing our behavior, echo our contempt for those courses, and finally for all that we do? Nothing we say could counterbalance the contemptuous message about LITCOMP given by the practices I have described. Deans, provosts, and presidents are bright enough to read our actions clearly. They can also read what we say about ourselves, and when we talk only about our theoretical confusions, and when our theories themselves seem to cast doubt on the very notion that we have something valuable to teach, it requires no very high intelligence to infer that we will have no real defense against further cuts. We cannot even compete in the prevailing competition for stars if what we do has no better justification than we usually offer. The result is that the big bucks leave the classroom and go to stars—mainly in other subjects.

We read, not only in the *Chronicle of Higher Education* but in the popular press, about the decision of this or that university to upgrade its national

3. Joseph Gibaldi and James V. Mirollo, eds., *The Teaching Apprentice Program in Language and Literature* (New York, 1981).

standing by buying up Nobel prize winners or their equivalents. Of course nothing is said, in such announcements, about increasing the university's national standing by improving the teaching of the modern languages and literatures; indeed there is no mention of the modern languages and literatures at all. How could there be, when the presidents know that they are addressing a public that think of us as incompetent guardians of usage? Nothing is said about how to make sure that every graduate has mastered at least one foreign language, or about how to make sure that every graduate can read and think and write.

Require that they be able to read a novel or poem on their own and say something worth saying about it? To take part in public debate? To appraise evidence in fields other than accounting and engineering or computing? Don't be absurd. I have heard of several campuses that will now require every student to own a computer terminal and develop competence in using it. How many colleges refuse degrees to all students who cannot write a literate, interesting essay about—let us say—the impact of computers on their lives?

Perhaps the worst consequence of this divorce of staffs and their mutual fear and contempt is the loss of critical correction across the battle lines. I hear complaints about trivial composition research spoken by scholars whose whole lives have been spent discovering and teaching trivia. I hear complaints about dry-as-dust literary scholarship spoken by composition teachers who never read anything if it's not in a freshman textbook and whose accounts of what they teach and how they appraise it are parodies of dry pedantry. Only those who fraternize in the no-man's-land between the two camps discover how badly the two sides need each other. Those from the front lines of composition teaching need to risk reading stuff from the "other camp," and then to risk writing about it, to discover how much their teaching of rhetoric depends on a steady diet of literary complexity. And those who engage in advanced scholarship, so-called, need the critique of good rhetorical theory and the "trying out" that only a non-specialized audience, those neglected undergraduates, can provide.

Too often, when people address the scandalous divorce of composition and rhetoric from literature and criticism, they talk as if the harm all flowed one way, against the teaching of writing. We forget that scholarship itself, which for many of us is still the raison d'être of the MLA, is a major victim whenever it forgets its own roots: the effort to free minds into critical understanding.

First, when we fail to test our scholarship by making its most important results accessible to non-specialists, we also lose our capacity to address, and thus recreate in each generation, the literate public who can understand its stake in what we do. While we conduct our internal battles about whether literature does or does not refer to anything real, or about that more old-fashioned issue—whether there are practical values implicit in the aesthetic—the public hears nothing from us that might explain why some experiences with verbal art liberate while others enslave. Our critical and scholarly jargons grow more recondite by the day. While there's nothing inherently wrong in specialized vocabulary for special subjects, there is something inherently pathetic in a profession that cannot explain its work to the public at least as well as the more articulate scientists manage to explain theirs.

Second, and perhaps most tragic for an association like ours, we lose our capacity to address each other, with force and grace and clarity, about our most ambitious scholarly findings. We produce more and more books and articles for fewer and fewer readers. No one can be blamed, of course, for producing as fast and as much as possible, since professional survival too often depends on the number of titles listed. But we can all be blamed for building a world in which professional survival depends on titles listed rather than on qualities of mind and heart, qualities that can be realized in scholarly writing only when the scholar has been given—or has taken—the years that are required for learning to share a deepening and refining inquiry. Once again here, as in the scandal about freshman courses, we have built a world that victimizes the young teachers—even those fortunate ones who are clever enough or lucky enough to earn promotion through early publication. I hear many a scholar complain, at forty, about having been forced at twenty-five or thirty into publishing a premature and finally embarrassing book. I hear many a colleague complain about how little that is published is worth reading. I hear a universal complaint from authors about how incompetently their books are reviewed. Such complaints may reflect, true enough, on the complainers as well as on our institutions. But why do I hear of no profession-wide inquiry into the causes and possible cures of the most embarrassing scandal of all: namely, that members of the profession most committed to teaching the arts of reading, thinking, and writing cannot address each other in critical understanding?

Here no doubt I should name names. But I name no names, leaving it to you to name your own names. Simply ask, of whatever scholarship you meet or practice, "Will this stuff, pursued to its proper end, really liberate any mind, even my own, to critical understanding of some human achievement *worth* understanding?" Only remember that if we apply that test honestly we will not find our results falling into neat piles under current labels: avant-garde versus traditional, critical versus historical, ideological versus objective or formal, rhetorical versus aesthetic.

V

Well, as I have told my private, slanted story tonight and offered my private, slanted exegesis, the world seems in danger of falling into its final collapse about our ears. Bombs and poverty, discrimination and cruelty abound, and I have heard it said that what our world needs most desperately is organized political action, not what we stand for here. It is sometimes said that to engage in teaching the modern languages and literatures is a cop-out, and it is more often said, these days, that because it is a practice without a single coherent theory, it is therefore ultimately indefensible. We are in crisis, we do not know what we are doing or why, we are wandering in a pathless wilderness. I have tried to suggest that, though we have no coherent theory to which everyone can or should subscribe, we do have a coherent task, one that to some degree unites us and that could serve as a rallying center for all of the activities we genuinely honor, even as we quarrel about other matters. It is an ancient and venerable task, but it is always a revolutionary one. What could be a more revolutionary political stroke, what action could make a bigger difference to the world, in both the short and the long run, than that of leading students, whether freshmen or those more recalcitrant folk, the Ph.D. candidates, from passive acceptance of the words that flow over them to critical understanding of those words?

To teach critical understanding, at any level, is always risky, because the teacher cannot predict the outcome. All we can hope for as the result of such teaching is a kind of person who will make a difference to the outcome. Anyone who tries to teach the arts of critical understanding will always be vulnerable to every good student who turns those arts back upon the teacher's own works and days. For all we know, our best efforts will be repudiated by those who learn best what we have to teach.

Thus we cannot even know whether teaching critical understanding will preserve or destroy our present institutions, our colleges, our professional organizations—the MLA itself. All we can know for sure is that whatever quality of heart and mind any future American society will reveal depends to a frightening degree on what we choose to do, now. Is it naive to hope for a profession that will violate less often and less flagrantly the central experience that its members care for most?

OCCASION 2 · *To Beleaguered*
"Composition" Teachers

Rhetoric and Reality; or, My Basics Are More Basic Than Your Basics

Yesterday in Colorado Springs I saw a girl wearing a T-shirt that read, "70% unique." This morning I wonder whether I shouldn't be wearing one that says "2% original," or perhaps "1% useful," or "Significant at the .005 Level." Certainly I could proclaim myself "98% humble" as I think of the unlikelihood that anything I can say to you will be really helpful, either in the public relations task of addressing the new demands of the public or in that age-old, nobler task of trying to educate the young.

Like many would-be public advisers, I have less humility about suggesting what teachers should *not* do than I have about offering positive advice. One of my freshman students this year told me of a class he took last year as a senior in high school. His oral account was so lively that I asked him to write it up for me, and I'd like to read some of what he wrote.

> The year I entered high school the more liberal English teachers had decided to experiment with a new concept of education. Reading and writing would not be given the priority that they had in past years and would be overshadowed by the student's "development as a human being." The result of this change of heart was a number of new courses which we would be subject to. Among the courses offered was the seemingly harmless Themes in Literature. . . .
>
> The first day of class we were led into an unfurnished group meeting room which had no windows, full carpeting, and a garish color scheme. Our "lecturer" was a woman in her mid-fifties who sat down cross-legged in the circle we had formed, her heavy jewelry shattering the silence as she positioned herself, and began to describe what we would be doing for the next two months in her class. Themes in Literature was based on the belief that before we could gain any understanding of the "true beauty of litera-ture" we must first understand ourselves and our relationship to others.

Slightly revised from the speech to teachers as it appeared in *The English Curriculum under Fire: What Are the Real Basics?* edited by George Hillocks, Jr. (Urbana, Ill.). © 1982 by the National Council of Teachers of English. Reprinted by permission.

She went on to describe how we could only learn to write by freeing ourselves from our self-imposed restrictions and preconceived notions of what
writing should be. . . .

We were all very open-minded about the class, at first anyway, and
every one of us looked forward to our next meeting; after all, we were the
experimental generation. The next class eliminated any doubts that I had
about just how far the concept of experience and encounter would be carried. When we arrived for class, we found the floor covered with an assort-
ment of pillows, bean-bag chairs, and big foam cushions. We were told to
make ourselves comfortable, relax, and clear our minds. Then the lights
went out. Mrs. X stood in the corner with a poetry book titled something
like *Reflections in an Empty Mirror*, reading with a penlight while the rest
of us made a serious attempt to release our inner beings. I really enjoyed it
at first. It was certainly more enjoyable than arguing about our papers or
taking notes, but after about twenty minutes of listening to that nonsense
about how we should leave our bodies behind in space and let our spirits
merge into the ever-flowing abyss, I wanted either to go to sleep or to tell
the teacher to shut up. Finally our tranquility was abruptly interrupted by
the inevitable joker who takes advantage of every opportunity to get his
hands into a girl's pants. First the girl started giggling, then out came
something like, "Oh, Paul, *stop* it!" Well, by this time even the people
who were asleep woke up and the class erupted in laughter. Mrs. X quickly
turned on the lights; she was noticeably embarrassed.

Well, now that we had "transcended" our senses, it was time for direct
sensory contact. Mrs. X randomly selected partners from around the room
and ordered them to touch each other in the most unlikely places (i.e., knee
caps, Adam's apples, ear lobes) and then describe out loud to the class what
they were feeling. It was insane. . . .

Well, to make a long story short, our one writing assignment consisted
of being led into a room full of incredibly corny posters, obviously ordered
from *Senior Scholastic* (i.e., the high school version of the *Weekly Reader*),
then choosing one which emotionally moved us and writing about it. Our
final most important project was an *art* assignment which we were to display to the class along with an oral presentation about how the project
symbolized our inner being. . . . I was not bitter about the class, after all,
we were the experimental generation. When our older brothers and sisters
were burning down college campuses while we were in grade school, it was
decided that something was wrong with our educational system. We were
going to be different. I had come to accept things like this as part of the
game and, believe me, this was not the worst.

When I heard about that classroom, I wanted to shout, as so many are
doing these days, "Back to the basics!" While John was lying on the floor
laughing at his teacher, he obviously was not learning any of the skills that
would have helped him be a better student in my freshman humanities

course. The world's literature and philosophy and history lay untouched as he lay there being touched. Whole domains of grammar and syntax were left as mysteries as he explored the mystery of his being. And the essential art of making one sentence follow another was unmentioned as he created a so-called work of art that he held in contempt.

Perhaps most of us want to get back to the basics, in one sense or another, but I don't have to tell you that we are not exactly united in a single conception of what the basics might be. We just fall into whatever comes to mind as "obviously essential," without taking a lot of time to think hard about it. Wayland Young once began a serious history and sociological analysis of prostitution, called *Sitting on a Fortune*, with the guess that nobody in the history of the race had ever before spent so much as four hours *thinking* about that ancient institution. Well, I'm sure that many people have spent at least four hours trying to think about education, but you wouldn't know it from the careless diagnoses and simplistic prescriptions that fill the air.

My anecdote about John itself requires some thought. It seems to suggest that what John really needed in high school was simply preparation for my college course, where the "basics" are reading fairly difficult classics and learning to write and talk about them: the *Odyssey*, Thucydides' *History*, Shakespeare, Freud's *Civilization and Its Discontents*, Karl Marx.

Karl Marx! Can you hear the great public scream? Karl Marx a basic? Meanwhile others fall, with the same sense of naturalness, into conceptions that seem to us even more absurd. I was amused when the associate director of the Council for Basic Education, talking about how widespread the back-to-basics movement is and how much progress is being made, offered this observation as a major piece of evidence: "People are talking about spelling for the first time in several decades. Grammar is coming back to the schools. It's no longer a dirty word." Well, spelling and grammar are not dirty words in my vocabulary either, but, like you, I know from experience what happens to an English classroom when such basics are made the center of instruction. What happens is that we produce graduates who say they hate English, who think of English teachers as pedants or torturers or both, and who do their best whenever in later life they actually meet one of us creatures who say we "teach English" to escape to more friendly territory.

So we have big differences, at least on the surface, between ourselves and our various publics. And these differences are represented within the profession, not just "out there." But I'd like to argue that beneath the differences we can discover common ground, that indeed the most important single task for this decade is to find ways of talking about our common ground so that we may educate ourselves and our various publics to its importance. Our task is thus both to discover whatever is really basic to education and to find ways of talking about it that will show why *what we care about doing* is *what the public really wants done.*

In other words, I think we are doomed to fail if we see our task as merely improving public relations or, as it is often put, "re-establishing our credibility with the public." We do want the public to believe in us, but if we are to find the language needed to talk to the public, we must first find the language to describe to each other our own commitment. And that will take more hard thought than most of our suggested cures seem to be based on.

I wish I had a respectable sample of the kind of talk that might persuade the public to trust us as we decide what to do next. Instead, I must address that preliminary half of our task, the effort to become clear with each other about *why we do what we do.* It could be argued that much of the public's distrust of what we have been doing springs from our own anxiety about whether what we do is really important. Because we have lacked collective confidence in our ways of teaching students how to read and think and write, we have let our subject be represented by every new fad under the sun. For all the public can tell from our statements, we teachers think that any old subject is as good as any other old subject, that learning how to read and write well has no priority over hundreds of other lively and novel subjects. We seem to demand that they pay us just as happily for practicing amateur Zen Buddhism or T-group formations or whatever elective occurs to us, as for developing literate citizens. When members of our various publics see us unsure of why English should be the center of the curriculum, and unwilling to defend what we do as essential both to our society and to every member of our society, they naturally feel some confidence in saying, "OK, *you've* given up on the job. Let *us* tell you what to do. Now what you should do is make a list of elementary standards for literacy, and then you should teach each standard, drill by drill, and then you should make up competency examinations to test each standard, and then we'll be sure that everybody you graduate is literate." [Addendum, 1988: I have not had to recast any of this to fit the new talk about "cultural literacy." E. D. Hirsch's nostrum—the 5000 or so "basic" keys to literacy—seems to have been "prophesied" by my worries in 1982! See note 9 below].

I am a bit troubled by the frequent suggestion that we should go about answering such demands by fitting into our classes short bursts of teaching that we ourselves do not respect, as if to say, "We'll spend the month or so necessary to pass the competency exams and save the rest of our time for genuine education." Good advice, perhaps,—for short-term survival. But when we do that, we are simply educating the public to believe in its own misguided notions—if they *are* misguided—and to believe in our hypocrisy, when we are found out. What is worse, our contempt for the competencies we sneak in will be all too apparent to our students, our most critical audience.

I would suggest instead that we go about it the other way 'round, that if we think hard enough about our own notions of the basics, and then teach with full devotion according to those notions, we will find the competencies following quite naturally. Such bold claims are hard to test. But I am convinced that any teacher who is fully engaged in learning to read and think and write—a lifelong task for us all—and who discovers how to engage students in wanting to read and think and write, any teacher who is *mentally engaged* with life, will find that the competencies the public really wants follow quite naturally.

A loose phrase like "learning to read and think and write" covers a lot of territory, and I can touch here on only one central plot in that territory, what some have called the "survival skills," the skills demanded of everyone who must cope with American life in our time. In other words, I'm not thinking mainly of learning how to read Shakespeare or Homer and of how to write passable critical essays on them; one can *survive* in modern America without being able to do that. Rather, I am thinking of the never-completed task of learning to understand what people are really saying, learning to look at what words really mean, and of learning to respond with words that do important work in the world. Sometimes we call such basics the "language arts," sometimes "communication skills," and sometimes even harsher terms than that. I choose to call this subject "rhetoric," though I know that to do so will seem to have already given the show away. I can hear someone say, "If you try to convince the public that what we are experts in is rhetoric, that what we are making of our charges is excellent rhetoricians, that public will *know* that they must now take over; we've lost our marbles." Well, maybe so. I surely don't want to quarrel over a name, and if you have a better name for the subject—the whole art of improving our capacity to interpret what other people say, to think about it, and then to say something worthwhile in return—then use that word.

It is certainly true that the word *rhetoric* has a bad press these days. As I was preparing these remarks, I read in *The New Yorker* the following statement:

> *La lutte pour la France* is over for a while—with casualties to the language which could keep a whole generation of *Académiciens* off the dole. It was a battle of words, and it went on for so long that by the time the French actually got to the polls to vote this spring, those words out of the litanies of left and right had lost any reference to reality they might have had and turned *completely senseless and rhetorical* [my italics].[1]

1. Jane Kramer, "A Reporter in Europe," *The New Yorker*, June 19, 1978, 71.

Similarly, in a recent *Wall Street Journal* I read a column headed "Rhetoric vs. Reality." The discussion was about the statistics of inflation, on the one hand, which are of course "reality," and what people are saying to describe inflation and to cure it, on the other hand—obviously something that is *not* reality, namely rhetoric.

But we shouldn't make the mistake of thinking that it is only the *word* rhetoric that has a bad press. It is our whole subject—the entire range of language and its resources—that is often meant when people contrast hard reality with the stuff you and I try to teach. Writing about her first book, Betty Friedan noted recently that her rhetoric was not "meant to take the place of action." "Wasn't it Marx," she asks, "who said, 'You can't fight a revolution and write a book at the same time'?" And a final example: the Suffragettes had a slogan, "Deeds Not Words"—as clear a statement as we could want that words are not deeds.

There are so many implacable moments in life, moments that can't be changed very much by words, that this way of distinguishing *something over here* as "reality" and *something over there* as "rhetoric"—mere style or language—comes to seem justified. After all, most of us believe that rhetoric, even when addressed to God himself, can't make a good crop grow unless the farmer has first done the plowing and planting. When the earthquake comes, rhetoric about architecture can't change the hard fact that some buildings are well built and don't fall down and some other buildings are badly built and do fall down. No wonder that most of us, even the professors of rhetoric, have developed metaphors for two quite distinct domains: words *approach* reality, we say, words *grapple* with reality, reach for it; they are a *tool* for dealing with reality, or a *lattice* or *screen* to obscure it. Without simplifying too much, we could say that most scientific achievements of the last three hundred years have been based on the effort to see behind or through our misleading words to some hard stuff: reality. You have only to look at the harsh words about rhetoric written by philosophers like Locke to see how deep this sharp distinction runs in modern thought. If we wish to speak of "things as they are," he says, then the figurative devices of rhetoric must be seen as a prime threat. They are "for nothing else but to insinuate wrong *ideas*, move the Passions, and thereby mislead the Judgment; and so indeed are perfect cheats." And he goes on to include all of rhetoric in his indictment.[2]

Two years ago one of Adolph Hitler's right-hand men, Albert Speer, published his memoirs, in which he tried among other things to understand how Hitler had been able to "take him in." Speer finally attributed Hitler's

2. John Locke, *An Essay Concerning Human Understanding* (1690), book 3, chap. 10, sec. 34.

otherwise incredible power over those around him to Hitler's knowledge of human psychology and his genius in using words to play upon the weaknesses of others. Commenting on Speer's confessions, a writer in *Encounter*, "R," observed that Hitler's primary skill was in oratory. His oratory

> was of the kind that speaks neither to the mind nor to the heart of his audience, but plays upon its nerves until they are strung to such a pitch of intensity that they shriek for release in action. . . . But it can only be practised by one who has a profound and subtle understanding of the secret hopes and fears of his audience . . . ; who can be a conservative with the conservative, a revolutionary with the revolutionary, a man of peace with the pacifist and a war lord with the belligerent, and on occasions all these things at once should it be necessary. Certainly Hitler was the greatest master of this type of oratory there has ever been, and I have stood among 10,000 people in the *Sportpalast* in Berlin and known that everyone around me was the victim of its spell. Who knows, if I had not been inoculated in childhood against the tricks of oratory, I might have succumbed myself.[3]

Notice that word *inoculated*. Rhetoric is in this view something to be inoculated against—and who wouldn't want to be inoculated against rhetoric like Hitler's?

Suppose we begin by accepting this negative notion: rhetoric as trickery or cover-up or obfuscation, the opposite of reality or genuine action. It would seem obvious that if we are surrounded by such stuff, dangerous as can be, one major task for students and teachers, regardless of what their specialty is called, is precisely to get inoculated against the dangerous disease. "We're surrounded by pollution; they're out there, ready to destroy us! Man the test tubes, mount the microscopes, start up the computers, so that we can exercise the manly art of self-defense, using reality against rhetoric." If anything is basic, surely such an art must be.

We really do seem to be surrounded by masters of "mere" rhetoric, many of them professional liars using rhetoric to trap us. Every day millions of Americans are taken in by public words that no educated person could believe after careful thought and investigation. I'm not thinking simply of the many hoaxes, the fake biographies of Howard Hughes, the equally fake but subtler fictions by Castaneda about his marvelous Indian guru.[4] I am thinking of the flood of falsehood and half-truth that spews from our presses and television sets daily.

---

3. R, "Column," *Encounter* 45 (November 1975): 44.

4. For a careful appraisal of the reasons for seeing Castaneda's "interviews" as a (benign?) hoax, see Rodney Needham, "An Ally for Castaneda," *Exemplars* (Berkeley, 1985).

The public has thus a vast interest, whether it knows it or not, in any education that attends to words and their ways. To a great deal of what is daily *uttered at them*, our students should learn to say an unqualified no. In judging advertising I can often say an outright no, without waiting for conclusive proof, because the motives for lying are so obvious. "Come to where the flavor is, come to Marlboro country." No, thanks, I'll stay right here, thanks anyway for the sincere invitation. "BP Oil is a new, 100% British company. As a new company we have a new slogan: Working harder for everyone. It's not advertising puffery. We actually mean it." No, no you don't! I can say no with great confidence. You *don't* actually mean it. You mean, "Buy BP oil!" "Asia provides the wonder, we make it wonderful!— Holiday Inn, the most accommodating people in the world." No, no, no!

Learning when to say no to words in the name of reality is thus surely one of the most liberal—that is, liberating, of all the arts. It can often simply be the no of laughter, the laughter of ridicule. Perhaps you have seen a recent collection of metaphorical boo-boos made by members of Congress. The collector, a Washington journalist, calls his little gems malaphors: not metaphors, not malapropisms, but malaphors. He has been listening to the way our representatives talk, and he hears them say things like this: "He threw a cold shoulder on that idea." Or, "Now we've got to flush out the skeleton." Or, "He deals out of both ends of his mouth." One thing that most of us teachers do almost automatically is teach our students to put up their dukes against such stuff—and in doing so we are really doing part of what the public wants us to do—or would, if they knew their true interests.

Now I don't think what I have been saying so far is false in any obvious way, but I hope that by now you are impatient with a certain emptiness in what I have offered, its negativeness, its defensiveness, its limited applicability. If your whole duty is to learn how to reject false words and thus get at a hard reality distinct from those words, how do you recognize *true* words when you see them? What should I do, for example, if I am a believer in Hitler and I hear a piece of very powerful oratory *attacking* his aims and methods. Should I congratulate myself on having been inoculated in my childhood against oratory? Obviously, a simple self-defensive suspicion will be of no help whatever to me there. The real problem will be to recognize that *now is the time to believe* the orator and give up my old beliefs.

But the trouble goes even further than that. It is not just that we need to study how to discover when rhetoric should be accepted because it *really reflects* reality; we need to study and teach a totally different view of what rhetoric is and what reality is.

In its simplest terms the error so far can be described as forgetting that rhetoric does not always either *reflect* reality, at best, or, at worst, *distort* it.

Rather, rhetoric often *makes* reality. The words and other symbols we use together often *are* reality, the truth, the world with which we must deal. And they often become a reality just as hard, in the sense of producing changes in other realities, as the most resistant stone or star.

Sometimes rhetoric makes a reality, *becomes* a reality, *is* a reality that is not just something suitable to the maker, not just a private illusion, but a reality that is real precisely in that basic sense we mean when we say that this room and those chairs and the flesh of your hand are real—a reality that has to be acknowledged by every honest observer. It dictates, in other words, what everybody else *ought* to say about it. We may not want to label it "objective" because in one sense we always have only our "subjective" pictures, and they can be encountered and tested only in our experience. But it is not simply subjective either, in the sense of depending on this or that person's private view. Perhaps for now we can be satisfied simply by calling it *real*. We might then use some word like *intersubjective* for our agreements about it.[5]

In talking of ways in which rhetoric makes reality, I'd like to use a classification that theorists have used ever since Aristotle. Some words (deliberative rhetoric) make the future; some words (forensic rhetoric) judge the past; and some words (epideictic rhetoric) change our views about, and thus remake, the present. Starting with that limp but useful triad, I'll work toward a point that I think Aristotle and many others have understated: when words make your past, present, and future, what they really make is *you*, and thus all of them have what might be called an "epideictic center."

We start with the future, where my case is the most obvious. Once you

---

5. Much literary criticism since the late sixties has approached this fundamental truth about truth from what may appear to be an opposite viewpoint: language never reflects, or refers to, reality—it is always "opaque." "All we have is language." "We make our worlds *in* language, as a system of 'signs' each of which finds its meaning by reference not to anything external to language but by an endless chain of reference to other signs, with 'real meaning' always 'deferred'." This seemingly new and shattering move by a special breed of rhetoricians will not disturb anyone who has pursued classical rhetoric seriously, though it will disturb anyone who, like Socrates as he deals with the Sophists, insists on searching for a single perspective on the "Good" or the "One" that might serve as a rock on which to build a church.

What is wrong with the extreme "deconstructionist" moves is not that they leave us with no firm ground to stand on but that they do not usually acknowledge—Derrida is *sometimes* a brilliant exception—the ways in which their own words make new realities. Obsessed with dramatizing the permanent gap between our words and things in themselves, they underplay, in curious ways, the "solidity" of the "realities" they work with—*make*—as they write and speak. But to do any kind of justice to current theoretical battles about how or whether "reality" eludes our educational efforts would require another kind of book entirely, one with the emphasis, but by no means all of the conclusions, of Robert Scholes' *Textual Power: Literary Theory and the Teaching of English* (New Haven, 1985).

think about how our words *make* the future, it is surprising that anybody could ever have thought that the language we teach only *reflects* reality. Everybody assumes, in practice, that debate about what to do next somehow changes what we actually *do* next, so that the future is made, at least to some degree, in how I talk about it right now. A family argues about where to take its vacation, and the reality of the vacation is changed by the argument. A teaching staff debates next year's textbooks, and authors' royalty checks show real changes. (Of course there are in such moments also changes in the reality of the present. If the argument is a pleasant one, the present is made more fun; if it is an unpleasant argument, the present is less fun. In either case the debaters are making some present reality *of that kind*.)

Such *deliberative* rhetoric, as it was traditionally called, can produce results as hard as bullets, since it often literally determines who will die and who will live. In a way everybody knows this. It is denied only when people talk theoretically about whether human beings have free choice, or when theorists of language just plain forget what language in fact does. When people say "Cut the cackle and get down to the hard facts," they exhibit in that statement itself a wish that the statement will change the future—that it will at least "cut the cackle."

You will remember my quotation from Betty Friedan, saying that her *words* were never meant to take the place of *action* that might change society. What do you suppose she turned to when she stopped "depending on words," as she put it? "Why," she said, "I threw myself into the action"— and the list of actions turns out to be: "I lectured, drafted statements of purpose, interviewed, kept a public diary, and wrote reports and articles." That's all the *action* she lists. That's "getting away from the words and getting down to the action." Her unthinking acceptance of the popular disjunction illustrates that we are talking about two kinds, or phases, of real action, not a distinction between rhetoric and reality.

Important as our deliberative rhetoric is in determining future realities, I am more interested here in the curious way in which its effects spill backwards, as it were, into the present. It was always clear that epideictic rhetoric could make the difference between good life and bad. When we praise or blame each other, lament our losses, celebrate our victories, eulogize our heroes and institutions, we can make or break a given day or year or epoch. How we talk about it changes what it is. But there is an interesting sense in which our deliberative or political rhetoric effects the same kind of transformation of reality. Since it is a process hardly ever talked about, and since the great public that cares about basics has an immense stake in it, I shall spend the rest of this speech trying to make that point clear.

Since there is some danger that some of you might consider my thinking a bit mushy from here on, I'm going to offer one of those queer things that every talk on rhetoric ought to have at least one of—a good solid *sorites*. Aristotle, you remember, says that a sorites—that is, a chain of syllogisms— should never be too long or too short. Sound advice, and I have of course followed it. The first syllogism:

Major premise: Individual freedom is a fundamental value we all pursue, and indeed ought to pursue, as essential to all else that we value. We could discuss this premise but I assume that we don't need to here.

Minor premise: Individual freedom depends on institutions that operate through politics—that is, through a political process of give-and-take, of talking things out, of seeking reasonable compromise—rather than through the imposition of force or the will of one leader or group. I must say something in a moment about this minor premise because it is not self-evident, but first, the conclusion to this first syllogism.

Therefore: Politics is a major value that we all pursue and indeed ought to pursue. Instead of being a naughty word, politics is, or are, the only defense we have against the tyranny either of a single tyrant or of whatever group at a given moment has the power to impose its collective will.

We should pause for a moment in our pursuit of rigorous logic, to discuss the minor premise that landed us in the embarrassing spot of saying a good word for politics. We could in fact spend considerable time on the reasons for saying that our individual freedom depends on politics. What I will do instead is recommend to you a fine little book by Bernard Crick, *In Defence of Politics*. Crick's brief and witty argument boils down to this: when interests of various groups and judgments by members of those groups clash, as they always will in any fully human society, how many ways are there to resolve the differences? There are in fact only two: either the stronger power will impose itself by force or the threat of force, or the contending interests will seek a political solution—that is, a solution that depends on accommodation among interests.[6] Crick puts it this way:

> Common usage of the word might encourage one to think that politics
> is a real force in every organised state. But a moment's reflection should
> reveal that this common usage can be highly misleading. For politics, as

---

6. The use of bribes could of course be considered a third way. But for clarity in this defense of rhetoric, all bribery can be seen as falling under either the use of force ("The amount offered was so large as to be considered coercive"), or as rhetoric: "Yes, George, I know that you consider accepting bribes immoral. But look at it this way. If you don't join me here, you are in effect being bribed by our common enemy. . . ."

Aristotle points out, is only one possible solution to the problem of order. It is by no means the most usual. Tyranny is the most obvious alternative—the rule of one strong man in his own interest; and oligarchy is the next most obvious alternative—the rule of one group in their own interest. The method of rule of the tyrant and the oligarch is quite simply to clobber, coerce or overawe all or most of these other groups in the interest of their own. The political method of rule is to listen to these other groups so as to conciliate them as far as possible, and to give them a legal position, a sense of security, some clear and reasonably safe means of articulation, by which these other groups can and will speak freely. Ideally politics draws all these groups into each other so that they each and together can make a positive contribution towards the general business of government, the maintaining of order. . . . But, however imperfectly this process of deliberate conciliation works, it is nevertheless radically different from tyranny, oligarchy, kingship, dictatorship, despotism and—what is probably the only distinctively modern type of rule—totalitarianism.[7]

Crick has now prepared us for the second syllogism. As in all sorites, our new major premise is the conclusion of the previous syllogism:

Major premise: Politics is immensely important to all of us, our only defense against tyranny.

Minor premise: The quality and success of any truly political process will depend on the quality of the rhetorical exchange among the participants— that is, you and me. We can here pick up from Crick's statement the phrases "listen to these other groups" and "means of articulation." Again this will take some discussion, but you can see ahead to our conclusion—

Therefore: Improving our rhetoric is our best defense, our only alternative to tyranny.

(Perhaps we should note that the threat of force in itself can be considered a form of rhetoric, but it is surely a degraded form, "mere" rhetoric often hard to distinguish from the use of force itself; it is in fact force disguised as words, words that indeed obscure reality.)

Again in this second syllogism, it is the minor premise that raises the questions. What can it mean to say that the quality of any political process depends on the quality of the rhetoric available to the politicians? Most of us have some general sense that this is true, but it is not an easy proposition to prove to anyone who is determined to doubt it.

Yet it is surely true. Perhaps it is most obviously seen to be true in the matter of public lying. A society that encourages lying and depends on it for

7. Bernard Crick, *In Defence of Politics*, 2d ed. (Chicago and London, 1972), 18–19.

its functioning obviously cannot long endure without tyranny. The exchange of reasons among contending interests depends on maintaining some level of integrity and hence trust, so that reasons can be in reality exchanged. It seems obvious that if any society ever reaches a point at which everyone can always assume that in all likelihood everyone else is lying, the political process in our sense is dead, and the resulting inhuman chaos will soon be resolved by some tyrannical takeover. Thus what we call political corruption is a *real* corruption, a corruption of rhetoric. If it goes beyond a certain point, always hard to determine, we are doomed. One often wonders how close we are to that point in America. I doubt that public lying has ever been as profitable as it is today.[8]

One thinks inevitably in this connection of recent books by Haldeman and Nixon, immensely profitable mixtures of lies, half-truths, and perhaps even an occasional truth, though there is no reason to expect it. I loved Sam Erwin's recent statement about Haldeman's book: "I would believe what Haldeman says only if it was testified to by all the apostles except Judas. It's not entirely unlikely that a man who has lied when under oath might conceivably lie when *not* under oath." But the trouble is that our lives are filled with too many Haldemans and Nixons for the Sam Erwins to keep up with them. And the point is that they are bad not just for our deliberative rhetoric: they pollute our political atmosphere, they degrade our lives—right now in the present.

Perhaps that is enough about the minor premise of syllogism number two, though many a book could and should be written about it. Let me hurry on to my third syllogism; again the major premise is the conclusion of the previous syllogism:

Major premise: Improving our rhetoric is our only alternative to tyranny.

Minor premise: Our best hope for improving our rhetoric is improvement in rhetorical education.

Therefore: Well, I'm almost embarrassed to say it, it seems just a bit self-serving to announce that you and I are charged by our society to teach one another and all we meet how to read and write, listen, think, and speak; that we are charged, in other words, with improving the arts of rhetoric; that we are society's front-line troops; not only against tyranny

---

8. Written in 1980 or 1981, the statement seems, in May of 1988, like an understatement; we now have a presidential crew who have in effect proclaimed lying to be their chief tool. Ask yourself whether you will believe, without checking some other source, anything that *anyone* in the White House claims.

in the future but against the dehumanizing of our lives right now. Embarrassing as any particular phrase of self-annointing may sound to our own ears, the fact remains: Everything we value in our society depends, directly or indirectly, on our ability to teach one another how to think about what people say—to teach not only the defensive rhetoric of smoking out the liars and thieves, but the affirmative art of sorting out the maybes, discovering our true friends and true interests, and marshalling the forces of language on behalf of our true interests, as we find them. I see no escape from the conclusion, self-centered or not, that liberal education as the study of rhetoric is our best hope for preserving free activity of any kind, including all other kinds of study, and thus any chance we have of improving our schools.

That might be a good place to end, but the discovery of our responsibility is obviously only a beginning. Where do we move, when the syllogisms have done what they can do?

The first point should be a warning about where *not* to move. Our inescapable political powers can avoid corruption only to the degree that they are not turned to the service of particular political factions. If we teachers try to organize our students, or talk them into lining up behind any one specific program that we happen to like, instead of teaching them the arts of rhetorical analysis and exchange, our pedagogical rhetoric will immediately turn into *mere* rhetoric, regardless of the virtues of our cause. Having taught them merely a line of action we think good because it may build some kind of desirable future, we will have neglected to teach them how to work thoughtfully and effectively on behalf of causes that you and I have not yet dreamed of.

The second point follows. Much of what we must do will not look like politics, and it will often be called something other than rhetoric. Though I have talked mainly of political rhetoric, as an example of how reality is made by rhetoric, I hope you can see how the same point applies to every nook and cranny of our lives. We not only affect future reality as we debate what we should do, we also affect the reality of our lives right now. We change ourselves with every kind of rhetorical exchange; and the changes then produce further effects. The reality that is most decisively made, in every kind of rhetoric our students meet, is people, the very shapes of their minds and souls. When historians, for example, make and remake our past, what are they really making? They are making new versions of you and me. I am in large part what I think my past was. If I have no roots, I am vulnerable. Give me good roots and I can flourish. Again, when the pseudo-anthropologists tell us that we are essentially naked apes or weapon wielders or creatures with a territorial imperative, they are making and remaking our very natures, so malleable are we all. And when novelists, playwrights, and poets tell us and our students that we are lost, miserable creatures caught in a life that is a swindle, a slaughterhouse, a madhouse, a rat race, a con game, a carnal house, a whorehouse, a raging inferno, a pigsty, the lowest circle of hell—to use only a few of the current metaphors they offer—they change not just our picture of what *other* people are, they change what *we* are, both as we read and as we move after reading. Such metaphors are not just the sea we swim in (though that is a much better metaphor than "the screen through which we observe" or "our tools for grappling with reality"); they are the air we breathe, or even better, our psychic food. We are what we have eaten. Our minds and souls have been made mainly out of other people's rhetoric.

It takes no very deep analysis of the current scene to conclude that we consume a daily diet that is nine-tenths poison. Half of the other tenth is pablum, baby food designed deliberately to keep us from ever growing up. Just think of the images of our human possibilities that are projected by what Tom Wolfe calls the one-hand magazines, by the novels we are most likely to pick up from the drugstore rack, by television ads and standard television dramas, by the typical political appeal. But once I get warmed up, I'll become more preachy than I've already been. I must resist that, and conclude instead with some suggestion about how my claims for rhetoric relate to the other aspects of our lives as teachers.

I have tried to suggest why what the public really wants is also what we want. We *are* the public, in the matter of consuming and responding to a flood of rhetoric that on the one hand seems nine-tenths lies but on the other is the very lifeblood of our democratic survival. "The public" says that it wants "good English," too often meaning by that simply writing and speaking that are cleansed of this or that horrendous error. We want to *educate*; we hope for graduates who will have been permanently "turned on" to self-education: readers, writers, thinking citizens of a republic more civilized than any we now inhabit. There can be no real conflict here. Students who are taught by teachers who are themselves reading and writing about what matters, students who learn to care about whether they get themselves *heard*, will want to learn the skills that make their thought accessible to others. Those skills go far beyond, but obviously include, whatever the usage handbooks contain that is worth knowing. (Some of it is not worth knowing, but that's another subject). When and where to fuss directly about comma splices, dangling modifiers, and the distinction between "affect" and "effect" cannot be decided in a general way, and need not be programmed for whole schools, districts, states, or nations[9]—so long as we keep our energies concentrated on educating the kind of student who will embrace learning to read and write as his or her own goal. Each of us knows this fact from personal experience in our own writing: it is when we care most about our rhetorical success that we are most determined to avoid whatever surface errors might lead to failure. We also know something that our public judges too often forget: that what is bad punctuation and grammar on one rhetorical occasion might be required in another, and that the details of what any rhetor does will usually depend on the desire to establish a bond with some other human being.

Perhaps it is obvious that the education in rhetoric that I am talking about will often be conducted under some other name, and that it is not the business of English teachers alone. It may be pursued under names like language arts or civics or popular culture or history or general science or film criticism or simply reading and writing. It may indeed be taught by teachers who have never heard the word *rhetoric* except as a term of abuse.

What I have said about rhetoric is only a sample of what we might want to say to one another about other values we care for. You may have noted that in defending rhetoric I seemed to have scuttled Shakespeare and Homer because, as I said, students can in some sense survive without Shakespeare and Homer, as they cannot survive without mastering the arts of rhetoric. Clearly I do not intend to scuttle the study of the world's great literature. I am convinced that we share with the public—in spite of the fact that many members of the public do not know it—as deep a common interest in *literary* education as in rhetorical education. But to make that common interest

9. (A postscript from the perspective of 1988): We have now discovered a public clamoring for a new kind of "basic," "cultural literacy," in the form of the list of terms provided by E. D. Hirsch, Jr., in his *Cultural Literacy: What Every American Needs to Know* (Boston, 1987). I fear the effects of any top-down imposition of such a list even more than I deplore the imposition of statewide, quantifiable, "competence" tests about more traditional lists. Most of what is in such tests, or any tests of cultural literacy that are likely to be devised, will in itself look unexceptionable: educated people "need" to know most of that stuff. The folly lies in thinking that since everyone ought to know, for example, that *Hamlet* is a play by Shakespeare, education will be served by teaching that fact as a raw fact. Hirsch does warn against such crude stuffing, but I fear that the warning will be attended to far less than his cries of alarm about the ignorance of our charges; besides, he does say that using Lamb's potted versions of Shakespeare's "tales" is one satisfactory way of feeding in the information kids ought to have. See my "Liberal Education and Cultural Literacy: An Open Letter to E. D. Hirsch, Jr." *Change*, July/August, 1988, 11–21, and his reply in the same issue.

clear will require of us much thought and many different efforts at translation of the kind I have attempted here concerning this other common interest. And the same can be said of any other deep value that the public seems to ignore when it calls for spelling bees: knowledge of history, of the physical sciences, of mathematics beyond arithmetical skills. What this means is that in electing to be educators we have elected to be educators of the adult public as well as of our charges. But it also means that we have elected to make a lifetime project of educating ourselves. Nothing of what we would defend can be defended by people who do not care for it enough to practice it as a daily habit. If we do not read and think and speak and write with a loving attention to how words can create or destroy, we'll never convince the public that its view of things is stunted and self-destructive.

To work at improving one's own education is hard; to try to teach other people how to improve theirs is much harder. But to attempt to improve a nation's educational climate seems at times an almost hopeless task. We do, however, have many resources on our side, you and I, including our vast inheritance of great novels, plays, poems, speeches, constitutions, philosophical works, histories, and theories of rhetoric and literary criticism. We also have, or so I like to think, a natural hunger for something better than we are fed on all sides. I may be wrong about that natural hunger. It may be, for all anyone can prove, that any culture whose children spend four to eight hours a day with television, and then spend their remaining hours in school with harried teachers who must teach from eviscerated textbooks designed by programmers trying to drill in one bit of information at a time— it *may* be that such a culture will be permanently crippled, molded in shapes of desire and fulfillment that make real growth impossible. I refuse to believe it, but the experience of every teacher today—from the first grade on—shows that even if education is our best hope, it is a slim one.

I would like to end on a more cheerful note, but I cannot. I do not *know* that we are not now on a hopelessly irreversible downward spiral. What I do claim, however, is that the issue at stake in our conflicts about the "basics" is the most important reality we know: the quality of our lives together, today and in the years to come.

OCCASION 3 · *To New Recruits to Teaching and Scholarship in the "Humanities":*

The Scholar in Society

> No one can predict what Europe will be like at the dawn of the twenty-first century; yet we know one thing about it. The men [and women] who will be in posts of responsibility then are already university students. The future of the nineteenth-century idea of a university is in their hands.
>
> Eric Ashby

Not one of your easy assignments, this one: "Say something *useful* to the would-be scholar about how to relate the scholarly role to society." What exactly is a scholar? And what in the world do we mean when we speak of society?

Is the invited essayist himself a scholar? People refer to him as a critic or as a rhetorical theorist. He has done some literary history, in his youth. He lists himself on passports as Teacher. When he reads *The New York Review of Books*, he thinks of himself as an intellectual. Are critics, rhetorical theorists, literary historians, teachers, and intellectuals *scholars?* And—whatever scholars are—what should be their relationship to whatever society is?

I

The scholar. Back in male chauvinist times, someone defined an intellectual as a man who has found something in the world more interesting than sex. Intellectuals have often contrasted scholars and intellectuals, to the detriment of the scholars: a scholar is a professional researcher who is paid to be pedantic, while an intellectual is someone who pursues ideas for their own sake. A scholar once replied that the difference between a scholar and an intellectual is that the intellectual has read an article on a given subject, while the scholar has read a book.

Commissioned by the Modern Language Association for the volume of advice to beginning scholars in the humanities, *Introduction to Scholarship in Modern Languages and Literatures*, edited by Joseph Gibaldi (New York: Modern Language Association, 1981), 116–43.

Instead of calling names, it should be more useful, as we struggle with an unusually ill-defined subject, to assume that there's nobody here but us scholars—that anyone who will risk being caught reading an essay like this in a volume of this kind obviously wants to be not a pedant but a genuine scholar, cares very much about learning for its own sake, and is willing to do what is needed to make sense out of the scholarly enterprise. Part-time intellectuals, part-time teachers, part-time scholars, we here consider what it means to be a scholar, a scholar *in* society.

"A scholar," we might say, "is anyone who sits alone (and often lonely) for as much as three days in a row, reading or thinking or writing about a single problem. She may or may not be paid for it. He may or may not publish.[1] But what makes a scholar a scholar is the willingness to sit alone, for long periods, trying to learn something that cannot be learned 'in society,' something that cannot be learned except through sustained, private inquiry." It might be objected that the privacy stipulation in this definition rules out team research. No doubt there are some problems that are best pursued in groups, but when such groups are examined they usually reveal the presence of only one or two scholars, who do a great deal of private thinking; the rest are flunkies, who carry out the experiments or data-collecting that the thinking dictates, or supervisors, who take the credit when the results are published.

The trial definition obviously embraces many people as scholars whom we ordinarily call by other names—certain business executives, architects, gamblers. It also suggests that many of us who are called scholars are scholars only during brief interludes. Many who sit at their desks regularly, "doing their own work," are not really scholars, because they are trying, not to learn something, but only to find a way of saying again what they already know: they are writers, or publicists, or self-repeating mechanisms, harmless drudges carrying out what amount to clerical tasks assigned by— well, by "society."

Where does the definition place me, asked by my society, the MLA, to sit alone (and increasingly lonely) at a desk increasingly messy with dis-

---

1. Could anything illustrate more clearly my own sense of being an occupied territory— occupied by society—than my discomfort in using *any* of the pronouns, or any alternative stylistic solution, that different readers would elect for this spot? The plural will sometimes work, but usually it weakens the point, as it would do here. In a first draft I tried alternating *his* and *hers* throughout, but two of my three official readers rightly objected that the experiment was distracting. So it will be *hers* throughout. Unfortunately, to make a statement like the following is no real solution: "Throughout this essay, all feminine pronouns should be read as referring to females and males alike." [1987 note: Since publishing this demurrer in 1981, I've read many pieces using the *she* ploy. It usually does not work very well. But I still think that it nicely fit my occasion *then,* writing as a scholar *in* society.]

connected half-thoughts about the scholar in society? I can see elements of the drudge, elements of the publicist, but where is the scholar? I must get to the library fast and do some scholaring on what other people have said about the scholar in society.

I find a book by Howard Mumford Jones, called *One Great Society: Humane Learning in the United States,* a report on what a whole commission of scholars thought about this matter. They all seem to think of the scholar as any serious student who is not a scientist. Scientists do scientific research. Scholars do humanistic research.

Suppose we try out their implied definition: "A scholar is anyone who sits alone for sustained periods trying to solve a problem that cannot be solved by a physical or biological or social scientist."

I must believe that I am making progress or I shall get up from my desk and lose all hope of being a scholar. But there are many difficulties here. I remember that Northrop Frye, who wrote the essay on literary criticism for the precursor of this volume,[2] made a good deal of the claim that criticism is a science; I remember also that much of what my scholarly colleagues do is indistinguishable in method from what scientists do. Come to think of it, for many modern theorists my definition will mean that a scholar works only on problems that cannot be solved at all, since solutions are the domain of the sciences. Maybe I can safely ignore this difficulty, because many other modern thinkers have given up the notion that even scientists ever solve problems once and for all. But I can't so easily dodge a further difficulty: the definition includes everybody who ever thinks about anything—advertising executives, who wrestle for days on end with the problem of how to sell plastic milk, or those geniuses at playing blackjack who think and think about how to keep the house-man from recognizing a new way of cheating.

I must try again. "A scholar is anyone who sits alone for sustained periods trying to solve a problem for the sake of interest in the problem and its solution, not for the sake of some practical achievement in the world like selling plastic milk or winning at blackjack."

This one at least has the virtue of explaining why scholars have always been so concerned about developing clear lines between what they do and what other people do when they sit at desks. As soon as somebody stops trying to solve a problem and starts exhorting people, she is no longer a scholar but someone else, someone who doesn't see sitting at a desk thinking as an end in itself.

I suspect that this definition might have satisfied the founders of the

2. James Thorpe, ed., *The Aims and Methods of Scholarship in Modern Languages and Literatures,* 2d ed. (New York, 1970).

MLA, if we had added the simple qualification, "a problem about modern languages and literatures." But it would exclude about ninety percent of what my colleagues and I do in the name of scholarship. It would dictate excluding an essay of this kind from this volume. Or at least it would require that if there were such an essay, its point would be to show scholars how to protect their work from the poisonings of praxis.

My efforts to define seem no more successful than those I find in the library stacks. But surely I am accumulating wisdom about my subject as I go. I can now at least list, like a good undergraduate who has done her "analysis" properly, six kinds of people who sit lonely in front of their desks, working over the modern languages and literatures instead of going off to hobnob with the gang at the club or at the national convention of (former) scholars: Intellectuals, who sit at their desks for no more than four hours on any one problem; Drudges, who sit at their desks working at other people's problems; Missionaries, who make *use* of hours at their desks; Publicists, who sit at their desks trying to find some new way of saying what they already knew when they first sat down; Scientists, who are ineffable; and Scholars, who are what we are all presumably trying to become. Some of the time.

Intellectuals we need not worry about; the more of them the better, provided we don't confuse what they do with scholarship. Besides, every good scholar is an intellectual too. Drudges we do not worry about. Whenever we drudge—and none of us can avoid it—our relation to society is fixed, so long as we remain Drudges: we *serve* it, often honorably, whether society is a senatorial committee or only that thesis chairman helping to get the damn thing out of the way. Missionaries we do not worry about for the same reason: when we become evangelical, our relation to society is also fixed, as we try to change it—honorable work, since every free society depends on vast numbers of thinking Missionaries to keep public life from freezing into its naturally wicked paths. Scientists we do worry about: for about three centuries we've spent a fair share of those hours at the desk trying to use or refute or adjust to the latest news from the lab.

The great public that never sits alone at a desk except to balance monthly accounts thinks that all scholars are Drudges, or should be: every scholar's labor should be as visibly useful to the world as the manufacture of safety pins. Drudges think that all scholarship must be drudgery, since they have never known it to be anything else. Missionaries think that all scholars are Irresponsibles. Intellectuals think that all scholars are either trivia experts or obscurantists. Scientists think that scholars are fakers. And the Scholars—what do they think?

Well, if they *are* scholars, they don't quite know for sure yet. Though they are usually sure that this unsureness is some sort of blessing, it looks like a curse to everyone else. To the public it is a curse because it means that scholars are always questioning what had seemed established. Intellectuals see it as a curse because it leads people to ask embarrassing questions about evidence and reasons. Drudges see it as a curse because it means that just as the dissertation is about finished, that untrustworthy director has changed her mind about the whole problem. Missionaries see it as a special curse because it makes organizing the world for progress so difficult. And to the Scientist, it is *our* special curse: to be radically confused simply means that *serious* inquiry has not yet been tried.

II

Society. Now, society is . . . well, society is like culture, which means that it is very hard to define. Gerald Holton, introducing *Science and Culture*, another volume that I found when scholaring, says that he can't define it, and he quotes anthropologists A. L. Kroeber and Clyde Kluckhohn, who can't define it either, quoting A. Lawrence Lowell's claim that "there is nothing in the world more elusive. One cannot analyze it, for its components are infinite. One cannot describe it, for it is a Protean in shape. An attempt to encompass its meaning in words is like trying to seize the air in the hand, when one finds that it is everywhere except in one's grasp."[3]

But of course we've already been defining society. Society, for the scholar, is surely all those other people: the mere intellectuals, the drudges, the missionaries, the scientists, the thesis supervisors or tenure committees, the editors of journals and presses, the great public. It is everybody who is not sitting right now at this desk. The only person in the world, right now, who is not society is me, or I, sitting here with society shut out so that I can work at this problem, which is mine, all mine. Society is the telephone, a long-distance call from a student asking why I have not returned his dissertation chapter; it is the daily mail, with a request from NEH; it is the committees, the family, the budget, the daily blasts of horrifying news. It is everything that will do its best to deflect me from solving . . . whatever this problem turns out to be, once I have thought about it for a few more hours, in private.

3. Gerald Holton, ed., *Science and Culture: A Study of Cohesive and Disjunctive Forces* (Boston, 1965). Most of Holton's selections were originally published in an issue of *Daedalus* (Winter 1965) based on a conference that in a sense was entirely devoted to our problem here—but with the word "science" substituted for our word "scholarship." To anyone interested in how our social role relates to that of the "scientist," I recommend especially the essays by James S. Ackerman, Don K. Price, Eric Weil, and Robert S. Morison.

Could anything be more misleading than that seemingly inevitable po-larity? Like it or not, every scholar is always in a society and could not be a scholar if she were not. It may be a small, clearly defined society, like the monastery that supported and restricted medieval monks and nuns who itched to inquire. More often it is multiple and poorly defined. For every scholar "*in* America," as we say, society is many societies, some of them formally named, like the MLA or NOW or the Democratic party or the board of trustees, but most of them unincorporated, like the growing num-ber of my past students requesting recommendations, the non-academic friends and relatives who express their wonder about what on earth I am up to, immured in the stacks.

But it is folly to think of society as the enemy, "out there." Society is *in* the scholar. Even when doing the purest scholarship, the scholar works as a member of many groups, belongs to a time and place, asks questions and performs tasks that are in no sense private. Even if we were foolish enough to try to invent our scholarship free of influences, any perceptive observer from any other time or place could easily recognize our origins. We should not need the Marxists to tell us that we can learn only what our time allows us to learn, because we can ask only those questions and use only those methods that are alive in our time.

There is no known instance of an isolated genius raised in an unscholarly society who invented interesting scholarship out of pure native wit. This deeply social truth is only slightly caricatured in the study of Nobel Prize winners showing that most Nobel laureates have associated closely with other Nobel laureates, either as their students or as their colleagues.[4] Every scholar, good or bad, becomes a scholar *by associating*, or, since that word has lost much of its force, we might say *by societing*.

No doubt many of us will continue to derive comfort from the myth that society is simply the enemy; literary portraits of embattled Arrowsmiths are inherently more exciting than sociological reports on how scholars do their actual societing. But even as we do so we will be enacting a role that our society, as playwright, has created for us.

III

If the scholar is someone who tries to learn by sustained private inquiry conducted "for its own sake" and if society is *in* every scholar, we can easily understand why scholarship has always seemed so fragile and why scholars have often seen themselves as in opposition to society. Scholarship as we

4. Harriet Zuckerman, "The Sociology of the Nobel Prizes," *Scientific American* (November 1967): 25–35. See especially the chart on p. 33.

have defined it is indeed fragile, a late-blooming flower in any civilization (when it blooms at all). It looks hardy in twentieth-century America, or at least it did until recent economic setbacks, only because society has agreed to reward its practitioners with academic positions. Despite current depredations, we still have a larger proportion of paid scholars, I suspect, than any other culture in history.[5]

That the institution of scholarship is fragile we know from history; though it has been often invented, it has almost as often died, or come so near to dying that its preservers—a few crazy monks in Ireland, say, or in Tibet—seem provided only by chance, or by the Great Provider.

That each scholar's impulse to scholarship is even more fragile we know from evidence closer to home: most scholars see its fires flicker and die many times in their lives. Even if we leave aside, reluctantly, the many who, in their forties or fifties or sixties echo those wonderful words of George Eliot's Mr. Brooke—

> I went into science a great deal myself at one time, but I saw it would not do. It leads to everything; you can let nothing alone. . . . I took in all the new ideas at one time—human perfectibility, now. But some say history moves in circles, and that may be very well argued; I have argued it myself. The fact is, human reason may carry you a little too far—over the hedge, in fact. It carried me a good way at one time, but I saw it would not do. I pulled up; I pulled up in time. But not too hard. I have always been in favor of a little theory: we must have Thought, else we shall be landed back in the dark ages. . . . (*Middlemarch*, chap. 2)

—even if we leave aside the many who have failed for many years to sit steadily at that desk, whether from anger or contempt or grief or drink, we find that most of us who affect scholarship manage to bring it alive only for brief, blessed periods: a summer here, a year's leave there, a six-week burst of exhilarated inquiry when society, including our teaching, was neglected while we tried to answer some question that had ambushed us. And then, for months, years, decades, not scholarship but something else.

As Yeats says about the poet, all things can tempt us. I see one friend, a "seventeenth-century woman," writing a freshman composition text, and another friend building his own house, nail by nail, and another deciding at

5. This statement may seem to understate the seriousness of current threats to our profession, but I do take those threats to be serious indeed. (See my little cry of alarm, "An Arrogant Proposal," Occasion 7 below.) We cannot know, in the midst of the current job crisis, whether the effects will be worse than those, say, of the Depression, or of World War II. But they *might* be, unless the profession finds ways to combat the loss of nerve that to many seems even more threatening than the loss of jobs. My essay here obviously has only oblique relevance to the latter, but the two losses are obviously close-knit. No scholar who ignores the plight of junior humanists without jobs can be said to be a humanistic scholar.

last to write his novel. I see but seldom hear from my A.B.D.'s out in the tules: they accept a chairmanship, take up photography, run for political office. I see myself reading *Time* magazine on the plane bound for MLA meetings. . . .

But we are also—young and old—lured away by quite different temptations. Most of us can remember a youthful time when we saw scholarship not only as contemptible but as threatening to what we cared about in literature. How we palpitated to Yeats's "The Scholars":

> Bald heads forgetful of their sins,
> Old, learned, respectable bald heads
> Edit and annotate the lines
> That young men, tossing on their beds,
> Rhymed out in love's despair
> To flatter beauty's ignorant ear.
>
> All shuffle there; all cough in ink;
> All wear the carpet with their shoes;
> All think what other people think;
> All know the man their neighbor knows.
> Lord, what would they say
> Did their Catullus walk that way?*

Today, along with such youthful and admirable contempt, we experience a different attack: after deeply theoretical, perhaps even scholarly, inquiry, many humanists young and old are announcing that scholarship is not just absurd but Absurd: it is not free inquiry at all but simply one way of preserving power.

So it is that the scholar, *in* society, inhabited by society, is slave to fate, chance, kings, and desperate men. She doth with poison, war, and sickness dwell. That she survives at all is a wonder. Is it a good thing that scholarly societies should tempt their members, young and old, further to neglect their scholarship in order to think about scholarship?[6]

Perhaps the answer will depend on the quality of the thinking. It is all

---

*Reprinted with permission of Macmillan Publishing Company, and of A. P. Watt Ltd. on behalf of Michael B. Yeats and Macmillan London Ltd., from *The Poems: A New Edition* by W. B. Yeats, edited by Richard J. Finneran, copyright 1916 by Macmillan Publishing Company, renewed 1944 by Bertha Georgie Yeats.

6. This is not the first time that the MLA has done so. Though the previous edition of this project contained no essay on this subject—in fact it gave very little hint that such a subject might exist—other publications show that the MLA has almost always tried to support a social climate in which scholarship could thrive. On the other hand, anyone reading through those publications will find that many members thought such matters proper only to organizations like the National Council of Teachers of English, the Conference on College Composition and Communication, or the National Education Association.

very well to circle about the thinker's desk as we have been doing, taking notes, but how are we to *think* about our roles, instead of simply extolling or lamenting them? Thought, presumably, should be in some sense sharable, "objective" at least in the sense of differing from the work of missionaries and publicists. But even to list the issues we face is to violate someone else's list of what the issues should be.

If I ask where the scholar should draw the line in acceding to society's requests, I am already granting society the right to put questions to us. If I ask to what degree a scholar should be held responsible for the ethical consequences of scholarship, I have already ruled into our subject a topic that others would simply rule out from the beginning. And if I ask how the scholar is to reconcile her scholarly life with her role as teacher, I am already granting to teaching the full status as rival that some would deny to it.

IV

In the history of thought about our subject, perhaps the most powerful statements have been those by champions of scholarly autonomy. A free scholarship did not come into the world without battle; it had to be earned with argument and, one suspects, with the powerful assistance of useful results in the world produced by a freed scientific research. In the many past statements defending autonomy, one can detect a short list of persistent fears that always underlay the formulation of issues. Every scholar today has reason still to share those fears, but, for reasons I have already touched on, we cannot allow ourselves to be led by them into a hopeless battle for an isolated and autonomous scholarship.

I must now proceed from fear to fear, attempting both to do justice to the reasons for past battles and to move beyond the fears to the issues that every scholar must think about. I shall not, of course, suggest what every scholar should think. But I do claim that every responsible scholar should think through each issue in order to be ready at any time, in a sense "on demand," to give to her many societies the grounds for deserving support. In an absolute monarchy, presumably, a scholar could perform this task by thinking only of the reasons she can give her monarch when the old girl quavers, "What, you need *another* thousand, for *research?*" But in a democracy, the task is immensely complex because our publics are manifold.

The Fear That Scholarly Results Will Be Measured by Unscholarly Standards and Unscholarly People

As soon as a scholar's work is made subject to judgments about its value to someone else, there is clearly a danger that relevance to immediate needs will prevail over scholarly priorities. Researchers in the harder sciences have always had, at least until recently, a fairly good reply to those who sought relevance: engineering made scientific results relevant so quickly after discovery that it was easy to show that pure research was usually practical, at least in the long run. (Now that the practical results threaten to be terrifyingly impractical, scientists have some more thinking to do.) But in the humanities a demand for immediate relevance to social needs would obviously exclude a large share of what we admire most. Is it not safer, then, simply to cut society dead, before it starts asking of us a closer friendship than we care to grant?

The unprepared, the unscholarly, the inexpert are, in a democracy, always ready to believe that one woman's opinion on any subject is as good as another's. America has never lacked a supply of confident critics like Senator William Proxmire, who knows at a glance whether a project is ridiculous enough to deserve his Golden Fleece of the Month Award.

The humanities in America have always been plagued not just by demands for practicality but also by demands that "men of affairs," "men who have met a payroll," dictate what and how the schools should teach. Those who *can*, do; those who *can't*, teach. Let those who *can* dictate to those who *can't*. "If *I* can't understand it, hardheaded down-to-earth type that I am, there can't be much in it." "You're filling the heads of the young with insane socialist ideas that make them totally unfit for the real world." "You talk of teaching them to 'understand literature.' Well, what *I* want to ask is, why subject them to that mad Kafka and that unreadable Faulkner and that gloomy Dreiser and that dirty-minded Joyce and all those corrupt foreigners, when you could uplift them with these fine works that our board's committee has recommended to you?"

A governor of Texas, Jim Ferguson, once vetoed the entire annual state appropriation for the University of Texas, saying that too many people were going hog-wild about higher education. His veto was finally overridden, but were not the scholars of the state of Texas justified in their fears for the independence of the scholarly domain?[7]

Yet when we try to translate this justified fear into a question to be thought about, it is by no means self-evident that a simple plea for autonomy makes sense. The question might be phrased like this: To what extent should the worth of a given form of inquiry be measured by standards set by someone other than the inquirer?

I suspect that most scholars today would answer, "To no extent at all." Is

---

7. "Is the story true?" the *scholar* in me wonders. The intellectual/missionary in me, needing the anecdote for his point, refuses to trace it down!

it not the very nature of genuine inquiry that it must be freed of all restraints except those imposed by the problem and the standards of a given discipline? Yet in recent decades an increasing number of academics have argued either that free inquiry is never attainable and that arguments for it are simply disguises for the status quo, or that it would be undesirable if attained.

Defenders of autonomy can point to innumerable follies committed when the public decides to mock or censor studies in subjects it does not understand; Senator Proxmire amuses us when we know nothing about his subject, outrages us when the subject is our own. Contrary to Jerome Bruner's claim that every subject can be taught in some form to anyone of any age,[8] we all know that a great deal of what we value cannot be explained to anyone but a specialist, at least not within real limits of space, time, and patience (see Occasion 19 below).

On the other hand, to every thinking layman—and we are all laymen with respect to most inquiries—it seems obvious that we should not be asked to support many projects that in fact now receive public funding. In every field but my own, I find myself ready to ask a simple and nasty question: "Just how many scholars of that kind does a society *need?*" An intelligent and well-read member of my university's Board of Trustees once asked me, as we chatted during a banquet, "How many Chaucer scholars does a society need?" He could have made the question even tougher by asking not about Chaucer scholars but about experts in, say, *Piers Plowman,* or the Marquis de Sade, or George Sand. But one need not point only at others. For about two years of my life the United States government supported me (with the GI Bill) while I spent most of my time investigating the history of the self-conscious narrator in comic fiction before *Tristram Shandy.* I have since read many articles and even a book on something like the same subject, and there are hundreds of scholars now working on topics related to that one novel. Just how many scholars devoting their lives to Laurence Sterne does a society *need?*

Regardless of what field we think of here, we find that we are driven to acknowledge two seemingly opposing points: no public is qualified to answer the question, yet every public must answer it by the way it allocates its funds and thus rewards (or punishes) scholars who pursue this or that line.

If a Senate Subcommittee on the Worth of Scholarship begins to inquire into the value of my history of the self-conscious narrator, I feel justly indignant as I dig in my heels and tell the senators to go mess with matters

8. Jerome Bruner, *On Knowing: Essays for the Left Hand* (Cambridge, Mass., 1962).

they know something about. But if you ask me whether scholars studying the self-conscious narrator are in general qualified as final judges about how many such scholars my society should support, my response is much less clear.

Must we have fifty specialists in *Tristram Shandy?* As Goneril and Regan say, "What need you five-and-twenty, ten, or five . . . ? What need one?" Society long endured without a single scholarly article on *Tristram Shandy*, and if all of the published scholarship on it were wiped out tomorrow, would anyone in the world except us Sterne specialists suffer a sense of loss? As an expert on the self-conscious narrator in comic fiction before 1760, am I the best judge about whether society—let us say through the National Endowment for the Humanities—should provide support for more of my kind of thing? How, then, can we justify a national educational system that rewards and encourages scholarly specialization of this kind, often at the expense of simple essential matters like teaching the young how to read and write?

The scholar is, after all, not always the best judge of what her work is worth. She has put too much labor into it, whether it is good or bad, to be able to judge fairly whether it deserves public support.

My wife asks me to go cut some roses in the garden for the dinner we're giving tonight. For perhaps five minutes I do the best scholarly job I can of selecting the freshest ones, and we make a bouquet together. During the dinner I notice myself noticing the flowers more than I would have if she had cut them. My investment. My product. My roses. I find the bouquet good.

The scholar is like that, after the thinking is done. Anything I have put a great deal of myself into becomes my property, in a good old sense of the word: I have in it a piece of my *amour propre.* If any silly Senator Proxmire comes along and scoffs at it, so much the worse for him, I say; I *know* it is valuable.

It is thus almost certain that I will overvalue the importance of my own work, even when I see its faults. And scholars in general must surely overrate the importance of what they do as a body. We see this happening clearly to our colleagues in other disciplines. All the scientists we know naively overvalue science and undervalue the humanities. Every historian thinks history more important than it really can possibly be. Every social scientist similarly. . . . Why can't they all see that the most important scholarship is what we do—we *humane* inquirers?

But who, then, is to judge the importance of what we do, if none of us can be trusted? Why of course it must be other people—finally it is going to be people not yet born, but right now it is going to be *someone else out there*—some other scholar, if the question is the importance of "my own work" compared with "your own work," and some non-scholarly collectivity when the question is whether what we do is more important than what other scholars or teachers or postmen do.

My various societies thus allocate their resources and boost or hinder me in my scholarly endeavors. They support research about Chaucer or *Tristram Shandy* or Alcanter de Brahm because they have become somehow convinced, as we are convinced, that preservation of our literary culture is a good thing, that somehow literary culture graces or enhances their lives.

It is obvious that they will do this allocating well only if we have managed to teach them how to do it. We scholars have taught, after all, in our role as teachers, every member of society who carries much weight in society's allocations. And we continue to teach them and thus to make our society, by the nature and quality of what we do; they learn from us whether or not to take our work seriously.

In comparison with most other cultures, America has done not at all badly in educating a public that believes in higher education and the scholarship that feeds it, or should feed it, from the top down. Abuses of scholarship are somehow seen as a necessary cost paid for scholarship's ultimate value. The treatises on trivia and the nonsense that nobody will ever read must be tolerated in order to preserve the treasures that make a culture worth having. Whatever the reasons for past support, future support will depend on our ability to deepen and strengthen that conviction. And that in turn will depend more on what we do in the classroom than on what we publish. What the senator remembers about his teachers of literature will affect his vote much more strongly than any suspect scholarly title he happens to stumble upon in a busy day. We must be able to look him in the eye and say, with pride and assurance, that we deserve even more support because a society simply cannot have too many *teachers* who, because of their scholarly training, can teach Shakespeare, or Chaucer, or Sterne, or Jane Austen, or Mark Twain, in the illuminating and life-enhancing ways that he experienced in school and college.

There is another form of teaching that might also affect his vote, one that is perhaps even more badly neglected than classroom teaching. Our increasing specialization seems to have led to decreasing interest in addressing our results to non-specialists. Most of what scholars were writing in 1900, or 1925, or even 1950, could have been understood by any literate non-scholar. It might have been found boring, but it would not have been found unintelligible. Too much of what we publish now is both boring and unintelligible. No doubt many of our new problems deserve to be discussed with specialists in specialists' language. But most of our important work deserves also to be translated into a language that will, by its very nature, teach the public that we are serious and that what we do can be important to more than a priestly cult. America has a distinguished tradition of *haute vulgarisation*—of chautauquas and lyceums and college lecture series and literary journalism. The tradition is not dead, but I have the impression that it is pursued these days more vigorously among scientists than among humanists. Where is the Lewis Thomas of literary critics? Where is the *Scientific American* among our journals of literary study?

How many Chaucerians does a society need? An unanswerable question, because we could get along with none. How many good teachers of Chaucer does a society need? Another unanswerable question, because there is simply no limit. Would it not make sense to say that a society in which everyone was able to teach Chaucer—that is, to discuss him with pleasure and profit—would be a better society than one in which only, say, five hundred specialists could do so?

Thinking about our question has not, then, led us to an unequivocal answer giving the scholar the sole right to judge the worth of what she does. The scholar who works as amateur, devoting spare time to scholarship, may let her own curiosity or pleasure dictate whether she studies Pushkin or the game of push-pin. But the scholar who is paid *for* her scholarship must either find ways to teach its value to the world—whether the "world" consists of students or senators—or be prepared for the day in which California's Proposition 13 will be remembered as a mere hint of the drought to come.[9]

Fear That the Quest for Knowledge Will Be Abandoned for Other Goals, Worthy or Unworthy

We have all known many attacks on the primacy of cognitive aims in education. When Emerson pled, in his great Phi Beta Kappa address, for an *American* scholar, his ultimate appeal was not to something known but to something wished for. When John Dewey and other pragmatists attacked a kind of cognitive education that dealt, as they saw it, in frozen concepts, and substituted a pragmatic appeal to experience, many scholars were horrified. When pragmatism was taken up, often in garbled form, and turned into a "progressive education movement," many scholars felt that the Vandals were at the gates. It became widely believed that the many indubitable aca-

9. Since such hot issues cool quickly in public memory, it should perhaps be noted that Proposition 13 mandated for California the first nationally publicized tax cut that had drastic statewide consequences for educational budgets.

demic deficiencies in entering college classes in the fifties and sixties were a direct result of the schools' teaching "not the subject but the child," substituting notions like "growth," "personal well-being," and "maturation" for intellectual mastery.[10]

An urbane expression of the fear of a different kind of corruption can be found in the essay on literary criticism in the precursor of this volume. Northrop Frye's bête noire is "evaluation" or "judicial criticism." The true end of criticism is "to add to the understanding of a writer" (Thorpe, 72), and if what is added is to have any standing as *knowledge*, it cannot be evaluative. "Value judgments may be asserted, intuited, assumed, argued about, explained, attacked, or defended: what they never can be is demonstrated" (74). "Judicial criticism is based on good taste, and good taste is a skill founded by practice on the knowledge the critic has; academic criticism [which is the only proper subject for the academic scholar] is a structure of knowledge" (74).

Frye states again and again that he does not wish to disclaim the usefulness of judicial criticism, *in its proper place*. But that place is not the academy, and it is clear that if it enters the academy the proper order of things will be destroyed. It is only after cognitive criticism has done its work of showing how "the form of literature as a whole becomes the content of criticism as a whole" that we can face—in a final paragraph or two and not as literary scholars but as moralists and social critics—the question of what literature "does for society" (81).

The study of literature will lose its scholarly status, the fear tells us, unless it yields knowledge comparable to the knowledge offered in the more obviously scientific academic disciplines. And it will not yield knowledge if we allow ourselves to whore after these false gods of evaluation, or cultural relevance, or public service, or retribution for past social wrongs.

As we begin in the 1980s, we have seen enough shoddy work motivated by social concerns to justify the most extreme fears. Much that is published in the name of various new "scholarly" causes is clearly motivated not by any desire to know or learn, in any sense of the words, but by the desire to make converts. And it is not hard to imagine what some of the more rigorous scholars of previous generations—the great editors, the great literary

10. My younger readers may not remember the popularity of such books as Rudolf Flesch's *Why Johnny Can't Read—and What You Can Do About It* (New York, 1955) and Arthur Bestor's *Educational Wastelands: The Retreat from Learning in Our Public Schools* (Urbana, Ill., 1953). In the sixties and seventies similar impulses were expressed in the popular slogan, "Back to the basics!" They have recently clustered under the slogan "Cultural Literacy." See above, p. xii, n.4, and p. 43, n.9. See also George Steiner's review of Hirsch, "Little-Read Schoolhouse," *The New Yorker*, June 1, 1987, 106–10 and Robert Scholes's "Three Views of Education: Nostalgia, History, and Voodoo," *College English* 50 (March 1988): 323–32.

historians—would have to say about the results of our forgetting their insistence on what one of the greatest of their time, Max Weber, called
"value-free inquiry."

But we cannot simply revert to earlier cognitive models of inquiry, now
that we know what we know about the dangers and errors in the assumptions underlying those models. The knower, we all *now* know, *is* entailed in
what is known, and the bonds are far more intricate than anyone suspected
before this century. Even the hardest of the sciences, we are now told
on what seems unimpeachable authority (I name only Gödel's proof, that
staple reference of all of us half-informed humanists), cannot prove their
own first principles or give a scientific or mathematical defense of their
methods.[11] And if this is true of the physical sciences, how much more obviously it is true of the humanities, in which the structure of thought is
always visibly entwined in fundamental convictions about what is in fact
valuable. Even when I try to inquire qua scholar, I inevitably serve *these*
values rather than *those*, and thus I should, qua scholar, bring into my work
a conscious and deliberate assertion and defense of the values I serve.

Our fears thus again turn into issues to be thought about:

Will what I am trying to discover in any way contribute to the vitality of
literary culture? Can I hope that anyone who reads it in the spirit in which
'tis writ will experience a stronger sense of the value either of the literature I
am studying or of this way of studying it?

Is my scholarly project something I would choose to undertake if there
were no institutional pressure to do research? If not, how do I justify spending my precious life on it?

Is my scholarly project as important to me or to anyone else as other
projects I might spend similar amounts of time on—teaching, for example?

In my project, have I taken hold of the handle that I honestly think is
most important? If so, how would I explain that importance to a skeptic? If
not, do I have good reasons to carry on as I am?

But before we make the burden of these questions more than any young
scholar should be asked to bear, we should listen to another fear.

Fear of a Novelty That Will Swamp Valued Traditions

Society is always up-to-date. The humanities can never be, try as they will.
They are always harking back, reconsidering, trying old tasks once again.
I can hear a voice—shall we call it not an elderly but a mature one?—say-
ing, "If you insist on encouraging the young to think about how their work

11. See Ernest Nagel and James R. Newman, *Gödel's Proof* (New York, 1958).

serves society, you may find—as indeed we all found in the sixties—that Shakespeare, Milton, Chaucer, Molière, and Goethe are being replaced in the literature classes by Norman Mailer on Vietnam or Erica Jong on how to talk tougher than any man."

The notion of the autonomous scholar was developed in societies with strong traditions that often opposed the novelties of the new sciences. But it was then found important to humanists whose traditions were no longer taken for granted by a public that had learned to admire the practical results of physical science and engineering. How do you defend Greek philology or Assyrian lexicography to a public caring only about the latest developments in airplanes, cars, and kitchen gadgets? Obviously you cannot, so the best choice is not to try: that is, to argue the *general* case for professional autonomy, leaving particular research tasks in the closet. Knowledge for knowledge, a discovery about a hitherto misunderstood diacritical mark cannot compete, in the public eye or even in the eye of the youthful scholar, with whatever sensation *Time* magazine or the little literary magazines will feature today. So the best line was often said to be simply, "Leave us alone and we'll at least do you no harm, because we preserve the past and we say nothing about the present or future. And we'll teach our young charges to do the same."

But of course a general defense of culture and its preservers will not make the problems go away, and the problem we face here is whether we can defend *to ourselves* the inquiries we undertake. We may be quite right in resisting any demand that we make our scholarship relevant to immediate interests. But we cannot be justified in undertaking research that we ourselves do not believe in, and the fact is that our profession has, for complex reasons, developed a strange capacity to generate a kind of research that is not only irrelevant to society but irrelevant to the interests of the researcher.

What right have we, then, to place the burden of judging on the young scholar, if "we," in our roles as senior professors and administrators, provide circumstances that will punish her if she chooses to be honorable. If we have in fact invented a system that encourages what we might well call *un*-scholarship—that kind of research that is not dictated by a desire to learn something—do we have any right to ask young people to combat that system at personal cost?

From the point of view of anyone pursuing our common welfare, it would be hard to say who is more to blame for the flood of unscholarship, the beginners or the veterans. All older scholars know that young scholars publish too much too soon, but we force the young plants by the way we play our roles in tenure and promotion decisions. Young scholars know that old scholars also publish too much, because the academic plums continue to fall to those who publish more and more, throughout a lifetime. And the young, who should ideally be the source of a rigorous criticism that would save the oldsters from providing steady evidence of their decline, are caught instead in such a flood of stuff to be read fast that they soon develop habits of non-attention that make serious criticism impossible. Go to the library stacks, O skeptic, and look at the books and unpublished dissertations in your own specialty; pick out any half-dozen volumes at random, and ask yourself whether the world would be the poorer if half of them had never been loosed on the world.

The issue to be thought about, then, underlying the fear of novel standards and ways, is this: Is it possible, without simply embracing every novelty, to invent ways to improve the quality of the scholarship we lead each other to produce? If we are to do so, the inventions will most likely come from the young scholars, not from the old. Can we find ways to reward that kind of inventive service to scholarship and to society?

V

The dangers for any young scholar who attends to what I have been saying are obvious: if she does not play the game as it is now designed, if she does not succumb to ambition, mendacity, or cowardice, and produce *instanter* that book or article that should in fact have five more years of gestation, the ax will fall, but not on me. It is scarcely fair of me to urge individual victims to go courageously to the slaughterhouse. What must be changed are the rules of the house, and nobody knows quite how to do that without losing more than we gain.

When literal thought fails, let allegory prevail. Let us imagine a visitor who comes to America from a strange land, Eupaideia, a land that has miraculously ordered its scholarship and teaching according to a reasonable ideal. Asked to testify before the new Commission on Rational Promotion and Tenure Procedures, this is what the sibyl says:

We order all these things better in Eupaideia, and we are able to do so because we know what it is that we want from our educational system. We have agreed that what we most need is for every citizen to be curious about how to make life more humane. Our schools are organized not around reading, writing, and 'rithmetic but around a sequence of Curiosities: Curiosity I, about what nature is up to; Curiosity II, about what is humane; Curiosity III, about what makes an admirable human achievement; Curiosity IV, about why things so often go wrong; Curiosity V, about why they ever go right; and so on. Our colleges are organized similarly, with Curiosity 101, 102, 103. . . .

We impose no norms about what words like "curious," "humane," and "achievement" are to mean, and we have learned that the local curiosity of individual teachers and principals gives a much better guide to curriculum building than any impositions from more distant authorities. But we do impose two absolute rules: no curriculum can be adopted without a free vote of all teachers on the question, "Does this program interest *you?*"; and every curriculum must be revised every five years by a committee of teachers elected from the school where it will be taught.

More pertinent to your problems are our ways of relating scholarly inquiry, publication, and reward. Both college and school teachers are judged, for retention and promotion, mainly according to whether they can arouse the elected committee members' curiosity about the subjects they teach. Each teacher whose fate is in the balance can choose any method for interesting the committee: published writing, unpublished essays or lectures, tapes, a prolonged group discussion. If curiosity is roused about where she will go next (that is, about what she might be able to teach them next time around), she is hired, retained, or promoted. Every five years each teacher undergoes the same test, throughout her life, and those who fail are, regardless of their age, given a one-year sabbatical to allow for preparation for a second try; if after a year of free inquiry she still cannot arouse anyone's curiosity, she is asked to seek employment in some line of work not centered on competence in the Curiosities.

What this has meant for us is of course that nobody writes and publishes unless that route has for her proved the best way to learn. We were a bit surprised to find that the amount of *writing* did not go down markedly, while the amount of *publication* dropped by about seventy-five percent. Obviously most scholars find that trying to write a coherent statement is the best way to learn, yet most find the results of the try not ready for publication.

I should perhaps mention that in carrying out this plan we were immensely aided by our National Tax on Verbal Profits. [Compare the surprisingly similar idea toward the end of Occasion 7. Can the sibyl be plagiarizing?] It was instituted long ago for different motives entirely: to remove the immense rewards, still so striking in your society, for corrupting life by abusing language. . . . It is simply a steeply graduated tax on all publications that make money for author or publisher: a standard income tax on anything up to one-fifth over the basic annual academic salary, rising rapidly to fifty percent on high income from advertising copy, best sellers (including textbooks), TV and movie scripts. The motive for becoming a deliberate miseducator is thus drastically reduced. The fortunate side effect is to remove all financial incentive for publishing scholarly works and textbooks. . . .

Thus you see that in Eupaideia no one ever writes anything unless she wants to, and no one is ever in the position of wanting to publish something no matter what. Why write a book unless one cannot *not* write a book?

I cannot overstate the resulting differences in attitude between your young scholars and ours. Our youths naturally postpone publication as long as possible—until they cannot resist the itch to spread their ideas through the world. Insofar as their thoughts are on future professional success at all (and that seems to be about the same as in your society) they are driven to think hard and long about how on earth they are to interest that review committee a few years on. And they soon learn that the best way to prepare for *that* is to learn how to rouse the curiosity of their students. . . . [I cut five pages of details here.]

Our entire professoriat is thus, you see, devoted to the task of discovering whatever is truly interesting in the world and to teaching the arts of such discovery. Not the least of the resulting blessings is that everyone who picks up a new scholarly book can be fairly sure that its author wanted to write it and believed in it as the best possible under the circumstances. As bibliographies have shrunk, the quality of writing has improved, and sales figures for individual titles have soared. Scholars have rediscovered the wisdom of ancient Slower Reading Programs: the fewer pages you cover in a given time, the more you learn. You tell me that in your society the slow reader is doomed. I can well believe it, because we were once ourselves in danger of becoming a nation of desperate skimmers. But now . . .

Needless to say, your problem of the opposition between traditional values and the novel idea or movement simply does not arise. Since the curiosity of well-educated men and women can be on the whole as well aroused by an old problem or old text as by the most recent novelty, people are free to pursue in their own way that great truth enunciated by Aristotle: All men by nature desire to know—and women even more so. You can see, then, . . .

Obviously no one could seriously recommend the Eupaideist's program to America today. It was designed for a less sophisticated society than ours, and for scholars who have not eaten of the tree of knowledge. But the naive stranger does dramatize for us how strange is our practice of leading thousands of citizens, especially the vulnerable young, to publish books and articles against their will, books and articles that nobody will read—except for other reluctant scholars who are led to "cover the literature" in their own unreadable first chapters.

We should remind ourselves that there are other ways of managing things. Less than a century ago there was no university in the country that required the Ph.D. for academic appointment and no university that insisted on publication for those who were retained and promoted. Though in America William James was already by 1903 writing his lament about the "Ph.D. Octopus," [12] in Germany, where teachers were paid a capitation fee depending on attendance at their lectures, Max Weber could complain that promotion and tenure decisions took no account of scholarship whatever (thus we see how the Eupaideist's scheme would actually work out in a fallen world: as Weber complains, lecturers learn to use the cheapest tricks to "interest" large audiences, instead of keeping their minds on scientific inquiry!). [13]

VI

How could a young scholar hope to answer any of the questions I have raised? How is she to know whether what she does is important enough to justify the time and energy taken from other good things in the world?

There can be no easy way, but a first step is surely to be clear about why attempting good scholarship is in itself a service to society, regardless of the subject. How can anyone claim, as I want now to do, that to be a good scholar is to perform a service that no other "estate," no other establishment, can perform?

Our service, whatever it is, will be performed at the frazzled end of a three-century history that every scholar knows by heart as the struggle for one supreme value, objective truth. Our world has been shaken by a series of scientific revolutions, from Copernicus through Einstein to more recent forlorn questionings about whether the physical scientists may not after all be probing into sheer chaos. Perhaps just beyond the next experimental step into the unknown will be a revelation showing not only that God does play dice with the universe but that there is simply nothing "out there" to be known. [14] Each major revision of our view of the world was initiated by cou-

12. *Harvard Monthly* 36 (March 1903): 1–9; reprinted in *Memories and Studies* (1911; reprint, New York, 1968).

13. Max Weber, *Max Weber on Universities: The Power of the State and the Dignity of the Academic Calling in Imperial Germany*, ed. and trans. Edward Shils (Chicago, 1973). See especially pp. 23–25.

14. "And now a significant number of our most thoughtful scholars seems to fear . . . the labyrinth with the empty center, where the investigator meets only his own shadow and his blackboard with his own chalk marks on it, his own solutions to his own puzzles" (Holton,

rageous scholars who followed truth where it led—so the history runs—regardless of how badly personal preferences were trampled in the process. It is easy for us now to debunk this myth by showing that none of its heroes really foresaw where the inquiry would lead—they were all, in Arthur Koestler's apt description, "sleepwalkers." But the myth was intellectually and morally powerful, with its implied metaphor of an "edge of objectivity" moving courageously and impersonally into the unknown; its inherent heroic appeal was steadily reinforced by the spectacular practical results that flowed in the wake of the ship of objective intellectual progress.[15]

It is scarcely surprising, then, that most serious students of human nature and its achievements should have emulated the students of physical nature. The ideals of objectivity that accounted, or so it seemed, for scientific triumphs should surely yield similar triumphs in the study of societies. Why not ultimately, then, even in the study of that most mysterious of all our mysteries, the creative achievements of genius? If God's wondrous creation could be demystified with such spectacular results, why should we not demystify the acts of creative genius? But clearly we can do so only if we are willing to cast as cold an eye on the works of mankind as we have cast on the works of God. Our duty will be to exercise as much courage and honesty in our work as the most dispassionate scientific investigator has ever displayed.

But the ideal of a "value-free" objectivity in humanistic studies has been inevitably troublesome to every powerful inquirer embracing it. One of the greatest of these I have already mentioned: Max Weber. He is often now described by subjectivists as almost villainously given to an irresponsibly impersonal social science. But he was in fact always struggling to combine his justified sense of the necessary scholarly virtues with his personal responsibility to fight, as scholar and as editor of *Archiv*, for the "values" he considered "higher."[16]

Science and Culture, p. xxix). Holton was writing before the empty-centered labyrinth and related metaphors—webs, prison-houses, aporias, *mise en abîmes*—had become commonplace in literary criticism, and it is clear in the context of his full statement that he does not himself see the universe quite in this way. It seems obvious that every scientist must disregard, except when theorizing, the fear that there is nothing to be known. If there is nothing to be known, both scientists and scholars should fold up shop and find some honest way to make a living. But of course every scholar, like every scientist, knows that genuine knowledge can be earned, regardless of what a given theory may claim to have shown.

15. The myth, as pursued quite recently by an intelligent believer, can be found in Charles Coulston Gillispie's *The Edge of Objectivity* (Princeton, 1960). A splendid history of the idea of objectivity, as employed by American historians, is given in Peter Novick's *That Noble Dream: The "Objectivity Question" and the Professional Culture of American Historiography* (New York, 1988).

16. Weber's most important work on the problem of objectivity in social science is found

Anyone reading through Weber's influential essays about academic freedom, or his explanations of how the editors of a journal of economics can and must both follow scientific truth wherever it leads, in value-free objectivity, and at the same time express their "ethos" by supporting the causes in which they believe, must be struck by the driving sense of social purpose that informed both sides of the scholar-citizen's effort.

Literary scholars seem not to have grappled quite so profoundly with these issues. But everyone in this century ought to have faced them, because every modern scholar encounters a tension between the undeniable scholarly "value"—pursuit of the "factual"—and the undeniable fact that every step in humanistic inquiry, from the choice of subject and problem to the choice of relevant data and appropriate methods, is value-ridden. And since scholars have inherited, along with their scholarly ideals, the conviction that about values there can be no rational inquiry but only personal assertion ("propositions of value cannot be derived from propositions of fact"), they can be shown to suffer a deep sense of conflict between their desire to honor the scholarly virtues and their awareness that their lives are devoted to discriminations of value and to the service of what is peculiarly excellent.

Now that we no longer need be defensive about a scholarship that carries the taint of value judgments,[17] can we restate the virtues required *for* scholarship (and thus *taught by* scholarship) in a way that can make clear why the service of a genuine scholarship can never be in opposition to the values that any defensible society would want to promote? (If the old-fashioned term "virtue" seems moralistic, substitute "powers," or "habits," or even that weasel term from the social sciences, "traits." Or "strengths." Or "characteristics.")

The first is obviously honesty. If all the thousands of exhortations to objectivity were assembled and collated to determine what virtue they shared, we would discover at the core a refusal to lie about something that we know, even if lying will serve something else that we value. In the days when it was generally believed that we could not *know* values, this virtue inevitably

in *Max Weber on the Methodology of the Social Sciences,* ed. and trans. Edward A. Shils and Henry A. Finch (Glencoe, Ill., 1949).

17. In 1974 I compiled a bibliography of more than a score of modern refutations or reconsiderations of the fact-value split, most of them purporting to demonstrate that the "ought" can be derived from the "is." See the appendix to my *Modern Dogma and the Rhetoric of Assent* (Chicago, 1974). Since then there have been many others, the most fully developed perhaps that of Alan Gewirth, *Reason and Morality* (Chicago, 1978). In *The Company We Keep* (Berkeley, 1988) I discuss this point somewhat more fully, and provide many more references (chap. 2).

led to the notion that to be honest we must suppress our commitments in the service of what we do know: we must be "objective." But if we do in fact know some values, then this virtue can now be seen, not as some separable quality that a scholar might well add to her character, but as the very basis for scholarly inquiry. Inquiry begins when one thing that we know seems to conflict with some other thing that we know, generating a problem that we must then—if we are honest—inquire into. All true inquiry is generated in this very practical kind of conflict between at least two valued convictions, neither of which can, in all honesty, be simply ignored.

What is impressive about Weber's continuing discussions of a value-free inquiry practiced by a value-ridden scholar is precisely his refusal to deny either side of what he knew. On the one hand, if I allow my personal preferences to contaminate my inquiry, what it yields may be worthless as knowledge; and on the other hand, if I do not pursue my highest values (which were, for Weber, not distinguishable on rational grounds from "mere personal preferences"), I lose all self-respect. That conflict generated thought, and at the same time it set a model of scholarly behavior that all of us might emulate. Reading Weber now, in his attack on the "operators"—the academic toadies who modulate their conclusions to please the powers—it is the moral fervor of the man that is infectious. And that morality is inseparable from his passion for scholarly truth. It is, in short, an expression of the same honesty—though not of the same drive for "objectivity"—that Weber shows when he tries to study how the world's religions really work without letting his own religious preferences get in the way.

What the scholar in our time must be honest about cannot be dictated by anyone but herself, but of course it will be dictated, in a sense, by every part of the experience she has made her own, including whatever societies she is made of. Some of the academic revolts that began in the late sixties have been precisely an expression of an honesty turned onto experiences that "objective" scholarship had ignored.[18] "Objective scholarship" could, for example, study the history of the novel without mentioning the biases of religion, class, race, and sex that even the greatest of novels reveal and that most of the scholars tacitly shared. An "objective" female scholar thus would not mention, surely, that her own soul was violated by this or that work, and she would not include in her account how she actually felt as she read. It may be, as some claim, that we now face the opposite danger, from polemicists who can too easily give an honest report of their justifiably angry responses to various biases, without mentioning their inescapable ad-

18. See Chomsky's "Objectivity and Liberal Scholarship" in *American Power and the New Mandarins* (New York, 1969), 23–158.

miration for qualities that accompany the offenses. Honest scholars can be moved to new kinds of honest inquiry only when they place what they know from traditional scholarly pursuits together with all that they find in personal experience. The alternative to a dry (and secretly biased) objectivity is not thus "subjectivity"—whatever that might be—but honest inquiry.[19]

The second untarnished virtue is courage. What the myth of the objective scientist held up for our emulation was a picture not just of honesty but of courageous honesty: the virtue practiced by the lover of truth willing to risk personal harm for the sake of proclaiming an unpopular or even destructive truth. Though the myth seriously understated the ways in which honest inquiry often will actually buttress social norms and commonplaces, it had this much truth to it: all honest inquiry destroys something, if only the complacent acceptance of two incompatible convictions in the same mind. In all genuine thought I must give up something, discarding one or the other of the clashing commonplaces with which I began or finding a new synthesis that leaves neither of the prior elements unchanged. Such destruction always takes courage. Thought is always to some degree threatening; it is always easier not to think than to think, whether the results of thought finally turn out to be revolutionary or conservative. As Piet Hein's little verse has it,

> Problems worthy
> Of attack
> Prove their worth
> By hitting back.[20]

The scholar is the only person charged by society to carry the burden of thought to its extremes, even when thought hits back. All professions require brain work, but only the scholar is charged primarily with exercising critical thought that will stick—will stand up to further criticism. Intellectuals appoint themselves, of course, to this same task, and their barbs are

19. It takes very little experience with the terms "subjective" and "objective" to recognize that they are almost useless for serious inquiry. Not only is it true that historically the terms have radically shifted meanings, but they are now both used as terms of praise and abuse, and they never mean the same thing for their proponents as for their enemies. A clear instance is David Bleich's *Subjective Criticism* (Baltimore, 1978). The subjectivity that Bleich and other "reader" critics would restore to criticism is not the "opposite of objectivity" that their opponents fear. After all, to ask students to respect and describe their first-hand experience, disregarding everything but the evidence of "experiment," is very close to asking them to exhibit one aspect of the "objectivity" that the myth tells us made the scientific revolution possible.

20. Piet Hein, "Problems," in *Grooks*, 4 vols., assisted by Jens Arup (Garden City, N.Y., 1969), 1:2.

often essential in goading scholars into thought. But the intellectual who would make her barbs *stick* must either depend on scholars to think out their implications or turn herself into a scholar—that is, sit back down at that desk and start looking at the *reasons* on all sides of the question. All scholars know, of course, that even their hardest-won conclusions may not survive for long. On the other hand, they may survive indefinitely.

Courage thus reveals itself as of two kinds, depending on what kind of threat is defied. The scholar must be willing to face conclusions that destroy her own intellectual comfort—conclusions that she "personally" would rather not believe. And she must be willing to profess conclusions that go against her interests in the world: she must be—to use a good old word that is rapidly losing its usefulness—disinterested. She will not follow the advice of one of our most prominent and successful literary critics, whose scholarship grows weaker and weaker as he heeds his own advice: to keep our ears to the ground and our noses clean and to pursue whatever is the latest critical fashion to its most colorful extreme.

To resist such advice requires a third virtue, one not practiced by the "mere" intellectual: persistence. Whatever future-shock the scholar experiences as citizen, as scholar she persists on some one line for as long as is required. If her problem is "What words did Shakespeare, or Calderón, or Goethe actually write?" she may persevere for a lifetime without coming to an end. Living in a world increasingly jumpy—a hopping, a saltatory world where everyone changes neighborhoods, spouses, professions, and crises almost as fast as she can flick the dial to a new program—the scholar necessarily digs in deep and long.

It is for this reason that those who accuse scholars of defending the status quo are quite wrong; the scholar often never even catches up to it, so persistent is she on that problem she began with before all these changes occurred. Day after day, year in, year out, she goes to that desk and faces that problem until it is either solved or proved pointless. Ask any scholar whose book or article has made a difference for you how long she worked on it. For most books the answer will be "from five to ten years;" often it is "all my life." The scholar persists—or stops being a scholar.

Like all other virtues, persistence can corrupt unless it is tempered by other virtues. Whether the world will view the persisting scholar as pigheaded or plain crazy depends in part on the accident of whether the world has any notion of what she is up to and in part on whether the goal pursued is clearly separate from whatever rewards may accompany success. As I see it, we in America are desperately short of models of honest, courageous persistence in the pursuit of anything but money or notoriety. Now that all of the fine arts except musical performance can be mastered—or so we are told—simply by letting one's genius hang out, without persistence, and now that the persistence required for athletic preeminence is increasingly focused on the money and not on grace in victory, scholarly persistence seems about the only source of models of that wonderful weird human quality of steady, concentrated, unrewarded labor for an uncertain and seemingly impractical goal.[21]

A fourth scholarly virtue we might call "consideration," though the word has lost much of its force. Good scholarship requires, contrary to some popular notions of the lone scientist or scholar inventing private truths, a steady habit of sustained attention to other people's reasoning. It is thus largely good listening and reporting. The floods of bad scholarship that we swim against have almost drowned out what was originally the clearest acknowledgment of this habit: the opening section of the book or dissertation, in which the "state of the question," as others have treated it, is "considered." In that opening, so hard to write and often now mere ill-considered summary and thus boring to read, one showed a consideration of the opinions of other scholars in preparation for one's own effort to carry the question further—with the implication that one is carrying one's colleagues along as well.

That opening section has become harder and harder to write as publications have increased. When I did my dissertation it was possible, though arduous, to read just about everything that had ever been written about *Tristram Shandy* (except, of course, in languages beyond me; like Casaubon, I did not know that some of my grappling had been anticipated by "foreigners"—in my case, the "Russian formalists"). Writing *The Rhetoric of Fiction*, again I read "everything" ever said about narrative point of view. It would be absurd to ask any student to attempt either of those tasks now, since both "literatures" have doubled many times. But the student who has discovered a genuine scholarly problem about either of these inexhaustible subjects will, must, attempt something like this considerate survey of what other people have thought, knowing that some of them will have something to teach her. Though the task of winnowing becomes more difficult as the bibliographies lengthen, no publishing *scholar* will ever want to ignore the sometimes glorious, sometimes disillusioning companionship and tutelage of those who have tilled this field before.

We often debase this point to the relatively unimportant matter of not

---

21. Practical skills and crafts survive, of course, and they all require at least one of the three virtues: persistence. More time and energy, and perhaps even skill, go into a typical thity-second spot for a network commercial than went into many an admired Restoration comedy, say, or impressionist painting. See *Thirty Seconds*, by Michael J. Arlen (New York, 1980).

wanting to say what someone else has already said, as if no truth should ever be said more than once. Perhaps from the influence of the hard sciences, where new discoveries seldom require much repeating before they begin to do their work in the world, we forget that most of the knowledge we care about in the humanities is of a kind that cannot be considered and repeated too often, provided that the scholar who does the repeating has found a way of reasoning about it that makes it come alive again for her.

In short, scholarship as we have defined it depends on a "decent respect for the opinions of mankind," past, present, and future. Scholarly problems as we encounter them would not exist at all without our heritage of opinions about literary works and how to discuss them. Any present effort to solve a given problem and present the results in written form would make no sense whatever if we did not "consider" ourselves bound to a society of scholars who will attempt to follow our arguments.

In this way consideration, in several senses of the word, must affect how we write as well as what and how we read. The scholar will always make her results as intelligible to other scholars as the inherent difficulties of the subject allow, and she will not be embarrassed if this means writing so that any literate person can follow. The inherent drive of scholarship itself is thus toward a considerate style that assists other people as much as possible in a joint endeavor: understanding this problem and this possible solution to it. We may find this claim a bit hard to believe in these days when mystifying opacities fill our books and journals. But we should remember that some subjects *are* in fact difficult, even mystifying, and that no reader can determine simply from a difficult or easy surface whether the author is showing a proper consideration.[22]

Every genuine scholar who ventures into domains other than bibliography and editing knows a sense of failure in this effort to find a style that shares, that considers, that joins a subject to a proper reader. Her problems are always complex, her solutions are usually uncertain and unclear until the last page is completed—at which point she should start over with page one and rewrite the whole thing. But since we do not live in Eupaideia, revision must stop before it should, and the final presentation is not as clear as the inherent complexities would have allowed.

22. A good account of some of the complexities that underlie our usual insistence on a clear, accessible style is given—in a fairly "plain" style—by Geoffrey Hartman in "Literary Criticism and Its Discontents," *Critical Inquiry* 3 (Winter 1976): 203–20. See especially Part 2. I have made several attempts (for example in "Do Reasons Matter in Criticism: Or, Many Meanings, Many Modes," *Bulletin of the Midwest Modern Language Association* 14 [Spring 1981]) to describe the dangers implicit in Hartman's defense of a deliberately "inconsiderate" style. See Introduction to Part 5, n. 3.

And it is not all a matter of insufficient time. The very respect for the opinions of other people that leads one to try for clarity will lead often into obscurity, because the opinions of the various factions one addresses will inevitably be diverse. It is not simply that each potential audience will expect, even require, a different rhetoric. It is that if one pays a decent and sustained respect to the opinions of one's "societies," one's original hypotheses become challenged, one's theses grow more and more complicated, and finally one's whole project may collapse in confusion or surrender to some new project more plausible in the light of the voices one has considered. Dealing as we do with value-laden concepts, we embrace them *as* laden with the values our readers (and those we have read) place upon them. To the degree that the opinions of our various possible readers come to us with the support of scholarly reasoning, they tend to become our own opinions, and they must then somehow be accommodated—not to persuade others, though that is part of our aim, but to achieve some sort of resolution of the problem for "oneself," that internal society of scholarly selves that every scholar has become as she receives her training.

Implied by these four virtues is a schooling, finally, in a fifth: humility. Attempting to do scholarly work is in my experience a deeper schooling in humility than can be found anywhere else except in trying to teach well and trying to be a good spouse and parent.

It is true that humility, like all the other virtues, can be destructive if uncorrected by those others, especially by courage. It is also true that arrogant young scholars often achieve—especially in the natural sciences—results that their humbled elders would never dare seek. But the fact remains that as we peer about the world seeking examples of people who have the humility that the best philosophers have taken as the root and fountain of all human excellence,[23] the only examples we find of *intellectual* humility (as distinct from various self-denigrations and inferiority complexes that must not be confused with it) are scholars who have tested their powers for discovering truth and have discovered instead vaster and vaster domains of ignorance. Only the scholar who has honestly, courageously, persistently, and considerately tried to solve one genuine problem can know how little she can do to reduce her own ignorance.

We have no single name for all of these habits of mind taken together. For some philosophers in the past, "reason" and "rationality" were rough synonyms for the collection as a whole. But like all words in the scholarship

---

23. The most forceful modern defense of humility I know is Iris Murdoch's in *The Sovereignty of Good* (London, 1970).

family, these have been narrowed in modern usage to suggest an insistence on an emotion-free, linear logicality that is at most a small part of what I am suggesting. Still, we do need a name for the virtues, and since they cannot be called simply the "scholarly habits" (after all, we know that they are shared in various combinations with non-scholars). I suggest that we think of them as the "habits of *rationality*." After all, with a little consideration of what our predecessors (before the last hundred years or so) thought that rationality entailed, we should be able to use the word, and the richness it connotes, as an aid in saying to our various publics that we stand for something that they too can respect.

Can we not say that the chief duty of the scholar "in society," as of the scholar at her desk, the duty without which all other services to society will be corrupted, is to practice the rational habits—to show not just a private commitment to them but to show in her public acts, in teaching, in publishing, as in all political and social life, an unswerving desire to honor the honest, courageous, persistent, considerate, and humble pursuit of that special kind of tested opinion that can be pursued only in the courts of a shared reasoning?

Not everyone can be a scholar. Not everyone should be a scholar. But there is no human being whose life would not be enhanced by earning some share in the rational habits. And it is our task to keep those habits alive. The book-person who sullies the name of a scholar by publicly abandoning those habits, by refusing to teach them to others, or even by playing the increasingly popular game of pretending that they don't matter or that they are simply indefensible values like all our other "mere" preferences—such a scholar is no scholar, no matter how long she sits in front of that desk. She is a disgrace to the profession and—if paid by society—a cheat. Whether society quite knows what it wants, as it pays us to be scholar-teachers, what it really seeks, more or less blindly, is to keep the rational habits passionately alive in the world. Only if we do that job well, by the way we think, the way we teach, and the way we write, can we claim that we have honored the society that we are in and the society that is in us.

The days of simple oppositions are past, if indeed there ever were such days. No informed inquirer will ever again believe that her scholarly inquiry is innocent of political bias or social effects. The way she inquires, indeed whether she will be allowed to inquire at all, will depend on the society in which she lives. And what she does—both the subjects she chooses to investigate and the modes she chooses for reporting her findings—will not simply affect her society; it will to a large degree *constitute* the society in which she lives.

When we choose to become scholars, we join the guild of professional inquirers, the guild of those who profess the rational habits. The rights and privileges of that guild are different from those of any other guild, as are its responsibilities. In our society, no other guild is charged specifically with preserving the rational habits. It sometimes seems that we may soon have no other guilds committed to *any* of the virtues.

Whatever happens to our society, we cannot afford to spend any time proclaiming our helplessness before its forces. As one of the most powerful of society's "estates," we can be sure that whatever conditions we find in the world as we continue our efforts at scholarship have been to a surprising degree of our own making. In what we write, and perhaps even more in what we teach, we make the society in which we shall continue to remake ourselves.

OCCASION 4 · *To Warring Factions in an Up-to-Date "English Department"*

"You Worship God in Your Way, and I'll Worship Him in His": On Some Current Discontents in the Graduate Study of "English"

When I was invited to talk with you today, I was told that the English Department was experiencing some degree of conflict, that indeed you were in some danger of resorting to open warfare. I had a hard time believing this report, since every other English department I know about is living in a state of blissful peace. In my own, for example, all is sweetness and light. Neo-Aristotelians and feminists, Marxists and Reaganites, Derrivadives and Lacanics, conventionalitarians and flycast fishermen all understand each other perfectly. When an argument is presented by any one of these in a departmental meeting, it is never dismissed as motivated by party spirit. Our oral examinations are models of an irenic, friendly, open, inquiring spirit. Our disciple of Lyotard abandons her personal passions when entering the examination room, and asks questions that startle candidates by sounding highly traditional; our convert to the recent prophecies of Frederick Crews sloughs off all conservative prejudice as he asks penetrating yet friendly questions about the deferral of meanings through labyrinthine texts.

Why, then, why on earth should your department be having trouble? The more I thought about that question, the more comfortable I felt about my visit, because it seemed obvious that I could just enter the scene and quietly, humbly, offer the ecumenical wisdom that one garners simply by virtue of living in peace elsewhere, *outside* the scene here. Having provided

Speech delivered to the English Department at Syracuse University in April 1987. About a third of the talk was earlier given at a conference of graduate departments of English sponsored by the Modern Language Association. A large part of this speech was printed in *Profession 87* (Modern Language Association, 1987), 36–39.

you with the key to all the mythologies, I could then escape with my hide intact.

Well, would the world of English studies be healthier if that opening could have been spoken without irony—if most English departments were not embattled, if there was indeed some simple harmony that we could offer each other, some post-post-structuralism, something beyond-beyond that would enable us all to work together in pursuit of fully-agreed-upon ends? I suspect, indeed I hope, that no one here would see such a heavenly condition as a healthy one, for those of us who want to keep alive in a discipline that offers many temptations to die on our feet. I don't mean to suggest by this that we should simply revel in a fine, lively condition of intellectual warfare, if it is that. No one could deny that the profession is plagued these days with a good deal of *unnecessary, meaningless* controversy—that too many of us are fouling our own nests with poisonous outbursts. But I do think it is important, whenever one enters into intellectual battle, to count at least the one major blessing that such battle means: it means that we are alive and free in our endeavors.

Just think what it would mean about the world of English studies if one could say that all who worked in it were in the kind of harmony about goals and methods that legend tells us reigned in the Harvard and Princeton English Departments some years ago, before our recent explosives hit the—shall I say "scene" or "fan"? Such harmony would mean, I think, either that hard reflection had been forbidden by some authority, some totalitarian regime, local or national, or that the capacity for such reflection had been simply lost or deliberately abandoned.

With that concession to the value of what Bakhtin calls "heteroglossia," to the absolute need we all have for counter-voices that insist on being heard, one must hasten to acknowledge a counter-voice to that one, a voice that in effect I heard from several of you as we planned my visit. That composite voice said something like, "We are in danger here of losing our hold on *productive* controversy, of turning, instead, to the kind of destructive infighting that might prevent our accomplishing anything whatever." I'll not offer a definition of the differences between productive and destructive controversy; we all have a pretty good idea of what they are. What I want to do instead is to suggest, first, a few points on which I would hope everyone could agree (knowing, of course, that any statement of such points will itself prove to be controversial) and then an even more obviously controversial statement about a possible unifying center to our work that I *wish*, without much hope, we could all agree on. Needless to say, it will be a practical, not a theoretical center, a program of action, not a reconciliation of theoretical differences which, since they are about essentially contested concepts, can never be eliminated.

I

Suppose we start, then, with some beliefs that I hope are shared by most of us.

First, what we label with the catchall term "English" is the most important of all college subjects. Some of us think it is most important because in our culture it is the major heir of a once-glorious liberal arts tradition. Call us the Ancients. Others of us think it is the most important because in our culture it is the standard-bearer of some new vision that is to replace the outworn purposes and fixed canons of the past. Call us the Mods. Both groups are aware that because of the basic requirements and elective systems in most colleges and universities, our elementary courses are the only ones that all students will be touched by—if they are touched at all. If students are ever to obtain an education that will help them become the kind of persons we hope they'll be (note my highly general language: all the terms such as "liberal," "humane," "free," "creative," are suspect), if students are not to become simply shallow, self-satisfied, intellectually lifeless cogs in the great money-and-power-machines offered by too much of the rest of the world, the transformation will occur in one of our courses. What's more, I think that most of us are convinced that as our society goes, our B.A.'s and M.A.'s and Ph.D.'s constitute at their best a saving remnant—though perhaps none of us would be happy with that old-fashioned phrase. When we have succeeded, our students practice a kind of sensitivity to language and to other people as they employ language—a kind of listening and responding that in its combination of sympathy and criticism is always, in every society, in short supply.

To get beyond such general claims, let me become an Ancient for a moment:

English appears to be the chief heir and last hope of a once-glorious liberal arts tradition. The arts that at their best liberate us from our natural provincialisms. . . . [I here cut about three pages of "Ancientism," a somewhat exaggerated version of the case I've already made in this book for the unique importance of "English" in teaching "critical understanding." The Ancient concludes as follows:] We do not justify our requirements by saying to Secretary of Education Bennett, "We're filling in those cultural gaps that you seem to care more about than whether students can function in the world."[1] We justify them by doing something *for* students that ought to be done. In short, we hope to educate readers who will write back or speak back profitably to demanding texts, people who can engage in a kind of discourse that is by no means shared by all cultures or by all within our culture, a precious exchange of ideas that, just because it is not by any means essential to bare survival, is always in danger of being lost. The hard fact is that most American students, graduate and undergraduate, will receive little or no liberal education, little or no liberation from the provincial dogmas of our increasingly crass culture, unless they get it from us.

Now this same case, as it would be made by a Mod, or rather a Post-Mod, is harder to summarize, partly because there are many different voices claiming to speak for what is truly the next wave. It is harder for me also, because the only one of the new voices that I might claim to have done real justice to, in my own thinking, is that of the feminists. But let me try anyway for a composite charge, risky as it may be:

What we call "English" should be considered the most important subject in the curriculum because, given our present requirement patterns, English classes are the only place where students can be freed from their natural tendency to slavish dependence on whatever texts fall into their hands, or ears. In teaching them how to read productively, creatively, rather than in mere passive reception, in teaching them how *not* to accept texts as givens and classical hierarchies as fixed, in teaching them to recognize just how subtly and oppressively standard readings and reading lists can impose norms of behavior and thought that are entrapments of the spirit, we can hope . . .

But here the voices diverge: some would hope to free males and females from the stereotyped, sexist notions that an uncritical reading of both contemporary and classical literature would impose; some would free us from impositions of class or racial or ethnic bias; some would free us from all solidities, all notions of presence, all binary oppositions of sex, class, quality, or genre, in the hope of graduating a kind of person who would take abso-

---

1. Perhaps this is the place for me to confess my (slight) embarrassment at being listed as a consultant for William Bennett's little book, *To Reclaim a Legacy: A Report on the Humanities in Higher Education* (Washington, 1984). The rascal ignored much of the advice that some of us tried to give, and then wrote the book as if we all shared his views. He has managed to write an entire book about the failures of American higher education without indicating how or why *the public* might take more responsibility and offer more support.

lute and free responsibility for an unfixed self in an unfixed universe. But we must ignore such complexities and continue with the imaginary voices in unison:

If they do not obtain these freedoms from us, where will they find them? Not in their social science courses, unless they happen to meet one of the newer branches of sociology or cultural anthropology. Not, in most universities, in their history courses, still taught in old positivist, objectivist ways. Not in their philosophy courses, at least not in most American departments. Not in their natural science courses, unless they happen to choose some especially alert version of philosophy of science. For most of them, their last chance for a genuine thawing out of frozen categories is their course (or if they are lucky, courses) with us.

II

Coming out from behind the mimicry now, I must underline the obvious point shared by the two voices: that curiously ambiguous term "English" names the most important subject in the curriculum, most important partly *because it is subversive* of values conventional or dominant in our culture; both Mods and Ancients have a stake in opposing at least some of the more self-evidently destructive, anti-educational forces of consumer capitalism, including the stereotyped responses of various "rights" and "lefts." We all seek to build people who can exercise a kind of critical, reflective freedom in the face of all the forces trying to turn them into automatons.

Before I move on to other sharings, does it not seem a pity, in the light of what we have seen so far, that we should spend our energies fighting caricatures of one another, when our common opponent, not to say enemy, is so powerful?

Last week a friend showed me a copy of a communiqué from a symposium director, addressed to those who plan to discuss "Literary Theory and Textual Scholarship." The letter begins with an attack on the standard notion that the goal of textual editing is "to establish [canonized] texts for others to read and criticize," the editor thus serving the interpretive critic. Such traditional editing, the director goes on to say, seeks always to "recover authorial intention," and it thus always produces the "phallotext," that is, the recovery of an implied author, *always* "phallocentrically determined. The notion of intention implies a text centered in a recoverable desire for unity, coherence, textual logic." Instead of pursuing that text, he says, editors should combat "patriarchal" editing with an editing that respects "*l'écriture feminine*," not only changing the list of texts to be edited but turning each traditional work into a "series of texts," their meaning, for editors and their beneficiaries alike, "endlessly deferred."

Now everyone, including the author of that invitation himself, can see that this new view of editing raises lots of problems. But are they such problems as to suggest no possible ways in which such an editor, seeking *not* the author's final intention but the history of texts as culturally multiplied, could give us knowledge worth having? Yet the photocopy of this relatively mild Mod manifesto was sent to me by an ardent Ancient with the note, "See what we're up against?" And the copy is marked up with the responses of some other anonymous Ancient. "Unbelievable bullshit." "Simple as that, eh!!!" "Since Foucault says it, it must be right?"

The epithets flow on both sides—I've seen a copy of *A Rhetoric of Irony* with obscenities scrawled in the margins by some troubled soul who had landed angrily on every word that has a possible traditionalist connotation.

While this kind of quarrel goes on—seemingly more intense by the month—can we not discern a second point of agreement between the Ancients and the Mods, namely, that our graduates, who are implicitly expected to know everything by the time they get the hood, offer in their ignorance ample evidence to both sides that we are performing badly: "You mean it's possible to get a Ph.D. from your university without having read a word of Aristotle, Sidney, or Samuel Johnson?" "You mean to say that it's possible to get a Ph.D. from your department without having read Derrida or de Man?" "You mean to say that you are producing Ph.D.'s who know nothing of linguistics, of rhetorical theory, of composition theory, of film theory, of feminist criticism, of folk literature, of . . . "—but as you know, the list of possible oversights could go on for some time. About the only boast we might all want to make is that our graduates, regardless of their specialties, probably read and write *somewhat* better than those who dodge our ministrations, though many of us sometimes wonder even about that: they may write better in one sense, but they have actually been corrupted to write like *that*. In any case, if we ask them what they are doctors *of*, what they profess to know, we receive answers as miscellaneous as the annual MLA convention program. The result is that most of us think that most graduates from most other institutions are ignorant of most of what they should know. Indeed, even the graduates from here—wherever here is—are woefully ignorant unless they happen to have taken a lot of courses from *me*.

Obviously the threat of multiple and unrealizable goals does not come just from new intellectual movements. The institutionalization of scholarship and the pressures for premature publication that we all help to impose have made it impossible any longer to expect that candidates "cover" any of the traditional fields, or even the previous publication about any one author. Something like a book a day is published on Shakespeare, somewhere in the world, year in, year out—probably no more than nine-tenths of it rubbish. There are now more than five hundred articles on one of Henry James's stories alone—as you might guess, it is "The Turn of the Screw." The bibliography of books and articles about Saul Bellow now lists more than thirty-five hundred items. A single year's entry for Faulkner in the *PMLA* bibliography covers five columns. There are more new books each month in critical theory alone than even a specialist in critical theory can hope to read. A field like mine, "rhetoric and rhetorical criticism," is by now no definable field at all. I would have to drive myself brutally to keep up with the publications on Aristotle's *Rhetoric* alone. No wonder that a colleague of mine was recently heard to say, when asked whether he had read any Derrida, "Read him? I haven't even lectured on him yet!"

What kind of learning, Ancient *or* Modern, do we expect of students faced with such a flood of stuff? What kind of supervision do we offer, knowing that we ourselves cannot "cover," and do not want to cover, all the literature on the subject? What is the point of producing doctors of a subject, Ancient-style or Modern-style, if they cannot be said to have mastered something or other about a subject well enough to be called "doctor" and to enter into productive dialogue with other "doctors" of that subject?

When faced with the more recondite or polysyllabic items from this new hodgepodge, my friends among the Ancients often cannot resist that cry of "bullshit." If I cannot understand something written in "my" field, either it must be nonsense or I am some kind of fraud. If we can just convince ourselves that we are attacked by a band of barbarians, then we know how to fight and what to fight for. But anyone who spends more than a few hours breaking through the barrier of new vocabularies soon realizes that the new feminisms, new Marxisms, new black critiques, and new deconstructions cannot be dismissed as worthless nonsense. My guess is that time will reveal roughly the same proportion of trash—rather high, I'm afraid—in all current modes of scholarly production, including my own: we have all bought into practices that force even the brightest among the young into premature harvesting, and even the most durable of us elders into increasingly self-indulgent, solipsistic repetitions.[2]

We might, even so, embrace all of this multiplicity, thus parting com-

---

2. *My* repetitions (like this one, of a point made in my preface) are of course productive, even essential, not the least bit self-indulgent or solipsistic.

All irony aside, I should underline the striking difference between my tone here, addressing (or so I expected) a group of established professors about students' ignorance, and my tone on Occasion 3, addressing fellow students about *our* common ignorance. At Syracuse I actually found more students than professors in my audience, and some of them reported after-

pany with both the Mods and the Ancients, *if* we could be convinced that someone else, in some other department of the university, was minding whatever store we see as the central supplier of the necessary goods. But for the most part the basic arts of reading and thinking, writing and speaking, under any definition that any of us would embrace, have been turned over to us, with an occasional assist from the departments of "speech," "communication," or even "rhetoric." If the writing and thinking of our graduates is bad, and even when not too bad is confined to a tiny corner of the intellectual landscape, "we" are in some collective sense to blame.

It takes no very wide experience with the first books and unpublished dissertations produced by our doctoral programs to see that something is wrong, and *that* something is not peculiar to either side of the Mod/Ancient debate. Even though there are dissertations and books that are polished in a professional way, with supporting scholarship that really bears on the thesis, our students mostly show scant mastery of the art of careful and respectful interpretation of texts, or of rigorous construction of argument.

The situation is not new. About twenty-five years ago I asked George Williamson, then editor of *Modern Philology*, what criteria he applied in choosing articles for that journal, with its obviously very high standards. He looked crestfallen. "Oh, I can't say that I *have* anything that could be called a criterion. I just hope to find for each issue enough articles that show *some* relation between conclusions and argument."

The anecdote dramatizes how hard it is to know whether our situation is really worse than it used to be. Perhaps our best work now is as good as or better than the best then; perhaps we are simply producing more students and asking them to publish more in order to get ahead. But it does seem to me that even fewer people these days than in the golden past show any concern about relating conclusions to argument, or any awareness of how their conclusions relate to any conceivable history of similar conclusions; often enough they are not even aware that the issues they raise have been addressed earlier, and at much greater depth, by authors who were once on everyone's reading list. In short, our B.A. and M.A. papers and our dissertations are produced by honorable, hard-working people who, lacking a general education, read and take notes in some isolated corner of the intellectual universe, and then do the best they can with the pitifully inadequate intellectual habits picked up in a miscellaneous list of courses, courses that have themselves too often been isolated from all influence of ethics, politics, history, logic, dialectic, or even grammar.

Some Mods may object at this point that I have suddenly shifted from

---

ward that my description of their ignorance was—not infuriating, as I might have feared, but just plain depressing.

my attempt to occupy neutral ground and have become an unabashed Ancient, as I lament the loss of what used to be called "the liberal arts." Or
some may want to say that I am trying to impose masculinist standards on
what should be a radical revolution producing a world in which we no
longer care about whether conclusions relate to argument. I deny the
charges: take as your standard not the learning and methods of argument of
any old guard you can think of, but rather those of the founders of deconstruction, or of those feminists or Marxists you admire most—the historical and philosophical groundedness of a de Man or Miller or Foucault,
the care with argument and the respect for texts of a Derrida or Hartman
or Raymond Williams, the sensitivity to complex historical influences of
a Jameson, Gilbert, Stimpson, or Jacobus. My lament is that because too
many of our degree programs, whether Mod or Ancient, are unsystematic,
undemanding, and uncritical, our graduates for the most part receive a miscellaneous set of uncorrelated indoctrinations, not what anyone would want
to call a "liberating" education.

It is true that they have been taught, many of them, how to mimic a
given vocabulary, on one side or another of this or that issue. They may
have been taught *something*, by so-called historicists, old or new, about the
techniques of assembling a collection of citations in a plausible order. Perhaps from this or that surviving Ancient or vigorous Mod they have learned
to do a plausible critical analysis, tracing an arbitrarily chosen theme or
"gap" through a text. Whenever I face a new M.A. class at Chicago, I can
usually count on only that one kind of general learning: they all have done
lots of papers, as undergraduates, analysing single novels, plays, or poems,
whether in the old mode of tracing a theme or in the new mode of tracing a
(preferably contradictory) metaphorical pattern. Until quite recently most
of those papers showed how the given work held together, in spite of all the
ironies and ambiguities that the clever author had embedded. These days
they tend to show how the work falls apart, in spite of the hapless author's
futile effort to make it hold together. But on either side of that divide, too
often one can predict, from reading the first paragraph, precisely what the
last paragraph will say—a sure sign that one is encountering mimicry, not
hard thought. What the authors of such papers show is that they have not
learned how to tackle a serious critical or historical or philosophical *problem*
and bring to bear on it what the major figures, Ancient and Mod, always
apply to *their* problems: the kind of sensitive reading and critical, responsible thought that can only be mastered through years of immersion in
work produced by first-class minds possessed of a liberated learning.

The ignorance of our Ph.D.'s is not to be blamed, of course, only on our
chaotic graduate programs. If we could count on the B.A.'s who come into

graduate work having been led by *somebody* toward *some sort* of good general education—in a goodly portion of those good subjects that I earlier ascribed to a classical education—we could then happily concentrate on whatever we now ask our candidates to concentrate on. Because then we could be sure that our candidates could build on a broad educational base, and therefore could become qualified to teach undergraduates in courses that go beyond the narrowest of "literary" topics.

But of course we cannot count on anything of the kind. We cannot assume that B.A.'s will come to graduate study knowing any history well enough to think historically, any languages well enough to read works in the original, any criticism or philosophy well enough to respond to complex arguments without reducing them to easily embraced or rejected polarities. In short, most of those who come to us for graduate work do so with very limited intellectual equipment.

What do we then do to them? I now arrive at a third opinion that I would hope most Mods and Ancients share, though few of us would want to confess it openly. It is this: We treat those fresh, unlicked, well-intentioned B.A.'s badly, and we educate them badly. We educate them badly by telling them something like this: Just take a miscellaneous range of courses, with some small measure of "distribution" that will fill in gaps—the "gaps" usually defined as some list of the classics, established or newly discovered, of English and American novels, plays, and poems. Then quickly choose an author or period or type or current school of criticism, dig into it for a year or two, say something about it that is more-or-less intelligible and preferably novel, and we'll give you the badge that just might get you a teaching job. We *treat* them badly, meanwhile, by saying to them something like this: "Oh, by the way, you will also begin teaching, right now, this very day, and with little or no further training for doing so, a required writing course, a service course that you will be asked to go on teaching until you earn the blessed right to abandon it, as those of us fortunate ones who hire you have long since done." Some of the more highly qualified ones we "reward" by freeing them from composition to teach literature courses, just as we bribe the seemingly best new Ph.D. candidates by telling them that they will teach only courses in what they call their fields: *no freshmen,* if you're lucky. Even if they thus get the prize of teaching "literature," not composition, their courses, in half-time loads that are roughly the same as our full-time loads, will include no historical, rhetorical, or philosophical works, only novels, plays, and poems (in those places where the new critical theories have penetrated, they may add some recent works of critical theory). They are thus likely, throughout their four to ten years with us, to read no philosophy, no history, little criticism written before about 1950, and no rhetorical theory (unless they happen to elect the rhetoric option, and even that may be intellectually slim indeed).

If they are gifted, they may in spite of all this do worthwhile work in their chosen areas—interesting feminist criticism, interesting deconstructionist criticism, interesting Marxist criticism, interesting neo-historical revisions, even interesting editing. If they are not gifted—and we must remember that no group, even at the best universities, will contain many who are especially gifted—they will remain uneducated: unable to apply original critical thought to the world of letters, or to politics, or to any other part of their world. If they do any serious work after their dissertation is turned into a book, as most of them will not, they will continue to work in the shoddy style that produced their dissertations. When they report on their sources, they will do so irresponsibly, as all of us who publish learn about the hard way when we encounter reviews by people who have not troubled to read the work reviewed. How—one asks oneself after licking one's wounds—how can "educated" people commit such atrocities?

And then one realizes the explanation: they have been taught by their own kind, which is *our* kind; nobody is minding the store, all along the line, and we have fallen into a downward spiral. Ignorant high school graduates, like the Wayne Booth of 1938, enter college and are taught—not by the kind of experienced teacher I found in Karl Young but by ignorant fresh B.A.'s, graduate assistants working in appallingly unprofessional conditions and for slave wages. Those B.A.'s have found themselves in graduate programs that leave them ignorant of everything but some tiny, specialized field. And when they teach, they teach courses that do not require them to make up for lost time: with no depth of rhetorical theory beneath them, they teach "service comp courses;" or they teach narrowly focused advanced "literature" courses that, Ancient or Mod, simply perpetuate the downward spiral.

A fourth point of agreement—or so I hope, though by now I can be sure that more and more of you are getting off my boat—follows from this picture of freshman classes taught by freshman graduate students. We all know that English teaching, in our society, is radically under-rated, under-supported, under-rewarded. It is true that many of us here do not feel this condition in our own bones: "I'm all right, Jack, so let those youngsters survive as they can—the way I did when I began." But how can we go on pretending that those courses that are most important, both to society and to our own departmental recruiting, the freshman courses, should be taught by the least fully prepared and most badly paid members of the profession?

To become not just a technician teaching grammar and spelling but a doctor—a teacher—of the liberal arts takes time, time for years of education and time for developing and practicing the arts of teaching. We deprive our youth of that kind of time by overloading them and paying many of them below the poverty line. As evidence, I offer here the results of a little intuitive survey I have made since I began here today: I can report that during this half hour, administrators around the country have cut 257 tenure-track lines from their English departmental budgets, replacing them with 752 low-paid part-timers and freshly graduated B.A.'s, many of the best of whom will soon get fed up with intolerable conditions and leave us for greener pastures. In doing so they will all blame those "higher-ups," the dean, the provost, the legislature, for tight budgeting. We are all tempted to do the same. But we should confess—those of us who are established in the profession, tenured, decently though not affluently paid, and given a choice of whether to teach freshmen or not—that we ourselves profit from the very conditions that we otherwise deplore. We have increasingly divorced the teaching of literature from the teaching of writing, treating composition more and more as a merely technical matter, rather than as a road to liberal education through the serious study of rhetoric. We have thus given all of our publics every reason to believe that we think teaching freshmen how to read and think and write is child's play, while teaching this or that literary work or fashionable or revolutionary bit of literary theory to advanced graduates is really where the action is.[3]

In these and other ways, we have been painting ourselves into a corner, a corner that we almost openly label, with some pride, Department of Useless Studies. I can't do justice here to the complex issue of just what notions of usefulness are harmful to us, of just how much aesthetic purity is good for us, of just how to protect ourselves from the wrong kinds of so-called practicality. Nor can I go into the good reasons for our past battles to establish an autonomy from benighted external social and political pressures; we were right to resist the powers who have not respected free academic inquiry pursued for its own sake. But while continuing to resist every Bennett-like effort from outside that offer us panaceas in the form of inert lists, we ought to ask ourselves constantly what sorts of service to our students and to the grand chaotic edifice of human knowledge might justify our existence.

The point might best be dramatized by acknowledging our own bifurcation, like this: "I am a member of the great public, and I am also a professor of English. What reason can I, *as citizen*, give myself, as professor, for supporting the vast machinery of what we call 'English'?" My answer will always be complex, but it boils down to something like this:

---

3. I argue the point further in "Litcomp," in *Composition and Literature: Bridging the Gap*, edited by Winifred Horner (Chicago, 1983).

You, Wayne Booth, deserve the support of me, Wayne Booth, because I think you are some kind of guardian of some kind of truth or light or set of practices that are finally useful to me and my kind, in making life worth living—in providing a kind of liberation from provincialisms, from the intellectual and aesthetic chains that make life nasty, solitary, poor, brutish, and short. As a member of the great public, *I* can see no reason for my tax dollars to support *you*, as professor, merely to write another book asserting that language does or does not refer to reality, or that critical theory is or is not grounded, or that Chaucer's Wife of Bath is or is not a feminist, or that Shakespeare was referring to this person or that person in his sonnets, or that fictional works are better addressed with a rhetoric of fiction or with some hotter theory of narrativity. But I have every reason to support you if you can claim that while, or through, pursuing one or another of those topics that interest you deeply, you are working vigorously to educate fellow citizens, whose enhanced lives, impinging on mine, will enhance my own days and justify the very existence of my so-called civilization. And I suspect that many of my fellows in the great public, who these days are putting their complaints about you in obviously reductive terms—"back to the basics," "back to the great classics of our tradition," "restore cultural literacy"—really have a dim notion of something much finer: a hope that you would take your profession seriously, as something more than an invitation to *la dolce vita*. More specifically, as a contributing member of the great public, I have a right to insist that you and your kind do your best to *educate*, not just to give professional training in this or that specialized literary field.[4]

If we agree that we have colluded in the construction of what threatens to become an irreversible downward spiral, with the increasingly blindered leading the increasingly blind, and if we can unite in a determination to do something about that collusion, what follows? Thinking about such complex problems, one often feels as helpless as Lear facing his daughters: "I will do such things—what they are yet, I know not!" (2.4.283–84). Something must be done, or we are sure to see English go the way of the classics: becoming not the one required subject in every college, but one tiny remnant elected by a few nostalgic folk wanting to preserve past glories. Some de-

---

4. According to Peter Novick, the Modern Language Association holds "the record for the number of separate [professional] divisions: seventy-six" (*That Noble Dream: The Objectivity Question and the Professional Culture of American Historiography* [New York, 1988]). Dare we ask ourselves whether the knowledge yielded by each of those special fields is important enough, not to some abstract society, but to *us*, to justify supporting it, if the support is *at the expense of* furthering the downward spiral I have lamented?

partments spend their major energy not addressing these problems at all, but simply trying to recruit stars in sufficient quantity to allow them to ignore the big problems: "Just give us a better national reputation, and we will then attract the best B.A.'s to our graduate programs, and we won't even have to worry about the low quality of our own graduates." More responsible departments have made the natural mistake of trying to address these problems by working only on graduate curricula. It is true that we desperately need new and imaginative graduate curricula, rather than piecemeal revisions of old requirements surviving long after everyone has forgotten why they were instituted. I do hope that we will regain our confidence and *require* some coherence in our programs. But whatever curricula we design will not do the job I have in mind, unless we at the same time design better combinations of graduate courses and *supervised, collegial* experience in undergraduate teaching: undergraduate teaching not just of how to read novels, plays, and poems, but of how to read rhetorical, historical, and philosophical works, ancient and modern; how to think critically about such reading; and how to integrate historical, philosophical, rhetorical, and literary experience. If all of our teaching assistants were asked to teach in college courses that included philosophy, history, literature, and rhetoric, *in the company of experienced teachers, meeting regularly to discuss what might be done to make this teaching count,* what a difference that would make, both to their future teaching and to the quality of their dissertations. (See Occasion 12 below.)

The English department that convinces its university to develop and support a Ph.D. program that educates real doctors (that is to say, teachers) of philosophy (that is to say, the pursuit of a truth worth teaching) will not gain an immediate national reputation thereby. It would be hard to think of a title for such a program that would be as jazzy and hence as "attractive" as some now on front stage. But in the long run, that Department of English, a Department of Liberal Education, could well become known as mother of the most important educational revolution of the century.

OCCASION 5 · *To a Banquet-Roomful of Sinful Colleagues*

The English Teacher's Decalogue

About three weeks ago there was a conference at Northwestern University on "Interdisciplinary Studies in English." I can't remember that I heard any mention, during the two days, of composition or communication, except by one man who was a specialist in communications theory. What struck me most was that there was a great deal of talk about the chaos in our profession and about the need for new definitions of literacy. We seemed unable to agree among ourselves about why people should study English, let alone why they should be required to. At the same time there was a lot of uneasy defensive talk about the importance of literature, and even of what was called the "old new criticism." The refrain was, "But why shouldn't I teach what I've been trained to teach? It's the only thing I know."

If I had been a non-academic citizen trying to decide, on the basis of what I heard there, whether to give any more money to English, I'd probably decide to cut off every cent—which is apparently what many of our citizens are deciding.

Maybe you've all heard by now Paul Olson's report on our man in Washington who said, "Nixon's knocked the crap out of our program—and the crap was the only good thing *in* it." We are attacked from outside by what, in our passion for metonymy, we call "Nixon"—all the forces of economic cut-back in league with the brute forces of accountability. But it seemed to me at that conference that we are attacked even more strongly from inside by our sense of guilty failure and our lack of clarity about what is worth doing. Even when we try to defend ourselves, we often sound like easy marks. And if we move from English in general to composition and communication, the plot ceases to be tragic or epic and becomes comic; we teachers of freshman English, as it is still sometimes nostalgically called, always knew we were mere pawns in the great game; and now, helpless as ever, we stand by and watch our departments lop off program after pro-

Luncheon speech at the annual Conference on College Composition and Communication, November 26, 1971, during the convention of the National Council of Teachers of English in Las Vegas, Nevada. First published as "The Meeting of Minds," *College Composition and Communication* 33 (1972): 24–50. © 1972 by the National Council of Teachers of English. Reprinted by permission.

gram. Our "betters" clearly hope that if they can only give up enough of what doesn't matter, of what is most clearly and embarrassingly proved to fail, at least by the crude tests of the accountability folk—if they can just give up teaching how to write well and speak well—the enemy may be satisfied and literary scholars may have peace in our time.

But there's no point in coming to Las Vegas only to add more evidence that we are in rout. The job is clearly—or so I told myself as this moment drew closer and closer—to prove that we need not be. Nobody, I told myself, nobody who has thought much about it believes that we have been as bad as we say to each other or as the public charges; nobody who has thought much about it will expect of me some simple, new, clear nostrum. What you must do—I more and more desperately urged myself—what you must do is find some way to convince them that we are

> . . . in blood
> stepp'd in so far that, should [we] wade no more,
> returning were as tedious as go o'er.

No, *Macbeth* clearly would not do. Perhaps I could invent some heroic imagery, or possibly even discover some scriptural solace. . . .

The days went by, the weeks went by, and nothing on paper! Yesterday in my motel room here, incommunicado, I was really growing desperate, staring at the blank pages before me. My wife suggested crossly that I might as well be downstairs gambling as upstairs grumbling. So I went down and began, at first idly, with nickels, then dimes and quarters; soon I was really into it, working two machines at a time, and had gone to dollars. Feeling like a character out of Dostoevsky, hooked to the table in spite of the dreadful deadline inexorably approaching, I paged my wife, while still pulling levers, hoping she would rescue me. But the page came back saying she had checked out of the hotel, leaving the message: "Flying back Chicago; told you wouldn't spend another these blasted NCTE Thanksgivings alone, and meant it."

Finally, at 4:53 this morning, exhausted and with only two dollars left, I looked up for a moment and saw a machine in the corner that I had not noticed before—a much more complicated-looking machine than the others, sort of a combination juke box and Rolls Royce radiator. Though I half noticed a tiny typed message below the level, "No Cash Payout on this Machine," I put a dollar in anyway and suddenly there was a great flashing of lights, a voice chanting, "York Jackpot, York Jackpot, Now Hear this, York Jackpot," and out came not a flood of dollars but a tape cassette. I haven't had time to listen through all of it, but I have no choice but to risk playing it for you now.

The Testament of York

And lo, there was a great gathering of the lost tribes of English in the city of York,[1] where men did say that there would arise unto them a new Word to lead them out of the wilderness. And verily the word was among them at York, yet they knew it not, for it did speak through each man in his own tongue, and the children of darkness knew not how to listen unto one another.

And there was a great Babel of voices, and each man and woman would say, "There is no Word but my words, which this generation of vipers heedeth not."

And there was much anger and bitterness among all those who were there, and they did murmur among themselves saying, "We were promised a great new Word, and there is no Word." And the British did murmur against the Americans for corrupting the Word with mechanisms and national curriculum studies, and the Americans did murmur against the British for speaking words that sounded like unto the words of their prophet-in-disgrace, John Dewey, and the Canadians did murmur against both the Americans and the British for worshipping Language Arts and thus betraying the literary monuments of Western culture.

And there was much flailing of phrases and gnashing of nominals.

But after many days, lo, a miracle was wrought in the land where English was born. Those who had been in the bonds of fear and despair did begin to abandon their autistic ways, to raise up their eyes and look at each other, to open their ears and hear each other, and what they heard was this:

"We have behaved unto each other in a strange but interesting way, yea, even as our students behave in our classrooms, which is to say, we have heard only what we were prepared to hear, we have been unable to learn except that which was already almost known.

"And there was a great questioning among us about why in our age and wisdom we should have behaved like unto children, and a theory did emerge among us that our minds were more like our students' minds than

1. "York" was the second of two international conferences on the teaching of English. Some two score of us critics, grammarians, historians, philologists, educationists, novelists, and poets—teachers all—gathered first for several weeks at Dartmouth College. After reports on our endeavors had been published, many of us met again, with many more teachers, in York, England, to continue the stimulating exchange. In one sense, "nothing came of Dartmouth or York," as some say, though the published reports are still worth reading. But by 1971 the conferences had produced enough discussion for "Dartmouth" and "York" to become buzz words, meaning something like "the (admirable/hopeless/promising/silly) effort by the profession to make sense of what we do."

we had once believed, and the likeness was as the great neglected American psycho-prophet George Kelly had said unto us long ago, echoing and expanding an ancient rhetorical truth: each mind is constructed of symbolic efforts to make sense of the world, and no mind ever meets another mind except when two systems of "personal constructs" find some overlapping where a jointure can be made, a joining of the symbols which our Lord the Logos hath given unto us.

"And each of us is like unto a child, in that we spew out untasted whatever meat is strange to us. What we say unto one another, whether in a conference or in a classroom, can only be heard if it somehow fits what we already have and are. Knowledge can only be taken by us, as by our students, when it can be fitted into the geography of whatever symbolic land the Lord hath in his glorious linguistic copiousness given unto us, even us who are mature and, unlike our wicked students, freed of Satan's temptations to remain ignorant."

And lo, it did come to pass that everyone spake in agreement one with another, though in different languages, saying: "It is always good to grow in our capacity to cope with our various worlds through language. We have sinned in many ways, but not least in pretending that we have no shared commitments and in saying that we therefore have nothing to teach our students or learn from them. We now see that we have all been traveling together toward the Promised Land. For lo, there is a great purpose that we all believe in and work for, a purpose which our many neglected prophets, living and dead, have preached unto us: it is always in all lands good for any person to grow in his personhood by improving his capacity to cope with the world symbolically, which meaneth to take into himself the selves of others. And we now see as in a vision that nobody at this conference or any other conference can really doubt the glory of working for such growth."

And we did look upon each other in great amazement, saying: "Here, yea, even here we have discovered, in *facts* that we know about ourselves, a common *value*; in our *subjective* experience we have shared an *objective* reality that we can depend on; in *reasoning* together we have rediscovered a great and unshakable *faith*."

But even as we came unto this new unity, there was one among us who said: "Although we have by dwelling together here for many hours and many days come to a great new determination never again to betray the Logos which is our inheritance, when we return to explain what it is that we and our colleagues should do, we shall once again find ourselves in a great Babblement, with many doubters saying that to preach growth through language, or to say that just as mankind is created in and through language, so men and women are saved only in increasing their symbolic copings—to say these things will produce a great scoffing, because men will say that we offer nothing to the world about what practice follows from our common faith."

And there were many among us who began to murmur, saying: "This skeptic hath spoken aright. We have discovered an empty generalization in discovering that all who profess writing and speaking profess the improvement of man's life by improving each person's capacity to grow in and through symbolic coping with the world. No man among us can say which definition of symbolic interchange, which definition of language, we should give ourselves to."

But lo, there was one among us who stood above all the others in understanding the Words of Kelly, and he did go unto the top of York Minster to consult with the Lord about what we should say unto all teachers about his will. And he was hidden from the multitude many hours, and when he descended, he did issue a press release, to wit, as follows:

COMMANDMENT ONE: *I am the Lord, thy Logos, which hath brought thee, through the meeting of minds, out of the protozoal slime; thou shalt have no other Gods before me, neither the forcing of minds, nor the conditioning of minds, nor the meeting of minds with machines. Though thou deniest me often and always, I dwell with you whenever there is among you a true meeting of minds through symbolic expression.*

And since I am dealing here with a bunch of niggling English teachers, I want to get my definitions straight from the beginning. This message is for English teachers, and in dealing with English teachers I shall be talking about symbolic expressions, and if I were talking to a convention of brain cells, I would deal with information exchange at a different level. And I should make clear now that when I say "mind" I do not mean mere calculating brain, as distinct from heart, gut, and gonad. When minds really meet, persons meet, and I'm getting sick and tired—I mean to say, it unstrings my withers when I see what some of you do with your abstract distinctions of thought and feeling, reason and emotion, logic and faith, and what not. Hast thou not read the words of my prophets Michael Polanyi or John Dewey or . . . [There's a hiatus here.]

But I am getting ahead of my story. I just want to say unto you because it is sure to come up later on, that I honor committee meetings and conferences, when they labor honestly to bring about a meeting of minds. Though many a conference has, I am sorry to proclaim, passed from my control into the hands of a former counselor of mine who shall be nameless, I want it to be known that I have given the gift of holding conferences to modern man as one last hope for making the center hold. He who scoffeth at conferences hath said in his heart, of his brothers, "Raca, thou fool," and as you might learn in Matthew 5 : 22, whosoever shall say, "Thou fool," shall be in danger of hellfire.

One final preliminary, before I move on to Commandment Two: The meeting of minds that I have in mind is not commanded in order to insist that ye agree one with another; it is only when you disagree and then allow lesser gods to prevent your understanding the ground of disagreement that you violate my command. But if ye succeed in understanding your disagreement, I am satisfied. I the Lord your God always try not to be unreasonable.

COMMANDMENT TWO: *Thou shalt not construct abstract tables of commandments about how to bring about the meeting of minds through language, nor hierarchical rulings about which languages are sweetest in my sight.*

And this goes for you guys who worship the language of the street just as much as for you pedants who worship the language of the study. If you'll just think about this one for five minutes, instead of shouting against each other so much, you'll see that where you all go astray is in supposing either that it is undemocratic to talk about real standards, or that I have a single path of improvement in mind, everybody having to pass from mulings and pukings to Shakespeare or Malcolm X in one leap. What I want for you all is what every one of you wants for himself: increased personhood through increased capacity to take in and deal with your experience in symbolic exchange—to give symbolic ordering, that is, to whatever I throw your way, regardless of how chaotic I make it seem. If you would only remember that I don't ask you to do anything for your students that is not commanded of you—at however exalted a position on my ladder you think you may stand—we wouldn't misunderstand each other so often.

I hate to have to remind you, but I said all this to you last year at the CCCC annual luncheon, through the mouth of my prophet Robert Heilman, in urging you to come to composition, to com-pose. I still can't get used to the way you all forget, from one year to the next, applauding a speech like his one day and then within a month mouthing speeches about how nobody knows what English is about any more, as if you had heard Heilman in a dream. Go back and read him again, lest I wax wroth.

COMMANDMENT THREE: *Thou shalt not make unto thee any graven concepts, thinking that it is in the power of man to utter any of my truths once and for all, or that it is comely in my sight for any of my servants to try.*

Graven concepts, whether in books or party slogans or private formulations, cannot further the meeting of minds. Even when they come to seem shared, whether by two men or by a large conference in its resolutions, as at Dartmouth, they are not a meeting of minds but a locking together of non-minds, comparable, in my no-doubt-limited view, to the copulation of insects. Of course I do not view the copulation of insects as contemptible; everything in my creation is good. But some things are better than others, and I have made you alone capable of loving each other together in the invigorating baths of half-truth.

COMMANDMENT THREE A: *Yet neither shalt thou worship the golden calf of thine own notion of what kinds of symbolic exchange are performed in my name. It is an abomination in my sight when thou sayest such old-fashioned things as "The unexamined life is not worth living;" or such newly fashionable things as "The examined life is not worth living." Thou shalt not speak against interpretation or for interpretation. There is often more genuine growth through meeting of minds in what you call unexamined lives than in the clumsy and hate-ridden exchanges that are sometimes undertaken in the name of examining life. And, as my good book often says, vice versa.*

COMMANDMENT FOUR: *Thou shalt not take the name of ANYTHING in vain, because when names are used falsely there can be no meeting of minds. Thou shalt neither say nor imply that it does not matter whether words are used deceptively or carelessly, in ignorance. When thy leaders call war "pacification," murder "protection," and mass murder in the service of tyranny "a noble effort to preserve peace, build democracy, and create a better way of life," thou shalt kick against the pricks, hard. But by the same token when thou who kickest call genocide what is not genocide, fascism what is not fascism, and totalitarianism what is obviously and tragically a great scattered and bumbling nation trying to build a tower of Babel in the name of an impossible and illusory bliss, thou shalt protest the protesters, because in such misnaming there can be no meeting of minds.*

Actually, though, I'm a bit worried here that you may misunderstand this commandment as exacting a spiritless and often mindless literalism. I myself have produced some of my best and most lasting effects with rhetorical figures like metaphor, hyperbole, and irony, because when properly used such things can produce an intensified meeting of minds. When my prophets have understood my irony, as when Job understood my question, "Where wast thou when I laid the foundations of the earth? declare, if thou hast understanding," then our minds have clamped together in a great and glorious and indestructible clamping. It is only when

*my people—and I'm thinking especially of you down there in 1971—
engage in private put-ons for their own exaltation instead of ensuring
growth through the meeting of minds—it is only then that I repenteth
me that I made man on the earth.*

COMMANDMENT FIVE: *Honor thy mental fathers and mothers, that
thy thoughts may be long in the rhetorical community which the Lord
thy God giveth thee and through which he created thee and will create thy
posterity—if any. Remember that there can be no meeting of rootless
minds, determined to be autonomous, original, creative personalities at all
costs. Thou art so made that thou canst not do thine own thing except in
madness. No mind is an island—a message I conveyed to one of my
favorites some centuries ago.*

COMMANDMENT SIX: *Thou shalt not kill other minds by turning them
into straw men, in order to gain easy victories. Because between head-
pieces full of straw, there can be no meeting of minds.*

   *I would like, in this connection, to call attention to the righteous ser-
vice of my newly converted prophet Ellsberg, not only for his courage in
battling to make possible a meeting of minds by sharing knowledge, but
for his way of conducting his defense. When Ellsberg had published his
argument that the Viet Nam disaster resulted from a vast and wicked
conspiracy to ignore what was known, one man he had attacked, Arthur
Schlesinger, Jr., was invited by the* New York Review of Books *to write a
rejoinder to Ellsberg, and Ellsberg was invited to reply to Schlesinger.
Whereupon Ellsberg chose to follow my commands rather than the dictates of SOP for controversy in 1971: he actually suggested that he and
Schlesinger talk together "in advance, in order to narrow grounds of difference and eliminate false issues." As Schlesinger reports it, after hours of
talk much disagreement still remained, but let me just ask you, oh my
people, when did you last observe two of your own number taking such
precautions against meaningless debate in your so-called critical and
scholarly journals? I shall not pause for a reply.*

COMMANDMENT SIX A: *Thou shalt not assume that any student or any
colleague hath no mind to be met, regardless of how hopeless he or she
may appear; remember that to ME thou appearest as hopeless as even
the most hopeless case amongst thy students appeareth to THEE, and YET
I continue to hope for a meeting with THY mind.*

COMMANDMENT SIX B: *Thou shalt not labor to kill budding thoughts in
other minds, however monstrous and ugly the buds may appear. Because
in all buds of all thought there is present the Supreme Principle of growth*

through symbolic meeting. Remember that in killing any part of any mind, thou killest part of thine own.

COMMANDMENT SEVEN: *Thou shalt not commit adultery!*

COMMANDMENT EIGHT: *Thou shalt not steal ideas either by plagiary or by taking what thou mistakenly callest thine own ideas and turning them into thy property. For in the day that thou labellest an idea as thine, thou shalt surely die. And thy competitive discourse with thy fellow professors and administrators will be nothing more than the clashing of symbols and the tangling of brass* (sic).

COMMANDMENT NINE: *Thou shalt not lie, whether to thy colleagues or to thy students. Because when any man liest—I mean lieth—there can be no meeting of minds. Indeed, any lie diminisheth the mind that utters it.*

COMMANDMENT NINE A: *Thou shalt not seek to appear wiser than thou art, because when thou concealest thine ignorance, there can be no meeting of ignorant mind with ignorant mind. The great and original sin against my name is pride; the original sin against my mind, and thine, is intellectual pride. Thy need for growth in language equals that of any man.*

COMMANDMENT TEN: *Thou shalt not covet thy neighbor's mental achievements, because thy mind is his mind and his composings can, without coveting, become thy composings.*
I have, as a matter of fact, a good deal to say about this matter, if there were time, but perhaps you can figure it out for yourself.

APPENDIX A: *Thou shalt never refuse to labor to provide reasons for thine ideas, when thy brother asketh for reasons, or to embrace his ideas when his reasons are superior. Remember the much misunderstood teaching of my great prophet Descartes, which in its original form, before scribes tampered with it, read: "We discourse together, as I write my meditation to you; therefore we are."*

APPENDIX B: *Thou shalt labor unceasingly to treat thy neighbor's objections to thine arguments as if they were thine own, and thine own arguments as if they were thy neighbor's.*
For it is my honest opinion, though again I may be wrong, that in matters like this you and your neighbor are pretty much on the same footing, and unless you work in recognition that you are on the same footing, you shall most surely come a cropper in the eyes of your father, the Logos, which hath, as I said at the beginning, brought you out of the

*protozoal slime. It yieldeth me great pain and wrath whenever I observe
you slipping back into it.*

APPENDIX C: *Though my clairvoyant powers are not what they were in
ancient times, I can horuspicate into your hearts and find, O my people, a
great and disastrous misunderstanding. In spite of all I have said, you still
hope—even those of you who have been attending to my words—you
still hope for a single prophet to lead you out of the wilderness. And you
still think that it is one of your main tasks to hunt out the false prophets
and expose them to stoning by the multitude. If I've told you once I've
told you a thousand times that there will be no single prophet and no
single way. It is a wicked and adulterous generation that seeketh one
prophet only, one new English or anti-English, one new rhetoric or anti-
rhetoric, one new discipline or interdiscipline, one new teaching device or
way of not teaching. Some of my servants are at this moment quickening
hearts and meeting minds with methods invented by Aristotle; others are
enabling minds to meet through "writing workshop" techniques that
would have made my ancient prophets weep, dogmatists that they were.
To me there is only one kind of false prophet, and this is the prophet who
has frozen himself into his formulation so that he can no longer improve
his capacity to meet other minds. As I have said before, many prophets
are called, but even more are—but I resist the obvious jest as beneath my
dignity.*

APPENDIX D: *Recent studies in developmental biology and social linguistics have shown that a newborn baby begins immediately to bathe in
the sea of symbolic exchange which is my Being. I would recommend that
thou addest to thy reading list the May 7, 1971, issue of the TLS, and. . . .*

[We elide about fifteen minutes' worth of increasingly pompous and trivial
law making and cut to the end.]

In my end is my beginning. *The message of York is this: Thou shalt
not despair, though the false prophets of thy time would teach thee to
despair. Thou dwellest not in a total chaos of conflicting values. In the
words of a student, overheard recently by my prophet Harry Finestone,
"Since I got converted to Isis, I see that chaos is getting somewhere."*
*All of you believe in the value of preserving and purifying the lan-
guage of thy tribe, not by imposing abstract standards of purity but by
enlarging every student's symbolic powers. You can do what you know
you should do only if you throw away these tablets, and all tablets, and*

return to your domain and station determined to listen, and through listening to save yourself by enlarging your mind.

Go forth and labor in love, which is the meeting of minds. . . .

The tape fades here. To my mind, the Lord makes it sound too easy, as he always has done. But what, I want to ask him, *what* do we do about rising teaching loads and falling budgets? What do I do about my student Jackson, who won't even talk with me, and what about Smith, who calls the fruit of my mind bullshit, or Zabriski, who says I'm irrelevant because I was once a dean, and so on? To find out, I tried another dollar, but nothing came out. I guess I must go back to Chicago with nothing but my highly skeptical and often despairing students to rely on. I wonder what it is, really, that Jackson, with his frozen silence, is trying to say to me.

PART II · *TO OUR VARIOUS "PUBLICS"*

You know what college I went to? I went to the college of hard knocks.

> Popular saying.

I don't know, Ma'am, why they make all this fuss about education; none of the Pagets can read or write, and they get on well enough.

> Attributed to William Lamb, Viscount Melbourne, addressing Queen Victoria

What we discovered was that the words we use really make a difference.

> Congressman, commenting on a budget compromise between Congress and the President.

INTRODUCTION · *The Occasions*

Most of the rhetorical demands set by the occasions for the following four talks can be inferred from the footnotes naming the organizations I addressed. But the last one, the talk to the top editors of *Time* magazine, calls for a bit of staging. In 1971 Edward Levi, president of the University of Chicago, suggested to the managers of *Time* that a couple of days spent on the University of Chicago campus would surprise and enlighten them. Our claim was that we were consistently underplayed by East Coast journals. We had noticed that whenever a story broke that called for expert opinion, we too often saw some second-rater from Princeton or Columbia consulted, while our bevy of Nobel laureates was ignored. When Harvard or Yale "discovered" some curricular innovation that we had practiced for decades, the story was covered everywhere; when *we* innovated, we waited for news about it until some Ivy Leaguer (or perhaps Stanford or Berkeley) adopted it. (Does my account seem biased? I can't see why!) So we hoped to capture the attention of at least one major journal from the benighted East.

To our surprise, *Time* agreed to send its top brass and a broad range of reporters to get a quick look at just what we were up to out here in the provinces. They came, visited classes, talked with faculty members and students, and finally attended a luncheon at which I was the speaker.

As I asked those visibly sophisticated folks, "Why Don't You Do It My Way?" I had a strong impression that things were going unusually well. They laughed when I intended laughter, looked thoughtful when I asked for thought, nodded their heads when I expressed my criticism of how they handled their inevitable mistakes. At the end, many of them jumped to their feet to give me the standing applause that memory tells me I clearly deserved. But suddenly they all plopped down in their chairs and applauded politely: Hedley Donovan, the chief, had not stood. He had remained in his chair, paws flapping unenthusiastically. They had seen, understood, and followed obediently. (Did I dream this failed climax? No, my colleagues who were there saw it too.) As we were leaving the dining room, Donovan approached me, praised the speech courteously, and asked if he could print it in *Time*'s house organ, *FYI*.

I sent him a copy, thinking no doubt that at last I had the media at my feet, where they belonged. They printed—*not* what I had sent but a totally emasculated version, one that removed every comment suggesting the least fault in *Time*. Only my opening words about *Time*'s importance, only the rhetorician's soft soap, met their standards of reporting. The meat of my suggestions—that they should educate their readers to some standard of critical response—simply disappeared without even ellipsis points. So much for *Time*'s interest in improving public rhetoric. So much for the power of rhetoric to sway *the* powers. Can we hope for other publics that will prove less impervious?

OCCASION 6 · *To Those Who Do* Not
Teach English, but Who Believe that
Something Called "English"
Should Be Taught:

Mere Rhetoric, Rhetorology, and the Search for a Common Learning

One of my earliest experiences with curricular reform took place at Haverford College in the early fifties. After some months of careful thought about what was wrong with an absurd accretion of requirements that had apparently never been thought through by anyone before, we on the curriculum committee had the instructive experience of seeing the faculty spend all of ten minutes on our report. The coup de grace—only a pretentious cliché can do justice to it—the coup de grace was administered by kindly old Ned Snyder: "Gentlemen"—and we were all gentlemen in those days— "gentlemen, we are already the best men's college in the country. Why on earth we should change is more than I can see!"

The Haverford faculty, in its wisdom, assumed that it had debated the subject adequately, and dropped the report without a vote. The document disappeared without a trace.

I do not know that it was a good report; I never had a chance to find out by testing it in serious discussion. What I know for sure is that our failure to debate its merits exhibited our bad rhetorical education, "highly educated" and well intentioned though we were. Skilled specialists, most of us, in the arts of reasoning in our specialties, we were totally unskilled—as many another faculty meeting of the time further revealed—in the art of reasoning together about shared concerns.

I must confess that having observed similar non-discussions in many a meeting through almost thirty-five years of curricular discussion, I find our

Slightly revised from "Mere Rhetoric, Rhetoric, and the Search for Common Learning," in *Common Learning: A Carnegie Colloquium on General Education* (Washington, D.C.), 23–55. © 1981 by The Carnegie Foundation for the Advancement of Teaching. Reprinted by permission.

failure haunting us here as we renew deliberation about general education.[1]

I may as well also confess that whenever I see a list of the essential ingredients of general education, I invariably feel that my own subjects have been radically underplayed. How could the Carnegie essayist [in the position paper for the conference] be so blind as to list "The Shared Language and Symbols that Connect Us" as only one of six co-equal subjects, on a par with those other interesting but far less important subjects, history, natural science, mathematics, ethics and political science? Have they not realized that the study of all the rest depends on the quality of the shared languages we use in that study? Have they not recognized that the study of how to improve our capacity to share symbols—what many of us call *rhetoric*—is thus the queen of the sciences?

I know very well that to succumb like that to the temptations of disciplinary imperialism is to destroy from the beginning any chance of building a general education curriculum. So I feel guilty about such thoughts. But I would feel guiltier if I did not suspect that others secretly respond in the same way. The historians will wonder why history, which is obviously the most important and most neglected of studies, should be degraded to one-half of one slot out of six, and labelled only as a "concern with a common heritage"—as if we did not live and have our being in that heritage! The natural scientists, the social scientists, and the philosophers similarly must each squirm a bit to see that what is for them central has been pinned wriggling to the wall-chart—and what is more, labelled with an alien name. And this is to say nothing about those other scholars and teachers who cannot find themselves on the chart at all. (You may have noticed how much we resemble, in our jockeyings for position in curricular debates, the various special interests in their responses to budget cutting proposals: insofar as we really care for our own territory, we almost inevitably place it ahead of all others.)

Such imperialisms aside, at least for the moment, I assume that we could all agree on something like the six-fold list in the Carnegie essay. We know that when our colleges graduate students who are radically ignorant and unskilled in these shared connections, the result is shocking. It is a scandal that so few of our graduates are even minimally proficient in more than one of the six fields. It is a scandal that even students who major in any one of the conventional fields that profess to deal with "connections"—I mention only English and philosophy—are often blind to the issues raised by words such as *shared* and *connections*. They have been systematically incapacitated for

1. At the original conference sponsored by the Carnegie Foundation, a series of public lectures and discussions at the University of Chicago.

sharing anything except expertise with other experts in some subdivision of current inquiry. If you think I exaggerate, ask the next economics B.A. you meet what her study has taught her that would be useful in dealing with our rising mass illiteracy. Or try to have a good conversation about politics or literature with your university's M.B.A.'s or "behavioral psych" majors.

So far we might all agree that sharing the six sharings will minimally mark a person as "generally educated," as someone deserving a *Bachelor of Arts* diploma. Presumably our next move is to discuss what particular consequences for educational planning might follow from such agreement. But experience teaches that trouble begins whenever we move from general goals to particular means.

Just think of the jealous responses we are likely to meet, within any one of the six general subjects. The sociologists, anthropologists, economists, legal theorists, and political scientists will quarrel, for example, about which of them deals best with our "shared institutions" or "shared activities"; the various schools of philosophy, anthropology, psychology, and literary theory will quarrel about which deals best with our "shared values"; and so on.

Or think of the academic rivals who might claim that they should provide the substance studied under the first category, "competence in symbol-sharing." Agreeing that students must become competent in "the shared language and symbols that connect us"—that they must learn to read, write, speak, and listen effectively—many different experts can make quite plausible cases for the centrality of what they do. Most obviously, teachers of composition and of elementary foreign languages will make their case for a basic literacy. But a basic literacy taught according to what paradigms? Offhand, one can think of at least a dozen disciplines claiming to provide the central theory both for elementary instruction in how to read, think, speak, and write and for advanced training toward degrees in linguistics, semiotics, logic, analytical philosophy, hermeneutics, communications theory, cognitive science, various kinds of structuralism and deconstructionism—not to mention (as we say when mentioning) the many versions of my own pet field, rhetoric. And what about the fields that the report does mention but does not include explicitly in the summarizing chart—the languages of mathematics, music, and the visual arts? Where are the symbolic sharings through the languages of film, photography, and TV?

We all know that the same kinds of rivalry can be found under each of the other five categories, even in the natural sciences. What, then, are we to do, when we turn from our general lists and try to design a general curriculum?

That question leads me nicely back to my own empire, rhetoric, just as it has led the Carnegie Foundation to place its money on the rhetoric of conferences and collections of essays, in the hope of making changes in the world. Whenever we are faced with a multiplicity of seemingly conflicting spoken or written claims, we turn to the art of rhetoric, the art of pursuing the understandings that lurk behind our surface symbolic disagreements, and the disagreements that lurk behind our superficial agreements. We think about how our discourse in these areas works and about how it might be improved. We analyze our terms and look beneath our verbal surfaces, searching for common grounds, from which we can then begin discoursing at a new and improved level.

In the ancient terminology of rhetoricians, we seek to discover the topics, the topoi, the places or locations on which, or *in* which, a shared inquiry can take place. Whatever conclusions we come to as we confer, we shall be practicing, well or badly, the arts of rhetoric. Whether we practice them well will depend only in part on the quality of the formal education we received in them, because our education—or miseducation—in rhetoric continues willy-nilly after formal schooling.

In using the much abused term *rhetoric* to cover everything any of us says at this conference, I know I take some risks. Rhetoric has always had a mixed press. When the International Society for the History of Rhetoric met in Madison, Wisconsin, in April 1981, one entire afternoon was scheduled for papers on the long history of *attacks* on rhetoric. But we do not have to go to history to discover that the term is suspect. At least nine out of ten references to it in the press today are unfavorable. In popular usage it generally refers to the sleazier branches of the arts of persuasion, often synonymous with bombast or verbal trickery or deliberate obfuscation. It is what we substitute for substantive action or genuine thought, what we fall back on when serious arguments are lacking. "Although the President's deeper purpose was concealed in the rhetoric, [he] sent a red hot message . . . in his speech last Wednesday." "But Miss Caruso dismissed Healey's statement as 'rhetoric' and vowed to bring in the second round of her proposed cuts." This is surely the standard usage.

You might then well say, "If *rhetoric* is such a bad word, why not just get rid of it and use the words stressed in the Carnegie essay, *symbol sharing?*" But it is not just the word that is debunked; it is what it stands for. "Reaction [to Mayor Byrne's announcement that she will move into the Cabrini-Green housing project] was mixed Saturday night, with many calling the move courageous but symbolic." Courageous—that's good. Symbolic, introduced with a *but*—that is obviously somehow bad, or at least inferior. "Alderman Danny Davis . . . said the move might be more symbolic than substantive." Obviously anything merely symbolic is not substantive, and if rhetoric is anything it is an employment of symbols.

If you detect a tone of defensiveness in these observations, just think how you would feel if you professed a subject that gets itself talked about like that, every day, everywhere!

What people usually mean when they dismiss other people's efforts as "rhetoric" or, more often, "mere rhetoric," is that words or other symbols are being used to deceive or to obscure issues or to evade action. Animals cannot tell elaborate lies, only simple ones. Animals cannot use symbols as evasion. Only a rhetoric-endowed species can produce an elaborate chain of lies to achieve a cover-up; or a multi-million dollar advertising campaign for products known to be either useless or harmful; or a diplomatic and political vocabulary for making the worse seem the better cause. Rhetoricians have often tried to wash their hands of such stuff, preserving the term "rhetoric" for cleaner efforts. But as educators we cannot accept that dodge. If we confer symbolic powers upon our students, we take on all of the risks of symbolic power. If we train our students in the arts of reading, writing, listening, and speaking, we inevitably empower them to do great harm in the world—to use rhetoric for private, anti-social ends, to break rather than build connections. I must return to this problem in a few moments, but for now perhaps we can simply label the whole domain of the deceitful rhetoric we deplore as "sub-rhetoric." Different people will probably have somewhat different examples in mind; hardly a day goes by without my adding to a list that exhibits, as its supreme moment, Richard Nixon's Checkers speech, when his family, and then his dog, won the hearts of a nation.

One step up from sub-rhetoric, we find the word "rhetoric" used to refer to the whole art of sincere selling of any cause, not just the trickery part or the disguise, but the genuinely persuasive parts too, including the logical arguments. In this sense, President Carter's rhetoric was said to be poor and President Reagan's is generally said to be good, meaning that, on average, people come away from their encounters with President Reagan having moved more or less in his direction. Almost every day we read that the United States must "improve its rhetoric throughout the world," obviously meaning "we must sell our case more effectively."

Though it is hard to distinguish this level of rhetoric, which I will call "mere rhetoric," from sub-rhetoric, obviously its uses can range from the most noble to the most dangerous, from Churchill's wartime speeches to the typical piece of campaign oratory. In some ways, mere rhetoric is more dangerous than sub-rhetoric, because those who employ it are sincere; they have a position that they hope will prevail, and they themselves respect the rhetorical devices that they employ. Presidents Reagan and Carter both seem to believe in their hearts that they are good medicine for the country. More important to our analysis than their sincerity, however, is that they always give the impression of having used their rhetoric to put across a position that was known in advance, before the work on the rhetoric began. The case is already known: "OK, Sam, let's whomp us up some mere rhetoric to put it over. Let's see, who's our best ghost writer on this subject? George? OK, George, you know what we want, now get cracking on the rhetoric." The fact is that most freshman composition texts, even those that have taken up with the renewed fashion of using the word "rhetoric" in the title, imply that one's case is found by some other art or science, and then one puts it over with mere rhetoric.

Even if that were our final definition of the art, rhetoric would still obviously be indispensable in all general education, since its uses are shared by all who engage in any kind of practical endeavor. But it is hardly the art that I could bring myself to defend as what we should use in debating general education. Presumably, as we discuss our various proposals we do not think of ourselves as coming out of the discussion precisely as we came into it. We want to discover something through our rhetorical exchange.

Aristotle's *Rhetoric* goes one large step further toward the definition we are seeking. Instead of referring to an art of persuasion about a case that is entirely known beforehand, rhetoric for Aristotle is the *faculty* or *capacity*, found of course *in the rhetorician, of discovering* or *inventing* "the possible means of persuasion in reference to any subject whatever." Unlike the arts of medicine, geometry, arithmetic (and presumably politics, too, though Aristotle does not mention politics in this context), the art of rhetoric "appears to be able to *discover* the means of persuasion in reference to any given subject." It is thus used by all disciplines, except insofar as those disciplines have available apodeictic proofs, what we call "demonstrative" or "scientific" proofs. Rhetoric in this view is not a dressing added to the case to make it persuasive; the rhetorician discovers the case itself, using the art of rhetoric as an art of discovery. When the search is successful, the case is persuasive, though the conclusions it leads to may not be true for all time and are certainly not demonstrated in any absolute sense.

This art, which I will call "rhetoric-B," is a marvel and a wonder. A scholar-teacher might honorably spend a whole career mastering its subtleties and passing the mastery along to students. Obviously it is a much more important subject than what most people call rhetoric. It will of course include the study of the inferior rhetorics—how otherwise could one distinguish the "bombast" and "empty verbal ornamentation" of one's enemies from the "true eloquence" and "sensitive verbal enrichments" of one's friends? But its true home will be what we call "value disputes": in the political arena at its best, when a Pericles or a Lincoln or a Churchill reminds a nation of its deepest commitments; or in literary criticism; or in quarrels about the law or about constitutions. It comes into its own in every part of life where simple appeals to obvious facts or unquestioned logical proofs are not available—and that surely means most of what we do, even as scholars. Clearly, such a subject is immensely important, well worth the hundreds of pages of close study that Aristotle and Cicero gave it, and the many thousands that later students have added. There is nothing "mere" about it. It is the very lifeblood of our daily lives together.

But is it finally what we seek, if we are looking for the art not just of discovering, but also of appraising the values we share? One obvious problem is that it seems to lack any limits on its power. It can be taught to villains as well as to saints, and it can be employed either for or against the good of a society. It is, of course, an immensely seductive art, because its mastery is the road to worldly success. Rhetoric-B is the art of knowing what you want and finding the really good arguments to win others to your side. It is the art of the good lawyer, of the effective business leader, of the successful fund-raiser, and it is not to be scoffed at or ignored. But it does not itself teach us what ends it should serve; it is still an art without essential restraints, other than those provided by the counter-rhetoric created by other warriors or competitors. The world it builds, left on its own, is a world of a free market of atomized persons and ideas, each privately seeking victory and hoping that in the melee a public good will be produced by some invisible hand. Thus all thinkers, from Plato and Aristotle on, have felt the need to subordinate it to some higher discipline capable of revealing proper ends or goods. We see what happens when such higher controls are lacking, as various spokesmen for this or that new rhetorical theory— "communications skills," "propaganda analysis," "advertising techniques," "information science"—show themselves to be, in effect, available to the highest bidder: they fail to provide, from within themselves, any hint about limits to how and when their techniques are to be used.

But to what discipline or art now on the scene might we turn for the controls that each of our three kinds of rhetoric so clearly require? It takes no great skill in rhetoric to recognize that in our society at this time, there is open warfare about whether any superior "good" exists, or, if it does, what in fact it is and how it should be pursued. We seem to share no single notion of the good, or of the proper methods of argument to be used in its pursuit.

If we did have such agreement, we might of course deduce from it the proper uses of rhetoric: something like, "Service of the one true Lord requires, as Augustine teaches, that rhetoric should . . . " or "To restore our position as the world's greatest power, it is obvious that our rhetoric should . . . " or "By studying the right list of classical philosophers, we can learn those truths that we can then sell with our rhetoric." But we in America have agreed on something else instead—that we are to be a pluralistic society in which many different possible first principles will coexist. Some of them, like some scientists' and mathematicians' notions of what can be known, would rule out as trivial or non-cognitive most of the proposals we offer each other about general education. Some of them would suggest a list of co-ordinate values. And some, like mine, would lead to a more aggressive kind of hierarchical ordering, with certain threatened educational deficiencies seen as much more important than others.

When first principles conflict, how do we proceed? One possible way is to use rhetoric-B to persuade other people to change their minds and accept the predetermined *true* first principles. Marshalling all of the possible means of persuasion in our situation, we would, in that view, try to win as many converts as possible.

But did the Carnegie Foundation's authors know, before they began to draft their report, not only how the report was to come out, but how those who read and discuss it were supposed to respond? Did I know, as I began to write, what general education program we all should fight for on our campuses, using the best rhetoric we can muster?

Clearly, we all admire most still another form of rhetoric entirely, one implied by my hierarchical progression from sub-rhetoric through mere-rhetoric and on to rhetoric-B, namely—surprise!—a "rhetoric-A." When we are working together at our best, we repudiate both the autocratic imposition of a program by some benign dictator and the warfare of fixed positions; instead we try out our reasons on each other, to see where we might come out. We practice a rhetoric of inquiry that is to some degree similar to what I label, in "The Idea of a *University*" (Occasion 19 below), as "rhetoric-3." But rhetoric-A could be employed in all the three rhetorics of that piece.

To invent a label does not mean, of course, that the art we seek actually exists, and it certainly does not say that we will attain to it if it does exist. But if there were an art that promised to aid us in going beneath the surface of our verbal disputes, in order to discover the common values that underlie them and to build practical programs on them, would not mastery of that art be, for any pluralistic society, a noble art indeed?

Is there a rhetoric-A? Is there a supreme art of inquiry through symbols that is designed, not to win by cheating, as in sub-rhetoric; not merely to win sincerely, as in mere rhetoric; not just to marshal all of the good reasons there might be for accepting what one knows already, as in rhetoric-B; but rather to discover and refine, in critical exchange, our ends, our purposes, our values?

Let me stress again the curious point that we have intuitively elected to practice that unnamed art whenever we engage in conferences that permit open exchange of ideas. What is more, I suspect that despite all our rhetorical faults as a nation, it remains true that no other society has ever committed itself so passionately to the search for rhetoric-A. Often this commitment is mocked, as people get impatient with committee work, with the cumbersomeness of representative government, with the absurdities of our thousands of national conventions, colloquia, conferences, workshops, and commissions. "Just think of all the time, energy, and money that is being wasted at this moment by hard-working, intelligent people, who travel thousands of miles to confer together in muddle-headed fashion, using dubious arguments about unformulated questions, appealing to unclear principles and leading to ambiguous conclusions!"

Well, that's rhetoric-A for you! We seem to be stuck with it, not only when we confer in person but whenever we seriously take other people's views into account. So let us try for a somewhat clearer definition of this rhetoric that we seek to practice together when we are at our best.

Is it not *the art of appraising the warrants for assent in any symbolic exchange?*

The definition may seem anti-climactic until we think about the ground covered by its four key terms:

Appraising—the judging of the real validity or force, the power or weakness of something.

Warrants—the reason or motives given by one human being to another as support for some belief or action or change of mind (note that we move here beyond notions of "proof" or "demonstration." Such ostensibly hard stuff becomes only a subset of all the more or less good grounds we can give each other for changing our minds and hearts).

Assent—rather than dissent, because, though the two notions of saying "yes" and saying "no" are indissolubly linked in all human exchange, assent is really prior. Of the many reasons one might mention, the most obvious is that "thinking together about warrants" cannot even be undertaken without a primal act of assent: "I" must assent to "your" equal right to a hearing in our mutual endeavors; note again the contrast with traditional notions of hard proof, sought usually in private inquiry by *dis*proving other people's views, the results then imposed upon a reluctant world. What is more, the "I" who assents or dissents was long since constituted in a series of incorporations of other selves. Hence:

Symbolic exchange—like the other, inferior rhetorics, this one is indissolubly bound with the notion that it takes at least two to tango. But unlike the other definitions, this one rejects the very notion of the private individual "self" thinking by "itself." We move, instead to a kind of thought possible only for a radically social self; the dichotomy between the individual and his past and present "context" is unreal. Good thinking in this view will not be quite like the "clear thinking" touted in so many handbooks of logic, something performed by the "individual" in opposition to all those sloppy thinkers "out there." Instead it will be "social thought" even when it is in some sense private; good thinking will be only that kind of thinking that takes into account what others have said or can say against it. And it will be, from first to last, richer than what could be said, or even thought, by any one party in the exchange.

It is clear that if there is such an art, it must include the skills of appraising arguments offered in the inferior kinds of rhetoric, and it must no doubt include the appraisal and placement of the various kinds themselves. In that sense, I have been trying to practice rhetoric-A throughout this essay. But rhetoric-A can be practiced in the simplest of exchanges—the argument with your neighbor over the smell of his gingko tree, the discussion with a student about a low grade, the debate in committee about whether to require competence in a foreign language. In fact, I want now to suggest that rhetoric-A is indeed the most general of all general arts, and that to neglect it in our general requirements, as, indeed, we too often do, is fatal. I know that I can trust you to discount the outrageous arrogance in such a claim. I fully expect other disciplines to make similar moves—and I ask only that, when they do, we insist on real argument in their support, not just the claim that freshman courses are needed to attract majors. The best curricula will emerge, I am suggesting, when each of our imperialistic claims is forced into the courts of communal discourse, where our various rationalizations are transmuted, under critical scrutiny, into that special kind of reasoning I am calling rhetoric-A.

II

To make my case, I must practice a bit of rhetoric-A on the notion of general education itself.

The trouble with all highly general terms like *general, shared,* and *connections,* is that, like *rhetoric,* they cover and sometimes even obscure essential distinctions. Some forms of generality are harmful—I offer the easy examples of totalitarian imposition of general aims and practices on a whole populace, and the soppy generalities offered by some "interdisciplinary" programs. Some sharings are dangerous—I cite only the exhilarated sharings that lead to mob action or national witch-hunts. Some connections are intellectually inhibiting—I cite only the ancient lumping of matter into the four elements, and the highly up-to-date and fashionable lumping of all narrative, including history, as "fictional" and therefore a form of lying. If we try to build our programs simply on what is shared or what is general, we shall be vulnerable to the first sophist who comes along and insists that we teach lying, just because all human beings lie, and proudful self-serving, just because all men and women are self-serving, and the arts of vandalism, just because scientific studies show that all of us share a capacity to take pleasure in destroying. In short, implicit in the Carnegie essay's emphasis on what is shared is a demand for distinctions of quality and kinds of generality. Once we limit ourselves to what we might call "generalities *worth having*," how many kinds do we find appealed to in the search for a general education? (Four of the following five kinds of generality, and the notion of distinguishing the four kinds, I borrow from that great student of rhetoric, Richard McKeon.) [2]

Education can be general, first, in the sense of being generally shared by all students in a given setting. Many curricular planners have found themselves giving up on the hope for a reasoned selection of the knowledge most worth having. "Who can say that everybody must know a given Dickens novel rather than the great Chinese novel *Monkey*, or Platonic thought rather than Zen Buddhism, or the second law of thermodynamics rather than how to do a regression analysis in statistics? Nobody. But we can say that it is good for students to share a culture, locally, so we'll make up a list of more-or-less arbitrary general requirements ensuring that they'll at least have something to talk about together." Rather minimal thinking, this, but no doubt better than nothing.

Education can be general, secondly, in the sense of covering the general needs of all citizens in a given time and place. That it should fill this function was the standard argument used by the defenders of the great Hutchins program of fourteen required year-long courses. Usually their talk was explicitly about preparation for citizenship, as if to say: "We seek an education that all Americans should have, because it would be folly to expect anyone to exercise the choices presented by our society without having the fourteen competencies our comprehensive examinations cover. All citizens will have to exercise these competencies, regardless of what the future brings; therefore they should share a standard preparation in them.

A rather different curriculum emerges if we emphasize a third kind of general sharing, the methods and subject matters that all the genuine modes of inquiry share. Proponents of "*the* scientific method" have argued that all genuine thought depends on certain paradigms of proof, and that general

2. Richard McKeon, "The Battle of the Books" in my collection, *The Knowledge Most Worth Having* (Chicago, 1967), 188–89.

education should build habits of thought that will be generally useful, in all fields, though such habits are obviously unshared by most citizens. Programs with emphasis on training in logic, semantics, linguistics, laboratory techniques, computer technology, and mathematics have emerged from such paradigms. They tend to show little concern about whether any two students have both read Shakespeare, or studied the Constitution, or thought about the role of law in public affairs, or developed skill in communicating their "scientific" results, or learned the same computer language.

Entirely different curricula have been suggested by proponents of a fourth notion of generality, based on what is common to all people in all cultures, as if to say: "Our deepest connections are with humankind as a whole, and nothing is worse, educationally, than our chauvinistic concentration on Western culture. What all students should learn are the experiences that join them to the rest of the world, not the narrow and elitist canons of Western taste. What could be more absurd, in the modern world, than the Western provincial who knows all about Beethoven and is ignorant of the Javanese gamelan?"

Finally, education can seek the general in the form of conceptual generalizations that serve as comprehensive overarching principles, under which each discipline performs its work—whatever generalizes all particulars in a field or in all fields. Surely if there is some "general field theory" it should be our center. Many mathematicians and physical scientists have pursued a truly general truth that could provide a capstone for all knowledge. As Morris Kline has recently said, mathematics offers all the values offered by any field, and, in addition, is "the paradigm for the best knowledge available."[3] For certain religious planners, on the other hand, it has seemed obvious that an education without a knowledge of God as a capstone is not education at all but a misapprehension of fragments. They seem to say: "Surely an education that does not lead the student to try to put it all together, to see not just connections but the ultimate connectedness, can hardly be considered really general, and is not worthy of being required."

III

At first consideration, this list of rival sharings may seem daunting. Regardless of where we would place our own planning, or that of the Carnegie Foundation, we are all aware that there are these rival views—that the shambles the report rightly deplores comes in part from the failure of educators to think through which of these notions of the general they are pur-

3. Morris Kline, *Mathematics: The Loss of Certainty* (New York, 1980).

suing, and why. All five build in a rejection of trivial or base kinds of sharing. But are all versions of each of them equally important?

I am almost sorry to report my daunting discovery that I am unwilling to give up any of the five. Though it is easy to see how special versions of each can be in direct competition with the others, it is obvious that each is radically desirable, in the precise sense that we began with: there is a kind of scandal in giving the B.A. to any student who has *no* common intellectual bonds with other students, with all other citizens, with all genuine disciplines, with all human cultures, and with all who seek to discover truths that are truly general.

If all five kinds are desirable, then we can begin to play an interesting game. Which of the many sharings on the Carnegie report's list, all of them good things to have, can make the best case for itself as indispensable, according to one or more of the notions of generality?

Again I shall, of course, leave it to others to make their cases for disciplines other than rhetoric. But I would not be doing my duty by an ancient and honorable discipline if I did not claim that rhetoric-A, the development of the appraisal (and hence the skillful use) of warrants for assent in human exchange, is an art unrivaled in its service to all five kinds of general education. I hasten to add that it is an art that need not be taught under the title of "rhetoric." I cannot think of any course in which some contribution to its mastery could not be made, if a teacher really tried. But it is too easily neglected when it is not given a clear and distinctive place in the curriculum; and when it is neglected, all the other disciplines suffer.

Turning then to the first kind of general education: if students on a given campus are to share educational experience, whether achieved through requirements or simply by living together, they will do so largely in their use of rhetoric, good or bad. Only to the degree that they learn to practice rhetoric-A, appraising together the warrants for assent that they and their teachers and texts offer, will they learn what to share and what not to share, what positions to buy and what to reject. In short, rhetoric is the very medium in which students share most of their genuine education, including most of their classroom experiences, even in the hardest of the sciences. The rhetoric may very well be of inferior kinds; even the best teachers may find occasional uses for hamming, tear-jerking, blood-letting, and swinging from the chandeliers. But surely our ideal of education is the sharing of *good* reasons for changes of mind, and since in most subjects that we care about there are no rigorous mathematical or experimental proofs available even for the simplest processes and conclusions, our hope must lie in rhetoric-A.

It seems equally obvious, secondly, that the primary need of all citizens, before, during, and after college, is a mastery of rhetoric. The business of

American life is, after all, conducted—perhaps more than was true of any previous society—*in* rhetoric. Unlike people in traditional societies, we get our jobs, keep them, or lose them, and actually conduct them, with rhetoric. *The Chronicle of Higher Education* has recently made the claim that more than 50 percent of all Americans make their living at what the *Chronicle* elegantly calls "symbol pushing." You would think, then, that every college in this practical land would have at least one entire degree program in how to symbol-push better than other symbol pushers. But if you have such a program on your campus, one that goes beyond the mere rhetoric of advertising skills, I shall be surprised, and I hope to learn about it. I shall be even more surprised if your catalogues list more than one required general course—*perhaps* Freshman English—that might conceivably be renamed "Improved Symbol-Pushing 101."

Rhetoric as vocational training is obviously far more important than we have recognized. But I would stress even more strongly its value in serving our universal need for *political* savvy. All our political life, except what is done through bribery and violence, is conducted in one or another form of rhetoric. Working together in symbolic exchange is in fact our only alternative to tyranny; either someone will impose forms of life upon us, or we must learn to embrace forms of life by trying them out on each other. And if we cannot manage to do the trying out effectively, if we cannot rise above sub- and mere- and B-rhetorics to an effective appraisal of our reasonings, we are doomed to some form of chaos, inevitably followed by some tyrant's takeover.

Our founding fathers did the trying out at a wonderfully high level; my students and I have been discovering just how high as we work over the rhetoric-A of Madison's *Notes* and the rhetoric-B of *The Federalist Papers*. (The Founders were highly skilled in the use and analysis of the lower rhetorical forms, too; what we might call our founding uncles, like Tom Paine, owed their astonishing popular success to a rhetorical range that any of us might envy.) What is more, every generation since theirs has offered its demonstration that unless effective rhetoric governs politics, money and violence will. The Constitution in this view is a marvelously shrewd effort to guarantee that rhetoric will have a chance, an effort to open up public spaces that will require, not just allow, that our many different would-be governors listen to each other and listen to the governed. The fact that we survive at all as a democracy is a triumph of that great piece of rhetoric-A— and of our willingness to talk and listen according to its rules.

Thirdly, rhetoric is general to all disciplines, in the sense of their depending on it in daily practice. Though many disciplines are described as if rhetoric were beneath their high-minded endeavors, one has only to look at the rhetoric used in each field, both in its publications and its teaching practice, to see the absurdity of the claim. The fact is that every field depends, often to a surprising degree, on the skills I am talking about.

I will not insist, as some rhetoricians have done, on the claim that even the hardest proofs in the hardest sciences are conducted *in* rhetoric: "the rhetoric of the laboratory," "the rhetoric of the equation," "the rhetoric of the graph."[4] But even if we grant the name of pure science to the processes of decisive and final demonstration, we know that most of the business of scientists, even when they are writing in their front-line journals, depends on obviously rhetorical arguments, like exploration of hidden or overt analogies, colorful metaphor, appeals to the character of the speaker and of supporting institutions, and direct or subtle manipulation of readers' emotions. We should not have needed *The Double Helix*,[5] or *Lucy*,[6] the new book purporting to reveal how anthropologists work, to teach us what a small portion of every scientist's scientific life is decided by scientific evidence.

The infusion of rhetoric, of our kinds of reasons, good and bad, is usually not noticed, especially when it comes in the form of appeals to certain root metaphors that everyone in the field simply takes for granted. When it is noticed, it is usually treated as a kind of impurity that could be washed away if only scientists were more scientific. But rhetoric is inescapable, even in mathematics and physics, to say nothing of all the other fields hinted at in the Carnegie report's list of sharings. Leaving aside the obvious rhetoric of the grant proposal and the seminar room, a very large part of what every inquirer in every field says in "scientific" debate with colleagues is not backed with certain proof. As Michael Polanyi has shown, in his great book *Personal Knowledge*, no scientist could ever prove scientifically most of the scientific beliefs he or she accepts.[7] In every science, scientists believe most of what they believe about it—all except their own very tiny specialist's domain—without even being able to follow, in detail, the proofs that other specialists would offer (see pages 312–16 in Occasion 19). This does not mean that they believe their colleagues on what is called "blind faith." They believe their colleagues because they have more or less reliable warrants for assent of the kind that rhetoricians have always studied. For example, no-

4. But see my description of "rhetoric-1" on Occasion 19.
5. James D. Watson, *The Double Helix: A Personal Account of the Discovery of the Structure of DNA* (New York, 1968).
6. Donald Johanson and Maitland Edey, *Lucy* (New York, 1981). For a fine semi-popular account of both the scientific problems and the rhetorical exchanges involved in the development of microbiology, see Horace Freeland Judson's *The Eighth Day of Creation: Makers of the Revolution in Biology* (New York, 1979).
7. Michael Polanyi, *Personal Knowledge: Towards a Post-Critical Philosophy* (Chicago, 1958; rev. ed., New York, 1962). See especially chapter 9, "The Critique of Doubt."

body could absolutely disprove any of the wild popular assertions of pseudo-science, the theories of Velikovsky or van Daniken, the experiments of hordes of para-psychologists, the reports of UFO-ologists, and what not. Yet all scientists of repute reject these schemes by the dozen, annually, without investigation; life would be intolerable for them if they did *not* reject them *without scientific investigation*, trusting to rhetorical warrants like authority, emotional commitment to "the scientific method," and pure hunch. On the other hand, all scientists accept dozens of new developments annually in fields outside their specialties, on grounds that can only be called rhetorical: the strength of personal and communal warrants that have nothing to do with scientific proof. Since such warrants never yield certainty, the people who make these choices sometimes turn out to have been wrong; occasionally a "wild" scheme later establishes itself, and an established truth is overthrown. But most of what we think of as scientific life would simply disappear if such uncertainties led scientists to insist on scientific proofs for every belief on which they act.

It is impossible to exhibit here the kind of field-by-field survey that might support my claim that rhetoric is essential to and practiced in *all* disciplines.[8] But consider the following three fields as examples.[9]

First, scientific linguistics. No one could seem more certain about his conclusion than the great linguist Edward Sapir, in his conviction that language is the defining feature of mankind. He *knows* that his particular truth is *absolutely* universal, though of course he has personally examined only a fraction of the tribes of mankind. Listen to him now as he leads to his definition of language by arguing that, though it is universal to man, language is not natural in the same sense that walking is.

> Speech . . . *seems* as natural to man as walking, and only less so than breathing. Yet it needs but a moment's reflection to convince us that this naturalness of speech is but an illusory feeling. The process of acquiring speech is, in sober fact, an utterly different sort of thing from the process of learning to walk. In the case of the latter function, culture . . . is not seriously brought into play. . . . In a very real sense the normal human being is predestined to walk [by biological heredity], not because his elders will assist him to learn the art, but because his organism is prepared from birth, or even from the moment of conception, to take on all those expenditures of nervous energy and all those muscular adaptations that result in walking. To put it concisely, walking is an inherent biological function of man.

8. Nor is such a full survey found anywhere in this book. The closest to it is the effort by "Raphael Hythloday," on Occasion 19, to show that everyone in the "University of Polytopia" discovered a common interest in rhetoric.

9. The examples that follow did not appear in my earlier published version.

Not so language. . . . Eliminate society and there is every reason to believe that he will learn to walk, if, indeed, he survives at all. But it is just as certain that he will never learn to talk. . . . [10]

My point in quoting this passage is not to raise doubts about its *certain* conclusions, though Chomsky and others within a few decades were doing so. The point is to underline the nature of the reasons offered. Sapir's truth is of the kind that can be revealed in "a moment's reflection." It is in opposition to "illusory feeling." It is presented "in sober fact," and "in a very real sense." It is believed because "there is every reason to believe it," and *in fact, in sober fact,* it is *certain.* The only experimental evidence offered is a mental experiment, that of raising a child outside a culture. The only facts cited are dubious claims (made in a section I have not quoted) that a cultureless child must walk exactly as we walk. In short, rhetorical analysis applied to this piece of "science" reveals that though unmistakably science it is also mainly rhetoric.

Next, consider the social science that is often called "the great grey science," economics; called "grey" just because, I believe, its works are reputed to be so fully freed of the exciting blandishments of rhetoric that they are dull. I will not dwell on the much-too-easy demonstration that most economists spend most of their writing time producing mere rhetoric, or at best a bit of rhetoric-B—appeals to our beliefs that haven't the slightest claim to scientific proof. Here is Milton Friedman, in the introductory paragraph to his book *Capitalism and Freedom:*

> In a much quoted passage in his inaugural address, President Kennedy said, "Ask not what your country can do for you—ask what you can do for your country." It is a striking sign of the temper of our times that the controversy about this passage centered on its origin and not on its content. Neither half of the statement expresses a relation between the citizen and his government that is worthy of the ideals of free men in a free society. . . . To the free man, the country is the collection of individuals who compose it, not something over and above them. He is proud of a common heritage and loyal to common traditions. But he regards government as a means, an instrumentality, neither a grantor of favors and gifts, nor a master or god to be blindly worshipped and served. . . . The free man will ask neither what his country can do for him nor what he can do for his country. He will ask rather "What can I and my compatriots do through government" to help us discharge our individual responsibilities, to achieve our several goals and purposes, and above all, to protect our freedom? And he will accompany this question with another: How can we keep the government we

10. Opening paragraphs of Edward Sapir's "Introduction: Language Defined," *Language: An Introduction To the Study of Speech* (New York, 1921).

create from becoming a Frankenstein [he means Frankenstein's monster]
that will destroy the very freedom we establish it to protect? Freedom is a
rare and delicate plant. Our minds tell us, and history confirms . . . [11]

Mere rhetoric. *Good* mere rhetoric, perhaps even a bit of rhetoric-B, but not
much. And no rhetoric-A.

Well, as I said, my main point is not about social scientists addressing the
public, but about social scientists doing their science with each other. If you
open any book of economics in which economists are led to address each
other's arguments, you'll find a great deal of what I find in a volume reporting a conference on research in income and health. They are all like this.
Mr. A. presents an argument, buttressed with charts and graphs and some
mere rhetoric. Ms. B. gets her turn, and says, "Mr. A's discussion shows
considerable ingenuity, but contains some errors in both logic and fact,"
which she then specifies. Mr. C then says, "Mr. A contends that the
usefulness of family income, expenditure, and saving data as indicators of
welfare and the propensity to consume is increased by classifying families
by expenditures per equivalent adult. No one will deny [note that: no one
will deny—but no evidence is given] the need for further exploration of
ways of making these data yield additional information nor the earnestness
and vigor [note well: the *earnestness* and *vigor*] with which Mr. A presents
his hypothesis and findings. With respect to his own proposals, however,
there is nowhere apparent the critical ability he displays in discussing the
use of classifications by family income. . . . Some readers may wish to take
issue with Mr. A on the relative values of his scale for various persons. But
even more important seems to be a shortcoming . . . Mr. A's discussion is
lacking in perspective. . . . " *Seems to be? Lacking in what? Perspective?*
Now let's see. What exactly is that?

Soon Ms. D gets into the act. "Implicit in Mr. A's discussion is an assumption that should be examined because it is fundamental to much of the
present thinking in this field. His entire argument takes for granted that a
single measure . . . can serve the multitude of purposes for which such data
are used. If this assumption is accepted, . . . the formula used is of considerable importance. If the assumption is not regarded as necessary, attempts to
construct and interpret combinations of the variables into one index may be
considered interesting and valuable as experiments [but] without serious
consequences. . . . There is, however, a simple and direct alternative . . . "
and that of course turns out to be her own favorite assumption, one that like
the first could never be proved with economic science!

Mr. E now gets his turn. "Mr. A's unfamiliarity with previous work on

11. Milton Friedman, *Capitalism and Freedom* (Chicago, 1962), 1–2.

these problems, has, I believe, led to the adoption of unsuitable methods and the derivation of incorrect results."

Finally, after many such interventions, Mr. A may have a chance to reply, "I must *plead guilty* to having criticized current procedures *without having adequately investigated the literature*. (And) Ms. D's observation . . . shows that for this scale of family size at least it cannot be assumed that the consumption patterns of large families are merely multiples of the patterns of small families. *I freely confess* that some such assumption was *in my mind* when I began the tabulation." (My italics.) You freely do what? Confess? The assumption was where? In your *mind* but not in the presented argument? You people sound just like a bunch of literary critics disputing an interpretation. Or a bunch of rhetoricians talking about how to debate together. The proportion of *mere* rhetoric has gone down, I'm glad to see, and you are occasionally rising to rhetoric-B as you examine your assumptions. But *science?*

You may think economists are too easy a mark—after all, none of us watching the recent TV series done by Milton Friedman had the illusion that what he was practicing, with those shots of happy workers in Hong Kong sweatshops, was the science of economics.[12]

Consider, finally, as representative of what plays a necessary part in every field, the kind of thing one finds in *Scientific American*. That wonderful journal brings a hazy sense of scientific developments to us laymen, but like its sister journals of general science it also provides, as I learn in talking to scientific colleagues, many of the beliefs that scientists themselves hold about sciences other than their own. Not long ago I read the following:

> The first test of Einstein's general theory of gravitation to be made on objects outside the solar system was reported shortly before the 100th anniversary of Einstein's birth. The opportunity for such a test presented itself with the discovery in 1974 of a radio pulsar that is a member of a binary pair . . . PSR1913 + 16. . . . Since 1974 the signal emitted by PSR1913 + 16 has been closely monitored by its codiscoverer, Joseph H. Taylor of the University of Massachusetts at Amherst, with the 305-meter radio telescope at Arecibo in Puerto Rico. In a recent issue of *Nature* Taylor . . . report[s] the results of some 1000 observations over four years. With gradual improvements in technique pulse-arrival times can now be established with an accuracy of about 50 microseconds.[13]

---

12. See Donald McCloskey, *The Rhetoric of Economics* (Madison, Wis., 1985), for a detailed account of how the *economic* thinking of economists depends on rhetorical modes that are not acknowledged in their stated ideals about how to do economics.

13. *Scientific American* (May 1979): 82, 86, 90.

Like wow! Little did I dream! Yet it must be true. *One thousand* observations! 50 *microseconds! Closely* monitored! At U. Mass! Reported in *Nature!* All of this is, of course rhetoric, mere rhetoric.

There follow three paragraphs of explanation, at a highly general level. In a state of happy, easy faith, I go on to the next item: "How Interferon Interferes." The conclusions of that one I also accept, sort of, because "the *remarkable* ability of the protein interferon to inhibit the multiplication of viruses in animal cells has *tantalized* biochemists and virologists ever since its discovery in 1957" (my italics), and also because a scientist from *The University of California* (!) at Santa Barbara, no less, has reported his work in *The Proceedings of the National Academy of Sciences!* Rhetoric. Not terribly good warrants here, once I think about them. Not good enough to satisfy me fully, especially if I am an astronomer or virologist. But we can be sure that every mathematician, say, or economist, who reads this will tentatively add this lore, as I do, to "what science has proved."

Since I am aware of how far my evidence here falls short of my vast generalization, perhaps I can just appeal to your own expertise. Simply think of the last article you read in your own field, one not addressed to the general public, and then ask, what proportion of the propositions in it that you accept could *you* yourself prove or disprove according to the standard of proof set by Karl Popper's test of falsifiability.[14] My guess is that the figure will run as low as 5 percent. There is absolutely nothing wrong in that— except when poor education in the intellectual procedures needed for that remaining 95 percent leads people to poor performance with their rhetoric.

I can do even less justice to the fourth kind of sharing—our connections with all cultures, all of humankind. It is perhaps self-evident that rhetoric in some form will be found in all cultures. As Sapir claims, the capacity to engage in symbolic exchange, the capacity to use statements about the world rather than mere pointing or brute force, is recognized by all anthropological schools as a distinctive feature—perhaps the essential feature—of human cultures. Though what constitutes a good reason, a genuine warrant, will vary considerably from culture to culture, I can be sure in advance of studying any new culture that people in it will have their own way of distinguishing good argument from bad, and that they will recognize a difference between those who are good at finding the right words and those whose words mislead or destroy. I can be equally sure that any chance we have of building understanding among cultures will depend on a rhetoric of discovery. What do we share beneath our surface differences? Let us inquire

---

14. Karl R. Popper, *The Logic of Scientific Discovery* (London, 1959; rev. 1968). See especially chs. 4–6.

together, in symbolic exchange. There is no other way except to eliminate differences by forceful domination.

So I must assume, without further argument, that rhetoric is a universally needed and practiced art, if there is any such thing as a universally needed and practiced art, and hurry on to the fifth and most implausible of all my claims today. Most traditional educational systems have sought to study and instill understanding of some kind of ultimate good, some supreme standard against which all of our interests and endeavors can be measured. In America today we can rely on no such standard. Our culture has no publicly acknowledged and universally accepted ultimate standard of that kind. Our question then becomes: Can rhetoric in any sense fill a gap that is left when theology, philosophy, the idea of scientific progress, faith in ultimate political revolution, and all other gods have failed?

To show how it might do so would be a tall order.[15] I can only suggest that when we ask the question, "What warrants for assent are *really* good ones?" we are forced to practice rhetoric-A at the highest possible level— one that indeed we may want another name for: meta-rhetoric, perhaps, or rhetorology? We are then asking the kind of question that the Carnegie essay calls for when it asks us to think about the "issues of values that we share in common." We are pushing ourselves to reflect not just on the warrants for assent in particular cases, but on the ultimate ways of grounding assent, the varieties of modes of assenting, modes of warranting. And we are likely here to engage in a good deal of comparison across fields and cultures.

The rhetorologist will be interested not so much in whether Mr. A or Mr. B wins in a particular debate as in the structures of assumption and proof that both share, and in how these structures might differ from the structures found in neighboring disciplines, or in the same discipline a decade before or a decade after. You can see immediately that there are a lot of rhetorologists around, traveling under other names. Indeed in most disciplines these days one finds people who are reopening "settled" questions about what constitutes good warrants for assent in that discipline—they are exploring the ways we think about the ways we think. One sees efforts everywhere to rehabilitate proofs that earlier thinkers tried to reject: "telling a good story" as one form of validation in history; analogy as one form of genuine argument in science; metaphor as inescapable in all inquiry; the

15. I am currently trying to address the problem in a largely unwritten work about "the rhetoric of religion"—especially the rhetoric of various surrogate religions that travel in secular guise. For a sample of the problems such inquiry raises, see my "Systematic Wonder: The Rhetoric of Secular Religions" in *Journal of the American Academy of Religion* 53 (1985): 677–702.

persuasive force of a speaker's ethos; appeals to tradition or precedent; even a legitimated and controlled reliance on emotional stirrings.

Even more important than the critical rehabilitation of these warrants rejected by earlier positivisms is the critical probing of basic assumptions within and among the disciplines. Suddenly everyone seems to be aware that human thought does not have to be either strictly deductive or strictly empirical but can be "topical," rhetorical. If you look at any statement that purports to be proof, in any discipline, you find that it relies on "unprovable" assumptions, sometimes stated, often left tacit: assumptions about what makes a fact in that subject, about the purpose of inquiry, about the self-evidency of certain principles and definitions, about the proper methods of moving back and forth between "unquestioned" principles and "undeniable" facts. The work of the rhetorologist is precisely to pursue the comparative worth of different warrants in different persuasive enterprises, and to invent—or if you prefer, discover—improved ways for minds to meet within disciplines and among seemingly different or conflicting disciplines.

To the rhetorician—though not to most other people—it has been clear for more than two thousand years that none of the individual disciplines provides a method for examining the basic assumptions necessary to the practice of that method. The lawyer does not use legal argument to establish the validity of legal argument; to do that requires some kind of political philosophy—either one derived from an established authority or an assumed good, like the divine right of kings, or one discovered in symbolic intercourse among those who choose to think about such matters—that is, by rhetorology. The physicist cannot prove, using the methods of physical science, even that nature exists, or that the proofs of physics are any more than game playing, or that evidence should not be fudged, and so on. Rhetorologists cannot "prove" such matters either, and they welcome what might be called the "Gödel bandwagon," that new growth industry that has convinced even the mathematicians that *ultimate, certain* proofs are not to be had.[16] The rhetorologist has always known what popularizers of Gödel are saying, that "truth" is a larger concept than "proof," that there are many truths that are "uncertifiable." For rhetorology this has never presented a crisis but simply a challenge to find new topics, new shared places from which any given rhetorical community can move, trusting to various degrees of warranting in the search for liveable truths, not certainties.

As I said earlier, most philosophies have hoped to school the vagaries of various rhetorics, to rein in the immensely frisky pony of mankind's free-

16. The best account I have seen of the revolution effected by Gödel's famous paper of 1931 is offered by Ernest Nagel and James R. Newman in *Gödel's Proof* (New York, 1958).

ranging symbols, by discovering some supreme single substance or method that all could—or should—adhere to; some metaphysics or meta*some*thing that could determine which first principles are *really* first and then establish the others in relation to it. There are of course many thinkers today who still pursue that kind of hope for a supreme monistic view of all knowledge. But I don't have to tell you that they move in many different paths to many different ultimate principles. And as soon as they offer to take us with them to their heights, as soon as they attempt to meet those of us who do not share a self-evident vision of some single ordered truth, they perforce must enter the domains of rhetoric—either the lower forms, attempting to win converts; or rhetorology, attempting to discover common ground between their programs and ours. Thus even those who hold to a faith that someday, somehow, a unified language of all knowledge will be discovered, with a universally accepted supreme substance or concept to validate it, are forced to work here and now in a pluralistic world of differences that are found not just on the surface but very deep, a messy world of dispute, of lines of reasoning that are only probable, not certain, of major questions about which there seem to be not just two sides but many sides.

In that world some people become skeptical and even cynical: if nothing can be finally demonstrated, everything is equally doubtful, and all claims to knowledge are spurious. But the rhetorologist has learned, from practicing the less comprehensive kinds of rhetoric, that to be uncertain is not the same as to be cognitively helpless. Having learned to use symbolic exchange to test the "maybes" in everyday affairs, the rhetorologist is not afraid to use such exchange to test the maybes that we dispute "at the top," as it were. The faith required to do so is not a blind faith, because it is perpetually rewarded with islands of clarity that make human life not only possible but rewarding. It will look like blind faith only to those who insist that there is only one kind of serious inquiry—the pursuit of certainty, and that all the rest is mere guesswork, or *mere* rhetoric.[17]

17. It is not appropriate to my argument to lay down the principles that I expect to be found by rhetorologists who think together long and hard about the grounds of their discourse. But one thing is clear from recent probings in various fields: metaphysical questions that many modernists thought settled once and for all, settled with firm answers like "God is dead" or "Values are man-made and therefore non-rational," are now reopened. The ancient "proofs for the existence for God," for example, have often been "shown" to carry no rigorous "scientific force." But they are coming alive again, sometimes in traditional vocabulary, sometimes in entirely new terms. See, for example, Iris Murdoch's *The Sovereignty of Good* (London, 1970). She claims to be proving only the reality of the good, not of God. But her proof exactly parallels one version of the traditional ontological proof.

IV

Clearly I have thrown caution to the winds and allowed my imperialism to run riot. My claim is not of course that those other good things on the Carnegie list should be discarded; in any college curriculum I could respect, all would be pursued vigorously. But I do fear that the Carnegie essay's careful rhetorology, its search for what we share beneath our differences of expression, may become quickly corrupted, when it gets into the hands of curriculum committees, corrupted into a list of six or eight required courses. Then, when the committee report is manhandled by the faculty council, the final new plan, to be hailed in *The New York Times* or *Time* magazine as the product of the Carnegie Foundation study, will cut the eight courses to four: one called Freshman English, the rest turned into distribution requirements in history, the social sciences, and the natural sciences. Category six, our shared values, the study of ethics, will simply be dropped, as it almost always is, as too hot to handle.

If we are to forestall that mutilation, we must push ourselves into thinking hard about what specific priorities we share, and about how to answer when some Ned Snyder pronounces, "Gentlemen, we are already the best men's college in the country. Why on earth should we change . . . ?

When Matthew Arnold was about to go to Oxford, his father, Thomas, wrote to the University to ask whether Aristotle's *Rhetoric* was required study there. "I could not," he said, "consent to send my son to [a] University where he would lose it altogether." Many, perhaps most, of our students "lose it altogether," and I rather doubt that many parents have threatened to withdraw them because of the lack. What they may complain about, these days, is the failure of the college to teach "the basics." Obviously, then, our problem is in one sense quite simple. Just teach the public the truth: namely, that what they mean when they cry "Back to the basics!" is "Back to rhetoric!"

With such an effort at a resounding peroration I dramatize that my program is circular: we must use a corrupted medium to improve that medium. But the circularity does not alarm me, because it need not be vicious. A vicious circle is actually a spiral, moving downward. It is true that rhetoric, especially political rhetoric, does sometimes work like that. But we have all experienced moments when the spiral moves upward, when one party's effort to listen and speak just a little bit better produces a similar response, making it possible to try a bit harder—and on up the spiral to moments of genuine understanding.

OCCASION 7 · *To Our "Employers,"*
Whose Fate Depends on Ours

An Arrogant Proposal—a New Use
for the Dyshumanities

That "the humanities" should be somehow useful to humanity has always seemed obvious—except to certain literary theorists and aestheticians who have set up polemical oppositions between the human arts and the practical or technical arts, or between the language of truth and the language of power, or between various higher useless purities and various other practicalities. Even the most extreme argument for pure uselessness can easily be reconstructed to reveal a higher usefulness. Whether artists and those who study their works have been seen as the legislators of mankind, or as the supreme courts, or as the revolutionary shock troops, or simply as a rear guard ensuring a saving remnant, all defenses finally claim a usefulness either for society, for a profession, or for the souls of those who pursue what is humane.

So we ought not to spend time asking whether we think that the humanities should be useful. The question rather is why, given the obvious centrality of the humanities to everything we value, *why* we are all doing so much to destroy that usefulness.

I thus have four sermons, addressed by four different speakers to four radically different audiences: the laymen of the humanities, the archbishops, the lower clergy, and the novitiate. (I make all of my spokesmen male, partly because I am a man and partly because to speak of a lay*woman* risks mockery.) Any sophomore will be able to show that the four sermons cannot be fully harmonized. What they have in common is a definition of the humanities and a plea for action to deal with what from all four views is a threatening catastrophe.

The humanities, let us say, in a fusion of several traditional definitions, consist of the highest achievements of mankind and of their appreciation and encouragement as achievements—not just, as Arnold put it, "acquaint-

Modern Language Association panel on "the humanities," 1976. Reprinted from *Profession 77* (Modern Language Association, 1977), 1–6.

ing ourselves with the best that has been known and said in the world," but acquainting ourselves with the best that has been made or done, making ourselves aware of what is good, or better, or best about it. Whatever any-one has made or done especially well—a novel or poem, a political speech, a constitution—can be studied for the sake of understanding its quality and encouraging more makings or doings like it.

The humanities were thus not invented when the term was invented, fairly late in our history. They were invented the first time one human being noticed that another human being had achieved something better than other efforts in a given line; enjoyed that achievement as something to mar-vel at for its own sake (as we later learned to say); and then began to talk about it and to encourage others to try to match or outdo it.

You will see that in this definition every discovery or invention in any field, considered as a human achievement, becomes a "humanity." Whenever anyone does something that other people can't do or can't do easily—whether making better mousetraps, better juggling acts, better con-stitutions, better philosophical arguments, better songs—and whenever other people talk about it with a sense that the quality of the making or doing matters, there you have the humanities.

Sermon One

THE LAYMAN IS ADDRESSED BY THE NOVICE

If I were a new Ph.D. (male or female) unable to find a job, I would want to say to the American public, the laymen of the humanities, something like this:

You are going to hell in a handbasket, a chrome-plated, TV-equipped, air-conditioned, mass-produced handbasket that has cost you so much money and time that you can't afford to finance the study of how to make or do or appreciate whatever is excellent. History offers, as perhaps I am not the first to notice, a nicely sustained series of national suicides. I admit that some of these, like the Nazi stupidities and atrocities, are more dra-matic than what America is now doing to and with its children and youth in education. But I can think of few examples in history in which disaster was cultivated with so little real need, so little real thought, and so little awareness of why choices were being made. To see one's own people de-stroying themselves through greed, pride, or blindness can seem either tragic or comic or infuriating or merely absurd, depending as much on whether one has a personal escape route or storm cellar as on one's own philosophy of life. But I have no storm cellar. And to see the wealthiest nation in the history of mankind sacrificing its children because, as everyone claims, it cannot afford to pay me to teach them—that is infuriating indeed.

What am I thinking about? First, I am thinking specifically of the living, flaming absurdity of community after community cutting school budgets to the bone, with some school districts cutting their school year by a third and some actually closing their doors—all this, while a majority of people in every one of those districts, even the poorest, enjoys what we mistakenly call a higher standard of living. I am thinking of high school English teachers with 160 students, of classes of 40 pupils each, few of them learning to read or write or enjoy the arts because their parents "cannot afford" to vote proper tax levies, so poor are they after they have provided those necessities of life—the cars, the TV sets, the outboard motors, the snowmobiles, the vacations . . .

I am thinking, secondly, of the vast sums available for study about how to reduce unique human achievements to easy formulas, programmable results, simplistic "behavior mod," computerized instruction. How could a country choose to waste fifty million dollars trying, unsuccessfully, to build translation machines, when it could have paid that money to human beings trained to teach other human beings in that uniquely human achievement, the comprehension of languages that are infinitely richer than any machine can encompass?[1]

Thirdly, I am thinking of our national habit of reducing humanistic values to those shibboleths, "the basics." The American public seems to be aware of only one failure of our schools: if they fail to teach secretaries how to spell and punctuate, everyone gets excited and says that we've got to crack down. Everybody gets less excited when it is explained that cracking down, even in such peripheral matters, will cost money and will mean attacking some of our prized institutions. And just about everybody gets off the boat when it is explained that every child (except for a very small number of the handicapped) can be taught to read and write and think and enjoy mankind's achievements, at a level that would make living worthwhile, if only we would turn our national energies in that direction.[2]

1. The story of the growth and decline of faith in "MT"—Machine Translation—is a marvelous case study in how contemptuous notions of "the brain," and hence of people, can mislead intelligent and well-meaning researchers. So far as I know, the full account, from predictions in the fifties that we would soon have perfect translations of Pushkin, to the present almost total disillusionment with the whole scheme, has never been written. But there have been many "confessions" and "conversions" by now. See, for a recent example, Joseph Weizenbaum, *Computer Power and Human Reason: From Judgment to Calculation* (San Francisco, 1976), especially chap. 7.

2. See Benjamin Bloom, *Human Characteristics and School Learning* (New York, 1976)

Finally, to cut a long list short, I am thinking of a nation that spends hours each week sitting in front of the boob tube, and provides irresistible temptations to all of its children to do the same, watching programs that are, by commercial requirement, designed *not* to be distressingly excellent, *not* to be appreciable as human achievements. The only real exception is athletics, one of the great humanities. But sports are rapidly following drama, fiction, poetry, music, science, and politics into the huge indiscriminate mess of the easy, the contemptible, the manipulable, the duplicable, the pablum that TV offers disguised as daily bread.

In short, the nation that cannot afford to hire me to arouse in its children a fascination with what's difficult, rare, and excellent has plenty of money and skill for designing and touting duplicable, soul-corrupting pleasures.

I think the thing to do is just possibly to take hold of all this and start over, from the top down. Offer me a plausible program, "revolutionary" or "reactionary," and I'll join it like a shot.

Sermon Two

THE LAYMAN ADDRESSES AN AUDIENCE OF ARCHBISHOPS AND BISHOPS

In spite of what that youngster just said about us, if we compare our national educational expenditures to that of other nations, we don't look too bad. That is to say, a lot of our money gets into the hands of you college and university administrators. It happens to be less money than it was ten years ago, and that will enforce certain economies. All to the good, if you made your cuts at the right joints. But you presidents and provosts and deans and chairmen are presiding over a wicked misapplication of the funds you have. Even if it were true that we are misappropriating our funds, public and private, I have to say that most of you are making your economies precisely at the point where they will do most harm to the humanities and thus to America's future as a nation with qualities worth preserving.

Where are your cuts being made? Obviously where they are easiest— at the junior levels of hiring, not in the buildings, not in the public relations offices, not in the departments whose graduates know only one language, computer talk. You are not cutting the deadheads with tenure.

---

for a powerful argument based on careful research, showing that "what any person in the world can learn, almost all persons can learn *if* provided with appropriate prior and current conditions of learning."

It is the assistant professors of English, philosophy, history, mathematics, and the sciences who are being dropped, while whole departments that would never be missed, by any society, remain well fed.

I look over your catalogue, and I see that you have hundreds of courses, and many whole departments, working on subjects that have no connection that I can see with producing a society that is humane. I note, for example, that you are spending more on . . .

And then there follows a list of examples and wasted funds. But I must cut this sermon short, because my composite layman cannot agree with himself about whether to attack exotic languages, or astronomy, or Greek, or Anglo-Saxon, or computer science. All he is sure of is that the administrators are simply passing the buck in the easiest way possible, feeding funds to the established departments and leaving them to make the cuts where they are easiest: eliminating those with the least power to fight back.

Sermon Three

THE PROFESSORIATE (THE PASTORS) ARE ·
ADDRESSED BY A CHORUS OF LAYMEN AND NOVICES

Perhaps the most visible sign of how you have allowed caste and class interests to control you is the way you have conspired with the administrators' natural temptation to work righteously and vigorously to cut faculty budgets where it will hurt least.

On the one hand, you work hard to tempt some second-rate star from the best institution you think you have a chance to compete against, offering a salary and perquisites that would hire from three to five junior men or women.

Here is a true story. Professor X at a state university is widely and rightly known as a fine teacher and scholar. He is teaching five courses a year, while doing some administrative work and supervising dissertations. He *feels* overworked and he *is* overworked. A neighboring institution offers him a named professorship, with a salary in the neighborhood of $50,000.[3] He shows the offer to his superiors. Knowing that to lose him would be a serious blow to their prestige, they give him a permanent position in their research institute, reducing his courses to two per year, and add perquisites that will make him, as people used to say, independent for life. The amount of his salary *increase*, counting perquisites, is roughly equal to what it would cost to hire two assistant professors. The depart-

---

3. Note that the date is 1976. In 1988 the figure could be $100,000 or better.

ment will now, of course, have to find some way to "cover" the abandoned three courses. Both of the bargaining institutions have thus lost the teacher.

Now, if the change actually helps produce first-class humanistic scholarship that would not have been produced otherwise, the bargain may have been worth it. But the chances of that are so slim as to be derisory. How many older scholars are there in any generation worth four times what is paid new Ph.D.'s—scholars whose work will in the long run make any real difference in the quality of the nation's life in the humanities? Shall we be reckless and say ten? But in the first place, nobody knows who they are; and in the second place, if they are really first-class they will write what they have to write anyway; and in the third place, by the time the institutions come to bargaining for them they are mostly already on decline. So what in the name of the Logos is this that you are doing, while turning many of the brightest prospective full-time teachers away from your doors and leaving your students to be taught in overloaded classrooms by part-timers and even cheaper teaching assistants just out of college?

Which brings us to your other hand, the left hand, which doesn't know what the right hand is doing. You spend your time sifting through those great piles of letters and dossiers from hundreds of applicants, seeing the current glut as a glorious opportunity to improve your take. A few of you have even simplified your lives by casting aside the application of anyone who has ever taught anywhere else, thus ensuring that you will get the most labor for the cheapest price.

And a few of you have even been so foolishly ambitious as to institute new Ph.D. programs, hoping to raise your prestige one small notch on the national scale. Meanwhile a generation of teachers will be lost.

Sermon Four

A REPRESENTATIVE OF THE PROFESSORIATE ADDRESSES THE NOVITIATE

Audience four consists of the novices who may find themselves without a teaching job, or with an "inferior" teaching job (that is, with less money and prestige than hoped for) or with no job of any kind.

The speaker is a kindly, generous, youthful-spirited professor sporting a white beard, a man now living in what he fondly hopes will turn out to have been his middle years. His only known weakness is his foolish hope that anyone suffering on the job market can be expected to listen to advice from someone who has one of the best-paid and most rewarding jobs in the profession. On reflection, I think it might be well to dress this speaker in a toga—and let us show him hollow-eyed from overwork.

Yes, yes, indeed! Your society is in many ways messing up *your* opportunities and *its* true needs, blocking your careers and thus blighting its own future. What, then, what in the name of your own true commitments, can I say to you?

It is mainly this: stop merely complaining and start living and fighting in the humanities, wherever you are. The humanities are not, never have been, never will be primarily a way to a job. It is, in fact, a rare thing when a society decides, as ours has done, to pay a great many citizens for doing what everyone who knows what's what will want to do anyway: to read and listen and look and think and learn.

When Karl Popper was a young man, just after World War I, he found himself living in what everyone agreed was a grim time. But, he says, it was an exhilarating time:

> Most of us had no prospects and plans. We lived in a very poor community in which civil war was endemic, flaring up in earnest from time to time. We were often depressed, discouraged, disgusted. But we were learning, our minds were active and growing. We were reading ravenously, omnivorously; debating, changing our opinions, studying, sifting critically, thinking. We listened to music, went tramping in the beautiful Austrian mountains, and dreamt of a better, healthier, simpler, and more honest world.
>
> During the winter of 1919–20 I left home to live in a disused part of a former military hospital converted by students into an extremely primitive students' home. . . . [My] father . . . had lost all his savings in the runaway inflation. . . .
>
> I had been doing some unpaid work in Alfred Adler's child guidance clinics, and I was now doing other occasional work with hardly any pay at all. Some of it was hard (road making). But I also coached some American university students, who were very generous. I needed very little: there was not much to eat, and I did not smoke or drink. The only necessities which were sometimes hard to come by were tickets for concerts. Though the tickets were cheap (if one stood), they were for a number of years almost a daily expenditure.
>
> At the University I sampled lecture courses in various subjects. . . . But I soon gave up going to the lectures. . . . [Reading the professors'] books was an incomparably greater experience than listening to their lectures. . . . I also started fighting my way through the *Critique of Pure Reason* and the *Prolegomena*. . . .
>
> I passed my "*Matura*" as a private pupil in 1922, one year later than I should have, had I continued at school. But the experiment had been worth

the year I "lost." . . . Two years later I passed a second "*Matura*" at a teachers' training college, which qualified me to teach in primary schools. I took this examination while learning to be a cabinetmaker. (Later I added qualifications to teach mathematics, physics, and chemistry in secondary schools.) However, there were no posts available for teachers, and after concluding my apprenticeship as a cabinetmaker I became . . . a social worker . . . with neglected children.[4]

And then he goes on to show how, while doing all these things in an impoverished time, he began to develop his major ideas and write his books.

Obviously the conditions Popper had to work in are not ideal. But most periods and places have not been ideal for those who would pursue human excellence for its own supreme kinds of usefulness. My college teachers all had to pass through the Great Depression, and many of them had to discontinue their education for several years to avoid starvation. My own generation did have enough money to get by, thanks to the G.I. Bill, but we had all lost, as you might put it, from two to five years in World War II—and many lost their lives.

Kenneth Burke once pointed out, at a time when his own so-called standard of living was so low that it would seem intolerable to almost anyone today, that consumer capitalism provides a marvelous opportunity for the true artist or philosopher: he can live royally on the leavings of the non-philosophers.

But of course to talk in that way will make sense only for those who in fact love the humanities. For anyone who has elected the humanities as a way of earning a good living easily, my advice may seem mere mockery. "How can you, with your cushy salary, have the nerve to advise me to be philosophical about not having a job!" An obscene gesture.

But I can't waste time today defending my own authenticity. I must simply report that if anyone finds himself or herself feeling bitter about having wasted, as I have heard students put it, four or five years getting a doctorate that did not finally yield a job, or a job at what is called a quality institution, I cannot feel sorry for his or her material plight. What I do feel sorry for is the spiritual emptiness, an emptiness that would tolerate playing a meaningless game for that many years.

"Ah, but you professors were the very ones who led me to waste four years by requiring me to do a dissertation on a meaningless topic!"

Nonsense [the cornered greybeard replies]. Or, even if that were in some sense true, that same excuse can be offered for every spiritual disaster. Patty Hearst was "led into it," right? And so was every tragic, or

4. Karl Popper, *Unended Quest* (LaSalle, Ill., 1974; rev. ed., Glasgow, 1976), 39–41.

pathetic, figure you can name. But the problem for you, now, is how to lead yourself out of it, whatever "it" really is. Meanwhile, don't expect me or anyone else to feel sorry that you were given a chance, whether you took it or not, to dwell in the humanities for four, eight, or twelve years. You have been given a chance at that very special kind of human freedom that is experienced only when we live in the achievements of mankind, for the sake of the quality of that life. Our society still happens to recognize, however fitfully, that people who do that, and do it well, and know how to teach other people to do it, are somehow, sometimes to be freed from having to make a living in other ways. And it has also "decided" that far more people should be freed to train themselves for that kind of calling than will actually get called.

Thus like all other societies, ours does not "use" adequately the training that it provides. Still, it is in fact far less brutal in shunting to one side the remnant than most western nations have generally been. (Compare our present cadre of people unable to get teaching jobs after obtaining the Ph.D. with the far larger proportion of intellectuals in other Western nations who, even now, are failed into "ordinary" jobs, as it were, at the age of fourteen or eighteen or twenty-two.) But your main problem is how to make use of the special chance you have been given to find human freedom. Now if I were you . . .

[And speech four fades into a prolonged inaudible drone.]

Well, now that my four speakers have alienated every possible audience, what do I, Booth, have left to propose? How can all this blaming be put together to make something other than a pointless lamentation? Almost to my surprise, I have some proposals.

I propose first that the MLA and other ostensibly humanistic centers set up a national lobby with the specific purpose of improving both the education and the professional fate of all teachers of the humanities. It would work both to increase funds and to redress the disproportionate rewards for "higher" and "higher" education. And it would offer support to any group of part-timers that chose to organize against those administrations that fail to initiate reforms.

The National Endowment for the Humanities has on the whole been a good thing, and I would not want to add my voice to the raucous chorus of those who would turn it into a national endowment for the encouragement of whatever is known *not* to be best. What has been wrong with our national and state efforts is not primarily geographical elitism, but vertical unfairness. Most of the money has gone to the last years of the educational ladder. It is a wonderful thing for the NEH to provide one hundred scholars each year with free time to work on their humanistic projects. I would not trade my own fellowship of last year for any other professional experience of my life, except teaching in the staff-taught courses at Chicago when I first began teaching.

But why should not similar sums be spent on projects for the improvement of humanistic teaching at the so-called lower levels?[5] We all know that a good high school teacher makes more of a difference to our national humanity than an equally good graduate teacher. We all know that elementary teachers can destroy or awaken souls far more powerfully than any college teacher. We all know, without the need for elaborate studies, that untold thousands of humanists who haven't the slightest personal desire to do publishable scholarship are spending time in hateful degree-grubbing and fruitless efforts to publish. But if the reward structures were anything like equivalent, and if the teaching loads were anything like equal, and if the chances for leave time were fairly allocated, thousands of us would spend our time more happily and usefully in teaching. Many of these thousands would love a crack at teaching in the earlier years, even the pre-school years, the most important of all. But who can be expected to make a deliberate choice, the way things are now, for slavery versus partial freedom? Does anyone in the world think that anyone can teach writing to one hundred and sixty pupils at a time?[6] You'd have to be a saint to elect to teach under most pre-college conditions today, if you had a chance at a college job. Our lobby would campaign not for ideal justice, just for some redress of balances, in pay and teaching load and leave time, and—here is the crux—for the hiring of the academically unemployed to assist in that balancing effort.

This is not the place to suggest what specific programs a national endowment for the teaching of the humanities might work for. But certainly the first order of business would be to save for the profession whoever among us really belongs among us. So I would propose the establishment of a National Teachers' Corps, analogous to the Peace Corps and the earlier Teachers' Corps, but more grandiose in aim and more free-wheeling in operation. Its purpose would be twofold—to get educational jobs done that are now being neglected, and to provide minimal income for the man or woman who would rather live as a poor humanist than as a comfortable mail carrier.

5. Since this was written, NEH has in fact developed several programs of the kind I had in mind. But the gap between what is spent nationally on recruiting and cosseting "stars" and what is done to improve conditions in the early years is still outrageous.

6. I must confess, gratefully, that I have met some teachers—one at a high school in Muskegon, Michigan, many at the "English Coalition" conference in 1987—who manage heroically to do so. But I have met many others who have—quite understandably—thrown in the towel.

The directors of such a Teachers' Corps would lobby for funds, and invent new educational positions, [both] in the formal schools and in newly founded schools, where those who love literature and the other arts could teach and learn to teach. The funds would simply be available to anyone willing to take what would amount to about half pay for a half-time load, in any institution willing to accept his or her services.

Just for dramatic effect, the stipends would vary inversely with the age group taught, that is, directly with the importance of the teaching. Let's say $5000 for teaching freshman composition, $5500 for teaching high school, $6000 for teaching elementary school, and $6500 for teaching in preschool programs.[7]

But there isn't space to spell out all the rich imaginative details, which are of course completely clear in my own mind.

I'll have to content myself with only one more particular suggestion for the lobby to work on: sabbaticals for elementary and high school teachers and for those colleges that do not provide them—with special refresher institutes for those who want to spend their sabbaticals that way. If you look at the NEH institutes you will find them for the most part again serving the star system: find the stars and make them starrier. Though the notion of curriculum building is essential to all of the institutes, I predict that they will mainly feed fancy ideas, most not as new or fancy as they look, into minds already too fancy for those difficult tasks of teaching people how to read and think and talk and write about the quality of our doings and makings. Let us, for the love of quality, have institutes that will help teachers at all levels explore how to teach good making and doing, especially in the earliest years. And let us invite into those institutes, as students, those college and graduate professors who are bored with whatever they've been teaching, and thus eager to try a new line.

How would I finance all this?

Why, of course, with an education tax on—well, my dream lobby would push for a tax on every para-educational medium—especially every dyshumanity. All advertisers, TV networks, makers and distributors of movies, organizations or persons now profiting from the "education" of our young people—*all* would be subject to the tax. Those who make money from railroads and highways are now taxed for the use of public resources. Some states now tax polluters for depollution costs. Well, people who make

7. Again, double the figures for 1988. My colleague James Redfield has proposed a plan that is probably more workable, since it in fact already works in France. Students who intend to become teachers could be totally financed by the government, in exchange for an agreement to spend the first teaching years in high school or elementary school. You'll have to ask Redfield or the French minister of education for the details.

money distributing cultural garbage to the young should pay special taxes to pay for the clean-up.

To put it that way, of course, might lead in the direction of a graduated tax, according to the quality of garbage or garbage disposal. And that would, of course, lead to a national censor. Fine, perhaps, if the censor could only be me. But since it wouldn't be, I'd better control my dream and simply put it this way: anybody who now profits financially from influencing minds will pay a special education tax, to be graduated not according to the quality of the "product" but simply according to the amount of profit. No employee who makes less than $15,000 [1988: 30,000], whether writing the most vicious TV drama or teaching high truth at the most prestigious Ivy League college, would be taxed at all. But the professor at the top of the scale would be hit pretty hard, and the TV executive or performer making millions by corrupting the youth would be hit very hard indeed.

Why should we go on allowing ourselves to pay hordes of people fantastic sums to miseducate us and our children, while we claim that we cannot afford to hire young people to work at real education? When the history of our decline and fall is written, our refusal to answer that question, in the name of a largely imaginary free-enterprise system, will seem very strange indeed.

OCCASION 8 · *To the "Powers" of Journalism, Urging Them to Join Us as Fellow Educators*

Why Don't You Do It My Way? Or, A Stitch in *Time*

I wonder if you gentlemen [they *were* all men] can possibly conceive of the kind of anxiety that your presence produces in us professors of humanities. Many of us are, after all, writers manqué: we too were going to be men of letters once—novelists, columnists, editors—men whose words would change the world, men whose words would even mean cash on the line. And here we face you who have not only made it, but made it big, not just editors but a double duodecimo of *senior* editors—not just the men who sent out the rejection slips we began to collect at age sixteen, but the men who established the policies that determined the rebuffs that strengthened our characters and made us what we are today. What's worse, in speaking to you we know that you have encountered every conceivable tone, every conceivable witticism. Like Tiresias, you have foreknown and foresuffered all.

But the soothsayer Tiresias is not really an adequate comparison. If you will think over the tones that might be adopted by those who speak to you on such a visitation, you will hear—I can *hear* you hearing—speeches that confer on you a higher standing. What I hear, in fact, is academic America praying:

PRAYER ONE, Petition or Supplication: We beseech thee, O *Time-Life-Fortune*, to praise this university throughout the land and for all eternity. Enter the hearts of donors and say unto them that the wicked among us have been purged, and that we are about our father's business. Etc.

PRAYER TWO, Confession: We have sinned, O Lord, how we have sinned! But thou canst announce to the public that we shall do better—starting after the troops are withdrawn, in 1972?

Slightly revised from *The University of Chicago Magazine* 64 (July–October 1971): 15–19. © 1971 The University of Chicago Magazine. Reprinted by permission. See the introduction to part 2 above for a description of this special occasion.

PRAYER THREE, Praise and Thanksgiving: [Here my scheme bogs down: I can't believe that you will hear any straightforward prayer of this kind, unless you have descended to institutions lacking all pride. What praise you get will surely be at least as well disguised as my implied praise for your wisdom, tact, and charity, contained in every critical word of this speech.]

PRAYER FOUR, Prophecy, Sub-Type A: I will tell thee, O *Time-Life-Fortune*, what wonders thou wilt see in this land, produced primarily by the wonder-workers in this much neglected university, by the year 2000. And I pray thee to proclaim the new Futurology in thy columns, and to feature me, the head Futurologist, in a cover story—if indeed it is thy will.

PRAYER FIVE, Prophecy, Sub-Type B (The Jeremiad): I will show thee many evils that stalk this land and that are leading it to its doom; indeed if thou art interested, I just happen to have with me an eighty-thousand-word manuscript that I submit for thy perusal. . . .

PRAYER SIX, The Blasphemous, Type A (Accusatory): Dropping the faked tone, I'll simply refer you here to Robert Maynard Hutchins' speech some twenty years ago to the Society of American Editors and Publishers. Sooner or later, on your junkets, you are going to hear a wicked and profane speech like that one, in which Saint Hutchins spoke truth to power, addressing the editors and publishers as fellow-educators who had gone astray. So far as I can tell, he produced little more effect on American publishing than to get himself anthologized widely in freshman textbooks and thus to contribute to the widespread conviction among the young that you are all bad guys determined to corrupt our minds. . . .

Well, what am I to do? None of these six will wash, that's flat. . . . Perhaps I could get by with a brief account of the book I'm working on, a brilliant analysis of the ways in which irony gets understood and misunderstood. There was that marvelous thing by William Whyte in *Fortune* many years ago, about the Universal Credit Card, the one that so many readers took straight—*that* might interest them and get me off this hook. Why (I go on procrastinating) *why*—come to think of it—*is* there so little irony in these men's pages? Clearly, it's because those pages are not edited the way they *should* be, for the audience they *should* have helped to create. And suddenly I face squarely the only thing I really have any heart for this noon—not prayer, not even Blasphemy Type A, but good old straightforward blasphemy of an older kind, that is, "taking on the prerogatives of deity." I've been fighting it for five minutes, but now I succumb: instead of disguising my fantasy of a take-over, by telling you what we try to do in the humanities and hoping that you will take the hint, I choose the unsubtle and totally unoriginal tack of imagining what I would do if I were king. In a time when—as a student not long ago wrote for me—confusion is amiss in the land, what would I do that you are not doing, if I had your power, responsibility, and brains?

My *general* purpose would not be terribly different from yours, I suspect. I infer from your pages that you want to do the best possible job of informing and educating the public without commercial failure. I, too, would want to stay in business, since if I do not stay in business I would cease to educate. And I would not want to try to turn *Life* or *Time* into the *American Scholar*, or *Fortune* into *Daedalus* or *The Public Interest*. What I find missing from your achievement, however, regardless of your purposes, is a consistent effort to educate your respective publics in *how* to think critically about what you present them—to educate them in the *how* and *why* of thought and judgment rather than the mere *what*. Of course I know as putative editor that I cannot do what our schools and colleges fail to do: that is, turn out from my subscription lists a stream of liberally educated men and women. But I look you in the eye—my courage rising as I move further and further out on this limb—and say that if I were to set my goal as reducing the number of Americans who think and behave as Spiro[1] and Howie Machtinger[2] think and behave, there are many, many things I could do that you are not now doing. The three I choose to talk about just happen to be at the center of our work in the humanities.

The first task would be a systematic effort, week by week, month by month, to raise the critical powers and mental habits of my readers. In attacking one of your rivals, *US News & World Report*, I once argued that in too many articles they cater to and reinforce a flat and stupefied credulity in the postulated reader; the audience is presumed to be incapable of asking that old-fashioned question, What's the evidence? The hidden presupposition of how a reader becomes informed about world affairs, in any field, is that he or she reads someone's explanation about it and then is just *informed*. The notion that critical thought is required, comparing *this* account with *that* account, *this* witness with *that* witness—the very notion of the kind of critical activity that goes on in your own editorial conferences, sifting reliabilities, rejecting suspect witnesses, comparing claim with claim—

1. Spiro Agnew, then Vice President and a vigorous, not to say frenzied, critic of the media.

2. Machtinger was as a graduate student a prominent leader of the University of Chicago's most devastating sit-in, in February of 1969.

this notion is in fact generally hidden from the public. Readers thus become habituated to intellectual passivity. Unless some demanding teacher has somewhere along the line taught habits of critical attention, the belief in established and fixed political and cultural truth is unshaken—unshaken unless the reader discovers, perhaps by accident, that your accounts are, like everyone else's, partial and controversial. In that case the kind of disillusionment sets in that makes it possible for any speaker in any university community to get a laugh by referring to the "objectivity" of your work.

Now I know that you try harder for accuracy and fairness than the myths of either the intellectuals or the Agnews give you credit for; but the myths and that resulting derisive laughter will prevail as long as you don't build into your editing a steady education in critical scepticism about your own work.

I would thus install, tomorrow, in every magazine in my immense and glittering domain, a page or two devoted to critical exposés of distortions and errors committed by other journals and by radio and TV. These would be not the sort of emotional attack that you occasionally print disguised as reports on magazines you don't like, such as *Ramparts* or *Rolling Stone*. What we need are specific exposés of the kind attempted, too often unsuccessfully, by the *Chicago Journalism Review*—lively but detailed explanations of how, in a given account of this or that hero or villain of the left or right or center, facts and quotations were invented, characters transformed, arguments distorted. This *Column-Contra-Credulity*, this *Guide to How to Read or View the Other Media Slowly, for Fun and Profit*, would of course be controversial; it would therefore have the nice effect, I predict in my role as prophet, of raising circulation.[3]

But it would not carry its full effect unless it was supplemented with another regular column of exposés of my *own* mistakes: not just corrections of errors of fact but analyses of how and why I went wrong in last week's prediction of election results, or of why my editorial policy about Viet Nam was wrong for so many years. I don't know of any American journal that does this kind of thing regularly; to read any one issue of any magazine, you would think that past judgments had all worked out well, and therefore that the present issue could and should be read in absolute trust. Imagine what it would mean to readers if they found *my* journals carrying a page of *mea culpa*s with an occasional *maxima culpa:* how we damned William Faulkner until he won the Nobel Prize, how we panned *Catch-22* until it was discovered by somebody else, how we predicted the death of rock music in 1958. Think of the excitement the following news items might create:

3. The *Chicago Journalism Review* died. So much for my prophetic insight into what will survive commercially!

In *Time:* "Early last Thursday morning, the phone shrilled on the desk of *Time* senior editor Blifil. 'Yes?' he barked—and then he listened for a long time. It was Doctor Anthrax from Berkeley, furious because our story of last week seriously distorted the nature and importance of the doctor's work. He is not in fact working on cancer but on botulosis, and in his own view the hope for cure is not just around the corner, as we put it, but at least ten years off. Readers could have discovered this mistake by referring to the more accurate account in *Newsweek. Time* apologizes."

In *Fortune:* "Last month *Fortune* reported on the efforts of American industry to curtail pollution. Unfortunately we failed to report, because we had not been told, that in 1970 industry spent ten times as much *advertising* their efforts to curtail pollution as was spent actually *curtailing* pollution. The Editors of *Fortune* regret this oversight, which readers could have discovered by taking a look at *Consumer Reports.*"

In *Life:* "Last week *Life* published a photograph of thirteen pregnant high school girls lined up for abortions at the school clinic in Santa Fe. Further research has shown that the city was actually San Fernando, eleven of the girls were not in fact pregnant but were stuffed with pillows, the clinic was not an abortion clinic but the principal's office; they were lining up to be expelled. The photograph was in fact a composite, as a careful viewer could have discovered by looking closely at . . . "

My efforts to create and appeal to critical Americans by a regular and systematic exposure of mistakes made by my competitors and by myself would lead, surely, to more careful and active reading and thinking. But I would add to it a second feature, a regular barrage of stylistic analyses, revelations of how writers betray themselves at the moment of writing. It would be a kind of running course in Freshman English, exposing not errors of judgment revealed by the passage of time but bad writing discovered in the simple, slow, intelligent reading of the words as they fall on the page. It would be in the direction of the newsbreaks in *The New Yorker,* which teach readers week by week that bad writing can at least occasionally have the mildly painful consequence of public ridicule. But I would do it more systematically and more savagely. I would try to find an H. L. Mencken, and I would regularly turn him loose on American writing habits, urging him to lash follies and to name names. With such a threat in the wings, our presidents and senators might try a little harder to make sense, to choose their words and arguments with more care.[4]

4. A fews years after this occasion, the National Council of Teachers of English founded the *Quarterly Review of Doublespeak,* edited by the Committee on Doublespeak (for subscription write NCTE, 1111 Kenyon Road, Urbana, Ill, 61801). The quarterly gives an annual Doublespeak Award "to American public figures who have perpetrated language that is

Such a column would try to be absolutely neutral, discovering its non-sequiturs and stupidities impartially in SDS[5] literature and presidential fireside chats. I offer only one example: President Nixon saying about the recent Washington demonstration, "These young people don't seem to realize that we are working not only for peace in our time, but for peace in their time too." Not one of you guardians of the public language caught that one when it occurred—and you ought to be ashamed of yourselves. In short, if you were mine, all mine, we would all find ourselves working very hard to purify the language of the tribe.

I have time for only one more major policy pronouncement, the craziest of the lot. If what I have been saying so far is that you editors are the unacknowledged English teachers of the world, what I turn to now suggests that for the American public you are to an astonishing degree the metaphysicians, theologians, moralists, philosophers of science, sociologists, and anthropologists. And if I am right, you have inadvertently been promulgating outmoded and discredited doctrines—dogmas that, like the rest of us, you took in with your mother's milk, since you were born and raised in twentieth-century secular culture. No one reading your journals would really understand that a vast intellectual revolution is underway, perhaps more significant than anything that has happened since the seventeenth century and certainly as earthshaking as the killing off of God that was begun in the Renaissance, completed by Darwin, and proclaimed by Nietzsche.

I must confess that you can hardly be blamed for editing your journals as if this revolution had not occurred, since many academics are still conducting their lives as if it had not. The very format of your visit here—science and "social science" one day, humanities the next—reinforces the old-fashioned view I think your pages perpetuate.

In that view, there are two kinds of human being, two kinds of mind. On the one hand there are reasonable people, *thinkers*, scientists, including one kind of social scientists, the "hard" kind. They know that the universe is cold and value-free, that we invent values rather than discover them, that values are thus relative to each inventor, or at best to each culture, and that values are unverifiable by any standards of knowledge or proof. What can be known is what is scientific. On the other hand, there are unreasonable people who *assert values* and who try to impose them on each other either

---

grossly deceptive, evasive, euphemistic, confusing, or self-contradictory." The 1987 award (vol. 14, January 1988) was given to Lieutenant Colonel Oliver North and Rear Admiral John Poindexter "for the language they used in testifying" about their shenanigans in the Iran-Contra mess. The "Review" does a noble work, but so far as I know it is read only by English teachers, and it does not usually analyze bad arguments, only deceptive language.

5. Students for a Democratic Society.

by "mere rhetoric" or by the threat of violence or by violence itself. They care more about people and persons and intuition and insight than about truth, so they have naturally been forced to give up knowledge and reason.

People on either side of this "modernist split" may be good guys or bad guys, "depending on your point of view," but the dogma requires us to make a choice between cold reason and blind faith. All thinkers of hard intelligence are atheists, because God is after all dead; only softies make leaps of faith against cold reason, and assert that God, or Satan, or Buddha, or Allah, lives. Interesting news comes about when values clash, but of course what are really clashing are only the motives and inner compulsions of the clashers, not real issues testable as matters of fact and subject to meaningful debate. It is a pity, as C. P. Snow says, that the humanities and the social sciences have lagged so far behind the sciences in developing scientific criteria of knowledge, but of course it is—according to the dogma—an inescapable pity; except for whatever is factual and value-free, nothing can be proved about the subject matter of our moral and political societies or our artistic achievements.

We should honor, of course, those interesting celebrities, those personalities, some of them quite saintly, who dare to assert traditional values: our dignity, our freedom, our hopes. We all want dignity, freedom, and hope, and it's nice to have such people become newsworthy. Here is Father Lonergan, whom many Catholics consider a great thinker; and *here* is physicist Michael Polanyi, who talks about personal knowledge and the tacit dimension; and *here* is Mother Theresa who dares to be a Christian: newsmakers all. But such grand figures sort of get mixed up in our pages with other asserters of value: the rediscoverers of astrology and black magic, the God-is-dead theologians, the reincarnated Christs who fill the land. It just goes to show, doesn't it, that as our freshmen all say, when it comes to values it's all a matter of opinion or intuition; what is right is what feels right to me.

Thus a kind of crude division of the world into fact and value, science and the humanities, the head and the heart, reason and faith, objectivity and subjectivity, is perpetuated by much of what you write. You edit yourselves as Americans live their lives—as if we had no choice but to act on the same dichotomies between logic and mysticism, reason and blind feeling, that Bertrand Russell was presenting to the world as daring new truth seventy years ago.

The great good news of the past several decades is that all of this seems, to most of those who have really thought about it, totally untenable, *intellectually* untenable. The whole effort to divide the world into cold factuality and warm values, the objectively known and the subjectively affirmed, has by now been radically repudiated by most original thinkers. It has in fact been old-fashioned at least since the work of our great American pragmatists and of Whitehead in explaining how values are inseparable from *what is*.

When Whitehead did his major work of integration, in *Process and Reality*, there were still many first-class minds who accepted and tried to live with the dichotomized world he attacked. But by now, there is hardly a professional philosopher alive, except in one small branch of existentialism, who accepts the crude dualism that for three hundred years supported the warfare between science and religion, or more recently, between science and the humanities. The entire skeptical, secular tradition that put religion on the defensive in the sixteenth and seventeenth centuries, forcing it to become a matter of "mere faith" or of "the heart," and then easily won battle after battle against a crippled enemy, culminating in our time with a *Time* feature on the death of God—this tradition, like the dogmatic religious traditions it both produced and attacked, has been dead for decades. Surely you should now conduct the appropriate public obsequies. How many of the readers of any of your journals would suspect that most professional philosophers have been rediscovering ways in which values and the world of fact or nature or science are not finally separable: that, as Lévi-Strauss and others have shown, some ultimate values are not relative to cultures but are common to all mankind; that, as Kurt Baier and Chicago's Alan Gewirth and dozens of other philosophers have been claiming to demonstrate, whether a given moral choice is right can be a plain matter of fact or truth, not dependent on whether the person thinks it is right; that, as Michael Polanyi has shown, science is value-ridden, and all value choices can be improved through rational thought; in short, that the universe as it makes man and as it is known *by* man is inherently value-ridden and value-creating.

Popular culture does not know about these and many other new efforts to reunite fact and value. Even popular academic culture does not know about it—it's still too busy conducting the old war by affirming values against "reason" or defending "reason" against "protest." Though the academies are where the revolution is taking place, we have failed to get the message across departmental boundaries even within individual universities. One result is that the public, seeing our impersonal scientific achievements (reported by you) on the one hand, and our value-affirming sit-inners and bombers (reported by you) on the other, concludes either that we don't believe in values or we don't have the guts to defend them. It is not at all surprising that the New Left and the New Right conspire together to destroy the academies, because, for both, the academies stand for the split, the inhuman, soul-destroying split, between truth and commitment, reason and faith.

What would I do about all this as editor? Obviously I can't turn over very many of my pages to Father Lonergan's careful arguments restoring insight to cognitive responsibility; or to physicist Polanyi's defenses of "tacit knowledge" and "indwelling" as cognitive; or to Richard McKeon's or Chaim Perelman's profound reunions of truth, value, and action in rhetorical "philosophies of discourse." Clearly my journals can't summarize each issue of those new periodicals, the *Journal of Value Inquiry* and *Philosophy and Rhetoric.* But there is one thing I *would* do: I would find a couple of well-educated reporters and plant them inside one or two of the great universities—I can think of at least *one* that would do—and leave them there for three to six months, with the simple assignment to find out what goes on there *intellectually*, beneath the surface battles and slogans of protest and response. Then I would ask for regular reports, which I would try to keep my cotton-picking editorial hands off, about what is really going on among the best minds in the country.

In short, what has been going on in university protest and response has been only a manifestation of something much deeper in American society, and part of that deeper crisis is loss of faith in the capacity to discover meaningful resolution of value differences without violence. And the loss of faith in discourse is in part a loss of faith in the meaning of life itself. You cannot do much about this crisis merely by editing yourselves in the old ways, taking sides as you see fit, affirming *these* values as against *those,* favoring the Viet Nam war this year and opposing it next; siding with the demonstrators this week and against them a week later. The public is grossly in need of re-education about the very nature of life itself, about life in political society, about the necessities and limits of human institutions, and finally about the grounds for our various faiths for resolution of conflict. When our presidents and SDS leaders seem equally to believe that principles can be taken up and dropped at will, that all value questions are simply reducible to political and physical power, we are in trouble.

In one sense what is at stake is the dignity and meaning of your own work. If one accepts the views of human nature, of science, of moral values, of the nature of the self, that you periodically and passively reflect to the American people, then *you* do not matter because *nothing* does: your journals are simply disguises for your power interests, and you have no more intellectual or moral justification for what you do than the most irresponsible bomber or assassin has. But if the intellectual revolution that I have hinted at is real, and if its founders are right, faith in reason is justified, to preserve standards of public discourse about values is terribly important, and we editors as a body are among the most significant men in the history of modern man. . . .

But with that imitation of Ciceronian rhetoric, leaving you with the difficult choice of being either on my side or being fools and knaves, I wake up from my Walter Mitty fantasy, descend from the heights, and return to my proper and natural humility: please don't go away mad, and come again.

PART III · *TO ASSEMBLIES OF MORE OR LESS RESTLESS LEARNERS*

Education is wasted on the young.
Plato and many others

Only the young are educable.
Anonymous

INTRODUCTION · *The Occasions*

I have no idea of how many talks I have given to assemblies of students—at Earlham College, at the University of Chicago, and at scores of other universities and colleges—perhaps as many as two or three hundred. Many of these have been about specialized critical, rhetorical, and political subjects not appropriate to this volume; many have been thrown away, and others no doubt should have been. But I confess that I've enjoyed nothing more, professionally, than those relatively rare occasions when speaker, topic, and audience somehow meet and a *real* occasion emerges, producing at each moment the smiles or laughter, the groans or deep silence that signify "we're with you," and then yielding at the end that most delicious of all elixirs, enthusiastic applause.

Every speaker soon learns just how deceptive such responses can be. A critical colleague at Earlham College once gave his debate class a spot-quiz on the content of one of my gloriously "successful" all-college lectures, and then gave *me* the deflating results: a most appalling collection of misunderstandings and skewed memories, together with a good deal of sheer inventiveness. I never again assumed that anything I said would be heard as I intended.

If it is true that no audience comes ready-made or leaves fully persuaded, it is even more threateningly true that anxious, tired, first-year students, called together in the midst of placement examinations to hear orientation talks like the one on Occasion 10, are not spontaneously inclined to listen critically. They will be polite; they will applaud vigorously no matter what you say. But they will really listen only if you create a drama that startles them, from the beginning, into expecting something they have not heard before.

That speech, like all of those I am reprinting, felt "successful" at the time of delivery: that is, they produced enough laughter at the right spots, and enough applause at the end, to make me think that I had more or less knocked 'em dead. Reading them in cold blood now, I don't find them quite as satisfying as they felt at the time. The introductions, on which I worked hardest, seem especially chancy. Obviously, they depended for their original success both on my timing and on the mood of the audience as it had been established by the colleagues who introduced me.

I find it interesting now, as I reconsider such student occasions, to note how much more politically insistent my tone became from 1965 to 1970.

(Compare, for example the speech given to freshmen in 1966, "Useful and Useless Education: New Letters of Screwtape," reprinted in *Now Don't Try to Reason with Me* [Chicago, 1970], with Occasion 9.) I had always been interested in politics—had indeed always thought of myself as considerably "left": in the forties and fifties, a "radical" or "socialist" (albeit a rather passive one), in the late fifties and sixties some kind of "anti-capitalist liberal." But I believed then, as I believe now, that the most valuable political act any teacher can perform is not to impose particular political views but to teach students to *see* the words that our society tries to inject into them unseen. I believed then, as I believe now, that strong forces in our society do not really want us to teach students to see—to think critically about their world and to learn how to speak and write powerfully to change it. That belief led me to assume, as I assume now, that genuinely free universities always exist on sufferance, in a kind of unacknowledged bit of plea-bargaining. (1) "We, the movers and shakers, know that many of you teachers are in some ways subversive of our values. But we tolerate you, indeed support you generously, because we need what you produce as you do your subverting: a clerisy who can do the work of business and government. We will leave you alone to work as you see fit, so long as we get our supply of clerks—and *so long as you do not organize yourselves as political entities.* On the day that you try to take over either business or government, we will of course crush you." (2) "We, the professoriat, agree not to organize ourselves as a political force, so long as you will let us teach as we please and write as we please."

Believing in some such non-intervention pact, I was from the beginning of the sixties deeply opposed to that branch of the student movement that expected the university as an entity to move militantly against policies in Washington. Though I spoke out "prematurely," as citizen, against America's moves in Viet Nam, joined students in 1967 in opposing the university's provision of Grade Point Averages to Selective Service, and felt a strong sympathy for the motives that led students to various excesses, I kept trying to say to them, in diverse ways, "We must defend the principles of independence that preserve the university *as a university*, because sooner or later [Note, 1988: I actually thought it would be sooner than has turned out to be the case] the 'conservatives' will be at our gates, saying, 'If the left-wing students can dictate to the university, so can we.' And they will have more power than you do."

Under the pressure of increased student activism in the late sixties, it is not surprising that my theme of education for freedom became more overt and insistent. When I became dean of the College in late 1964, Chicago had not yet been hit by any kind of student sit-in. We were still congratulating ourselves because *our* students, seeing the obvious differences between us and a Berkeley, would surely continue to appreciate what we offered. By late 1970, we had barely survived, or so it seemed. We had had one minor and two major sit-ins, the worst of them culminating just the year before in the expulsion of more than forty students, some of whom ended in the Weathermen and on the FBI's most-wanted list. "Kent State" had occurred in the previous spring, and our faculty council, by now almost as politicized as the students, had voted to suspend classes for one week in the coming term, to allow students to engage in political work. It is thus hardly surprising that my speeches of 1968 and 1970 reflect their occasions by revealing a "sub-text" of exhortation to some critical thought about current leftist slogans.

Can they therefore be called "conservative"? I think not. I could now give something like the same speeches to young "conservatives," urging them quite radically to think behind the mindless and heartless slogans that too many are being fed by our political and economic leaders.

The last two talks to students were presented on relatively simple occasions: meetings with volunteer audiences who had come to hear a talk *from me* and *on this subject*. I could consequently spend somewhat less time and energy on establishing ethos, and I felt less need to insert those little periodic dramas—seeming digressions that must always carry forward the true subject if they are to earn their keep—designed to call all wool-gatherers back to attention.

OCCASION 9 · *To About a Thousand Undergraduates Gathered (Voluntarily!) To Take Part in a Three-Day Liberal Arts Conference*

Who Killed Liberal Education?

One of the best-kept secrets on this campus is that the administration—or rather, a tiny little group of us super-administrators—has access to a special computer, one that goes far beyond every other known computer in speed, complexity, and judgment. Judgment is not, I know, ordinarily attributed to computers, and I can hardly expect you to believe me when I say that this machine, which for reasons that will appear later we call the MANIAC 2000, has consistently shown better judgment than all the rest of us put together. Indeed, some of us have begun to feel that there is no word except *wisdom* that can do justice to the faculty this machine has of guiding us, time and again, to do precisely the right thing at the right time. Those of you who have been overwhelmed with admiration for the unfailing shrewdness with which the College has been run since I became dean in 1964 will understand what I mean when I say that the MANIAC 2000 is the greatest thing to hit the College scene since Hutchins.

Naturally whenever I am to give a speech I consult old MANIAC, and sometimes I even let him—her—it—write the speech for me. This time I thought I'd try to do one of my own, but I wanted help at the beginning.

"What shall I write on?" I typed into the thing, using that mastery of FORTRAN for which even my best friends have never given me enough credit.

"The future of liberal education," said the printout.

"But I don't know anything about it," I complained.

"Ask me," it said.

"What is the future of liberal education?" I fed in. Came this printout: "Liberal education died."

"How?"

There was a fantastic clatter and whirring that went on and on and on—

Speech delivered in 1968 at the University of Chicago.

157

try as I would I could not stop the thing to get a word in edgewise—if that is how one gets a word into such a conversation. On and on it went—for exactly six thousand words of printout. Not being a speed-reader, I had been unable to keep up, and when I saw the last words, I was astonished: "End of speech for Liberal Arts Conference, 1968." I chose one of our luxurious easy chairs—you wouldn't believe how luxuriously our inner sanctum is furnished, paid for out of your hard-earned tuition—I settled, as I say, into an easy chair and read what I shall soon, following old MANIAC 2000's fantastic orders, read to you. The title was "The Death of Liberal Education, As Seen from the Year 2000."

It had never occurred to me before that MANIAC's powers included prognostication, and I was rather disillusioned to think that my favorite machine had fallen victim to the disease of two-thousandism that Daniel Bell and so many other social scientists have contracted these days. On the other hand, there was a kind of logic about all this. After all, if liberal education dies, there will be nobody left to give an educated account of its demise—except possibly some super-machine with a memory bank like MANIAC's. So I decided to read on, though not without keeping all my critical faculties alert.

Today, April 3, A.D. 2000, with the death of Professor Zukunft, the last educated man alive, liberal education died. Just before his death, he ordered his "History of Liberal Education in the Last Third of the Twentieth Century" programmed into this machine. His history reads as follows:

[I must confess that these wheels within wheels annoy me, but that's the kind of age we live in. MANIAC's big point seems to be to have so many narrative voices that you and I cannot make out what is really being said. Obviously we must keep our wits about us here. Back to Professor Zukunft:]

I am the last educated man alive, and nobody knows it but me. In fact, everyone in the world today feels quite complacently well-educated. Ninety-five percent of the world's populace now goes through colleges whose curricula are determined by student votes. Everybody learns a great deal and everything that is learned is thought to be relevant. Consumption of books and magazines has reached new heights, and just as Mr. Charles Silberman could, in 1967, hail the rising educational level of *Look, Life, Time,* and *Newsweek,* so we can now show that the educational level, so-called, has reached a point beyond which it cannot go: every magazine is now edited to appeal to an audience with eighteen years of formal education. Everyone consumes more art and literature and music and even philosophy than ever before. But to me the world is full of cultivated idiots, a new kind of *idiots savants* who know the price and use of every work and the value of none. The simple value of cultivation of the powers of thought, for the sake of the value of thought itself and not for some ulterior practical use, has disappeared; the massage of the media has finally produced a gloriously comfortable and permanent mental torpor.

Why did it happen? Who killed liberal education? Before I too die, I should like to attempt an account, in the no-doubt-vain hope that someone in the future, bored to distraction by his own cheerful vacuity, may read it and be joggled back into some kind of human existence.

Liberal education was weakened, first, by forces from outside that drew away those who had once practiced it. Even in its heyday there were never very many teachers who cared about educating people for the sake of what education did to them as persons and not for some utilitarian value for this or that segment of society. But there was a time when most such people were in the classroom, and liberal education would not have died if they had stayed in the classroom. But in larger and larger numbers they left— they left to join research institutes, they left to work for the government and for industry, they became deans and foundation officials, they received graduate professorships that required little or no teaching, or they discovered that they could earn twice as much teaching Tamil, Urdu, or Amharic to three or four graduate students as they could teaching Montaigne or Goethe to undergraduates. Nobody has been able to trace the decline back to its exact beginnings. Some say it was when the first Ph.D. was granted; some say it was when the first research grant was made. And some say that it was when the first teaching assistant was hired to take over entire responsibility for a course, with no supervision from experienced teachers. But everyone seems to agree that a simple, deadly process, noticeable to men like William James from the beginning, was visible from about 1900 on to the end; teachers with strong, original minds, who had once spent most of their working hours teaching their juniors, no longer spent their working hours teaching their juniors. More and more of the best minds ceased to teach altogether except through articles and books, which teach in a way that everyone from Plato on has recognized as a very inferior (though necessary) kind of teaching.

Soon deans of university colleges, like presidents of liberal arts colleges, were finding that young scholars labored harder to publish premature books than to challenge their classes. One dean found that one of the best teachers in his college, a man who had always spoken contemptuously against those who neglected teaching, moved, on November 15, 1967, to a research institute position with no teaching duties—as soon, in fact, as he had the chance. That same dean received memos like the following: "As you know, the second term of Ms. Smith expires this year. The personnel committee has met, and we have reluctantly concluded that although Ms. Smith is the best of the fifteen men and women teaching course X, we cannot recommend promotion to a professorial rank (assistant professor) of anyone who clearly has no intentions of carrying on frontline research. We are quite sure that anyone we may get to replace her will not teach as well, but a professorial position, which might build expectations of tenure, is out of the question."

But it was not only that many teachers were tempted away from college classrooms. Those who remained were too often drawn into uneducational or even anti-educational forms of teaching, force-feeding the young geese in order to collect the foie gras of professional training.

There is no need for me to detail here the fantastic professionalism and specialism that triumphed throughout American life in the mid-twentieth century. I cite in my bibliography 2,757 items, most of them speeches to educational conferences, describing the trend that was summed up when Cornell finally accepted the advice of its President Perkins and eliminated liberal education in order to allow students to specialize as soon as they arrived. This might not in itself have been a serious blow to our victim, if secondary schools had been able to provide liberally-educated graduates to the increasingly specialized colleges. But the high schools had long since suffered both of the trends we are describing: many of their best minds had been bled off to the colleges, or to business, and those teachers who remained had long since come to see their task either as hopelessly uneducational baby-sitting (for the lower tracks) or as joyless cramming for college entry. According to my figures, by April 1 of 1968, only 5 percent of the students then in college had ever discovered what it might mean to learn something for the sake of learning it, so steadily were they subjected to the notion that one learns something only in order to climb a professional ladder. Even that low figure steadily declined until today, Easter 2000, when there is not a soul alive who will understand what I am saying. . . .

[I must skip some of Zukunft's rather long-winded account.]

The phenomenon of the "flight from teaching" was often, indeed monotonously, described by critics of that time. But it was not often noticed that those who spent their time deploring that flight were not teaching while they did it, thus exemplifying the flight they described; indeed, the deplorers, claiming to be friends of liberal education, became as a group the second main team of assassins. It was not only that when deans spent time at liberal arts conferences attacking graduate departments and research institutes they were not minding the store; it was also that the methods they used in their attacks were too often in essence anti-educational. In short, liberal education was killed more by the bad thinking of its friends than by the rivalries and animosities produced by the technological age. At one conference held at a major university in 1968, for example, most of the participants—students, faculty, and visitors alike—fell into the most shameless cliché-mongering imaginable. Out they poured, the stock counters of the anti-establishment brigade. A dispassionate observer might have concluded that a small and well-established series of games were being played against the establishment, according to certain clearly *established* rules. One of these games was called Wholemansmanship. It went like this:

> x (a teacher in a liberal arts college): You graduate scholars are destroy-
> ing undergraduate teaching, because you teach dry subject matter and
> fail to educate the whole man.
>
> y (a dean of a graduate school): You undergraduate buffs are so concerned
> with students' personalities and psyches that you are failing to educate
> them at all, whole *or* part.
>
> x : Nonsense! What you forget is that a subject is meaningful only inso-
> far as it becomes real to the subject, meets his concerns and needs,
> takes on existential relevance.
>
> y : Double nonsense! No man can claim to be whole these days who
> has not mastered a special field. Your whole man is maimed by
> incompetence.
>
> x : You are a son of—perdition. You ignore the flesh-and-blood creatures
> you would teach. They have passions, they must make vital choices,
> and you, in your ivory tower, would teach them dry facts and irrele-
> vant theories. Your departments are medieval bastions of irresponsible
> autonomy. . . .
>
> y (thinking he has heard the word "bastard"): You're another . . .

And so on. The counters in this game were clearly marked, the moves all laid out in advance; nobody had to think to play it. About the only restraint shown by participants in the game of Wholemansmanship was that no one except an obscure dean in 1968 ever accused an opponent of acting Wholer than Thou.

[Somehow this reminds me of where we are, and I must interpolate an exhortation: I think that anyone looking at the program for this confer-ence might suspect that it was set up as a test match in Wholemans-manship. It was not, but we cannot prevent its becoming as deceptive and unproductive as the games described by Berne in *Games People Play*, un-less we determine here at the beginning to *think* for three days rather than to defend previously held positions. Most of the players Berne de-scribes are defending psychological positions, and it is clear that some of us in educational debates are doing the same: defenders of graduate research who are working out their guilt over having abandoned undergraduates; attackers of graduate schools who are angry because they were refused tenure at good old Perish State University. But the indictment of universities that I am sure Mr. (William) Arrowsmith and Mr. (Edgar Z.) Friedenberg will offer here cannot be defended or attacked without thought, and that will require us to go beyond game-playing to look at the complexities behind our claims for the Whole Man.

End of interpolation. Back to old Zukunft.]

Another game played by 98.2 percent of the participants at 97.6 percent of all educational conferences in the sixties and seventies was Polarities. In that game the contestants vied with each other to see who could reduce the most complexities to two opposite poles. The policy of Publish *or* Perish—for or against? Relevance *or* Irrelevance—for or against? The Establishment *or* the Good People—for or against? There were, of course, sound reasons for the rapid increase in the popularity of this game in the late sixties: war always polarizes, and an undeclared and unpopular war tends to polarize everything that is touched by it. A young man who must choose whether or not to accept the draft cannot resist polarization: there are only two boxes to be checked—yes or no. He cannot, by taking thought, invent a third box, "None of the above." So it was not surprising that *everything* came to be viewed in polarized terms.

For liberal education, the most destructive of these polarizations was that between research and teaching. Are you for research *or* for teaching? One of the most intelligent of the defenders of liberal education, Mr. William Arrowsmith [a conference participant], often fell into the trap of talking as if it were possible to choose up sides on such a question. He even recommended that the country should set up research institutes in large numbers, divorcing research almost entirely from the colleges where, presumably, the truly liberal learning would go on. That a man with as much true learning as Arrowsmith's could have recommended such a thing shows just how hard it was, in 1968, to think clearly about the causes and possible cures of the decline of teaching. Whenever hard thought about real causes and processes is replaced by a melodrama of the good guys versus the bad guys, liberal education dies from within, and that is, without question, what happened mid-century. Wherever one turns in the literature of the time, one finds people playing games with simple pairs of opposites, indulging in a kind of opinion juggling, two Indian clubs only, with neither club standing for anything except an abstract concept in the juggler's head. For David Riesman it was *professional* versus *intellectual*, making it impossible for anyone to aspire *both* to the

fullest professional competence *and* to the intellectual's passion for ideas.[1]
For many graduate professors it was *professional* versus *incompetent*,
which had the same effect but with a rhetorical push in the opposite direction. For Martin Duberman it was *student-initiated learning* versus
teacher-initiated learning, and the resulting polarity was so compelling
that even when a great many of his students complained that they hadn't
learned enough because he refused to teach them anything, he dismissed
their complaint with the charge that they had been corrupted by their
early training.

Here I should like to quote [Zukunft goes on] from an unpublished
speech by an anonymous dean, dated April 1968, at the University of
Chicago Liberal Arts Conference. It is clear that at that time it was cus-
tomary still to hold Easter festivals of learning, and that somehow there
was in the popular academic mind an obscure connection between Christ
and Athena, or perhaps even Apollo, with their resurrections of the spirit
of learning. Be that as it may, at one of these festivals this harried dean
said the following:

"The absurdity of blaming research for bad education can be shown
quite simply:

"First, ask yourself who have been the really valuable teachers in your
own life. Then check those who have been actively engaged in some kind
of research and publication which they themselves cared about. For me the
figure comes out to better than 95 percent of the good teachers I have had,
including my high school teachers. Mr. Arrowsmith, Mr. Friedenberg,
Mr. [Henry] Kamen, and Mr. [Roger] Hildebrand all do research, and the
results of their research become part of their teaching, both in print and in
the classroom. I have studied under only two non-publishing good teachers, and both of those were doing what I would call research—they were
actively engaged in inquiring into questions other scholars had not yet
answered.

"Secondly, make a list of the teachers whose classes were for you absolutely worthless. Note that I am not asking you to make a list of people
you consider bad teachers. That might come later. When I make such a
list of worthless teachers, I find that all but two on the list were *not* doing
any kind of research, let alone publication. Three were, I admit, publishing
the crummy results of crummy research. But the point here is that four of
my five *worthless* teachers were worthless because they didn't know
enough; they had nothing to teach me, or at least were unable to *show*

1. David Riesman and Christopher Jencks, *The Academic Revolution* (Garden City, N.Y.,
1968).

me what they had, though at least two of them thought of themselves as genuine teachers devoted to their work.

"Third, add to list number two those teachers who you think were bad simply because their techniques were bad or because they neglected their teaching in favor of research. Then ask, how many of these would have been better teachers *if they had spent less time on research and more on their teaching?* I find only one woman I feel clear about here. The rest would have been just as bad if they'd spent weeks of preparation on each class, and worse if they had done no research.

"I conclude from these three simple mental experiments," the worthy but obscure dean goes on (in a learned allusion to David Hume), "that to talk of research and teaching as antithetical gets us nowhere. It cannot be research itself that leads to the obvious neglect of teaching, and it cannot be a simple decline in what we call 'teaching' that produces the decline in liberal education. As for the tendency to blame graduate schools for the decline, we must never forget that every graduate professor, every institute researcher, and every graduate student was once an undergraduate somewhere. What he or she is must in part be a result of what occurred in the four years of college. If no liberal education occurred, who is to blame?

"But of course many graduate professors *are* liberally educated, and they are, pace Arrowsmith, conducting liberal education with their graduate students. If we searched America today to find where genuine cultivation of the mind occurs, with professional and social consequences left to fall where they may, we would surely find as much of it going on after the B.A. as in the undergraduate years—in a few law schools, some business programs, an isolated English or philosophy or classics department. I know one graduate professor of physics who gives his Ph.D. candidates, belatedly, a liberal education. Graduates of famous liberal arts colleges, they still are barbarians when they come to him, but they leave him fundamentally changed."

But I must leave the dean's rather shrill rhetoric and continue with my own dispassionate analysis [says Zukunft, and he goes on as follows]:

Besides the Wholemansmanship players and the polarizers, the chief culprits responsible for the worst crime of the century were the many inventors of plausible substitutes for the real thing. Defenders of liberal education were fairly well-armed, after all, against their open enemies. When businessmen asked for more 'practical' courses, colleges knew the answers in advance, and resisted. When government tried to force indoctrination programs onto the colleges, most colleges knew the right answers in advance, and resisted. When graduate research programs stole money and equipment and time from undergraduate classrooms, they may have in part succeeded in the theft, but nobody was fooled into thinking that what they did was done in the name of liberal education, or that nothing had been lost. But when the defenders of liberal education themselves grew more and more confused about what it was, then there were no true defenders left.

All of the proposed substitutes for liberal education, offered in the name of liberal education, were of course good things. They could not have been dangerous, and finally effective, if they had *not* been obviously good things. Perhaps it was inevitable that in a time when most educated people had lost their faith in all other institutions, they should have called upon the universities and colleges to take care of all of the values remaining in society.

Probably the most important of these was love. With the church dead, at least in the opinion of most faculty members and students, it was natural to demand that the colleges should provide a loving community of the saved, an institutional embodiment of everyone's hope that, even in these non-Christian times, love might save the world after all.[2]

I quote from a statement by a graduate student of 1967: 'With one exception, Hannah Arendt,' he said, 'I doubt that any of my teachers cares whether I'm around or not—so long as I learn what they have to teach.' When asked if he didn't think that *teaching him* was from his point of view the most important form of caring, he denied it: 'When teachers care too much for the truth, they become inhuman. I'd even prefer Professor X, who, unlike Hannah Arendt, has a mediocre mind, but who really cares about his students and makes them care for him, to Professor Y, who will trample everyone in his way as he struggles to get at the truth. The university is really cheating me out of my tuition if it makes a God out of truth. Truth simply is not an end in itself—it is a means to the end of developing people.' And then he went on to say that he thought it his own duty as a teaching assistant to shock his freshmen into changing their lives, not to teach them simply how to be effective in the world of ideas.

And so he and others called for a loving community of the saved, living together in spiritual equality, like primitive Christians. In such a community, what could be more inappropriate than grades—can we grade anyone's soul? And why should we make false distinctions between faculty members and students? In the kingdom of love, it is 'one man, one vote.' What is wrong with the kingdom of intellect, in contrast, is that it presupposes distinctions between wisdom and foolishness, between knowledge and ignorance, and finally between teachers and learners.

But if such distinctions violated love, they even more obviously vio-

---

2. For a fuller discussion of "The College as Church," see my *Now Don't Try to Reason with Me* (Chicago, 1970), chapter 12.

lated the principles of egalitarian democracy. And since most faculty and students had lost their faith in government and political parties as embodiments of their highest political aspirations, it was natural to demand that the university and college become the last, best manifestation of democratic political ideals. Of course in practice this meant that the university was viewed as a kind of state or city, to be manipulated or used for particular political ends. Professors were found demonstrating against a major university because it banked its money at a bank that loaned money to a wicked country. Other professors were found leading demonstrations demanding that the university ban certain persons from the campus. One advanced graduate student in one of the traditionally liberal disciplines, when reproached for violating the right of free entry to the campus, said, 'Let's not have any of that civil rights bullshit!' Of course he felt very moral as he said it, because he was speaking on behalf of participatory democracy, and participatory democracy was obviously a very good thing. It's true that the motives for seeking egalitarian universities were not always quite this pure. One spokesman for what in those days was called the 'New Left' was quoted as saying that if you're traveling on the *Titanic*, there's no point in going steerage. But liberal education was not killed by such grubby, envious motives; had there been anyone around to defend it, such attacks would have meant little, but too many of those who might have been defenders had gone whoring after other Gods.

Thirdly, it was natural, when civil society found itself no longer able to support a genuine shared cultural life (except for sporadic outbursts like the Beatles phenomenon), it was natural, I say, to ask the universities to become patrons of the arts, sponsoring every good thing, because every good thing would die if it was not sponsored by the university. Theatre, modern dance, contemporary music, architecture, cinema—older societies found private or governmental means to fulfill their ends in these arts. But the universities found themselves with orphan after orphan dumped on their doorsteps—and who could be so cruel as to let the orphans die?

And speaking of orphans, social services were increasingly left to the universities. With the local, national, and state governments no longer able to solve social problems, what more natural than to ask the universities and colleges to cure all social ills? When universities found themselves spending more money annually on their brand new departments of urban studies than they spent on required courses in liberal education, the end was in sight. A few shrewd educators, seeing into the future, transferred from college positions to departments like urban studies, and labored subversively in them, teaching students how to think freely, using urban problems as subject matter. This worked for a while, until the free thought got in the way of the doctrines of the urban planners; then of course the practical demands won out.

So the process was clear and inevitable: asked to become church, political savior, patron of the arts, and social worker, college after college simply forgot what it might once have been to be thinker and teacher of thinkers. The university should relate to society in one or more of these ways, everyone came to say, without even having to think twice about it; the truth was so obvious that soon no one remembered that before two things can really relate, they must really be two things, different from each other. If a university is just an extension of society, without a unique and essential role of its own, it cannot relate to society; it *is* society.

By 1984[3] no one was left to state such counter-truths, and nobody felt compelled, consequently, to attack the ivory tower. But a decade or so earlier there were still a few traditionalists saying that universities were, or ought to be, somehow distinct and unique, and consequently young folks could still feel quite self-righteous and courageous in attacking what one of them called "the Complacencies of the Academy: 1967." I shall quote from his article, which was printed in the first issue of what pretended to be a new and radical journal, the *New American Review*. Pleading for the obvious virtue of courageous outspokenness on public issues, the author, Professor Roszak, after some rather feeble ironies about the failure of academic education to ennoble those who imbibe it, made four comparisons:

> Let us suppose, then, that an instructor in American history takes an active part in organizing a thoughtful, well-conceived campaign against capital punishment in his state. He musters the students to the cause and succeeds in engaging public officials and people generally in a searching debate of crime and punishment. Has he not made a more genuine *intellectual* contribution than if he had written a definitive study on the decline of cotton factorage in the American South for the period of 1865–1894?
>
> Or, again, suppose that a psychology instructor, feeling that the politics of his community has gone slack, undertakes to run for Congress, with an eye to stimulating serious public discussion of pressing local problems. His campaign is responsible from start to finish, and he forces his opposing candidates to take clear-cut stands they would otherwise have avoided like the plague. How shall we assess the man's *intellectual* behavior? Is it more or less valuable than an exhaustive study of olfaction in the unrestrained rat?
>
> Suppose an English instructor devotes a large amount of his time to organizing "freedom schools" in the slums and conducting a creative writing workshop there. Should we, [not] for purposes of promotion and ten-

3. Remember: I was speaking in 1968.

ure, count his *intellectual* efforts as highly as if he had produced a critical study of Golding's translation of Ovid's *Metamorphoses?*

Suppose an anthropology instructor busies himself organizing a teach-in on the Vietnam War. Perhaps he even travels to Vietnam for the Inter-Universities Committee and then writes a solid analysis of the effects of the war on the rural population for the *Atlantic Monthly* or *The New Republic.* Is his work worth more or less—*intellectually* speaking—than a study of unity and diversity in the celebration of cattle curing rites in a north Indian village?[4]

Now we can leave aside the obvious point that Roszak clearly thinks that the academic studies he describes are trivial or contemptible. We can also forgive him for not knowing that each of the studies he pooh-poohs turned out during the next three decades to have unpredictable practical consequences (we all remember how important Blitz's study of the olfaction of unrestrained rats turned out to be in making possible the survival of the human race during the Great Smog of '88). Leaving all this aside, what kind of mind do we see revealed here, and what conception of the operations of mind? Are these supposed to be *arguments?* How is one to judge the worth of "a solid analysis of the effects of the war on the rural population for the *Atlantic Monthly* or *The New Republic"*—except that we are told that it is "solid," which must make us all very happy? The organizing of 'freedom schools' in the slums and the conducting of a creative writing workshop there would obviously be achievements of the highest order, if anyone ever succeeded in doing them well, and they are achievements that would obviously require a good mind. But to place them in competition with writing a critical study, even if Roszak had played fair and referred to *significant* research, is entirely misleading. The world did not need one or the other kind of activity: it needed both, but it did not get both, because it pretended that they are achievements of the same kind.

Roszak went on to make quite explicit his notion that "thinking" and "acting" are not separate, since analysis and discussion are political *acts,* and "to think, to speak, to teach, to write: all these are forms of doing" and are thus "indispensable parts of the political process." And since this is so, the value of a man's political actions, especially if they are in the "dramatic form of civil disobedience," should be taken into account when promotion comes. In 1967, mark you, Mr. Roszak complained that "the barest handful of schools in America took 'citizenly conduct' into account

4. Theodore Roszak, "The Complacencies of the Academy: 1967," *New American Review* 1 (1967): 103. Revised and reprinted in *The Dissenting Academy* (New York, 1968).

when making professional decisions." But we are now in a position to see how quickly that situation was reversed. Having been taught by Roszak and others that "citizenly conduct" was equivalent to intellectual achievement in the academy, universities and colleges were soon hiring and firing according to the instructor's social value. At progressive institutions, faculty committees found themselves trying to decide between Smith's creative organization of protest demonstrations, Jones's good teaching, and Brown's good book. At conservative institutions, committees of course fired Smith for leading demonstrations, but they had a hard time weighing Doe's good work for the John Birch Society against his study of Emerson. Incidentally, my research has not been able to uncover what form of reward was given to the professor who helped to organize the creative demonstration reported in a newspaper article carrying the headline "BURN COMMUNISM," PITTSBURGH STUDENTS URGE DURING RALLY:

> Pittsburgh, January 26 [1968] (AP)—Two hundred chanting, flag-waving students, most of them of draft age, marched through downtown Pittsburgh today in support of war.
>
> "Burn Communism, Not Draft Cards," "Smash Korea," and "U.S.A. Is No. 1," read some of the placards.
>
> Two coeds carried a sign that said, "If the Boys Won't Go, We Will."
>
> One of the girls, Juanita McCool, 18 years old, said her husband was leaving for the Army next month.
>
> The snake-like procession stopped in the plaza at the Federal Building. Four students dressed like the figures in the painting "The Spirit of '76" led the cheers.
>
> "All the way with the U.S.A," the students shouted.
>
> The students attend the Educational Institute of Pittsburgh, a downtown business school.

Ah, yes, one sighs, those wicked graduate schools that failed to recognize the need to make teaching relevant to the modern world and its needs. We can see now that they were, in fact, the last and strongest bastions against the loss of one of our great values: the cultivation of intellectual power as a good thing in itself. Though all of the colleges had, by 1984, ceased to teach any subject except as it could be proved useful, a few graduate schools went on believing in knowledge and the pursuit of knowledge and mental excellence as self-justifying goods until—well, until the end. By 1984, in other words, every college student in every minute of the day was engaging either in public service, in political activity, in industrial work projects, or in that minimal amount of study necessary to get into graduate school. But it was not until 2000, this very year, that the last graduate department officially gave up the ghost.

That school was not, as people in mid-century would have predicted, the art department, or the music department, or the English department, or the philosophy department: these had long before declared disinterested curiosity out of bounds. No, the last bit of free curiosity pursuing its own ends was located in the business school, where a group of professors got together once a week to discuss a variety of theories about why no student had been heard laughing for at least two years. They all got very excited by their theories and they neglected 'their own research' terribly as they conducted their studies of what had happened. Finally one man hypothecated that the students were joyless because they were no longer curious, and then somebody suddenly noticed that nobody teaches curiosity any more, and yet curiosity is surely one of the things that modern businesses most want—and why don't we have any courses in curiosity? So they voted a proposal to the business school faculty for a program of six courses in Curiosity—Curiosity 101, 102, 103, 111, 112, 113. Everybody thought it was a very good idea, because certainly all graduates of business schools should be curious, and curiosity was finally enshrined, perhaps forever, in six dull courses at Gradgrind University.

But I have no heart to continue. Why should I continue? With everyone leading useful, happy lives, how can I hope to interest anyone in the death of a value—especially a value the usefulness of which can never be demonstrated to anyone who is not already convinced of that value. How could I hope to persuade anyone, now, that it is a good thing to be curious and to have curiosity satisfied and to learn how to do a good job of satisfying curiosity, and especially of satisfying that supreme curiosity about what curiosities are most worth satisfying? It used to be said that it was natural for human beings to want to learn. We have now proved that civilization can overpower such a seemingly natural urge, that the most luxurious of all societies can get along without the luxury of liberal learning. Everyone, as I said at the beginning, is very happy about our successes. There are no educational problems when every high school knows that its task is to prepare for college entry, when every college knows that its task is to prepare for graduate school, when every graduate school knows that its task is to prepare the nation's human resources for industry and government and consumerism, when every researcher is pushing for results and for publication whether there are any real results or not, when every teacher is willing to doctor the truth in order to give the students what they want to learn, when every student has learned to parrot what the charismatic teacher says.

I am told that last week, at my own university, from which I retired in 1992, the students *voted in* a new Ph.D. program in Feelie Science. Some of the older professors of subjects like Video Science, Cinematographic Chaos, Creative Collage, Controlled Hallucinogenetrics, Hermeneutalismics of Happenings, and Entertainment Journalism opposed the program on the ground that the feelies as an art form did not yet have enough popular support to justify a whole Ph.D. program in Feelie Science; they thought that the M.A. went far enough. Besides, there was only one slot left open in the computerized time table of Ph.D. programs—the program in Free Logic and Loose Analogies, and the professors in those subjects were strong in defending these traditional disciplines. But the day was lost when it came out that nobody, not even the professors themselves, could explain what logic was or how analogies work. The Committee on Liberal Education recommended that there could be no education truly worthy of the name 'liberal' if it could not *freely* accommodate the new disciplines as they came along, and the vote was assured.

As for myself . . .

Professor Zukunft's manuscript and MANIAC's printout end here, leaving me terribly puzzled, not to say curious. *Why*, if Zukunft is so hot on totally disinterested, non-practical curiosity, why should he want to communicate with anyone else about it? Shouldn't his idle curiosity have been enough, in itself?

OCCASION 10 · *To About Six Hundred Freshmen, in Orientation Week*

What's Supposed To Be Going On Here?

I

When I was asked to speak tonight, I accepted because I wanted to say that what goes on at Chicago, or what is supposed to go on, is the development of an important kind of freedom. That was nearly two-and-a-half months ago, but since that time I've found that everywhere I turn, somebody or other is claiming to offer freedom. I turned on the car radio as my family and I were driving through the western mountains, and I heard a voice from Texas saying, "Now folks, if you want our pamphlet showing how Communist influence in the government is every day taking away more of your freedom, just send twenty-five cents to Freedom School, Box 882, Dallas." A few moments later I saw a bumper sticker that read, "Scientology, the Key to All Freedom." During the summer I must have heard about ten different rock records hailing ten different brands of freedom.

Another complication in my plan to offer education as the road to freedom came when I went to a conference and met the president of a small western university. I knew that he had a Ph.D.—it turned out to be in computer technology—and he let us know very early that he had been given three—not one, not two, but three—honorary degrees. The conference was on what all conferences are on these days, how to keep our doors open by responding to or dealing with or refusing to deal with student protest. Such conferences are usually boring enough at best, but this one was really ruined by the uneducated behavior of this degree-toting ignoramus. I won't take time to describe all of the intellectual and personal faults he committed, but it really was pathetic to see how he lumped all students together as agitators—filthy ones, at that—and then treated them simply as obstacles in the way of his plans for the growth of *his* university. A composite of his remarks during three days would go something like this:

Well, now, I think the American people have just about had all they'll take of our shilly-shallying in the face of violence and protest and dissent.

From the annual "Aims of Education" address to beginning students in the College, University of Chicago, September 1970.

What I have told my faculty is that the future of our university depends on our showing the public that we have some standards. All over the country the universities have become visible symbols of the *lack* of standards, and every time some long-haired hippie comes along and shouts "Gimme this," the faculties climb all over themselves hurrying to give what is asked. It's crazy, plain crazy, to scurry around, for example, to find more black faces just because students say you should, and we're holding the line on that one. It's just as crazy to let behavior on campus be set by students, and we've now got a code that you ought to take a good look at: it covers beards and sloppiness, it covers love-making on the lawns, if covers alcohol and loud hi-fi's and sex in the dorms. We have an arrangement publicly announced—we believe in being absolutely fair and above-board—we have an arrangement with the FBI that anybody caught with marijuana on our campus will be turned over to them to deal with. What I tell my faculty is, that with a little more attention in advance to these problems we could have them licked; I'm thinking of admissions, especially. You can tell the potential troublemakers, most of the time, just by looking at their pictures; though it's true that some of them dress up for the photos, you can usually tell by the look in their eyes. And the folders give little hints that any half-bright admissions officer should be able to spot. We just don't have to put up with this stuff, and I think we can't put up with it if we expect to maintain first-class educational institutions where teachers and students have freedom to live decent, respectable, scholarly lives together.

In one of the coffee breaks, I asked this free brother what sort of reading he'd been doing lately. For the first time he looked a bit embarrassed. "Well, ah, you know what a president's life is like. I don't get much time for reading these days except for the memoes that come crawling across my desk. Ha, ha." But then he brightened. "I do make it a point to read *Time* magazine every week and the *Reader's Digest* every month; a man has to keep up on things."

Since he was very clear about what we should do in Viet Nam—go in and win and then get out, none of this shilly-shallying—I asked him what he had read about Viet Nam. "What's there to read?" he asked. "You know without reading that you don't win a war by sitting on your hands."

Well, here was a man who had undergone at least twenty years of formal schooling, who was responsible for the education of three thousand students each year, and who, so far as I could discover in three days, was totally unable to think for himself, totally unwilling to make the intellectual effort that might free him from the stereotypes and clichés that his society poured into his flabby receptacle of a mind.

173

How could this happen? Could it happen to you? [Long silent pause]

My guess is that something like it just now happened to at least some of you. How do you feel about that college president? A pretty hateful guy, isn't he? Or he would be, *if* he existed. [Another silent pause, then giggles and groans.]

I won't ask for a show of hands, but I wonder how many of you were willing to accept a phony story like that as a true one? How many of you reacted uncritically, unthinkingly, to my imaginary portrait, as I laced into it the symbols I could expect you to detest automatically? And how many of you made the mistake of thinking that *I* must be a good guy since I was attacking such an obviously bad guy? About the only thing I left out were my fictional villain's opinions about literature and music, but it would have been easy to make him even more hateful by having him lace in appropriate attacks on Mahler or Dylan or Aretha, or on Hesse's *Siddhartha* or Heller's *Catch-22*.

Some of you, on the other hand, resisted; some few of you have learned how to resist public speakers, and you said to yourselves something like, "What's this phony up there trying to do, wearing that beard and turtle-neck and spouting those clichés? Why *is* he wearing that trimmed beard and no necktie anyway? Is he describing that scapegoat president merely to make himself look good by comparison? And when is he going to stop the softening up and start *saying* something? The fact that he attacks a caricatured hawk doesn't prove that *he's* trustworthy."

Some of you may even have learned to think so critically that you were able to decide that everything I said was false. [Pause.]

I'm sorry to say that some of you are by now cheating. You naturally want to think yourselves clever, you want to join the precious critical few, and you have begun to send your actual previous responses to this talk down the memory chute. By the time you've left the hall, you'll be talking about all those other gulls from the sticks who were taken in, but you, being a person of high critical intelligence, were *not* taken in; you were free to think for yourself, unlike those slobs who did not have the advantage of going to the kind of first-class school *you* were educated in.

At this point in my manuscript, I had another tricky turn, but I don't have the heart, or the guts, to take it. What it says here—just so you know what I almost did to you—is this: "Well, now I've got news for *you*: my story was really true, there really was a conference, I really did listen to that awful college president and he really said all those terrible things. And I really am a good guy because I recognize that all those things he said are terrible. Do you believe me?"

Well, now, my friends, we approach the end of the introduction to this year's "Aims of Education" speech, delivered by a good guy to this year's crop of well-educated freshmen. The point of the introduction, as you may have guessed, is to leave you folks a little less sure of your automatic judgments than you were: if at any moment so far you have felt any more than about five-percent confident either in accepting or rejecting *anything* that I have said (including this) you have surrendered your intellectual freedom too easily, on the basis of inadequate evidence. You are like Laetitia Snap, the heroine of Fielding's *Jonathan Wild the Great.* Wild would most surely have ravished Laetitia, says the narrator, had not her "ready compliance" forestalled him. As men and women of great compliance, you have not behaved as free men and women ought to behave; rather, you have behaved as most of us behave most of the time, slaves to our prejudices and emotions and impressions of the moment, prisoners of our stereotypes—the automatic response mechanisms programmed by our past to respond in easily predictable ways.

Last year at the annual conference of the United Nations Student Association, in Liverpool, a mimeographed sheet was distributed to all conferees. You were given copies of it as you entered tonight.

BACKGROUND PAPER ON THE SITUATION IN THE ARGENTINE

Recent material has just become available about the disturbing situation in the Jujuy province of the Argentine, where local Indians and poor whites have been engaged in an exhausting struggle against Argentine oppression. The Jujuy province is a high altitude area (12000 feet at places), with tiny villages huddled at mountain feet. The Jujuy people's struggle dates from 1968 when their subsistence-oriented life was broken by the discovery of rich tin deposits in local veins on the Bolivian border. An American survey, financed by South African–Jewish millionaire Avram Globstein led to the formation of the New York–based Jujuy Tin Development Corporation, a large holding company which is believed to embrace C.I.A. interests. The mining operations have been started, using the displaced local farmers, at wage levels which amount to slave labour.

The son of a local tradesman, Stefano Camille de Yavi, is believed to have been the founder of the rapidly growing Jujuy Accion Movimento (J.A.M.), which may well have gathered the remnants of Che's ill-fated band after their leader's decease in Bolivia. The movement was at first dedicated to the cause of peaceful protest but their early badly-organized strikes among the tin-miners were savagely repressed by troops, sent directly from Buenos Aires for the purpose. Since then the movement has realized that only an armed struggle has any relevance in a revolutionary situation. Their arms are mainly stolen from the ill-trained and rebellious Argentine troops, whose morale is sagging due to the climate, poor living conditions and bad feet.

Conditions in the province have vastly deteriorated since the intervention of the troops to protect American influence. Troops are themselves reduced to stealing food from the under-nourished local population. The sacreligious [sic] and hostile soldiers have committed many well-documented atrocities, offending the well-being and religious sensibilities of the Jujuy people. For instance, no longer are the Jujuy headmen allowed to boil their pots over a naked flame, an essential part of the ancient Jujuy ritual, because of the danger of fire in surrounding scrubland. Anything which interferes with the tin-mining operations is strictly controlled by vicious Argentine vigilantes, supplied with spiked clubs and steel helmets by the Jujuy Tin Development Company.

Stefano Camillo de Yavi was himself shot after being accused of consorting with the wife of the local army commander but a new leader has arisen in the person of Enrique Halatoso, a leader with years of experience in the Bolivian campaign.

The military junta of the Argentine announced in La Nacion, "this is only a minor insurrection by illiterate Indians, provoked by foreign agitators." Information about the situation is very limited. Indonesian observers, invited by local chieftains, brought the difficulties of the Jujuy to the attention of "Le Rouque," France's equivalent of Black Dwarf. Since then articles [have appeared] in various Latin American publications, some translated into German.

Meanwhile shares in the Jujuy Tin Development Corporation have risen on Wall Street by $6.59 in a recent 3-week period, no doubt at the expense of more Jujuy lives.

After the conferees had had a chance to read the sheet, a resolution was passed supporting "in particular with critical sympathy of their situation, the Jujuy Accion Movimento of the Argentine." Then the new student president announced that the delegates, who thought of themselves as the cream of British intelligence, the most highly selective student group in the world, had voted to support a non-existent movement, protesting a non-existent corporation. The paper is a hoax from beginning to end; about the only thing true in it is that there is a Jujuy province of the Argentine. The report I got did not say whether the new student president, responsible for showing up his electorate as uneducated men and women, was lynched by them or not.

But now I have a confession to make. I first reported this episode in a speech at the University of Sussex, and what I said then was, "The whole thing is a hoax. There is no Jujuy tribe. . . ." And then, after the speech, I *thought* a bit, and I looked it up, and there *is* a Jujuy tribe. My own prejudiced desire to make the anecdote reflect as powerfully as possible against the uncritical students had led me into the very fault I was condemning. Things get complicated, don't they?

So far, then, I'm simply reminding you of an ancient truth: most of us most of the time are easily manipulated by other people and are to that extent not free.[1] Every advertising executive and campaign manager knows and uses what I'm talking about, though most of them are not quite as blatant about it as Mr. Thomas Bertsche, described as "one of the country's rising geniuses in the field of political advertising and image-making," who recently said the following about his role in the campaign to defeat Adlai Stevenson:

> When this campaign is over, people are going to believe that Adlai Stevenson stands for what *we* say he stands for, not what *he* says he stands for. And I don't think our interpretations of his positions are necessarily inaccurate. They're just paraphrased and interpreted to suit our particular needs. But every ad will be based on research and solid fact.[2]

We like to think that it is the other fellow who is vulnerable to Bertsche's kind of dishonest manipulation and to other forms of automatic triggering devices. But in fact we *all* are, except when we happen to know how to avoid it and happen to remember to bring our knowledge into play. My argument tonight is that it is the chief business of education to make such happenings—such moments of freedom—somewhat more frequent, not just in politics but in all aspects of life.

II

Liberal education was originally called "liberal" because it was supposed to liberate men to apply their minds, their critical thinking, to the most important decisions of their lives; how to act, who or what to love, what to call good or true or beautiful. We all know, of course, that much that traveled under the name of liberal education did not in fact liberate, because it was not in fact a removal of ignorance but an indoctrination with new forms of ignorance; or because the ignorance it removed was trivial, and the knowledge substituted was not of how to use critical intelligence but of how to use a collection of information, more or less inaccurate, for social climbing. But

---

1. This bit of exaggeration, perhaps typical of liberal rhetoric in mid-century, now seems to me at best a dangerous half-truth. If every moment of surrender to the influence of others is a sign of our slavery, we are all helpless slaves from birth. My emphasis in 1970 on "education for freedom *from other people*" can be justified, perhaps, as a warning to those would-be free spirits that left-wing appeals to freedom can impose their own bonds. But it should be read in the light both of what I said later in this speech about "renovation" of old ideas and of my repeated argument about how we make selves only by taking in other selves. See my *The Company We Keep: An Ethics of Fiction* (Berkeley, 1988), chapters 8 and 9.

2. *Chicago Daily News*, September 19, 1970, 12.

these perversions do not destroy the value of the genuine article: in the great educational philosophers, from Plato and Aristotle through Newman and John Dewey to whoever is your favorite of today, we discover a kind of perennial philosophy of liberating education. They all say that only in knowledge, only in the right kind of knowledge, can we liberate ourselves to make free choices. Without knowledge we may have the illusion of free choice; we may embrace political programs and schools of art and world views with as much passion *as if* we knew what we were doing, but our seeming choices are really what other people have imposed upon us.

Now if you're listening to me critically—and I hope you are—you will already be troubled with a lot of questions. Some of you will be wondering whether I'm against spontaneity. Some will be worried about the possible selfishness of cultivating free minds while the world burns (what *use* is freedom?). Some will want to ask whether I'm not just delivering a disguised bit of brainwashing, trying to *impose* an institutional doctrine to protect you from the educational efforts of SDS or the Black Panthers or whomever. I like to think that I have answers to such questions—every speaker would like to think he could answer *all* questions—and I hope some of your objections will be met as I go along. Keep them in mind, in any case, so that we can then discuss them later on, and let me try for the moment to explain this notion of mental freedom, a notion which is not original with me by any means but which is different from much of what gets said these days.

There are many ways of talking about the arts of liberal education, the arts that genuinely liberate. At the risk of being gimmicky, I'd like to suggest a way of reviving that tired old list, the "three R's." Reading, 'riting and 'rithmetic made up a highly simplified, minimal list of the arts of liberation: to be able to read is to be free to learn what other men know; to be able to write is to be free to teach or move or change other men with your words; and to be able to calculate is to be freed from enslavement to other men's calculations. Without scrapping arithmetic, which raises additional problems I can't go into, I'd like to expand the first two of these into four. The new list would have reading and writing mixed up in every one of the four, and it would run like this: first, the art of Recovery of meanings, the seemingly simple but never finally mastered ability to learn what other men have known or believed; second, the art of Rejection of whatever is false or enslaving in other men's meanings—what is often called critical thinking; third, the art of Renewing or (the thesaurus yields lots of "R's" here) Renovating or Recognizing or Re-presenting what is valid or worthwhile in other men's meanings; and finally the art of Revising or Revolutionizing thought by discovering genuinely new truth.[3]

3. Yes, I really uttered all of these *mens*, to an audience about half of whom were

Both critics and defenders of current education seem these days to be far more interested in the last of these four, revolutionary novelty, than any of the others. Under the names of "creativity," "originality," or novelty, educationists often talk as if a little institutional doctoring would make it possible for everyone to become intellectually revolutionary, thinking bold new thoughts that nobody else has ever dared to think. Well, maybe. Nobody knows precisely the limits of our creativity. All I can say is that genuinely new ideas seem to me terribly rare, and if it is the goal of education to produce them most of us seem to be doomed to perpetual second-class citizenship. Maybe I can dramatize what I mean by saying that so far as I know, there are no original ideas in this speech. It is true that the whole thing is brand spanking new in one sense: my various sub-points under the theme of education for freedom have never been put together in quite this shape before. But anyone who has the slightest acquaintance with the history of thought will find all of my ideas expressed by many before me, often expressed in better form than I can manage. So I'm going to leave genuine revision or revolutions of thought to one side for awhile, and concentrate briefly on the three R's that to me are more important to liberal education: more important, first, because they must be mastered before creativity has a chance, and more important, second, because they are available, in some degree, to every student who is willing to seek them out, regardless of his past educational experience. If I offered to teach you how to be a genuine intellectual revolutionary, I would be a fraud, because I don't know how it is done (believe me, if I *did* know, the world would be paying more attention to me than I seem to be able to get it to). But I *can* look you in the eye tonight and promise you that here at Chicago, in classes or on your own in the library or in conversation, you can learn how to free yourselves, maybe a little, maybe a lot, never totally, but enough to make a difference—to free yourself by working on the arts of recovery, rejection, and renovation. In the process you will not necessarily make yourselves happy; the liberal arts will not save you from disease and death, or from anxious pride and personal anxieties and the suffering that all human beings seem to inflict on each other. But they might save you—could save *all* of you, and almost certainly will save *some* of you—from the special forms of slavery that only these arts can remove. Nobody can force you to become educated, nobody can even convince you in advance that to become educated is worth doing. But the curious fact is that most of you do not need to be convinced; you already want this mysterious thing. The big problem is how to go about getting it.

---

women! And I heard no protesting groans, then or later. If you feel unbearable pain here, please turn to Occasion 11, and then perhaps come back later.

III

The first step toward this elusive kind of freedom is learning how to recover other people's meanings and thus make available to oneself what others have already learned. You and I were born as ignorant as the most ignorant newborn baby in the most primitive corner in the most backward moment in man's history. We were born ignorant provincials in time and space. But we were thrust immediately into a world buzzing with knowledge (and with misinformation disguised as knowledge). We must either learn to recover what is really known or be doomed to drift through seas of confusion.

There is no reason to think that a modern college is the only place, or even the best place, in which to earn this freedom. For some people a job as a newspaper reporter would be better, and for some others prisons are better places. I know of no more moving account of how freedom comes to a man when he learns how to recover meanings for himself, how really to listen to what is there on the page, than Malcolm X's story of his prison reading.

If you haven't read his *Autobiography*, you ought to, and you ought to pay special attention to chapter 11, which he calls "Saved."

First, he says, talking of how learning saved him, he literally re-copied every word and definition in the prison dictionary, determined to master the world of words. Think of that, ye innovators. *There's* innovation for you, and interdisciplinary at that!

And suddenly, he says,

> for the first time [I could] pick up a book and read and *now begin to under-stand what the book was saying*. Anyone who has read a great deal can imagine the new world that opened. Let me tell you something: from then until I left that prison, in every free moment I had, if I was not reading in the library, I was reading on my bunk. You couldn't have gotten me out of books with a wedge. . . . Months passed *without my even thinking about being imprisoned. In fact, up to then, I never had been so truly free in my life*. . . . No university would ask any student to devour literature as I did when this new world opened to me, of being able to read and *under-stand*. . . . I have often reflected upon the new vistas that reading opened to me. I knew right there in prison that reading had changed forever the course of my life. As I see it today, the ability to read awoke inside me *some long dormant craving to be mentally alive*. . . . My homemade edu-cation gave me, with every additional book that I read, a little bit more sensitivity to the deafness, dumbness, and blindness that was afflicting the black race in America. Not long ago, an English writer telephoned me from London, asking questions. One was, "What's your alma mater?" I told him, "Books." You will never catch me with a free fifteen minutes in which I'm not studying something I feel might be able to help the black

man. . . . Where else but in a prison could *I have attacked my ignorance* by being able to study intensely sometimes as much as fifteen hours a day. [Except for the word *understand,* italics are mine.][4]

Even in this isolated quotation we can sense the miracle of freeing that has occurred. Every time I read that chapter I feel that there in that strange moment of human history, there in those seemingly binding circumstances, lies the full wonder of what education ought to be about: "I had never *been so truly free in my life.*" Malcolm Little, freed to become Malcolm X, still had a lot of mental chains upon him, as he himself says; we all do. But he had begun to learn the *ways* of freeing, and he went on to new and surprising freedoms throughout the rest of his short life.

It is important to look closely at what really happened in that first moment. The curious thing is that Malcolm X in fact already knew how to read, in the usual sense, long before he went to prison. In chapter 2 we learn that in seventh grade he was at the top of his class. As a thirteen-year-old boy he could, it is clear, read and write far beyond the average of his age group. But what happened later in prison, as his own emphasis shows, is that he suddenly became "able to read and *understand.*" What the words before him were really saying became for the first time available to him, and he "*attacked his ignorance*" and became freer than ever before in his life.

Unfortunately, freedom to recover meanings, freedom to understand, is not as simple as my account so far would suggest. As Malcolm X would have been the first to admit, there is understanding and understanding, and there is a tremendous problem, even for highly literate folk, of deciding what meanings are worth understanding. Even that voracious and highly intelligent prisoner sneaking his gulps of learning behind the backs of the patrolling guards far into the night could not cover more than a fraction of the books that are worth reading. Our library here contains more than two million volumes, every one of them thought by somebody—if only its own author—to be worth reading. Even the speed readers among you, reading an average of a book a day for four years, will cover at best only around a thousand of those books, fewer than one two-thousandth of what is available: and meanwhile, during those four years, something like 150 thousand more books will have been published in America alone, scores of times more than you have read in the four years. Clearly nobody is free to recover knowledge in that quantity, and if anybody tried to he would soon crack up under the strain.

I am frequently told that your generation is "better educated" than any

4. *The Autobiography of Malcolm X,* edited by Alex Haley (New York, 1966), 172–73; 179–80.

previous generation, partly because you have picked up so much knowledge from TV. It may be true that you have recovered, in this sense, more information than your predecessors, though from what little I see on TV I would say that more of it is misinformation than not. Even if our minds are filled with information, we could still be totally enslaved in the sense I'm talking about (and that Malcolm X was in part talking about), unless we had mastered that very different kind of knowledge—the knowledge of how to reconstruct what other people really mean by what they say or write. And *that* includes the knowledge of how to guard against one's temptations to misunderstand. It sounds simple, but it is one of the most difficult arts in the world—the art of recovering what other people mean and not what we'd like them to mean. It is an art that is not highly honored in the world around us: all the value is usually placed on reacting to meanings without discovering first what the meanings actually are. Our intellectual lives are for the most part lived about on the level of our TV watching: you can tell the good guys from the bad guys by simple symbols, and the heroes and villains shift from day to day without real thought. One day [Herbert] Marcuse is our hero (though don't ask how many have actually *read* him) and the next day he is attacked, still without really being read. It is all done with simple catchwords and slogans: Is he *for* the movement or *against* it? One day Paul Goodman is so besieged with invitations to campuses that he can't keep up; the next day (still without really being read or listened to) he is down and out, because he has accidentally pushed this or that button marked "Bad Guy."

And poor Goodman is left, in a recent poem called "The Young," lamenting

> When young proclaim Make Love Not War
> I back them up because it's better
> and some are brave as they can be,
> but they don't make love to me.
>
> He brought petunias to the Be-In
> and fed a lump of sugar to a policeman's horse,
> but me, he said, he didn't like my vibrations.
> For this I didn't need to trudge to Central Park.
>
> Sure I am heartened by my crazy allies
> and their long hair looks very nice on some,
> but frankly, more of them were interesting
> before they all began to do their thing.[5]

5. Paul Goodman, "The Young," *The Nation*, June 20, 1970, 794. Reprinted by permission of The Nation Company, Inc., copyright 1970.

If I am right, then, the chief threat to our intellectual freedom is not illiteracy, or censorship committees, or boards of trustees firing radical professors, or the heckling and shouting down of speakers without caring about what they have to say. Though all of these are bad, they are openly bad, as it were, and few of us are fooled into thinking that they are good. More threatening to you and me is the subtler mental violence that occurs when people who think they are listening with an open mind actually wrench complicated or new or unacceptable messages into simpler, ready-made categories of old ideas. The person who reacts passionately for or against what was not actually said or written is a slave to his own ignorance, no matter how gloriously free and spontaneous and righteous he feels as he reacts. Yet the shameful fact is that most of us most of the time reduce other folks' meanings to nonsense that we *can* reject. After all, if it's shit already, I don't have to try to digest it.

Jim Hoge, the editor of the *Sun Times*, told some of us freshmen last week that he often cannot recognize quotations attributed to him by other journals, particularly the weeklies. The fault of mis-hearing and mis-reading is indeed so common, among the so-called educated professors, journalists, and politicians, that it is difficult to find counter-examples, examples of the painstaking recovery of what the other person knows or claims to know. *You* think you are an exception, I'll warrant. But bright as you are, full of information as you are, clever as you are at checking the box marked "None of the above," quick as you are at deciding whether this or that item from the past is relevant to your lives, I would be very much surprised if there are three of you here who could read a dialogue of Plato or an essay by Hume and reconstruct what is said in a form that Plato or Hume would recognize. I look you in the eye, you marvelous promisers of future freedom, and say something even more insulting: I doubt that many of you could write a summary of a speech by President Nixon or Senator Fulbright that *he* would accept as a genuine recovery of his meanings. I have no doubt whatever that you could write colorful *criticisms* of what you *thought* he said, criticisms that would pass for relevant because they wouldn't miss the target any further than most of what gets printed these days. But you're not free to learn from Plato or Hume or Fulbright, or even Nixon, and therefore you are not free to accept or refute them, until you are free to find out who they really are.

Just to show you how serious I am in this arrogant little part of this arrogant little speech, I am going to make an offer: to any one of you first-year students who can write a summary of *this* speech, in 100 to 250 words, a summary that really reconstructs what *I* think I mean, I hereby offer twenty-five dollars, tax free. In case there is more than one more-or-less successful entry in the Booth Recovery-of-Meanings Prize Contest, twenty-five dollars will go to the best entry, and five dollars to each of the others. Just remember: all I want is a summary or précis, the kind of thing that English teachers used to ask for before they got up-to-date and began to ask students to do what they call "research." And all I ask is that I will be able to say, "Yes, that's what I really said."

Some of you at this point will be wanting to ask, "Who are *you* to judge?" "How can *you* be objective?" To which I reply, "Who else?" For the contest, it's *my* meanings we're after. Then we can move on to your refutations. If anyone insists, however, I'll be glad to appoint a review court, students of your choice. Anyway, don't be afraid that I'll be trying to protect my twenty-five bucks. I'm pathetically eager to be understood; I am praying for a winner this time, because I want to feel that I have not been talking into that great, garbling meaning-chopper that often seems to swallow all our meanings at one end and spew out nonsense at the other.[6]

Everyone who has ever been reported in the press, and especially in the weeklies, has felt the effects of the meaning-chopper. Norman Mailer, who almost always seems to me to misunderstand everyone else, is very good on the subject of how it feels himself to go through the meaning-chopper of the media: "The papers distorted one's actions, and that was painful enough, but they wrenched and garbled and twisted and broke one's words and sentences until a good author always sounds like an overcharged idiot in newsprint." Mailer sometimes makes the mistake of talking as if the meaning-chopper worked only out of malice—if people would only be friendly all would be well. But finally he recognizes the truth: "The average reporter [can]not get a sentence straight if it [is] phrased more subtly than his own mind. . . . "[7] In our terms, the "average reporter," whether a professional reporting for other readers, or simply you and I trying to record for our own future needs, is not free to recover meanings that are richer *than his own mind*. And the first goal of education is thus to prepare your minds for the free conversation with other minds that can only take place if you really know what those other minds are offering.

Unfortunately, this first freedom, freedom to understand, is even more complicated than my examples have suggested. Even experts, dealing calmly with issues that are not tied to survival or burdened with emotions or cluttered with business, often have trouble understanding each other. Philosophers always claim to be misunderstood by other philosophers. Hegel is said

6. To my surprise, there were three winners. The first prize went to a young man who wrote his summary in an excellently formed sonnet sequence!

7. Norman Mailer, *Armies of the Night* (New York, 1968), 80–81.

to have lamented on his deathbed: "There never was but one man who understood me—and even he did not understand me." The reviewer of scholarly books who can discover what the books attempt before damning or praising is a rare bird indeed. And of course none of us ever becomes free, in this sense, in very many subjects. I cannot, for example, recover the meanings of current papers in mathematics or atomic physics; even the popularized papers on these subjects in *Scientific American* frequently throw me. To this extent, I am unliberated in these subjects; the only freedom I can hope for is the freedom that comes from knowing my own ignorance. But this in itself is no mean thing, as Socrates taught the world. To know *when* you don't know and *what* you don't know is in fact probably the most important step in earning the first freedom, because unless you know that you are ignorant, you will not know that you are enslaved, and you will have no motive to "attack your ignorance."

IV

My second and third "R's" are Rejection, on the one hand, and Renewal or Renovation, on the other. I won't discuss them at length tonight, but just describe them briefly. It is obviously not enough just to feed back accurately and justly what the other speaker or writer meant. We must be able to sort out, distinguish the sound from the unsound, and then *re*-present old meanings in forms intelligible and useful in new situations. The freedom to reject falsehood and renew truth by transmitting it to others is in effect the freedom to exercise power over the world and over other men's minds, and it thus clearly includes (though it goes far beyond) what we mean when we talk about "learning how to speak and write."

There's a lot of talk in America these days about how we professorial ignoramuses have failed to teach you student ignoramuses how to write. Supervisors of Ph.D. dissertations blame college teachers, college teachers blame high school teachers, and the public blames us all. But most of the complaints I see from the public are trivial, concerned only with spelling and grammar. The real failure we ought to be concerned about is that hardly anybody seems to be concerned with writing in the sense of composition— com-posing in the sense of testing, with hard mental labor, whether ideas really fit together. The writer who matters to us is the one who has faced honestly what happens when ideas are recovered and set free in a free mind. What happens is that some of the ideas fit together and some do not. The complacent, uneducated mind does not worry when ideas do not fit. Such a mind can believe, or believe that it believes, both that all men are brothers, or children of the same divine father, and that a particular man, whose skin color is wrong, can be used as a machine convenient for economic purposes, thus ignoring his humanity and brotherhood. The mind struggling to free itself can't do that. It looks at the two ideas and they start nagging at him: "One of us two has gotta go." The uneducated mind can accommodate the belief that "the students must be put down" because they are all immature, dirty, paranoid revolutionaries with the knowledge that particular students—Jones, Kozol, and Grziack—are mature, clean, reasonable people, deeply devoted to their studies in a university of which they are proud. The uneducated mind will accept slogans like "students are the most exploited class in America today," even though it also knows that migrant workers and black workers have been immeasurably more exploited and have a right to be insulted by the comparison with affluent middle-class students. The mind struggling to free itself will never rest easy with such plain and living disharmonies of words with words and of words with deeds. It cannot believe that to napalm a village is to liberate it, that to destroy a country is to bring it a better way of life, or—on the other side of the political fence—that the misery or even death of this particular human being now standing innocently in my path does not matter, so long as it is required in order to build a beautiful revolution. From this point of view, the ultimate expression of the enslaved mind would be something like that of the fathers of the Inquisition, who could kill a man to save his own soul, or the California cultists, who are said to have killed in the name of liberating the victims. But most of us can find examples in our own ideas and practices of equally crude disharmonies.

Note that I am not saying that an educated man has no ideas that clash with other ideas. All of us struggle throughout our lives, until we die or die on our feet, with many incompatibles or seeming incompatibles. But it is the mark of an educated, free mind to struggle with its seeming incompatibles and to try to remove them without cheating. And it is one mark of anyone with this special kind of freedom that he has developed some skill in doing it: some capacity to take the various notions in his head, clarify them, sharpen them, reshuffle them in application to the manifold new situations that come thrusting at him from all directions. Such skills can of course be used in evil causes, and just as it is possible for an uneducated man to be a good man, it is quite possible for an educated man in this sense to be a bad man. But he will never be satisfied with the slavery of deceiving himself.

I don't have to remind you that what I am saying about rejection and renovation, old and tested as it is, conflicts with a great deal that we are told. Everywhere you look, in the press, in art and movies and novels and books and essays about where we are in this decade, you can find claims that the effort to reason about things in this sense is old-fashioned, irrelevant, or even downright destructive. The medium is the message; linear thought is passé. We are in a time of "electronic simultaneity," of "iconic vision." Don't try to sort out the various messages and think things through for yourself: let yourself go, sink blissfully into cosmic pools of illumination, and you will find truths beneath truths, mystical roads on which nonsense is sense, contradictions are harmonies, everything anyone says is equally beautiful and equally true. And if you need intellectual support for re-pudiating the intellectual endeavor and believing anything you damn please, why there is the Freudian tradition, teaching that ideas are simply super-structures for our deeper, and hence realer, psychological and sexual mo-tives; and there is the Marxian tradition, teaching that ideas are really only superstructures for historical and sociological motives that are deeper, and hence realer. Or there is the tradition of popular sayings, like "A foolish consistency is the bugbear of little minds." Or there are the Spirovian prophets [the reference is to Spiro Agnew, the already disgraceful Vice President, who was only later publicly disgraced] who address their stirring words to members of the silent and blissfully unthinking majority, telling them in effect not to worry about relating notions of right and wrong to U.S. actions abroad: that if there were "only" one-hundred Americans killed in Viet Nam this week—how I marvel at that "only"—things are getting better all the time; or that the evils of American life are caused by the "reds" and "radicals" who insist on pointing them out. Or there are the current anti-theorists of mindless activism: "Principles-Schminciples," a "Weatherman" wrote two years ago, when some of his SDS critics argued that deliberate and unprovoked violence contradicted certain clear principles of SDS. Or there is the philosophical tradition, promulgated by men who claim to be educated, telling you that the universe is itself proved to be ab-surd, and that true intellectual power comes from recognizing and surren-dering to its absurdity, not from trying to penetrate the fog and find islands of clarity. Or there is the message found in so much of contemporary fic-tion: not only the universe, but every institution in it is absurd. After all, all values are only relative anyway; even *Time* magazine teaches that these days, so it can hardly make sense to try to wrestle with seeming inconsis-tencies between value X and value Y.

When I consider the floods of mis-education of this kind that have bap-tized you daily since your birth on that unlikely (but of course star-studded) day back in 1951 or '52 or '53, I am almost surprised that you haven't lynched me by now for casting doubt on the true church of freedom-as-caprice. But of course nobody can ever be fully baptized into hopeless absurdity. We all come strangely equipped with Malcolm X's "dormant craving to be men-tally alive," a hunger for reasonableness that can seldom be totally repressed. We are, it is true, equipped with many other hungers that often overwhelm this one, and this kind of psychological disharmony has sometimes been used as evidence that disharmony is at the heart of things. But the fact is that we all have a natural resistance to contradictions, we all feel violated by them *once we see them clearly*. And if I am right, it is the main task of education to help us see our contradictions clearly and, more importantly, to teach the methods of bringing contradiction to the surface, of working out genuine harmonies, and of presenting the results persuasively to our fellow men.

There are many complications to be explored in all this, if only we had time. There is, first, the plain fact that if I spend too much time trying to get all my ideas clear before I act, I may never act, and while I cultivate my precious mind, the needed actions may not be performed by anyone. I can't pretend to a satisfactory solution to this problem, since I am often torn between the need to act *now* and the desire to think some more. But what I do know is that the conflict is not between simple and easily realizable impulses to act for good in the world and simple and selfish impulses to cultivate mental freedom. On the contrary, more harm is done in the world by well-intentioned and mindless action than by a failure to act. Arthur Koestler has argued that in fact the chief cause of man's suffering in all ages has been group-oriented altruism—that the man selflessly committed to a noble cause, acting—or so he thinks—for the good of his group, usually does more harm than good. Just as it is true that only the man who is free to love is of much use to those who need love, so it is true that only the man whose mind is free is of much use to his fellow men—in any task, but especially in the task of freeing their minds. Was Malcolm X being selfish when he spent his time mastering those books? In this, as in so many things, it turns out that true self-fulfillment yields the greatest possibility for true service.

There is, secondly, the complication that just as everything under the sun, including slavery, travels under the name of freedom, so does everything under the sun, including grossly inhumane and irrational behavior, travel under the name of reasonableness. And there is the third complication, that pleas like mine to educate free critical intelligence imply a radically misleading notion of independent, isolated thinking "atoms." Modern western civilization has contributed to perversions of "reason" by isolating an imaginary construct, the critical intelligence somehow belonging to an isolated individual ego. One of the main contradictions we moderns must wrestle with is between this fictional critical calculator of independent thoughts and the world of passion and feeling and shared values and traditions and collective inquiry that in fact creates what we call the "self" and makes it able to function in the first place. Much of the present youthful revolt against abstract rational calculation divorced from value is thus justified, and it would be a mistake to defend education of the critical intelligence without taking into account what we now know, or should know, about our "selves." In-dividuals simply cannot go it alone intellectually, as autonomous logical calculators, any more than they can go it alone morally and emotionally, ignoring the needs and promptings of their brothers and sisters.

And there is a fourth complication: How do we preserve ourselves, as we seek an education, from the influence of indoctrinators disguised as educators? (Am I an indoctrinator, for example, or have I been an educator tonight?) Everything I have said implies that there is a sharp difference between indoctrination and education: indoctrination enslaves us to the opinions of others, often by making us believe that we have thought for ourselves; education—if there really is such a thing—liberates us to recover and renovate ideas by making them our own. Even if this difference is, as I am claiming, real and fundamental, it will never be an easy one to recognize.

Each of these four complications deserves hours of discussion, but I think none of them invalidates my general claim: It is the main goal of education to liberate minds otherwise enslaved, by developing the skills, first, of recovering meanings, then, of rejecting the ones that do not hold up under a close look, and finally, of renovating, re-synthesizing those that do. About the fourth "R," the art of intellectual Revolution, I really have nothing to say; we must leave it to the geniuses.

Well, my time is up—and I've necessarily only scratched the surface. There are no doubt worst disasters than never learning to think. Never learning to love, never learning to enjoy laughter or music, never knowing friendship—these kinds of binding would seem to me even more tragic than never learning to think. But if anything is clear about recent experiments in anti-rational lifestyles, it is that even loving and laughing and friendship and making music can be poisoned by thoughtlessness. I suppose that "every man trusts his own consciousness-expanding devices," and I know that I am preaching to a generation that wants to believe that there is more education in a sunset than in Plato. But I hope I have shown that whatever crisis we face in education is made of our own fears, not of any real lack of value in our disciplines. To pretend that college education is an empty farce is to make it into an empty farce. But the age-old task of imparting the four arts of freedom is at least as important as it ever was, and it is as important as anything else in the world. Let's get on with it, all of us, celebrating the good fortune of living in a time when what we are doing here is not only allowed by our society but encouraged and rewarded by it. What could be a better gift than to be freed, for the next few years, to pursue the meaning of freedom together here?

OCCASION 11 · *To a Few Score*
Undergraduates Who Responded to
an Announcement of a Lecture on
"Liberal Education"

Is There Any Knowledge That a *Woman* Must Have?

About thirteen years ago, our College ran a Liberal Arts Conference, so-called. Incredible as it may seem to you, the College Council voted to suspend classes for two or three days, to allow for about a dozen big public lectures and scores of panels and discussion groups packed into a very tight schedule, centering on the topic "The Knowledge Most Worth Having." We were initially warned—those of us who thought the conference a good idea—that U. of C. undergraduates could not be tempted to attend so many weird and dubiously profitable events, and as the conference approached we found ourselves almost in panic, as delegations of concerned students arrived to warn that vast hordes of students were not even aware of the conference yet, let alone planning to attend. Several of us then went from dormitory to dormitory talking it up, gadflying about the questions the conference would deal with. We plastered the campus with enough advertising to carry the Chrysler Corporation through a bad year.

This is not the place to describe all that happened. But I must confess that the happiest moment I can remember as dean of the College was when I arrived at Breasted Hall to give the opening statement and introduce the first major speaker, fearing that "nobody would come," and found so many people that we had to walk over to Mandel, and filled it! The whole College, it seemed, had gathered to listen and think about what we're thinking about here today—the goals of liberal education.

As some of you know, I later revised and expanded my brief statement that opened the conference to make the opening essay in a little book that came out of the conference. I called the essay "Is There any Knowledge that a Man *Must* Have?" The piece ended up in the *Norton Anthology of Ex-*

Speech delivered to undergraduates of the University of Chicago at the invitation of the Liberal Arts Forum, December 1980.

positary Prose, and I began to get letters about it. At first the letters were friendly, but as the sixties turned into the seventies, there was a flood of letters (well, there *were* three) from women who were angered or shocked by what they took to be the male chauvinism not only in the title but in my use of "man" for humankind, and not only in the title but throughout the essay. I answered those letters as well as I could, on the assumption that obviously I was not guilty as charged. But I didn't get around to re-reading the essay until last week, when I sat down to prepare this talk.

What I found rather shocked *me*. The essay *is* male-chauvinist, at least to some degree. It is not only male-centered in the sense that the author is clearly a male seeing the world through masculine eyes. It is chauvinist also in the sense of failing to think about how its language would strike *female* readers, consciously or unconsciously. I ask you to remember, as a kind of self-defense, that it was written before the feminist critique of language and literature had got well under way. It was written by a man who had all his life attended and taught at co-educational schools. He thought of himself as considerably more enlightened on the subject of women than most men. He had contracted formally, when he married at the age of twenty-five, to be responsible for 50 percent of the housework and child-rearing—and that was in 1946, mind you! What's more, he believed, or said he believed, in equal careers for women and men. Needless to say, however, he had not lived up to the contract: the fifty pecent had shrunk, as the children came along and his professional commitments came to seem more and more important to him, to forty, then thirty, then perhaps twenty, with only brief bursts of one-hundred percent at times of illness, pregnancy, or uncharacteristic self-reproach. And of course the "equal careers" had quickly been thrown off balance, leaving Phyllis's "half" to wait, as we put it, until the children were in school.

Well, that flaming liberal, that youngish dean, talking about liberal education for all people, not only let himself ring a chime of scores of "man"'s and "men"'s where words like "people" or "students" or "human beings" would have done as well,[1] he let himself write a passage like this:

> The distinction between natural and man-made beauty might give me trouble if you pushed me on it here, but let me just say, dogmatically, that I would not be satisfied simply to know natural beauty—women and sunsets, say—as a substitute for art.

Now of course I did not mean even to hint at the notion that women, unlike men, are merely natural objects designed to serve as ornaments for a

---

1. Compare the similar language in Occasion 10. In Occasion 9 I have experimented with removing the sexist usage.

man's world. I can remember defending myself to one protesting woman by saying that my point was about people, and that it could just as well have been made about women admiring male beauty. But does the point really go as well the other way round?

Let's try it: "A woman should not be satisfied simply to know natural beauty—men and sunsets, say—as a substitute for art." It seems obvious that no woman would ever have thought of putting it that way, unless she were trying to make a dishonest buck writing for *Playgirl* or trying to make an ironic point about men. Yet that way seemed to me an acceptable way to write and talk.

Most of that essay, I'm glad to say, translates fairly easily when we switch sexes. In fact, I thought for a wild moment last week that I would try the experiment of simply delivering the same talk, with proper changes of nouns and pronouns, cleaned up like this:

> Second, the woman who has not learned how to make the great human achievements in the arts her own, who does not know what it means to earn a great novel or symphony or painting for herself, is enslaved either to caprice or to other women's testimony or to a life of ugliness. You will notice that as I turn thus to "beauty"—another old-fashioned term—I do not say that a woman must know how to prove what is beautiful. . . . Here we are asking that a woman be educated to the experience of beauty: speculation about it can then follow. My point is simply that a woman is less than a woman if she cannot respond to the art made by her fellow women.

Something's wrong, there. "By her fellows"? Not too good. "By other women?" That loses the force of community sought in that word "fellow."

Thus I discovered that I could not make an effective verbal translation. But even if I had been able to, the essay would still trouble me. I simply cannot stretch it, try as I will, to cover the ideas that occur when we ask the simple question that obviously never occurred to me at the time: "Is There any Knowledge that a *Woman* Must Have?" Or, to read it with the intonation that the original title was supposed to have, "Is There any Knowledge that a Woman *Must* Have?" If there is, we may decide that men will want it, too.

I'm going to dwell on that question for a while today, but I should hasten to make clear, first, that I am not taking a stand on the much-debated question of whether women are essentially different from men. My hunch is that, except for the anatomical consequences of the ancient dictum "Know Thyself," there is no essential difference in what men and women must know to be liberally educated—that is, there would be no essential difference *if* men and women found themselves in essentially similar circumstances in the world. But we all know that men and women do not find themselves in essentially similar circumstances. In our society, every woman's circumstances—her "surrounding positions," to translate that tired old word—are largely constructed by men, men who, even after some decades of consciousness-raising, have seldom even tried to imagine what treating women as equals might entail. We might, of course, try to imagine a utopian world in which those circumstances no longer existed, a world like Plato's imaginary one, in which men and women were treated exactly alike from birth and therefore experienced no different educational needs. But we do not live in that world, and our thinking about liberal education, an education that would in fact liberate, ought to have some connection with the world we all live in—from birth, through graduation, to death.

Women in our society need, then, to learn something that men don't need in quite the same way: how to cope with men, men who think of women largely in reductive metaphors labelled "woman" or "chick" or "broad" or "better half." One way of coping is, of course, to take on protective camouflage, to learn to think and act like a male. Some of you may be fearing that I shall now try to tell women what they need, instead of sitting back as I should and letting women tell *me* what they want. Well, like every other male academic, I do have some ideas about what women need, and I shall no doubt offer some of them before I'm through. But I hope that I'm a bit more sensitive to the ravages of egoism than I once was, and I'm more interested today in what a male can teach himself about liberal education, using the simple device of asking a simple question: What were you led to overlook because you failed to think about the special needs and problems of women in a male-dominated world?

So I'm going to dwell on the shortcomings of that original essay for a while, salvaging briefly what seems to me still valid in it, from the perspective of one whose eyes are slowly opening. Then I'll go on to add a bit about what it conspicuously ignores. We shall find, I'm sorry to say, that what it ignores runs far deeper than the simple failure to sprinkle in a few "she"'s or "her"'s.

II

My speculation about education, like almost everybody else's, began with a critique of other people's wrong ideas. The first two-thirds of the essay dismissed a passel of wrong-headed notions, starting with the widespread claim that we can't really *think* together about why some kinds of knowledge or pursuit of knowledge are superior to other kinds. With a passing shot at the conception of knowledge as mere information, I then gave a perfunctory refutation of the chief rival to my enterprise—the view that education should be controlled by social utility. In what seems to me now a misleading dichotomy between social utility and personal fulfillment, I took pot shots at a couple of easy targets, in order to leave the field clear for the question that really interested me then, and that still interests me now: "To be human, to be human, to be fully human. What does it mean? What is required? . . . Who—or what—is the creature we would educate?"

After six pages, I come at last to a section that I can still read without embarrassment. It classifies educational theories under four notions of human nature, three of them metaphorical, only one of them literal. Human beings, I argue, are not likely to be educated well if educators think of their charges as merely complicated machines, or rats, or ants. People are really people. I would now put my rejection of the three destructive metaphors differently, because I have discovered since then just how difficult it is to criticize a metaphorical view cogently enough to make those who hold it sit up and take notice. It seems obvious to me now that the few pages I devote to each metaphor work better as rhetoric addressed to the pre-converted than as rhetoric addressed to those who *think with* one or the other of the three metaphors. But it still seems to me true that genuine education, whether for men or women, is threatened by those who think of themselves as programming complex machines, by those who think of themselves as conditioning complicated animals, and by those who think of themselves as training units for an ant-like social utility.

So it is mainly the last third of the essay that leaves me squirming, the constructive third, the third that offers the knowledge that every . . . woman must have. What it offers to you women is the overwhelmingly original doctrine that to achieve your full status as human beings, you oughta just take good courses that teach you first how to think about what is true, second how to respond to what is beautiful, and third how to choose what is good.

Now obviously I'm not going to quarrel with such bromides today: they say nothing downright false. When I think, for example, of the education I would have wanted for my two daughters, I do not find myself having to discard anything that I said about what every man, meaning every man and woman, should have. I would still want to stress as strongly as I ever did the need for steady and sustained attention to the three domains I described: the speculative, the aesthetic, and the practical; or if you prefer, the domains of science and philosophy, of art, and of politics and ethics. I would feel about my daughters, as strongly as about my son, that they would be maimed in life—not just life in our time but life in any time of human history—if their natural curiosity about the truth of things were allowed to wither, or if they had no regular loving experience of the beautiful—that is, of those things in the world that are lovable for their own sake, without utilitarian qualification (and I would hope, incidentally, that they would not confine their appreciation to natural beauty—"men, say, or sunsets"). And I would hope to see them steadily growing in what Aristotle calls "practical wisdom"—able to make their way through the moral tangles of modern life with some sense of the difficulties, the excitement, and the sense of wellbeing ("happiness," "eudaimonia") to be derived from carving out a character for oneself, a character that can in turn to some degree master the choices life presents rather than being mastered by them.

But you see how general such talk is, and it was not much more precise in the developed speech. Instead of trying to cover the whole range once more, for the rest of my time today I'd like to concentrate on those matters that the young half-chauvinist either left undeveloped or didn't even mention. And instead of trying to think about the education every woman needs, in every age or clime, let's try to think about the education every woman needs in the 1980s.

To do that would seem to require us to describe what the world is like in 1980. If we are to educate ourselves to live in the eighties, we ought to know what the eighties are. But nobody knows for sure how to describe a given period, present or past, let alone what the future will bring. Every seemingly literal description I might offer you would be at best a part of the whole, and thus not really a literal picture at all but a reduction: a selection of parts that I would ask you to accept as the whole. In short, even the most literal picture would be metaphorical, in the sense of the word that includes that good old term *metonymy:* the part standing for the whole. And thus, in choosing how to describe our times, we are already engaged in the task of criticizing metaphors, selecting those that somehow do least violation to the actual richness of our lives.

Some people, searching for an accurate picture of the condition of women in our time, might attempt a hard social survey on income or expenditure, or purchasing power, or expressed goals. We might ask NORC [National Opinion Research Center] to do a poll, a vast questionnaire duplicating the coverage of the census. My sampling technique is slightly less scientific in appearance, though perhaps no less reliable in the long run.

I just happen to have with me this afternoon a beautifully edited little treatise on the nature and condition of women in our time. This glossy 250-page vade mecum to the good life, the good life for both women *and* men, was purchased by more than five million people last month, including me. Like Aristotle, the editors knew that all men, all *men*, I say, desire happiness, and all men pursue the good. So what they offer us, us *men*, is an unremitting picture of what the goods are in life that will produce happiness.

Look at the cover with me for a moment. This treatise on the good life is called *Penthouse: The International Magazine for Men*. Five million of us men bought copies of it last month, no doubt because many of us half believed that happiness could be found if we just had a "penthouse." A penthouse—that is, by implication, a place where unlimited and totally irresponsible sex can be had three times nightly, and twice as often on Sundays—a penthouse, we infer from this cover, is a place where it is okay to bind, and strip, and presumably whip certain anonymous females, whose eyes are mercifully shaded from us. Along with the photo of the writhing lady that we see here on the cover, we are offered an article entitled "Women Who Flirt with Pain"—that is, obviously, women who like to have us international-minded men, us cosmopolites, inflict pain on them.

Women who flirt with pain! Wow! We American males buy that, in more ways than one. We buy this version of happiness in a penthouse, at three dollars a throw, and we turn eagerly to the section on the pain women flirt with. Saving for later the "Free 31-inch by 21-inch Pet Poster Inside," saving the article on teenage sexuality, saving the "Forum" of fantasies fulfilled, we hurry to the series of paintings by Pater Sato, with the heading Sato-Masochism: "A Japanese master illustrator [Sato] . . . evokes the electricity of desire in women flirting with pain." Each painting shows ecstatic women either suffering or inflicting that marvelous electric shock they are supposed to enjoy whenever pain comes their way. And the paintings are accompanied with selections of poetry, so-called, all by males, of course, poetry that reads like this:

> Hurt me with kisses, kill me with desire
> Consume me and destroy me with the fire
> of blasting passion

That's Aleister Crowley. Or—

> My passion excites the tormentor.

That's Baudelaire. Or—

> I have placed you
> In the hollow of my hand
> Little toy-woman,
> And I gaze at you disdainfully.

That's by somebody named Joseph King. Or—

> No stirrup, no saddle.
> Just a touch of my boot, and you're off.

That's from a poem called "To my mouse twin" by Tristan Corbière.

The best metaphor for happiness, then, is a toy-woman who wants you to hurt her. Right? With a sense that my education in women is moving along nicely, I turn next to a sequence of photos of a lovely, gamboling, naked young woman called Tamara. Here the quotations claim to be from Tamara herself, though they were very likely written by flunkies in *Penthouse*'s editorial offices. "I like to take unsuspecting men by storm—like a friendly cyclone!" Tamara says, as she runs through the jungle in what the caption calls "savage splendor." Tamara is described, as some of you will, I'm sure, remember, as "The Pet of the Month"—to be replaced, in her mindlessness, by another pet of next month and another of the month after that. I can't bring myself to read aloud—not from prudery but from sheer impatience—many of the inane words that *Penthouse* puts into her mouth, a mouth that, so far as one can tell, is always breathlessly open. But I give you two of *Penthouse*'s visions of bliss, free for nothing: "Becoming a *Penthouse* Pet, claims our jubilant jungle lady, is 'a marvelous high—it appeals to my natural cockiness!'" Get it? She admits that her power over men has always been considerable. "'They tend to fall harder than I do,' she says. 'Even if a man stalks me [note that metaphor!] and claims me [*claims me*] for the night . . . there's no guarantee I'll be there when he wakes the next morning. I'm very young and very restless, and I'm not ready to settle for one kind of man or one kind of life.'" And Tamara goes on—that is, they go on for her: "'I think I radiate a certain kind of animal appeal that makes a lot of dialogue unnecessary. . . . I would love to see myself on the giant screen. It would be similar . . . to appearing here in *Penthouse*— knowing that thousands and thousands of otherwise indifferent men would be sharing one common passion: Me!'" And she concludes: "'I hate to say it, but when it comes to getting my attention, nice guys finish last!'"

Well, like, man! I turn fifty-nine this week, and I confess that all my life that's exactly the kind of woman I've been looking for, a *real* woman who is *all* woman. None of this nonsense about having to *talk* with her, none of this nonsense about having to be *nice*. The un-nicer I get, the more she'll like it. The less chatter I get from her empty (and for the most part almost invisible) face, the better. Sheer mindless passion is what I have always longed for and somehow have never been able to find. Where do they *find* these wonderful creatures who will guarantee that when I wake next morning they won't be around to interfere with my life? Clearly there are thousands and thousands of these creatures *somewhere*, eager to be screwed without being nailed. They are so eager, indeed, and loving, that they somehow are forced, *Penthouse* implies, to spend their whole time masturbating. Here they are, page after page, so desperate for a one-night stand that they have either to masturbate, or, for want of a male, to make love with other women.

I spare you most of the details of a long photo sequence called "The Art of Loving," featuring two women flopping about in wet paint and ending up in position sixty-nine, but I must share one bit of immortally poetic prose: "Breasts and buttocks splashed with rainbows of color [rainbows of what? color? Know any other rainbows?], voluptuous loins warmly massaged with sensuous brushstrokes. . . . 'You're a work of art,' breathed the sorceress to her swooning apprentice. 'Please excuse my free-form lust!'"

So now we men know what happiness is. Or at least we know something about it. It is inflicting pain and degradation on mindless and faceless animals who *want* nothing but pain and degradation. In a penthouse, don't forget. And—to make a long summary of the rest of the magazine short—wearing denim. "For the man who doesn't try too hard. He doesn't have to. Things come easy for the man who wears denim." Or perhaps he is sprayed by Chaz, "the fragrance that's almost as interesting as the men who wear it," or English Leather, because "all men wear English Leather . . . or they wear nothing at all"; drinking Ballantine's, "the oldest and most expensive scotch in the world"; smoking Winston cigarettes, for men "whose taste has grown up," or Camels, which offer satisfaction, since "some men taste it all"; listening to Panasonic stereo, which offers "for your eyes: sleek, sophisticated lines, a contemporary look and a dazzling display of fluorescent meters and light emitting diodes," and for your ears, an "incredibly smooth, clean power"; all the while driving a new rotary-engine RX-7 Mazda, the "seductive sedan."

Well, that's perhaps more than enough time spent on that kind of thing. My point is not to tell you women how to read *Penthouse;* most of you know how to reject such trash by virtue of being who you are. The point is that you are surrounded by men who read *Penthouse* and its kind, men like me whose fantasies about the ideal life are fed by such tripe. Five million copies in one month!—for only one of the scores of magazines selling the metaphor of happiness-as-the-quick-lay, the instantly gratified desire, the totally irresponsible pursuit of you and your sisters as machines of gratification, candy machines that ideally should cost nothing and that at most should cost somewhere between the world's most expensive scotch and the world's best stereo. Do not think that the man sitting next to you this afternoon is above all that. Go inquire, I dare you, at our university bookstore as to how many copies of *Penthouse* they sold last month, as compared with copies of any novel you love that shows women as human beings. The best novel I have read this month is *Plains Song: for Female Voices,* by Wright Morris. It is a loving hymn to three lonely women who suffer much from their uncomprehending menfolk. If Wright Morris is lucky, he may be read by ten thousand readers, a majority of them women—even though critics have called *Plains Song* "the perfect novel," and good old Dick Cavett has interviewed Morris about it on TV.

You are surrounded, I am saying, by men whose education about who you are is partly conducted by the sort of thing I have read to you. What kind of education might help you cope with that?

I'm afraid I don't find much in my earlier essay to help you. It describes what you need in a general way, when it says that all of us need to learn how to read critically, how to distinguish between the beautiful and the ugly, and how to make practical choices in the world. Sure. But *what* choices—and how do you learn how to make them, except by making all the bad ones and then suffering the consequences, perhaps fatal?

My essay gave scant help in how to choose models for one's self, in how to protect one's *self* from seductive models or metaphors that are offered by those who pretend to be friends but who are really exploiters; and it did not even mention how to combat the basic threats to the self that come from a given social or political order. Aristotle once said that you can't become a fully good man (read "woman") in a corrupt state. But Wayne Booth did not even mention the possibility of a corrupt society that might threaten anyone's effort to achieve freedom in each of his three lovely domains.

In short, I ignored the arts of self-defense, what today we shall think of as the womanly arts of self-defense. Self-defense can be a misleading concept, if we think of it as simply preserving selves that are already complete and whole. But if we think of the metaphor as suggesting our need both to build a self and to protect it from all of the social acids that might dissolve it, we may get somewhere.

I am suggesting that I did not think in these terms then, because I was in fact thinking more about males than about females. And I suspect that it is thinking about women's special needs now that leads me into this talk of defensive stances. One need not read very far in feminist literature to see that as soon as women start thinking about themselves in our society, they start thinking defensively, and then quite naturally they start thinking of aggressive strategies that might fight off the forces that too often destroy them. I won't debate today the question of whether women are in fact more vulnerable to self-annihilation than men. A good case could be made, on another occasion, for the claim that more women achieve full selfhood in our society, or achieve it earlier in their lives, than men. In fact, if I am right, it is the special failure of men to grow up that constitutes the main threat to women. But for now we are thinking of women, and doing so leads us to think of their special vulnerability to exploitation and loss of selfhood, and we are looking for ways to help diminish that vulnerability.

I have in mind four neglected liberal arts that every woman must, in our society, master if she is not to end up less than herself. They are, of course, arts that every man ought to master too—now that we've thought about them they become just as important for men as for women. Please relax: they are not the quadrivium, though they will be practiced best by those who master those traditional arts too.

The first one has long since occurred to many feminists here. But on the whole it has been practiced very badly. It is the art of strategy, the art of planning a political or military campaign in such a way as to win. In preparing a talk recently for the PERL program [Politics, Economics, Rhetoric, and Law], I noticed a peculiar omission in the disciplines that PERL covers. The PERL program claims, as you may know, to educate people liberally while preparing them for practical affairs in government or business. When we devised that program we tried to think of the arts or disciplines that are indispensable to the practical man or woman who intends to engage in what are sometimes called "public affairs." We thought of law, obviously indispensable. We thought of political science and of economics, almost as obvious. We thought of ethics and history and sociology and anthropology—and ruled them all out, sometimes for good reasons, sometimes just because we couldn't get anybody who teaches these subjects to take an interest in our program. We even thought of rhetoric, sometimes considered as merely the art of winning with words, but considered by us to be the whole art of thinking and communicating with various human languages. What we did not think of was one that was automatically included in many ancient programs designed to train citizens: strategy—how to outsmart your opponent and ensure victory. So far as I know, it never even occurred to any of us, though we can be sure that in some law courses and in some political science courses it has been taught under other names. I suppose if we *had* thought of it we would have rejected it, on the grounds that strategy connotes military strategy, and we would have shrunk from having PERL identified with the Viet Nam War, or indeed with any war. So far as I know, there has never been a required course in strategy in this or any other non-military college in this century, and the result has been, I suspect, that whenever American citizens spot an enemy, foreign or domestic, they tend to conduct their strategy very badly. Believing, as I long believed, that the very notion of trying to outsmart somebody was wicked, we find ourselves, when the occasion to fight occurs, falling back on a very simple repertory of devices, which depends on whatever is fashionable. If sit-ins are in, we sit in. If strikes have been tried with some success, we strike again. If hiring an advertising firm to change our image is what people are doing, we compete for the advertising firm that charges most. But what we don't do is study strategy.

This is not the time to relate all of the ineffective strategies that have been used by feminists in their efforts to combat male chauvinism. Nor can I claim to know many better strategies that might have had more chances of success. But it takes no very subtle analysis to see that American women have on the whole not fought the feminist wars very successfully. If ERA is not passed,[2] we shall all of course blame the arch-conservatives for the defeat. But if ever a constitutional amendment had everything going for it—except the strategic ignorance of us defenders—ERA is it. We defenders of ERA had no know-how at all about how to win a political battle. How could we have obtained that know-how? Not in most college courses. The very thought of introducing such a course would have led to branding the proposer as illiberal or commercial or anti-intellectual. Learn how to think about how to win in a good cause? Terrible. Corrupt. Let's read more D. H. Lawrence or Ionesco or Stevens instead.

Just think of the energy that we academics have expended trying to get our professional organizations to boycott the cities that are in states that have not ratified ERA. Boycotting Chicago to punish Illinois is, after all, a piece of strategy, a piece of strategy that has been employed by a fair number of organizations, including some I belong to. So far as I can tell, the chief effect has been to make enemies for ERA. Boycotting, useful in some contexts when other methods of persuasion have failed, was unthinkingly and self-righteously adopted as appropriate to a situation in which the problem was to win the votes of legislators. To win votes in regions where your policies are opposed, you do not set out to punish people in other regions where your policies are approved, thus confirming the worst prejudices that your enemies already hold. To win votes you attempt to win votes. Mike Royko has playfully suggested that we feminists should learn to win votes in the Illinois legislature with bribery. That would be immoral, but it would at least have some chance of success. But the boycott of Chicago to punish

---

2. By 1988 we have several whole books, and many articles, about why the ERA amendment failed. See Janet K. Boles, *The Politics of the Equal Rights Amendment: Conflict and the Decision Process* (New York, 1979); Mary Francis Berry, *Why ERA Failed: Politics, Women's Rights, and the Amending Process of the Constitution* (Bloomington, Ind., 1986); and Jane J. Mansbridge, *Why We Lost the ERA* (Chicago, 1986).

Springfield is both immoral and almost certainly ineffective. It is just plain bad strategy.

I do not know what an effective strategy for ERA might have been (I'm afraid that the past tense looks more and more appropriate). But I do know that lots of people know a lot about such matters, and that it is a curious gap in our general education that we do not require of everyone some experience with current strategies for political victory. Courses dealing with strategy would seem to be required both for self-defense—how can you fight 'em if you don't recognize what they're doing to you—and for offensives, when we see a good cause that deserves our support.

You may want to point out that we do have, in America, plenty of courses in strategy: courses offered by advertising departments and business schools. That's true: professionals do spend time and money training, or claiming to train, in the arts of producing the *Penthouse* magazine kind of advertising copy, and its hundreds of equivalents, some of them even having nothing to do with sex. But where are the courses designed to train us in the art of combatting the image-makers who make their livings by degrading us?

(Incidentally, if you want an account of what we're up against, I suggest you take a look at the TV criticism written by Michael J. Arlen. His little book called *Thirty Seconds* describes the the enormous care and skill going into a single commercial spot; it is especially revealing about the way the advertisers study how you and I tick, in order to hit us where we live. Or you might look at his recent piece in *The New Yorker*, where *Thirty Seconds* originally appeared, this one on how television sells political candidates. Interviewing, a "television media consultant," David Sawyer, he reports on the strategies that apparently work on those of us who do not have counterstrategies for self-defense.)[3]

I have time only to touch on the second art, which is not quite so badly neglected as strategy. I mean the art of persuasion (I won't call it rhetoric), conceived of as an arm of strategy. To learn how to speak and write in such a way as to increase the chances of winning is by no means the whole end of education in speaking and writing. But it is no mean art, and in a world in which too many people see themselves as winning by deception or by preventing thought in language, the art of using thought in language to persuade people to a cause is a relatively noble one. I've talked about it so much around here on various occasions, however, that I can perhaps take it for granted for today and hurry on.

The trouble with both of the first two arts, important as they can be, is

3. Michael J. Arlen, *Thirty Seconds* (New York, 1980).

that they presuppose practitioners who already have the right view of the world and of themselves, and who thus can wholeheartedly plunge into the effort to sway the world to their correct views. But some of you are old enough to have discovered that the cause you fight to support one year may actually turn out to work against your own true interests, and that the self you fling into combat today may look pretty puny and misguided tomorrow. The third and fourth neglected arts, then, are arts of criticism: first, the criticism of metaphors for human life and metaphors for the self; and second, the criticism of situations or circumstances.

The first of these twin arts, criticism of metaphor, I've been engaged in most of the time today. When I made fun of *Penthouse's* metaphors for happiness, what I was trying to do was to stimulate you to think about what a woman really is or *is like*. It is clear that *Penthouse* magazine has decided that all people, not just women, are reducible to one of two metaphors. Everyone I meet can be considered as *either* a useful tool, an exploitable means to some end I care about, a kind of tool box; *or* as a candy machine, a source of pleasure that will be mine when I insert something into a convenient slot. The only limits to exploitation of people as tools or as candy machines are the limits of the given market; other markets exploit the hardcore audience, and others still, the hard-core with open violence.

We all reject, or I hope we do, the notion that other people are merely our tools or candy machines, but what, then, are they, really? They are, we say, people, persons, selves. What it means to develop a self—what used to be called a soul—is never easy to say. The history of thought is full, in fact, of efforts to find the right metaphor, or analogy, for what a soul is. We used to be told that men are made in the image of God, meaning that the closest analogy to the mystery of selfhood is the mystery of universehood. The soul, like God, is too complex to be compared with anything else that is. For Plato, the soul is more like a commonwealth than like a god: a healthy soul is like a well-ordered state, in which each of many complex parts does its proper job, in harmony with the other parts, all under the direction of the part that *should* be in charge; a corrupt soul is one in which insurrection has occurred, this or that inferior part taking charge. Aristotle's picture is in some ways the same, though it could be argued that his good man's soul, identical with the happy man's soul, is far less turbulent than Plato's, far less subject to insurrection, far less like an angry and threatened slave master beating down the revolutionary forces of anger and desire. In Aristotle, the goal of life seems to be quite clearly cultivation of a self whose deepest desires and appetites are for kinds of activity that by definition preserve the soul's integrity and defend it from its enemies.

Though Aristotle's notion may come closer than the others to being literal and distinctive to human nature, it is still essentially metaphorical, since it inevitably reduces the soul to a finite and literal range of parts and habits, something that each of us struggling to find a self knows that a self is not. What is more, it comes uncomfortably close to the metaphor of a programmed machine, as we can see in various corrupt Aristotelianisms that have been offered throughout history.[4]

In my original conception of this talk, I had planned to offer at this point a section on some of the metaphors for the self that feminists have themselves employed. For completeness, the talk should take on some of these serious efforts to construct an image that might rival in its richness and power the traditional views I have mentioned. But time's a-wasting, and I must just ask you to take my word for it that there is almost as much need for critical acumen in appraising metaphors offered by would-be feminists as in reading *Penthouse*. Perhaps the need is greater, because I suspect that for most women (unlike most men) the crippling metaphors offered in a work like Erica Jong's *Fear of Flying* (say) will be more seductive than anything offered in the popular media. Women can simply dismiss the hacks of *Penthouse*, except insofar as males are seduced by them. But the serious contenders for a feminist vision require a criticism as subtle as we can manage: Just what *is* a model for a life worth having?

My point is that there is an immense gap in almost all programs in liberal education: the study of how to appraise metaphors. You will look a long time in any catalogue before you find a course titled "Criticism of Metaphor 101," or another, "Metaphorical Defenses Against Reductive Metaphor 299, for fourth-year students only." Yet every day selves are being destroyed before our eyes for lack of effective defenses against plausible metaphors.[5]

I must hurry on to a fourth art, one that can be developed above and beyond the art of winning though strategy or rhetoric and the art of criticizing metaphors. The trouble with both strategy and the rhetoric designed to win is that, though both are necessary in our world, their use depends on our accepting a basic and uncriticized metaphor for our circumstances: the metaphor of warfare. And they assume that we know who we are and what we want. Who we are can be stated easily: we are the decent folks who want what's good and right. What we want is victory over those fools and knaves who are essentially beneath consideration: people we can deal with only by fighting them.

4. Postscript, 1988: I have recently discovered a fine philosopher, Charles Taylor, whose work on who or what a person is would have been helpful to me here. See his *Human Agency and Language: Philosophical Papers I* (New York, 1985).

5. I develop this point in chapters 10 and 11 of *The Company We Keep* (Berkeley, 1988).

But we don't have to be sentimentalists to recognize that when we treat each other as unreconstructible enemies, we usually make disastrous mistakes. I think that Mayor Byrne, for example, has let herself fall into frozen postures of opposition that may very well destroy her and bring our houses down with her. Watching her, I have no doubt that she is sincere, courageous, convinced of her own rectitude, and frightened because she is surrounded by enemies who can understand nothing but power. She *is* surrounded by enemies, of course, more of them every day. And she seems to have no suspicion that there might be a kind of strategy, a kind of rhetoric, a kind of metaphorical criticism, a transforming art of thinking that would refuse to accept her *circum-stances,* her surrounding positions, as fixed, and then would seek imaginatively for metaphors other than the stand-off, the battle-line, the righteous last-ditch defense of truth and justice against the selfish monsters who have no public interest.

Just how she might do that I cannot pretend to know; my education in the higher strategies and the higher rhetoric of diplomacy was faulty. But the sad truth is that the first woman mayor of Chicago, probably the first woman leader of a city of this size in the history of the world, seems so badly educated in the arts we are talking about that she is "blowing" one of the biggest opportunities anyone ever had to show what she can do. And I don't have to tell you that she is surrounded—again those *circum-stances* —by hundreds of thousands of men who are secretly pleased to watch her painting herself into corners: "Just what we would expect, from a *woman.*" From a *woman.* Woman as metaphor, again, the proper metaphor for political ineptitude and shrill intransigence. One hardly knows what to be angrier about: the men who think this way, Mayor Byrne for falling into these traps, or a culture that educates us all to be as ignorant as she is about how to remake our selves and our circumstances by exercising habits of freedom.

I have suggested four arts that every woman must master, if she is to achieve any kind of genuine liberation in a world that from her birth seems determined to bind her to its enslaving metaphors. Two of them are arts of winning, given the selves and circumstances we find ourselves in. The other two are arts of reconstitution, the reconstitution of selves by a vigorous criticism of metaphors for the self, and the art of reconstituting circumstances, by a vigorous criticism of metaphors for situations. These arts are not dispensable frills on education. We cannot afford to leave them, as we now do, to the accidents of teacher preferences and the vagaries of the registration schedule. They are matters of life and death, sometimes quite literally, as when a Janis Joplin is killed by a society willing to use her and use her and use her, until what self she has is used up into nothingness. They are more often matters of life and death metaphorically: the life and death of our selves, our souls, depends on our mastery of these arts.

You may have noticed that though I began by talking of education as simply a kind of glorified self-defense, the distinction between what is defensive and what is constructive has somehow disappeared. Whenever I work to *defend* my self I am simultaneously *constructing* my self, building habits of self, habits of courage, skills of thought, powers of action. I thus want to conclude, as perhaps I should have begun, with some hints about what seem to me the ultimate rewards of thinking about education in these ways.

The woman who successfully resists the reductive metaphors I have described, and thus builds a self for herself, discovers somewhere along the line a marvelous and perhaps unexpected reward: friendship has become possible. Instead of conceiving of happiness as we are told Tamara conceives it—a solitary gambol through the jungle, with pauses only to masturbate and to drift "restlessly" (her word) from one-night stand to one-night stand—this self will conceive of happiness as the knowing of other selves and dwelling with them.

Some people, some selves, manage in a miraculous way to get beyond warfare and manipulation and achieve a mutual relation of loving respect, a relation in which each party works as hard to develop a self for the other as for her self. In such relations it is not just that number one wishes for the welfare of number two, because number two is necessary for number one's happiness—a very refined tool box but a tool box still. No, here number one simply loses track of which is number one and which is number two. Both become number one for both. In the words of E. E. Cummings' poem:

> now i love you and you love me . . .
> there's somebody calling who's we . . .
> we're anything brighter than even the sun
> (we're everything greater
> than books
> might mean)
> we're everyanything more than believe
> (with a spin
> leap
> alive we're alive)
> we're wonderful one times one[6]

6. Copyright 1944 by E. E. Cummings; renewed 1972 by Nancy T. Andrews. Reprinted from *Complete Poems 1913–1962* by E. E. Cummings by permission of Harcourt Brace Jovanovich, Inc.

Now you'll look a long way in current literature about education before you'll find someone saying that the knowledge most worth having is the knowledge of how to become a self capable of true friendship, of how to multiply one by one to get one. The goal is certainly implicit in much that your best teachers try to teach you, but it is also repudiated in many of the good things we try to do together in the academy. In most graduate study it is either repudiated directly, as in the economic theories that reduce friendship and love to their cash value, or it is simply ignored. Perhaps more surprising, even in our so-called liberal education, even in our required courses, too often the subject matter, aims, and methods seem almost deliberately chosen to reduce education to an exclusive training of what is called the "mind," rather than education of what I am calling a "self."

I cite only one example. For decades here at Chicago, Aristotle's *Ethics* has been taught in many required courses. It has often been taught well, and it has no doubt had fine ethical effect in leading students to recognize that if happiness is one's goal in life, one had better stop *pursuing* it, as if it were something that could be advertised in *Penthouse* or *The New Yorker*, and learn instead to develop a self, a character, capable of happiness. But so far as I know, no one in all those decades of required reading has until this year ever led first-year students to read the two books in the *Ethics* on friendship and the final book on pleasure and happiness, the books, note well, that provide the metaphoric culmination of the work and thus reward us for our journey through the whole treatise. Students have thus been left to discover on their own that for Aristotle the reward for studying ethics is a self capable of living in friendship.

But it is not my point to indict but to incite. I should like to incite you all, male and female, to turn your lives towards the active reshaping of yourselves and your circumstances. You are not helpless clay in the hands of Hugh Hefner and Bob Guccione[7] and all they stand for. And you can begin to fight back by turning each course you take, each book and magazine you read, into an active critique of the basic metaphors for human life on which it depends. Further, you can seek out those courses that will help you develop the rhetorical and strategic skills for combatting—both within yourselves and in your circumstances—those who, for good motives or bad, are busily reducing your metaphoric world to tool boxes, candy machines, and sophisticated biofeedback mechanisms.

It should be obvious, here at the end, that this knowledge that every woman must have is a knowledge every man must have, too. But there is

7. Editors of *Playboy* and *Penthouse*.

one kind of knowledge that every man should have that is not available to women: namely, how to listen to those who have been the chief victims of our vast hordes of hirelings, our hack metaphorists. The chances are very high that each of you men, sitting here, has been seriously maimed already by your culture. The chances are high that you have, even during this lecture, thought occasionally of the woman sitting next to you as a toolbox, or as a candy machine, rather than as a potential friend who might teach you something about how to become a self.

How do I know? Because it takes one to know one. Let's step over into the corner here, and I'll tell you a wonderful joke about this beautiful chick who comes into this bar, and she walks up to this cool stud, and she says . . .

Will you let me finish that story without criticism? If you do, you're no friend of mine.

OCCASION 12 · *To Fourscore Graduate Students Training To Be Teachers*

What Little I Think I Know about Teaching

As I was thinking last week about what should be said to a bunch of graduate students preparing to be teachers, I met a colleague in the corridor of Regenstein Library. A winner of the Quantrell Prize for Excellence in Undergraduate Teaching, he had just seen the announcement of this event ["The Student as Text"] and he growled: "You know and I know that all that stuff is crap. Nothing is really known about how to teach well; the most that could be known would be how to make students like the class and the professor and thus believe, probably erroneously, that they have been taught something worth learning." Greatly encouraged by this outburst I happened to meet a professor of education here in the hall, and I asked him, "Phil, what is really *known* about teaching?" His reply: "Not much! I'm just reviewing an eleven-hundred-page book summarizing educational research. In my view, the book is pretty discouraging. There's really not a lot of hard knowledge to report."

I next looked into a little book sent me by a former student, *A Celebration of Teachers.*[1] I found some wonderfully inspirational memories by fa-

Opening talk to a day-long workshop at the University of Chicago, 1987.

1. National Council of Teachers of English (Urbana, Ill., 1985). The card catalogue of my university library indicates that we own something like fifteen hundred books about teachers and teaching. And that's not even counting the great philosophical works—Plato's at the head of the list—that teach about teaching by sheer force of example. How many of these, I wonder, would have helped me become a better teacher? Some that have in fact helped are: Sylvia Ashton-Warner's *Teacher* (New York, 1963); Jacques Barzun's *Teacher in America* (New York, 1945); John Erskine's *My Life as a Teacher* (Philadelphia, 1948); Gilbert Highet's *The Art of Teaching* (New York, 1950); R. K. Narayan's *The English Teacher* (Chicago, 1945); John Passmore's *The Philosophy of Teaching* (London, 1980); and Joe Axelrod's obscure little pamphlet on "The Discussion Technique in the College Classroom" (or some such title), published sometime in the late forties and now, so far as my own shelves can tell me, lost to the world. More important than any of these have been thousands of staff meetings and conversations with colleagues in America and England, especially Harold and Connie Rosen and James Britton. I am of course not even beginning to list the many works that have influenced my

mous people, mostly writers, describing the unsung great teachers who changed their lives: Peter de Vries telling how John De Boer, his first high school English teacher, teaching one of his first classes, made his pupils into "kindred spirits, . . . responsive . . . to his dazzling mind, his richly humanitarian spirit, and his deep love of . . . literature"; Madeleine L'Engle remembering a sixth-grade teacher, also in her first teaching job, who "was the first person in all of my school life to see any potential talent in this shy, introverted child"; Bernard Malamud saying that Clara Molendyk "was very fond of her students and made us feel expansive, free, and useful"; Art Buchwald blessing Mrs. Marie Egorkin, at P.S. 35 in Hollis, New York, who, finding that Buchwald could not resist clowning, gave him the "opportunity to perform in front of the class in exchange for shutting up when she was trying to teach grammar." I wonder how many of you would be able to respond with similar memories, if asked—memories about some one or two teachers who made all the difference.

In any case, since I could find no clear line of pursuit in all that, I turned to a new book called *Distinguished Teachers on Effective Teaching*.[2] Again I found such a plethora of seemingly contradictory suggestions as to make me almost despair about our project today.

Clearly we should begin cautiously and humbly, though I hope not despairingly. We're talking about the most difficult and important of all arts. Like all arts, it surely must depend in part on knowledge, but like all arts it depends on knowledge that is elusive, manifold, and resistant to clear formulation.

In short, if generalizations are dangerous, and I think they usually are, they are especially dangerous about teaching. There is no recommendation that will work for all teachers, or, as my colleague James Redfield likes to say, "No teacher, not even the best, succeeds with every student, and there may be no teacher who succeeds with no one."

Suppose we begin by trying out three generalizations.

Good teaching is dramatic, colorful, lively, entertaining. Right? A dean at Earlham College thought so once, and when bad reports came in on the teaching of Mike Bossett, assistant professor of American history, he called the poor man in and told him to jazz things up a little. Bossett thought

---

thinking about rhetoric or about *what* I ought to teach.

Readers who are curious about how post-structuralists think about teaching will find guidance and challenge and even considerable wisdom about the dangers of pedagogical certitudes (what I later call "the good teacher as threat") in *The Pedagogical Imperative: Teaching as a Literary Genre*, ed. Barbara Johnson, *Yale French Studies* 63 (1982).

2. Edited by Peter Beidler, as no. 28 in the series New Directions for Teaching and Learning (San Francisco, 1986).

about it and appeared before his class in History of the American Frontier next day sporting a Davy Crockett costume, shooting off a cap pistol and shouting "Yippee-ee-ee!" The result, *almost* needless to say, was disastrous. Last year a professor of physics at Harvard taught his unit on jet propulsion by putt-putting himself into the classroom in a jet-propelled wheelchair, repeating the act later as he left the hall. I can't help wondering whether his students were as contemptuous, deep down, as Mike Bossett's.

At the opposite extreme from such shenanigans is my memory of one of the teachers who taught me most in graduate school. George Williamson violated every technique of good teaching that anyone has ever thought of. He would come into the classroom and shuffle, shifty-eyed, to a little platform, open an attaché case in front of him in such a way as to preclude all eye contact, focus his eyes alternately on the text and a far high corner of the room, and proceed to explicate T. S. Eliot's poems. It took me several weeks to realize that I was learning a lot, far more than I had learned in many a more engaging class.

Try another generalization: *Good teaching results from passionate engagement with the subject.* Well, of course it sometimes does, but I've known, indeed I now know, teachers who are deeply learned in and passionate about their subjects who just don't get through to even the best students, except at the most advanced levels, and then rarely. By the same token I know others whose learning is superficial and casual, who care more indeed about the stock exchange than about scholarship, but who in teaching younger students manage to wake up the sleepy, convert the hostile, and change lives in what I consider good directions. Perhaps even more significantly, I can honestly say that my own worst teaching has often been about those subjects on which I consider myself expert. The novel that I have taught most ineptly, the one that I now refuse to teach, is the one I did my dissertation on, *Tristram Shandy*. I just know too much about it—and I try to stuff it all in at once.

Third generalization: *Good teaching results from caring for students; from "teaching the child, not the subject," as the cliché goes; from "teaching the whole person"; or, in the terms of our program today, from taking the student as "text" rather than, say, Socrates, Shakespeare, Thucydides, or the second law of thermodynamics.* Since most of what I want to say might seem to be a recommendation of this one, I won't dwell on the exceptions to these claims—there's no use in turning you off at the beginning. But I do want to underline the following warning: Perhaps more bad teaching has resulted from a misapplied concentration on personality exchange, in the name of serving the student rather than the subject, than from any other one practice.

Having offered those warnings against any generalizations you hear from anybody *else* today, I shall now of course offer some hard, indubitable truths about teaching, my own deep wisdom acquired through four decades of perpetual anxiety and frequent failure.

Actually I have only one, a big one, one that I really believe in, with no surrounding ironies or discountings: *Bad teaching most often results from a pursuit of the wrong ends,* either because the teacher is unclear about his or her purposes or because plausible but harmful purposes get in the way of good ones. Of course there are many legitimate purposes of teaching, depending on different subject matters and circumstances. But I want to suggest that in America today one purpose that is legitimate for some occasions has been allowed to intrude harmfully on too many occasions where it is not only inappropriate but destructive: I mean the aim of conveying information, of *covering material.* We are an information-burdened society, and the loading of information into minds conceived as memory banks has come to dominate far too much of our educational practice. Much of the information-loading is of course described in fancy, respectable terms. One current prominent movement in my field calls it "imparting cultural literacy" (see Preface, note 4). In science courses it is often disguised as something called "problem-solving." That title makes it sound active and somehow connected with thinking, but the student is too often left going through the motions that no real problem-solver ever went through—the abstracted paths that were worked out as a retrospective explanation after the problems had been solved. In history, information-loading has long been deplored, but it is still, I would judge, the main goal of far too much instruction.

Of course there are many occasions when information-loading is proper or even necessary. But I think they occur mainly in the pre-college years. We are here talking about *college* teaching, and there is one crucial difference between teaching a sixth-grader, say, and teaching a college student. The pupil has to go on to the seventh grade whether he or she wants to or not; the college student is free to drop the subject permanently at the end of the course. As our appalling attrition rates tell us, college students are free to proclaim, "Never again."

So I like to think about a different goal, one that doesn't prevent all imparting of information, but one that certainly complicates our thinking about what we are up to: *Good college teaching is the kind that promises to make the teacher finally superfluous, the kind that leads students to want to continue work in the given subject and to be able to, because they have the necessary intellectual equipment to continue work at a more advanced level.* A crass way of putting this goal is to say that the good teacher is out to make converts to his or her field—not necessarily to turn students into ma-

jors or professionals in the field, but to turn them into adults who will continue learning in that field, either as professionals or as amateurs. William
James once said that you could tell an educated person by his or her way of
reading the daily newspaper. (Of course James said "his", not "his or her").
That may seem like a fairly low-level goal. But what kind of success could a
teacher claim if a student, ten years later, meeting the subject in some journal, popular or learned, turned away from it in disgust or with the conviction that only boredom lay ahead?

What follows for teaching when the teacher tries to ensure that students
will *want* to continue and will *be able to* continue after the end of ten weeks
or a year or four years? Note that our goal is not that the student should
want to continue *with this teacher*; that kind of loving attachment is relatively easy to obtain—and often dangerous when it comes. Love of the
teacher is not a goal of teaching but a dispensable and often dangerous by-
product of the goal, which, to repeat, is freedom from the teacher and critical
attachment to the subject.

First and most important, it follows that any given course should be
viewed not primarily as a preparation for some future course or future experience but *as an end in itself*. It may seem paradoxical to say that if you
hope for a future that includes your subject, you must not teach to that
future but to a delight in learning *in the present moment*. But it's not a
paradox. Love cannot be prepared for with hate, at least not usually. What I
have loved today I will want to have more of tomorrow. This means that
ideally—and no teacher realizes the ideal—each day's class should be so
rich in the excitement of learning that every student will say, at the end of
the day, "The high point of my day was that class. I can't wait to see what
we'll learn there tomorrow."

Obviously this doesn't mean that Mike Bossett was wise when he chose
to dress up like Davy Crockett. Primarily it means for me that I can never
be satisfied if I think students are not led, by the situations I set up, to take
an active responsibility for what is going on now and what will go on next
week. To deliver a lecture and assure myself that all the students are dutifully taking notes may give me the illusion that they are learning actively,
and of course some kind of activity is going on even when notes are taken in
boredom or hostility. But that kind of receptive role, even if the student
retains some of what is received, I think of as passive, though educationists
now seem to agree that there can be no such thing as utterly passive learning: to learn anything at all one must have an activated mind that *grasps* it,
in whatever form. This must be so, if we mean by "passive" a simple blank
indifference. And it is certainly true that the theorists I admire most, in con-

trast to what many prophets of artificial intelligence seem to say, agree that whatever the mind does is done by constructing, constituting, grasping, not just by "taking in" or receiving or containing or retaining. (If all those metaphors and the differences that they suggest interest you, I recommend a fine book about current controversies over the constitutive role of metaphor, *Metaphor and Thought,* edited by Andrew Ortony.[3]

Perhaps a better contrast would be between *responsible engagement* and *obedient receptivity.* The kind of active learning I always hope to see more of is the kind that takes responsibility for where a given moment is to go, in contrast to the kind of receptivity that leaves it entirely to the teacher's authority to determine where things are to go.

If we take that contrast seriously, if we really pursue a responsible engagement, certain things follow about classroom practice. First, what does it say about the proportion of lecturing and discussion, and about the kind of lecturing and discussion we engage in? It clearly does *not* say that we should never lecture, or that all discussions will produce responsible engagement. But I think it does follow that a teacher has failed if students leave the classroom assuming that the task of thinking through to the next step lies entirely with the teacher. And I suggest that that doleful effect, that hurrying away after class to something else that is really engaging, is produced much more often by lecturing than by seriously planned and executed discussions.

It is no doubt true that highly skillful lecturers can earn the kind of engagement I have in mind. A good lecture, like a good essay or book, demands the thoughtful engagement of everyone within earshot. It's also painfully true that so-called discussions that simply drift, with no one holding anyone responsible for saying anything worth saying, and no progress made on some recognizable question, can leave students even more disengaged than if they had heard a good lecture. Some decades ago here in our College a group of teachers conducted a careful experiment comparing lectures and discussions. They chose a group of teachers who were thought to be among the best lecturers, and another group thought to be among the best discussion leaders. They then made audio tapes of their classes, and played them back to individual students. At regular intervals they would stop the tape and ask the student, "What were you thinking about at that point?" Recording the incidence of distraction—"I don't like the color of his tie"; "I don't like her hairdo"; "I can't think what to say to my boyfriend tonight"—as compared to the incidence of concentration *on the subject,* they got what were for them disappointing results. They were enthusiasts for the glories of discussion classes, and they found that the lecturers had

3. New York, 1979.

the attention of more students more of the time than did the discussion leaders. Shocking. So they went back and asked a different set of questions, focusing on the incidence of *active thought about where the current topic should lead or about how to do something with it.* On that one they found that discussions did considerably better than lectures. The bad news is that, as I remember it, neither lectures nor discussions did very well—I think about the best anyone managed was to keep about 25 percent of students, on average, away from distractions—though of course there were high points when nearly all were engaged, and other moments when almost no one was.

If there were time, I would be glad to offer you my complete and final list of principles for good discussion. But time is running out, so here are only three that follow obviously from our principles:

1. You gotta get them talking to each other, not just to you or to the air.

2. You gotta get them talking about the subject, not just having a bull session in which nobody really listens to anybody else. This means insisting on at least the following rule in every discussion: Whether I call on you or you speak up spontaneously, please address the previous speaker, *or* give a reason for changing the subject.

3. You gotta find ways to prevent yourself from relapsing into a badly prepared lecturette, disguised as a discussion. Informal lectures are usually worse than prepared ones.

Second, certain practices follow for reading and writing assignments and testing. I ask you to think back on the assignments you have been given, and the testing you have suffered—and then to think about just how little of that pile of stuff really *engaged* you in self-education. My own thinking in this way leads me to use fewer examinations, fewer quizzes, and more essay assignments, including frequent one-pagers that require students to come up with pertinent questions and possible answers to them. You don't know anything about a subject until you can put your knowledge into some kind of expression. Trying to put it into a form of intelligible expression is usually the best path to active engagement rather than obedient receptivity.

Finally, in this little list of untrustworthy generalizations, I would urge you to resist planning too far in advance. Just how far too far is may be hard to determine, but it is extremely difficult to teach engaged responsibility when you have fixed all the fights from the beginning. Leave room for improvisation, even as you are walking toward the class. It was Art Buchwald's teacher's improvisation at a specific moment that leads him to honor her now. Leave the reading list to some degree open, so that when you discover an unusually well-prepared or badly-prepared group you can shift gears. Above all, leave room for your own learning—for the chance to discover and teach something you didn't know when the course began. After all, our basic choice of purposes here should apply to you as well as to your students: will *you* want to continue learning about and teaching this subject a year from now or ten years from now? Not if you've gained nothing from what happens in the encounter—nothing more, that is, than the sense that students came out with what *you* had when you went in. That's not enough; every class should be for you as much as for the students, and it cannot be that unless there are many moments of opening out into unforeseen learning.

The art of teaching a given class or student a given body of data is one thing. The art of building a life as a teacher is quite another. Good teaching, whether judged by what is good for the student or good for the teacher, might be identified by a simple thought experiment that I sometimes conduct for myself when I feel discouraged about how little my students seem to learn. Picture either the student or yourself at the end of the year, thinking back on the course, or at the end of four years, thinking back on many courses. Word comes over TV or radio that that nuclear war we all dread is upon us, Chicago has been targeted by the enemy, President Reagan's "Star Wars" is failing as badly as everybody of any sense predicted it would, we are doomed to die horrible deaths in five minutes. Looking back on the year or years of education in that final retrospective flash, would I say to myself, "Damn it all, I did all that preparation for a future that will now not come. All that career building—and no more career! I wish I had spent my time on this or that other more valuable or pleasurable activity"? Or would I, and would my students, be tempted to say something like, "Well, if I had known what I now know—Oh, oh! There goes the first blast, off above Evanston—I would have spent these last years, these last months, this last week, just as I have done, on that most distinctively human of all human activities, learning how to learn"?

PART IV · *TO HIMSELF—AND TO THOSE HE TRIES TO TEACH*

A TEACHER'S JOURNAL, 1972–1988

One [of my students] was T. S. Eliot, who subsequently wrote a poem about it, called "Mr. Appolinax." . . . He was extraordinarily silent, and only once made a remark which struck me. I was praising Heraclitus, and he observed: "Yes, he always reminds me of Villon." I thought this remark so good that I always wished he would make another.

    Bertrand Russell

Oh, Mr. Booth, it's so good working with you—you must have had to learn things the hard way!

    Student at Earlham College, after a grueling two-hour private conference on how to write an essay

INTRODUCTION · *The Occasion*

A sixty-seven-year-old smiling public man, I have now taught between eight and twelve thousand class hours—depending on whether you will let me count my "tutorial" hours working with groups of from three to six students. Private conferences with individual students must number somewhere from twenty-five to fifty thousand.

Am I burned out? I would be, if those hours were in any way mere duplications, or if the distresses outweighed the rewards. But they do not—as I hope somehow to convince you. Will quotations from my "Teacher's Journal" do it? Just three years ago, on March 13, 1985, the morning after what was almost certainly my eleven-thousand-eight-hundred-and-fifty-ninth class, I wrote the following:

7:45 a.m.: Feeling partially liberated. How can anyone claim to "love teaching" if he feels such relief when it's *over and done?* Two more classes, easy ones, ahead, then months and months, perhaps eighteen months, without classes. What bliss in prospect. Yet I don't feel like retiring completely yet.

But why does a class like yesterday's, the final class of Practical Criticism, seem so scary in prospect, so difficult in execution? It was really not very good, truth is, because I was tense and pushing—*telling them* rather than *teaching them.*

That may sound to some like burn-out, not the sort of thing to attract anyone into this line of work. To me it sounds more like evidence that this profession can never become boring. If I get bored *here,* it is my fault, not the fault of anything in teaching. Teaching is impossible to master, inexhaustibly varied, unpredictable from hour to hour, from minute to minute within the hour: tears when you don't expect them, laughter when you might predict tears; cooperation and resistance in baffling mixtures; disconcerting depths of ignorance and sudden unexpected revelations of knowledge or wisdom. And the results are almost always ambiguous. No, it is never boring.

But it is a profession that can seem, on a bad day, after a bad class, quite simply intolerable: "I've just got to get out of this, fast. I'll phone this afternoon to check into that early-retirement scheme." An hour later, a day later, the vocation can feel as fresh and rewarding as it looked on that day long ago when I said, "All right, then, I'll *be* an English teacher, even though it does mean I'll always be poor." On the good days, I always find myself thinking what a coup it was to win *all this* and to be paid for it too.

In the following pages gleaned from forty years of memories and relatively recent journal notes, I can't hope to have captured how the mixture of pain and joy feels. The pains are perhaps understated, though one reader of an earlier draft has claimed that too many of the episodes that I now see as funny seem simply painful to him. In any case, there is an inevitable prettying up, or at least simplifying, inherent in any account of this kind. Like the rest of the book, this record was designed and written mainly in the hours when I was feeling, if not actually "productive," as we say of ourselves, at least constructive enough to resist TV, Ngaio Marsh, the latest *New Yorker* and all other forms of escape or despair, and to "take pen in hand." (The journal entries were mostly typed or dictated immediately following class, in moods ranging from triumph to despair. But often enough I was too tired to record anything until late evening or the following morning.) Just as the speeches I print represent the relatively acceptable final versions, not the stacks of messy revisions produced in hours of confusion and even anguish, so this journal simply wipes out whatever could not be well accommodated to it: the moments when I could not write or teach at all, the experiences too painful for memory to retain, the abominable sentences and paragraphs that did not survive, the descriptions of anger or despair or even triumph that simply "don't work" when read in cold blood. Even the failures that I report here are no doubt to some degree transmuted in the telling; to write about them is, after all, one way to accommodate them. To see past disasters as funny turns them to good account.

I admitted earlier to the hope that some of my younger readers might be tempted to enter teaching by what they find here, and that some others might be tempted to stay in it. Though this motive by no means accounts for the whole book, it now comes into full play. But perhaps I should repeat the warning I gave those graduate students at the end of part 3: of all professions, this is the one about which generalizations are least reliable. What I have found in teaching, you may not find, and the reasons I offer for my failures and (presumed) successes may have little to do with the actual causes. Indeed my own past predictions about whether this or that student would become a good teacher have often proved to be far from the mark. In short, you'll never know whether "the most demanding of all professions" is for you until you have given it a serious try.

OCCASION 13 · *A Teacher's Journal, 1972–1988*

I · The Rhetorical Problem: Whose Successes, Whose Failures?

Interesting modern accounts of the daily life of the teacher are rare. Favorable accounts are even rarer. Though many novelists and poets have earned their keep as teachers, their reports on their experiences are almost always negative, or in any case satirical. I could name a score of novels and plays that show teachers—and their students—as clods, satyrs, slobs, toadies, maniacal sadists and frauds, but I can think of hardly any that portray college teaching and its related scholarship in a form that any serious teacher would recognize, let alone emulate. An occasional work will succeed with a respectful or even sentimental account of *secondary* teaching: *Goodbye, Mr. Chips, To Sir with Love, Up the Down Staircase*. But only a few modern stories or essays have managed to show, as Lionel Trilling does in "Of This Time, Of That Place," or as John Berryman does in "Wash Far Away," how it feels to try to teach literature, composition, or LITCOMP. Most of them follow the lead of Dickens with his Mr. McChoakumchild, his Mr. Squeers, and his Mr. Creakle, in showing the teacher as fool or knave, standing in the way of the child's natural capacity to learn.[1]

When they do try to get beyond such caricature, they usually do best, as Trilling does, with the moments of failure. Is that because failure is always more dramatic, more decisive, more emotionally persuasive than success? Or is it that success is always a bit dubious in any teaching worth doing— teaching that goes beyond imparting information and simple skills? Perhaps it is only that readers spontaneously enjoy accounts of bad teaching and of the miseries of bad teachers—they've all suffered from so many of those tyrants and bumblers, and it's good to see *them* suffer in revenge.

See the introduction to part 4 above for a description of this occasion.

1. Ancient authors are of course another matter entirely. The dialogue of master and pupil was a major literary form during most periods, from Plato through the Renaissance. Socratic dialogues can be described in many different ways, none better than as a demonstration of what it is like to pursue teaching as a vocation. (Since writing the above, I've seen the movie *Educating Rita*, which does provide many moments that might suggest why a grown-up person would think teaching English—and even composition—worth doing. But the film is very careful to cover its "sentimental" tracks with ample ironies against teaching and on behalf of "real life.")

No literary portrayal of a teacher's anguish is more powerful than D. H. Lawrence's portrait of the seventeen-year-old Ursula Brangwen's terrified encounter in *The Rainbow* with a class of hostile, brutalized pupils. Like many another fictional teacher, Ursula succeeds only when she abandons her ideals and learns how to beat her charges into submission.

> But she had paid a great price out of her own soul, to do this. It seemed as if a great flame had gone through her and burnt her sensitive tissue. . . . Oh, and sometimes she felt as if she would go mad. What did it matter, what did it matter if their books were dirty and they did not obey? . . . Oh, why, why had she leagued herself to this evil system where she must brutalize herself to live? Why had she become a school teacher, why, why? (Chapter 13, "The Man's World.")

The failures we teachers meet will vary, of course, depending on where we're placed. I have never had to face the physical threats that many a secondary teacher now faces daily; I have never had to threaten violence, let alone actually use it. I can only guess at the kinds of torture that in other circumstances I might have given or received. But I have known my share of psychic torture and visible failure—enough to help me recognize why it is so easy for authors to portray *only* failures, comic or pathetic.

October 31, 1978

My freshman, Jerry,[2] comes late to his appointment to talk about his paper. His writing has been so poor, his responses in class so sodden, that I have about concluded—against my professed principles—that he is hopelessly short on natural ability. Maybe he's simply one of those rare mistakes made by our admissions office. Maybe he's just what we used to call dumb. Thick. Hollow between the ears. Whatever his native ability, I have to conclude that this sullen, unresponsive creature is *slow*, slow in his reading (he cannot read aloud without stumbling badly), slow in his writing ("It takes me four hours to turn out one page"), slow in responding to my questions here in my office, offering responses that are often off-track, uninformed—dumb.

I resist the obvious conclusion and continue my effort to break into his world. Breaking and entering—that's my business, always on the assumption that some sort of treasure is inside if one can only get by the burglar alarms. An arrogant, sometimes brutal business this is, almost as brutal as Ursula's caning. But if you can't break in, you can never hope to help them break out. So I keep slugging away at it, trying first this move, then that—getting nowhere.

---

2. I have used the student's real name only when the anecdote reflects unequivocal credit, as it *almost* does here. Jerry's real name was of course Barry.

"Let's look at it this way. Have you never enjoyed . . . ?"

No, he has never enjoyed . . . whatever I name.

"When we were talking about the fat woman in [Flannery O'Connor's] 'Revelation' [*he* is fat], did you . . . ?"

No, he did not.

Finally, in desperation:

"Well, let's stop talking about the course for a while. When you're not being nagged by teachers like me, what do you really like to do?"

He looks even more withdrawn than before—not really hostile, exactly, just passive with a touch of sullenness.

"Isn't there *anything* you really like to spend your time at, anything that grabs you?"

In such moments, one "grabs" for whatever slang one happens to have available—always at least ten years behind whatever the student would recognize as the way his kind of person talks.

A pause. Then:

"I like to watch football on TV."

"Well, then." Hearty, now. My opening! The prospector has found his lode. "How would you feel about writing your next paper about—ah—whatever it is that—ah—grabs you about the—ah—current football scene . . . ?"

I am cursing myself for not even knowing which teams are which. . . .

"No, I don't think I could do that."

The hour ends. I am exhausted. He leaves without thanking me for my unsuccessful try.

I learned, a year later, that he had survived, after a disastrous quarter or so. As a sophomore he did better-than-average work. In his fourth year, I met him on campus, a better-than-surviving Economics major, and he told me that it was only when he got into my *colleague's* humanities course that things began to make sense. *Somebody* got to him, but not me!

The percentages of such failures will vary from teacher to teacher, from year to year, from decade to decade, even from class to class in the same term. But there are always some failures.

You can fail with the bright as well as with the slow. At Chicago we get our share of students who think they are educated already.

November 7, 1979

Lisa, who is sure to get on the dean's list, because she can turn out slick work on any assigned topic (a "prize high-school debater," she lets us know at every turn), comes to me at mid-term:

"Why do I have to waste my time listening to those assholes bullshitting when my father is paying good money for my education here? I want to hear what *you* have to say."

No, I did not make that up. Nor did I surrender to my impulse to slap her. So far as I can tell, Lisa learned nothing from me or from anyone else during four "successful" years—nothing other than how to win debating points.

Why is it, I ask again, that we generally find it easier to write and read accounts of such teaching miseries than accounts of the times when the true vein is struck and the student starts digging? Is it no more than original sin—our natural interest in failure, disaster, shame? After all, teaching is not the only life that gets a poor press in fiction and drama: troubles outnumber triumphs on every page and stage. Our very language is weighted toward failure: there are far more words in my thesaurus for loss, grief, evil, suffering, vice, and failure than for happiness, virtue, and success. Is it just that all happy teaching experiences are alike—while each miserable moment is miserable in its own way—and therefore more interesting?

February 14, 1982

My friend Anne, who teaches in the adult division of a neighboring university, writes me this week about her class of fifteen part-timers; all of them carry full-time jobs and attend classes only in the evenings or on Saturdays.

"I finally decided to ask the author of our textbook, who teaches nearby, if he would visit our class. He did, and it was wonderful from beginning to end. My students' image of an author of a book led them to expect a stiff, formal hour, and it was great to see how pleased they were when he turned out to show interest in what *they* thought and felt. Cherice was especially turned on. She had been looking forward to his coming for weeks, and she came to class all dressed up—usually she wears jeans. She started off the semester with an attitude of 'Oh, God, what's this stuff!', because everything about his book's cover and its opening pages suggested an intellectual world not just foreign to her but hostile to her kind. That took four or five weeks to change, and for the past month and a half or so she's been telling me that she walks around having conversations with the author in her head. And before this she's never even been aware that she *had* an intellect, much less valued it. . . . The whole class has been going marvelously ever since."

Most teachers chose the field they're in because some teacher, early or late, led them to some experience like Cherice's. You might expect, then, that we'd have a flood of literature about those experiences: novels of conversion, short stories about seeing the light, testimonials in our professional journals about "how Professor Smith turned me from slob to scholar," about Professor Rybine's gratitude for his chosen profession. But we do not.[3] We have grown so used to poor-mouthing what we do, so bludgeoned into thinking that the way to talk about teaching is to satirize it, that we seem to have lost the very vocabulary of celebration. Is it because talk about success and gratitude too often, like the following, lacks dramatic specificity, literary vitality?

February 6, 1987
Both classes seem to be going wonderfully. Cannot remember ever enjoying classes more. A wonderful bunch of freshmen, struggling coura-geously with Aeschylus, then Thucydides, then Sophocles. Then it will be back to Thucydides again, and Euripides. They are so gloriously eager, most of them, that I come away from class feeling blessed (unlike last quarter) for having been able to talk with them for an hour. And my graduate class, Introduction to Literary Criticism—those 25 kids are a de-light. In previous years I've always found, when the first papers come in, a radical decline from the level of class discussion; these two classes seem to write almost as well as they talk. How do I put this together with all the public lament about a national decline? And how can one express, without sounding impossibly square to this generation of institution-rejectors, one's simple sense of gratitude for the institutions that turn up these many responsive souls year by year, the high schools and college admissions procedures that turn them over to me for my "use"? Left to "my own devices," how could I ever locate such wonderful colleagues?

We just don't seem to talk very well about successes and thanksgiving, we who are properly contemptuous of the many phony optimisms touted by our political and commercial leaders. We do produce many articles, in journals like *College English, College Composition and Communication,* and *The English Journal,* reporting enthusiastically *to one another* about how this or that new teaching method has worked for us. But when we address "the public," portraying the profession in general, we tend to foul

---

3. See however the collection of testimonials in *A Celebration of Teachers,* National Council of Teachers of English (Urbana, Ill., 1985), and the essays collected by Peter Beidler in *Distinguished Teachers on Effective Teaching,* New Directions for Teaching and Learning, 28 (San Francisco, 1986). See also the fine recent book that I wish I had known before writing the bulk of this one: Philip Jackson's *The Practice of Teaching* (New York, 1986). Like the wit-nesses assembled by Beidler, Jackson's essays treat "teaching respectfully, which is to say that they treat it as being important, as an activity to be taken seriously, not only by its practi-tioners but by the world at large" (p. xi).

our nest, like Philip Roth, one-time English teacher, in *Letting Go* (1962), or Simon Gray, in *Butley* (1971), one of the most popular productions ever by our campus theater (it was produced twice within a decade). The witty center of that play is a middle-aged, failed English teacher, Butley, contemptuous of his profession and of his fellow teachers. In contrast, the "good teachers," those who have not failed colorfully, those who do not insult and cheat their students, are imperceptive, unoriginal, stodgy, prissy, dull—fitted only to serve as comic butts. We who attended the play all loved it. What fun to hear that cruel, clever slob turn on his students and move them to tears with his sarcasm.

As Butley's student reads her abominable paper he tears her to shreds:

> MISS HEASMAN: . . . "and thus of forgiveness on the theological as well as the human level."
> BEN: Level?
> MISS HEASMAN: Yes.
> BEN: The human *level?* . . .
> MISS HEASMAN: . . . "Paradoxically, *A Winter's Tale* of a frozen soul—"
> BEN: Bit fish-mongery, that.
> MISS HEASMAN: (*laughs mirthlessly*) "—is therefore thematically and symbolically about revitalization."
> BEN: Sorry. Re-whatalization?
> MISS HEASMAN: Re-*vitalization.*
> BEN: (*gets up and goes to* MISS HEASMAN) Thematically and symbolically so, eh?
> MISS HEASMAN: . . . "As we reach the play's climax we feel our own— spiritual—sap rising."
> BEN: (*after a long pause*) Sap?
> MISS HEASMAN: Sap.
> BEN: Sap. Sap. Yes, I think sap's a better word than some others that spring rhymingly to mind. Good. Well, thank you very much. What do you want to do—I mean, after your exams? . . .
> MISS HEASMAN: Teach.
> BEN: English?
> MISS HEASMAN: Yes. . .
> BEN: Teacher of whom?
> MISS HEASMAN: Sixth forms, I hope.
> BEN: Isn't it more exhilarating to get them earlier? Sixth-form teachers are something like firemen called in to quench flames that are already out. Although you can never tell—recently I've enjoyed reading almost as much as I did when I was twelve. I do hope I didn't slip through their net—it makes one lose confidence. But I'm sure *you'll* be all right. Perhaps books are just my *madeleines,* eh? . . . I'm not really myself this afternoon, what do you want to do next week?
> MISS HEASMAN: We have to cover at least six Shakespeares.

BEN: From what I've heard already, Shakespeare's as good as covered. . . .

MISS HEASMAN: Believe it or not, you can be as rude as you like. I don't take it personally.

BEN: That's another good way of taking the fun out of teaching. Good afternoon, Miss Heasman. . . .

BEN stands at the open door, gestures obscenely after her. Then, aware that he is holding her essay, pinches his nostrils, holds the essay at a distance, makes gagging sounds, pantomines gas-poisoning as he goes back to his desk. MISS HEASMAN has come back to the door, stands watching him. BEN drops the essay onto his desk, stiffens, turns slowly. He and MISS HEASMAN stare at each other. MISS HEASMAN turns and goes quickly from the room.

Butley later throws the stack of students' papers on the floor and stomps on them. My friend David Bevington, a fine teacher, said he found the scene excruciating: he wanted to get down on stage and rescue those papers. Me, too. But the audience—me, too—were laughing and rejoicing: what fun to shit upon our profession. That's the sort of thing we all enjoy as a portrayal of our lives in teaching. But of course for most of us the portrait is a gross exaggeration of the worst we could imagine about our roles. All of us who survive in the profession for as much as ten years enjoy and suffer a far more complex mixture of successes and failures, a day-by-day kaleidoscope that no brief portrait could capture.[4]

If we put the hours spent being a scholar to one side awhile, just what is that life?

—It is a life lived in the face of towering obstacles to success, some of which I turn to in the next section.

—It is a life that constantly threatens the ego, because no teacher knows enough, either about the subject or about students' needs, to do what needs doing.

January 2, 1972

On my way to my first class of the quarter, I meet Philip Kurland in the corridor. Both of us are carrying an armful of books and notes.

"I know what you're thinking, Phil, carrying all those heavy law books to your first class. You're thinking that this is the time they are going to find out just how much of a fraud you are."

"Yes," he laughs, "and I know how *you* know!"

---

4. Nobody knows just what proportion of those who start stay the course—or perhaps we should say "the courses"—from first teaching assignment to retirement. My guess is that it is far more than half—lower than one would find in better-paid professions like medicine, higher than in less personally rewarding, non-tenured professions like journalism.

Every teacher I've talked with about teaching has had a collection of remembered disasters, humiliations, moments when a genuine weakness was
revealed. I shall of course treat my own moments of that kind tenderly. But
here's a sample:

*Sometime in October 1950, a memory from the first year at Haverford,
of a three-man tutorial of students in my freshman course. The three are
supposed to be doing constructive criticism on their papers for the week:*
MARCHAND: [Oh, yes, I remember his name, though I can remember
the names of only one or two others from the class of twenty] Mr. Booth,
I wonder if I could be excused to go and take a nap? I have a "jitter-session"
[oral examination] in an important history class later this afternoon. . . .
WB: Well, ah . . . I don't know, Mr. Marchand. Uh, you know, if
you'll stay I'll try to make things a little more interesting. . . .
Or words to that effect, not spoken sarcastically but pleadingly. The
crawling, the impotence, the shame of it—felt even now! Why could I not
call on even a smidgen of Butley's cruel, nasty wit—precisely what I now
suspect would have waked Marchand up? Later on, we'll see more of this
character failure—the fear of not being loved, the fear of conflict.

—At the same time, and with only seeming paradox, teaching is a life that
offers daily temptations to egotistical triumph. This obstacle to real teaching
is more easily satirized than discussed sympathetically (as I tried to do in
"The Good Teacher as Threat," Occasion 18 below). A class of eighteen-
year-olds, each of whom knows that "success in life" depends in part on
how this absolute dictator assigns final grades, can be the most misleading of
all captive audiences except cowed citizens in a police state. How can they
not laugh at my jokes—so long as I make them obvious enough? How can
they *not* use flattery, subtle or blatant?

Here is an attempt to show how that works, in a freshman class-hour
excerpted from my someday-perhaps-to-be-completed novel, *Cass Andor*.
Jeremiah Gemissant, a minor character, is in effect showing the world how
much smarter he is than poor Cass, a freshman who has made the mistake
of baring her soul in her first assigned essay:

Assistant Professor Gemissant was playing one of his favorite games,
Stamping out Naïveté, and most of the kids in the class were loving it, and
him. It was one of the moments when he felt best about his teaching, this
moment late in the second week or early in the third, when he read aloud
from one of the more amusing essays and commented as he read. Bursts
of laughter were by now greeting every sentence, whether from the essay

itself or from his witty commentary. But it had taken a few moments of careful guidance to bring them to this point of bloodthirstiness.

Here is what they had heard so far:

"'Some people feel that you can make conclusions about life itself or about the whole modern world of today by looking at written evidence like what you find in newspapers.'

"Whenever I read a phrase like 'some people think' I wonder, which people? Does the author have anyone in mind, really? If so, why doesn't he or she . . . incidentally, I should just mention that I make it a point always to preserve the anonymity of the student when I read from a paper, unless the student himself, or herself, chooses to break the secret." Cass was already blushing so deeply that anyone looking at her knew the paper was hers.

"But as I was saying, who are 'some people'? Nobody, that's who." Only a smile or two, so far; they're not getting it. "'Some people feel' . . . the author surely means think, since there are no feelings mentioned." Still only faint smiles. ". . . 'that you can make conclusions'—I wonder if the author has asked himself or herself whether to 'make a conclusion' is a better thing to do than simply to conclude?"

Gemissant has mastered, self-consciously, that special rising intonation used by the younger generation to turn an indicative sentence into a bland interrogative, with a rising diphthong. "And I conclude that the author has not thought about it at all, but simply felt that to 'make a conclusion' is somehow fancier and thus more appropriate to college-level discourse than to conclude.

"'Conclusions about life itself'? Anybody know any life that is not life itself?" Titters. "But life itself does sound somehow more imposing, so it was slapped down, again presumably because it felt good." More titters; now we're coming; they're getting the pitch.

"'About the whole modern world of today'? Now we're beginning to discover the pattern of a kind of mind here, folks. 'Life *itself*' and 'the *whole* world.' Like wow!" Real laughter at last.

So now he had them; every sentence a boffo. An act like that can go on for a long time, even if you're not the victim. So I spare you, as Cass was not spared, his comment on her second sentence: "But anybody who thinks about it at all will see that newspapers report mainly the bad things about life or the world." But here he is again, on the third:

"'The old saying goes, if dog bites man, no news; if man bites dog, that's news.' I must say, class, that I've been reading student papers now for five years, and I had begun to hope that I'd live my professional life to the end without having to read that tired saying for the one-hundred-and-fiftieth time. But here it is, and the self-protection of 'the old saying' doesn't really help it much."

And the fourth:

"'Well, I would like to suggest . . .' Well, if you'd sort of like to suggest, why don't you go ahead and suggest instead of backing into the sentence this way, like a shy high school girl going to her first prom." Real guffaws now; got em! But many of those who were laughing hardest were by now—and Jeremiah Gemissant did not know this, indeed never discovered this to his retiring day—already inwardly drying up, thinking: If he objects to all that, nothing, nothing I can ever say can get past him, let alone please him. I'm doomed, doomed, we're all doomed, but meanwhile let's make sure that this rival is dead; grading here will be of degrees of badness, and let us hope this is the worst.

"'. . . that the saying should read, if man strokes dog and dog returns stroke with deep and lasting affection, no news: if dog bites man, news— if the man is an important citizen; if dog bites man and has rabies, then that's news!' Note how the epigrammatic quality of the original saying, banal as it is, has now been turned into preachy sententiousness." Alas, there was no one there to note that Gemissant was allowing himself certain stylistic latitudes denied to all the rest.

"But let us hurry on. 'I would suggest . . .' Oh, no, not again, shy creature . . ."

And so on Assistant Professor Jeremiah Gemissant went, line by line, phrase by phrase, through the most miserable hour of Cass's hitherto almost carefree life.

The self-flattery can spill over from class to paper-grading time. How smart can Jeremiah appear to himself, sitting alone with red pencil flashing?

Mechanics: B
Style: C
Argument: F

Dorcas Andor
Freshman Humanities
October 5, 1967
Mr. Gemissant

A good clean paper, Cass -- but one that says nothing. I'm afraid we must talk about it.

What I believe Most Strongly:

Meaning?

What I believe most strongly is that the universe is love, and that all human beings deserve love and can learn from love. God created the world so that people could learn how to love and how to learn, and he gave every person the essential equipment for progressing in love. The misery in the world is caused because people have failed to give other people the love that they need. If

all?
Hitler?

even idiots?

redundent

230

why don't they if God created them?

everybody would just <u>work harder in loving</u>, the main troubles of the world would be solved —e.g., war, crime, political conniving—all these are <u>obviously</u> the direct result of lack of love.

evidence?

evidence?

I believe, secondly, that the world is progressing. Though there have been many ups and downs throughout recorded history, on the whole, more and more people are learning the importance of love, and practicing love in the world. Though I have already read in this course some authors who think the world is getting worse rather than better, to me what they say seems just <u>silly</u>. Everybody I know of is constantly improving, <u>except for those who have not been given the love they need</u>. Some-times when I think of the whole universe, getting better and better as more and more people learn how to love, I could almost burst with the feeling of being part of all that. And I sometimes <u>cannot help wondering</u>, when it feels so wonderful to me, why so many people take so long in discovering the joys of love and progress. This is one of those things I would like to find out⓪what is holding things back.

name calling not evidence!

proof?

look up sentimentality

weak

pn

wordy

Third and last, I believe in education. There is so much to learn that everyone can have a whole life time of learning if he wants it. And if there is a life after death (I don't list that as something I believe strongly, but it seems to me the <u>most plausible hypothesis</u> of all hypotheses I can think of) then we could go on learning forever, and that would to me be a great thing. I can't believe that God would plan (this) desire for eternal learn-ing and growing in me and then frustrate it by making my death from this life final. Surely there is a (divine plan) that includes all my beliefs and many more that I will learn about in my next life.   *new topic?*

evidence?

not clear why

antecedent?

new topic?

you grow shrill here. Is it because you suspect that you are talking nonsense?

—The teaching life is at the same time a life that offers many genuine rewards, though the rewards are always suspect if scrutinized with the very kind of critical attention that is required in practicing the profession: "What's your evidence?" If, after a couple of weeks in the term, you decide to yourself that you are doing a splendid job, and that *they* are, too, you can fully expect that in the next week you will discover unmistakable signs—perhaps when you give a quiz, or when you read the first batch of papers—that you have apparently so far taught them nothing.

And nobody else's testimony is any more reliable than your own.

May 12, 1978
Mary was in today to say how my class has changed her life; indeed she is going to become an English major as a result.

"Well" (you always ask yourself) "does she mean it, or is she just working for an A? And if she does mean it, is that good? What sort of service is it to someone to turn her into an English major? How will I ever know?"

The phone rings and it is the dean telling you that you are to receive an award for excellent teaching, based partly on the students' evaluation forms and letters of praise. You glow for a few minutes or hours or weeks, but sooner or later you remember just what you have always said about the unreliability of student evaluations. And before long your triumph turns to ashes and thence—if you are lucky—to an ironic awareness that you just don't know whether you are any good or not.

—For these and other reasons, teaching is a life that exposes every flaw of character. It requires impossible measures of such old-fashioned virtues as courage, persistence, humility, and attention to other people's needs, even when they seem to conflict with your own. You are granted what at first looks like a great gift: unusual freedom of choice about how to spend your time. But that means unusual temptation to slack off. For most of us the specified hours amount to around six to twelve hours per week of class time for only nine months a year. During the nine months, you can simply cancel a class here and there, at least if you have tenure, with no serious tangible consequences, and your summers *can* be spent fishing or dealing in real estate.[5] Thus only what used to be called "inner resources" will prevent some kind of decay.

5. This year, 1987, one graduate assistant I know of—not in English—was discovered to have canceled nine of thirty scheduled classes. She will not be re-hired, but I have known professors who got away with worse track records.

February 20, 1984

What is hardest is staying fresh. Freshpersons meet, after a few years, stalepersons. I've taught "Soliloquy of a Spanish Cloister" perhaps 20 times by now, and I know the poem by heart. So what is there to prepare? I can go into that classroom, on this Monday morning, two weeks before the end of term, and coast, with no visible signs of staleness. They'll think the class OK. But I'll know that I'm going through the old motions.

In the shower, I am trying to think about what to do with the Princeton lectures, already anguishingly close upon me. And I am simultaneously trying to think about how to improve the draft of the Nebraska paper on Pluralism.[6] But suddenly, from another layer of anxiety, I am thinking about how Browning relates to the short stories I read Saturday by Jonathan Penner [*Private Parties*, New York, 1983]—splendid short stories, subtle inferences demanded—just like "Soliloquy" really. Ah, that's it. We can begin that class, we will begin that class, with a short reading from the opening of one of those stories, then a brief discussion of how we read the signs of character in such stories and in poems like "Soliloquy." And then we'll be really into "Soliloquy," which they'll be already thoroughly prepared on because of having to hand in a paper this morning on what they know, or can guess, about the characters.

The point is that the Penner has sprung into my plans from an unconscious level demanding that I make this next class go—tired or not, stale on Browning or not. I care about that class, now, and I am exhilarated about facing it an hour from now. "Soliloquy" no longer seems old; rather, it is an instance of what is perpetually new.

It is never clear just how long one can keep that process going—the interest in teaching that takes over the mind involuntarily in the shower. (Of course it is precisely that interest that prevents me from getting any of my "real work" done when I have any kind of teaching schedule. When the subtler levels of the mind are working on the next class, they are not working on a rhetoric of fiction or a theory of pluralism—except on those blessed occasions when the needs of the course jibe with the current writing project.)

On many a morning, what I have called the "process" simply grinds to a halt.

6. "Pluralism in the Classroom." *Critical Inquiry* 12 (Spring 1986): 468–79.

January 20, 1981

"Phyllis, I just don't think I feel up to meeting my classes today. I think I'll just stay in bed. I'm sure I have a fever; I think that thermometer must be broken. . . ."

I lie there, throat sore, mind sluggish, except for panicky images of facing the class without a word to say. "What *did* we do yesterday? What *was* it I promised to take up today? Where *are* last year's notes on [Zora Neale Hurston's] *Their Eyes Were Watching God?* What *were* those reasons I gave myself last week for thinking this the best of all professions?"

In spite of the temptations to abuse our freedom, most of us most of the time find a way, unlike Butley, to keep the business going: we leave that bed, load up on this or that cough medicine or tranquilizer or stronger elixir, and drag ourselves to the campus, hoping that something will happen to turn this into one of the better days. Yet all the time we have the threatening knowledge that if we don't turn up, or if we turn up unprepared, or if we don't read and comment on that last batch of papers, indeed even if we decide to call in sick and take the week off and go to Las Vegas, only the neglected students will likely notice.

March 3, 1975

As I am leaving Cobb Hall, our central classroom building, I meet a colleague, a man once judged to be one of the best teachers on campus, now known to be having a "little trouble with alcohol."

"How are things going, Hank?"

"Not so good, Wayne. You know about my divorce? That's taking most of my time. Actually I'm fed up to here with my teaching, just coasting, if you want to know the truth. Fortunately the students can't tell the difference."

Actually the campus is full of students' complaints about Hank's decline as a teacher. How might I help him? I see no way.

Now it strikes me that I didn't think hard enough about how to get through to him. The point is that he could have gone on like that, or even worse than that, indefinitely, with no consequences except perhaps a salary slightly lower than that of his functioning colleagues.

This particular story, unlike many such, has a cheerful ending. Hank "suddenly" became his old self again, teaching vigorously, no longer drinking, no longer kidding himself about what it takes to do a good class. Somehow his character finally came through. I suspect, however, that in most other professions he would have met external constraints, and perhaps even supports, much sooner.

II · Some Obstacles to Good Teaching

It is long since time to attempt a somewhat more systematic account of some of the obstacles that can not only turn good teachers into bad, but drive them from the profession entirely

OBSTACLE 1: WORKLOAD, PAY SCALE, AND PUBLIC MISUNDERSTANDING

I won't dwell on this obstacle here, since so much of the rest of this book is devoted to it. But it is important to say once again, as strongly as possible, that the disparity between what our various publics expect of us and what they are willing to pay is a major source of our failures.

Meanwhile, every teacher knows—though it's difficult, perhaps impossible to "prove"—that to teach reading and writing and thinking requires personal, individual attention to students' responses, and that, up to a point, the smaller the student load the better the results. It is true that some studies purport to show that class size makes no real difference. But nobody who has tried to teach English to more than twenty or thirty students at a time will believe those studies. To teach English, at whatever level, means to teach writing, and teachers of writing, if they have too many students, and if they are conscientious, burn themselves out fast, faster than any teachers except those who work with the handicapped and delinquent. The burden, the cross, of English teaching is the task of reading and responding personally and intelligently to batches of "bad writing."

I am really puzzled, Arnie [a freshman], *by what happens in this one, as compared to your first two. Did you simply put things off until too late? Your second paper said something that interested me and the students in your tutorial. This one—well, we must talk about it. You spoke well in class about [William] James's argument against abstract reasoning. Why don't you give a single quotation here as evidence for your claim that his argument is mistaken?*[7]

7. Italicized comments are verbatim copies of what I have written to students over the years. I have had to work hard to resist the temptation to make up smarter ones for my purposes here.

March 10, 1987

I'm surprised to be surprised by the fresh discovery of what I've discovered so often in the past: how much harder it is to *teach every student* in a class of 25 freshmen than in a class of 15.

When I taught Introduction to Humanities two years ago, I took pleasure in attending to each of the 15 students. That meant not only attending to each of the fifteen during our class discussions—no one can be allowed to hide. It meant also a lot of hard work on individual writing and reading problems. It included some nursing of wounded psyches and listening to life histories too much like too many other life histories I've listened to. It even required a couple of hospital visits, when "mononucleosis" (or some psychic simulacrum) struck a couple of them (as it always seems to when the pressure is on), and a couple of letters home to support the students' desire to stick it out in spite of unpromising starts that discouraged the financially pressed parents. After twenty weeks with me and ten with Gregory Colomb, all fifteen were in there pitching; all fifteen finished their first year honorably, and they were all back as sophomores—and again as juniors! Most of them are here again this year, and I'll have the pleasure of seeing them receive their diplomas in June.

This winter, in contrast, I "picked up" twenty-five, in a section of Greek Thought and Literature. Of course by now, in the tenth week, I "know" them all pretty well, in one sense. I've long since sorted out the names and faces, and distinguished those strange stereotyped pairings that often plague me. (Carolyn Heilbrun has reported that Lionel Trilling never managed to distinguish her from the only other woman in a graduate seminar; she claims that "women" were for him somehow all alike. My final problem this term has been distinguishing dark, handsome Kathleen O'Leary and dark, handsome Pegeen McCarthy—all that Irishness—and with yet another Kathleen in the class! That task took me about seven weeks, with my mind of course always on "higher things.")

Now, in the tenth week, I do not feel that I have really *taught* all twenty-five; I've *met* head-on only about ten of them, if by *meeting* one means an encounter that is likely to make a permanent difference. Though I've had private conferences with all, and my teaching intern and I have conducted several five-student tutorials with all, and though they've all written four substantial papers and one or more re-writes, I've managed to attend to the *particular* needs of only a small number. One young man in danger of failing college has taken endless hours of my time and of David Hanson's time and of various counselors time in the Student Resource Center; we may salvage a C for him, perhaps even a B, since his last paper was a B−. [He did not return for a second year. Where *is* that poor lost soul in May of 1988?] But meanwhile, I didn't get around to phoning Jeff when he was absent four times in a row (yes, it *was* mononucleosis, and he got all the reading done while lying in bed, so he'll survive—but even so, he might have been lying dead in a gutter for all I knew). And I didn't find time to talk with Sandra about the death of her mother, or with Sacha about his brush with the Swiss Army when it tried to draft him.

Why is it that even a College as proud of giving personal attention and "small-class instruction" as ours cannot understand that every freshman needs to be treasured in at least one group of no more than twelve to fifteen students? Almost any student who receives the kind of attention I can give, and do give, in a group of that size, can survive any amount of benign neglect in other courses. But when students find themselves anonymous in all four "small" classes (25 to 35, or even larger), how are they to discover the excitement of this place?

I am trying to dramatize a national failure to spend our money on the most important single problem—the education of citizens who can read and listen and think and write and speak effectively. The lack of individual attention is acute in every field, but I think it is most harmful in the teaching of "composition," "rhetoric," "communication"—*writing*. Learning to write requires more individual attention from the teacher than any other form of learning—far more than even the closest rival. (My own choice of "rival" would be learning to play the cello: what would I have learned, when at the age of thirty-three I "took up the cello" for the first time, if I had been taught in a group of twenty-five or fifty other learners, by a teacher trying to deal with three, four, or five similar groups?) Obviously our failure is most damaging in our elementary schools, high schools, and junior colleges, where English teachers—often called by other titles—frequently find themselves trying somehow to teach as many as two hundred students in four or even five or six sections. In such circumstances the students often write nothing; or if they write anything it is not read or is read inadequately. If the teacher is initially conscientious, he or she is quickly driven to despair. The plain truth is that almost no one with any fiscal responsibility has recognized the preconditions of any successful writing course.

Working with Ph.D. dissertations should be different, one might think. Written by prospective "doctors" of the subject, they surely don't need the detailed attention one gives to freshman essays. Not so: even those rare ones that are written with some fluency and care require detailed attention to every page—the same sort of rigorous attention one has to give to one's own first drafts.

I THOUGHT I had understood your outline and prospectus, Arthur, but by now in this chapter [his second draft of the third chapter] *I am utterly baffled about your organization. Where ARE we?*

In spite of the spirit-crushing loads, most of us keep on trying to say something hopeful. Though I cannot pretend to have got beyond "unread MS neurosis" I have found a kind of solution in the typewriter and—even better—in the word processor. Instead of filling the pages with innumerable abbreviations in red pencil ("gr.," "pn.," "par.," etc.), most of which most students ignore unless they are required to submit revisions, I usually manage to type discursive comments, trying to make them intelligible as direct talk to the student's specific problems. I ask myself "What is the problem that *this* student can most profitably concentrate on *now?*" Then I match my comments to numbers in the paper's margins.

Once I get at the task I positively enjoy it, because I'm "talking" with somebody about something that interests me. (Getting at the task is something else again. It is almost never a pleasure in advance.) The student receives what amounts to a letter from me about the project, and ideally he or she does not get the impression that writing the next paper is a hopeless task. It is true that my "letter" does not take less time than "grading" used to take me when I felt responsible for marking every comma splice and dangler; it usually takes more. But the time does not feel like something robbed from my life.

As I sort of anticipated, Anna [a junior], *yours is one of the papers that interested me most—in fact, it almost meets what you take to be* [J. H.] *Hexter's supreme criterion, by being fun. We must talk about it, but meanwhile I have to start qualifying the praise with the obvious point that the paper is really a pretty poor job, if judged by the standards it sets for itself. It implies that its author is ready to take Hexter on at his own level, to meet him in combat, and to defeat him. But (as you may suspect—who knows?) Hexter could wipe the floor with you. . . .*

Do you know the old story about Emerson (I think it was, or maybe it was William James, or maybe Channing) attacking Plato in his first paper at Harvard? The teacher wrote, "When you shoot at a king, don't miss." Hexter is not a king, but he's a lot tougher prince than you make out.

I know that my solution cannot be used in the same way by everyone. I can use it only because my student load is relatively light, because my students come to me already accustomed to turning out half-passable two-page essays, and because I type fast. But I have found that even the most badly prepared students respond when the teacher applies the principle, "Fewer Comments of Higher Quality."

Since I write 150–300 words on most short papers (and for B.A., M.A., and Ph.D. research papers it is often much more than that), I figure that I must have written something like eight million words in this peculiarly drab literary genre. If you add to those words the half million or so churned into letters of recommendation, I begin to rival the great letter-writers like Voltaire—in quantity. Of course, if you then divide by the number of repetitions—of catchwords, of "encouraging phrases," of expressions of alarm—the total number shoots down by 573 percent.

Is *that* a good way to spend one's life? Surprisingly enough, even after re-reading just now hundreds of these comments in cold blood, I still think so. But let no one pretend that essay-reading is sufficiently rewarding, in itself, to justify giving any writing teacher an eighty-student load.

The first par. is not as bad as you led me to expect, Eli [a junior], *but it's not a grabber. It does run over your conclusions—but not in a way that raises interesting problems for the reader. You assume a ready-made reader (me, I suppose), who knows the memos cold* [the assignment was to appraise the rhetoric of three memos from a dean who must do some firing] *and who won't really be interested in reading about them once again. Why not assume (and let me in on the act as an observer) some- one who has read them badly? Then raise a problem, rather than just announcing results.*

OBSTACLE 2: RIVAL INTERESTS AND DEMANDS

Probably every age tries its best to keep teachers from teaching well. Every age presents rival interests, rival pressures, rival ideals that teach teachers to undervalue what they do. The governess and tutor in the upper-class family of the nineteenth century were "told" by every social arrangement that what they did as teachers was not as important as what their higher-status charges would do, after they were taught. The business of the world has always been "business," not teaching. Though teachers in our culture may in fact receive more encouragement than they would have in earlier times, "everyone who is anybody" still clearly values other matters more than conducting a good class.

March 6, 1978

This morning, sitting in my library study with the door locked against all intruders, where no student can reach me no matter how serious his/her problem. . . . No, no. Try: where no students can reach me no matter how serious their problems? The revision weakens the particular image. In any case, I am thinking of a particular young woman out there, desperate about how to read the third sentence of paragraph three of the Hume we are to discuss tomorrow—wishing that she could ask Mr. Booth about it, dropping by my office and hearing the secretary say, "I don't know *where* he is this morning. No doubt in the library, working on his book." Sitting where no student, as I was saying, can come to be taught, I must begin revising chapter 5 of *Critical Understanding*. Instead, I am scribbling about teaching. The scribbling is as much an obstacle to actual teaching as revising chapter 5 would be. Surely the chief obstacle to my teaching is that my so-called scholarship is honored for several hours each day, by both my institution, which provides this private study and requires me not to meet students here, and by my ego and curiosity, which require me to keep at this resisting book, whatever the costs to my teaching.

Am I to dwell, then, on that outworn topic, scholarship versus teaching? Publish or perish? Bromide!—as my college teacher, P. A. Christensen, would have said. Platitude! Clichéd false dichotomy! Indeed it *is* a misleading dichotomy. Just think of all that can be said against it: If I had not engaged in "scholarship," would I not now be dried-up *as a teacher*?

1. No scholarship → no learning; 2. No learning → too much repetition of increasingly tired truths; 3. Too much repetition → growing hatred of students who demand it. Just last week I heard a colleague say, "If I have to teach *War and Peace*—a book I once loved—just one more time I'll go mad." What's more, my "scholarship" profits from my teaching.

Yes, all that can be truly said, in a hundred different ways. But the fact remains that this quarter I am teaching no classes, having pled "overwork," and the overwork consists of finishing my book, reading manuscripts for our press (and one for Princeton), reading dissertations and other scholars' manuscripts, lecturing at other colleges (o ho! o ho! as Caliban says; here's a confession indeed): my *chief* business these two terms, my busyness, is lecturing on eight other campuses, two days each, for Phi Beta Kappa. That's surely *not* pure scholarship. Do I count it as *teaching?*

Start over: The *chief* obstacle to sustained, serious teaching for me in my time is the racket I've got into of barnstorming other campuses, moving in for the one-shot kill and moving away fast, so that nobody can pick the holes in my brilliant, witty, learned presentations. I have become a sophist—like how many others? In theory we might defend ourselves as *good* sophists, able to construct a solid defense of our rhetoric as the center of education, eager to reconstruct what a good Sophist, talking with Socrates, would really have said in reply to Plato's unfair attacks. But in practice I often become a bad sophist: a "speech preparer," trained to make not just the worse cause, but any old cause seem like "the better one."

March 22, 1978

These lectures I have prepared for those undergraduates at Cornell, St. Lawrence, St. Catherine's, Augustana, North Dakota, Chicago Circle, St. Olaf, and Lehigh, are designed to stimulate hard thought. But they are at best the preliminary to teaching, not teaching.

Being on a campus two days is better, of course, than being there for one appearance, as I often have been in the past. Students do get a chance to come up and ask whether you really meant what you said, and you can then say, "Not really. What I should have said was . . ." But not often, not many. And meanwhile, there is that young woman back in Chicago, puzzling over Hume, being taught this quarter by God only knows what kind of incompetent, cruel, ignorant, indifferent betrayer of the cause, longing for a talk with somebody who will take the time to work through the paragraph with her. And I, I am . . .

April 26, 1978

On the road, I find myself wondering how I ever got into this. What strange combination of greed, ego, and altruism led me to think that it would be either service to the world or a tolerable thing in itself, to visit eight colleges for two days each, giving identical lectures at college after college?

As the year drags toward the end—two more colleges to go—I dread the next flight, the next attempt to screw up my energy and make a show of it. When I fly this afternoon to St. Olaf, I'll find myself already beginning to feel the tension. Even today, my "day of rest," I have gone through the two speeches for tomorrow, making a twenty-minute version of one for the chapel service, revising the other slightly because of yesterday's discovery that something didn't quite track. Chatauqua! Lyceum!

I think of all those lyceum speakers who used to come to Brigham Young University when I was a student. The lucky ones had some poetry to read: Carl Sandburg, Robert Frost. The hacks read their old lectures—was it Carl van Doren who lost his place one night and couldn't find it again? The great Tabernacle in Provo would be packed—how could that be? Have I misremembered?—and I would listen with every nerve, hoping for news from the great world.

I now know that many of these speakers had news from nowhere, had spoken those words already too many times. And here I am, doing the same thing. By now, the points—an attack on simplicities, a defense of rhetoric, "Can Art be Bad for You?"—seem not just labored but simple-minded, distorted, possibly bad for my listeners. I've had more than enough of this—I should be back home, teaching my own classes in the kind of sustained way that alone makes any difference.

May 1, 1978

But now I have been to St. Olaf, and the whole crazy process seems entirely justified. The speeches, which seemed drab when delivered to drab audiences, seem just fine when delivered to responsive audiences. The twenty-minute version, cut from the one-hour talk, "It's More Compli-cated Than That," seems positively inspired, as the three hundred or four hundred students laugh and applaud. "Critical Pluralism," given to faculty members who actually have faced rhetorical problems, seems to me almost profound. The social hour turns into a stimulating discussion. The plea-sure all this gives tells me just how much I do want to make a difference, and it changes my sense of why it was that I undertook this Phi Beta Kappa stint in the first place: I thought that I *might* make a difference.

How much of a difference? Well, when you think of the 2500 colleges in America, or of the 875 Phi Beta Kappa local chapters, you can't believe that visits to eight colleges, two of the visits quite drab, are going to trans-form the American educational scene. But would the same energy put into writing a book addressed to all such audiences have accomplished a lot more? I'll never know.

May 10, 1978

The *chief* obstacle to my teaching *at the moment* is my half-baked plan for a book about teaching. The truth is that I am sitting in my library study, at 9:30 of a Wednesday morning, "officially" finishing off, even thinking of killing, chapter 5 of *Critical Understanding*, but actually work-ing up these notes for *Teacher*—a book about a teacher who, instead of working with his students on Hume, spent his time in the library writing a book about teaching.

Why did he do that? "Officially" because it is important not just to teach your immediate students. The world of 1978 (it'll be 1983, '84, be-fore it comes out?)—the world of 1984 needs to be reminded of the serious-ness of teaching, of the presence on our scene of thousands of dedicated teachers and students. What they do is not ludicrous (all of the time); teaching and learning are graces of their—our—lives.

Yet—is this my point?—yet there *is* a kind of befouling of my life as teacher in the act of escaping students (*and* my scholarship) to begin writing a book about the importance of teaching English as a rhetorician. If that teaching is so rewarding, why don't I get on with it, rather than moving into this totally private world, the door safely locked against students, to write about it?

No matter what I choose to write here in the library, should I not worry that even this university, which values teaching more than most universities, cares more for—rewards more visibly—what I do "in here" than what I might do "out there?" If I had been the best undergraduate teacher in the country when I was at Earlham College for nine years, even if I had been *known* to be the best, pronounced best in the Sunday *New York Times Magazine* (what a fantasy!), no major university would ever have sought me out to bless their undergraduates. Only with the publication of a *book* did the great world suddenly decide that I was valuable. My point is not now to decide whether "the world" was wrong in this judgment (see "The Scholar in Society," Occasion 3 above, for the complexities plaguing any such judgment). It is rather to underline one reason why even those of us who have tried to learn how to teach have been so often deflected from teaching.

OBSTACLE 3: THE HECTIC PACE

By Thursday afternoon of each week I breathe a sigh of relief—except when I have Friday classes: I have almost made it through another week without disaster. Major disaster would be a complete unmasking of my gross ignorance. Minor disasters seem to fill my life, in surprisingly diverse forms:
—A student or colleague mentions an "essential" book that I not only have not read but have not even heard of.
—The phone rings and someone says, "Why have you failed to come to the oral for Louise Jefferson?" Or, "Did you forget that you were to speak in Mandel starting ten minutes ago?" (Yes, that one actually happened. James Redfield has recently suggested a new word, "clong," for the awful tightening of gut and brain that such moments bring.)

1978, undated, Friday afternoon
   Last week on Monday the phone rang.
   "Hi, Mr. Booth. You all set for Friday?"
   "Friday?"
   "Yes, you know. The talk to the 400 junior college teachers, Friday at noon."
   "Oh. [Brief pause, brief as I can make it.] Is that *this* Friday?"
   Long pause.
   "Yes, yes. This Friday. Noon. Have you forgotten?"

"Let me look at my appointment book."

I look at my appointment book and find that the speech is indeed pen-cilled in, for 3 o'clock in the afternoon, then crossed out, for reasons that I cannot now discover.

So the week was full, not only with my usual teaching, and with catching up from being away the week before, but also with preparing a 45-minute speech for those teachers—a speech that then had to be reduced five minutes at a time, down to twenty-five minutes, as I sat through other speeches.

This week has gone without *many* disasters! A typical week, threat-ened only by my always being pushed to the extremity of my limited knowledge about too many fields.

Monday, a.m.: Library, writing this book and other "assignments."

1:00 p.m.: Henry Anderson, Ph.D. candidate, to talk about his Special Fields Exam on Intellectual Texts from 1850 to 1940. At 12:30, munching my sandwich, I had scrambled through piles of unread manuscript trying to find his exam, but never found it.

"I sort of want to protest about that exam that you prepared."

"Oh. Was something wrong about it?"

"Well, it seems to me that it was distinctly unfair. You really asked me to construct the whole history of thought, using the texts on my list, and I was all prepared simply to talk about them one by one. I didn't feel I had a chance to show what I knew."

"Why didn't you then try to make something out of the question that you *could* do something with?"

"Well, I tried to. But I don't think it went very well."

I shuffle through my papers again to see if I can find the exam after all. It is still missing. I begin to believe that I've never *seen* the exam. I phone the department office. The secretary is sure that she put it in my box.

Anderson and I talk awhile about it. I assure him that if it seems to me that the question has been unfair—when the exam turns up—he will have another chance.

What I should have done, as I think about it later, is to try harder to put the burden back on him for being such a pedestrian student that he expects to be asked only one kind of question. The kind of thing I was asking of him would have been not only routine but perhaps a bit un-demanding if asked of certain other students I know.

Much too general, Henry [Ph.D. candidate]. *What you say may be true, but from the evidence you give one might just as well argue the opposite—that it would have been a better story told in the* FIRST *per-son: "I became aware that my body had turned . . ." Too often through this chapter I find mere assertion, not argument.*

2:30: Josh, a freshman, arrives to talk about the structure of his paper on Descartes. It is clear that he has not really managed to make Descartes' problems come alive, but he's bright—a very bright sixteen-year-old—and we have a lively talk about how to reconstruct the philosopher's problems.

Perhaps the most serious weakness in your treatment, Josh, section by section, is your failure to dig into the reasons Descartes offers for his position, leaving you (as at #5), simply asserting a contrary without a genuine encounter.

4:00: Steven Poltzer to talk about why the College at the U. of C. doesn't do more to get faculty members from various departments to talk together frequently and easily. I tell him that we do talk together frequently and easily, but that unfortunately students are usually excluded.

5:00: Special tutorial for the group of four freshmen who are going to conduct, later in the week, a class on *The Tempest.* I find their plans loose-jointed, vivacious, and worrisome. The class is sure to be loose-jointed, possibly not the least bit vivacious, and worrisome. We agree to meet again Wednesday night to make further plans, after they have got together on their own and come to a clearer notion of what will be worth doing.

5:30: Deborah Katz, my teaching intern, to discuss her anxieties about having to teach the class tomorrow, her inability to read Descartes with pleasure and comprehension, her worries about how to become a good teacher. A perhaps useful but exhausting hour.

7:30: Graduate seminar on Walter Guevara's paper dealing with Descartes' metaphor of building construction, deconstruction, and reconstruction. Good discussion. Guevara, lively, intelligent, witty, carries a great deal of the load. Animated good will in the group because Krispet is not there. Students talk to me afterwards about Krispet, wondering how we can keep him from terrorizing everybody.

Find myself wondering how I could capitalize on the accident that my freshmen as well as this advanced graduate student are working on Descartes. Can think of no way.

One student says, after all others have left, "The difference between your seminar and the one that many of us were in last quarter is like the difference between night and day." At first I choose the flattering interpretation, but later I can't be sure whether he said "night and day" or "day and night"—it makes all the difference. Am plagued by some anxiety, as I go to bed, about whether seminar is total or only partial failure—one word of possible criticism from one student can throw me from euphoria to despair. Decide, before falling off, that I must reproach Krispet once again for dominating and for showing his contempt for other students.

You have announced a fixed fight, Tod [Krispet—3d year Ph.D. student], *rather than drawing me into an inquiry. As you proceed in your writing for the Ph.D., this one point can become extremely important for you: Engage yourself, and your reader, in inquiry, by confronting opposing reasons. Your ex cathedra manner, both in seminar discussions and in your writing, is likely to prevent your learning from others and their learning from you.*

Must do a bit more thinking myself about Descartes' method, which seems to me more and more confusing, the more I study him—even as my admiration increases.

Tuesday Early a.m.: Re-read *The Tempest*, read student papers.

In spite of these objections, I like this one a lot, Cosh. May I have a copy please?

10:00: Freshman class conducted by intern Deborah K., in a competent but very nervous manner, along lines that I would never myself pursue about *The Tempest*. Hard work for me, sitting there silent, resisting temptation to take over. She is learning fast, she will be a good teacher, she cares immensely about the students and about *The Tempest*, and they know it. They respond like angels—giving her every benefit of the doubt, working hard to make the class go well, and in fact making it a profitable experience, so that later I can honestly tell Deborah that she is doing fine.

12:15: I buy a sandwich for lunch and read papers for the four o'clock seminar for today. Feel some sense of leisure because I still have almost three hours before class. The phone rings and David Smigelskis wonders why I am not at the steering committee meeting—clong! another one of those dreadful moments when I have forgotten my duties.

1 to 2:30: NCD [New Collegiate Division] Steering Committee meeting. Vigorous arguments, with some tension and mutual mistrust, mostly unspoken, trying to figure out how to conduct the Philosophy of Discourse class next year, and how to allocate our limited resources for the whole operation of the Committee on Ideas and Methods in the NCD.

The four of us are, so far as I can see, only remotely approached by any stereotype that I have met in any academic novel. All are serious and effective teachers, though in different styles; all are committed teachers and scholars. Any one of us could be easily satirized, of course, but it would be almost impossible to capture the intense seriousness about our task that has informed the whole hour-and-a-half.

The debate is not of that directionless kind that results when staffs simply quarrel about what books they want to teach. Our differences run deeper: just what kind of rhetoric course will qualify both as an essential step toward liberal education and as one of four required year-long courses in the new PERL program (Politics, Economics, Rhetoric, and Law). David Smigelskis clearly thinks that our previous two versions have been a bit unsystematic and more than a bit "academic." In place of "Philosophy of Discourse," he is pushing for something that could deservedly be called "*Practical* Discourse." Two of us like what we have been doing, and we resist his proposed changes. What comes out is essentially his plan, though modified by our criticism. We'll not know till we've tried it whether in fact the change is an improvement—and in one sense we'll never know: the variables in all teaching "experiments" of this kind are too complex for decisive appraisal.[8]

More of this bringing up of objections would help, Marvin [youngest student in the seminar]. *All of our inferences in these matters are chancy.*

4:00: Krispet comes to the seminar, and at first I regret it. But for once he behaves himself, partly because I begin with a sermon on how to deal with other people's ideas without turning things into a battle or a zero-sum game, and partly because [Robert] Inchausti, whose paper is our center, handles suggestions with great irenic openness and some skill. The group is beginning to jell. Seminar not a failure after all! Indeed, after two hours in which I have to say very little, I am high as a kite, and after fifteen more minutes of talking with students who linger on, I am thinking, as I walk toward dinner with visiting star Barbara Herrnstein Smith, that this is a marvelous way to make a living.

This is moving toward a fine paper, Michael. Your detailed observations about "The Dead" are sensitive and persuasive, and I think that the use of Longinus is beginning to pay off. Too much of the time, though, the allusions to L. seem forced, partly because you don't give me much about what L. was actually up to. Perhaps a clearer exposition at the beginning of how L. goes about his task would lead into a better explanation of why you want to make use of him, rather than simply doing your own private job on JJ [Joyce].

Wednesday. This morning I should really work at my book, or at my coming lectures, or at a dozen other things, including the papers due to students tomorrow, papers I promised to return *yesterday.* But my calendar says "read [Rufus] Cook's exam," "read Ken Frieden's paper," "read Doug Moller's exam," "re-read Peter's paper for 11:30 conference."

I'm afraid this revision doesn't work very well, Peter. In the first place, you waste your first par. on material that should have been some sort of

---

8. I describe a modified version of the course in "'LITCOMP': Some Rhetoric Addressed to Crypto-rhetoricians about a Rhetorical Solution to a Rhetorical Problem," in *Composition and Literature: Bridging the Gap*, ed. Winifred Bryan Horner (Chicago, 1983).

separate note or appendix. It does not invite us into the paper but merely informs us about your "study" background, then tells us what "the paper hopes" to do. Why should I read on?

Even more important, when you come to your conclusion, it turns out to be not much more than an assertion of a fact AS a fact, not as something that needs argument. We must talk about this one—along with the earlier version. You can easily learn to make better use of your revising.

So I do all that reading, just barely finishing in time for the 11:30 appointment with Peter, who proves to be friendly, open, and responsive to my suggestions about how to make his paper better. His paper is about O'Connor's "Parker's Back," a story I know very well, so for the first time this week I feel fully, whole-heartedly competent to give the student the help he needs. And he receives it well, so why am I dissatisfied? Is it that all the suggestions seem to be mine? Where are his?

12:00: Lunch again a sandwich in my office, because I have not yet re-read Krispet's paper. Also have not yet prepared my brief talk for dormitory house at dinner tonight.

1:30: Discussion with Cook about this exam. Prepared by three of us, it now seems much too broad, covering just about every major thinker since Aristotle: the questions stretch me beyond *my* limits.

2:30: Conference with Ken Frieden about his paper, "Narratives that Make Selves" or "Self-Making Narratives." Much continental jargon, much difficulty understanding each other, but a stimulating conference, as indeed was Cook's.

3:00: Tense but useful conference with Krispet. I think I got him to see that his brilliant ideas—and he *is* cleverer than our average—are besmirched by his carelessness of presentation, particularly his indifference to clear transitions and ambiguous pronoun references. It is difficult to bring him down from the heights to consider such matters, but when I revealed two actual grammatical errors, disguised by polysyllabic jargon, he did seem to begin to listen. A hard man to make an impression on.

4:00: The secretary reminds me that the letter of recommendation to NEH for Harold Hampton, who completed his doctorate five years ago, is overdue. The original seems to have been misplaced—did we fail to keep a copy?

I am pleased to write on behalf of Harold Hampton, who is applying for a Summer Fellowship. Mr. Hampton is unquestionably one of the ablest etceteras I have ever etcetera-ed. His dissertation, on etcetera, was given honors by the department. . . . He taught as my intern in Freshman Humanities, and I was much impressed by his etcetera. . . .

When the first draft is finished, I note how bland and general it is, so rush to my collection of dissertations and re-read a few pages in his, to bring Hampton back to life.

Sure enough, his work *is* a fine start on his problem—but why hasn't he turned it into a book yet? He'll never get it done in time for his tenure decision now. Mustn't worry about that—back to the letter, filling in some precise virtues where at first I had made him sound like every other young scholar. By 4:30 the letter looks passable, ready to be typed and possibly signed before 5:00.

4:30: Doug Moller, whose M.A. exam I have just read, comes in to explain why he thinks it shouldn't be passed and why he thinks he ought to leave the profession. Forty-five minutes spent pulling him together, like somebody propping up Mr. Smallweed. By the end he is beginning to consider the possibility that he might have a remote chance of becoming the really outstanding student that I think he already is. His work on a variety of rhetorical theorists and ethical critics is fascinating, work that might make a difference to the "outside world." [Note, 1988: Where is he now? He just disappeared on us!]

I like this one a lot, Treese [first-year M.A.], especially since I came to it after a string of papers that were a bit depressing. May I have a copy please? I think you strike about the right balance between mimicking Kenneth Burke's style to the point of parody and not mimicking at all. And you seem to me to have captured his main point. I especially like the details of your reading of Silas Marner.

I don't like the points where you seem to fall into KB's garrulity and lack of clarity in organization. Should I give you credit for imitating his lousy paragraphing?

5:30: I go for two hours with dormitory students to "sherry hour." A small turnout that embarrasses the student chairman, because she thinks everybody in the house ought to be there to hear me. We pass a gang of students around the pinball machine on the way, and she is tempted to harangue them into attendance. I hold her off.

A responsive discussion about irony and my professional commitment to "understanding." One student comes up afterward and asks if she could be in my section of Humanities next quarter, so much has she enjoyed the show. I am of course vulnerable to this kind of flattery, but unfortunately will not be teaching freshmen next quarter.

A fine conclusion, Tony [first quarter freshman], to a quarter in which you have improved rapidly and impressively. I hope that you can see as clearly as I can how much better this last paper is than your early papers. It is almost entirely free of your former elementary errors, it makes a serious case, and it argues that case with vigor and intelligence—with the exceptions noted below. You still have trouble "enforcing" your sub-points—making clear to your reader how each step is required to arrive at what you think is and is not worth studying in a "poetry" course.

You create a good sense of your own fairness, Amy [another first-term freshman], by conceding one main point to William James before showing his inadequacy on the other point. As you read further in philosophy, you'll note how different occasions call for different degrees of rigor. Later on, you'll want to press yourself about whether that inadequacy is real in James. You hit things about right here—for a short paper, written at the end of the beginning quarter, where superficiality could almost be said to have been "assigned."

9:00 p.m.: I walk to Woodward Court [dormitory] in order to meet with the four freshmen who will teach the class tomorrow. We work for two hours, each of them going over what will be attempted in 20-minute segments next day. Fatiguing work, because their pace seems so much slower than mine, and their essential good sense is hard to locate in the animated, pleasant, but chaotic discussion. I am tired. But they are beautiful kids, and they are really grappling with *The Tempest*. What's more, all four have by now a better grasp of the details of fact and scene than I do. The two women seem to have the precise page and line references needed in making their argument. At the end of the two hours I tell them that whatever happens the next day, they at least have a mastery of the play superior to that of many who have published about it.

Thursday: Up at 6 in order to be able to correct papers steadily, and in some tension, so that they can be returned by 10 o'clock. . . .

The fact that a word exists, Alan [another freshman], is no argument for using it in a given spot. My point about "spatiotemporality" is that it is pretentious in this context. If you want to be fancy, why not be really fancy and talk about "chronotopes"? I give you the word free of charge, with the understanding that you will also consider the possibility of something simple and direct, like "space and time." Or "places and times," or . . .

A whole page, Georgio [MA student], without a single bit of evidence from the texts! Throughout the paper you do not give yourself the fun of looking closely (as you seem to have done in your reading) and then playing with alternatives. Give your readers your evidence, and then lead them to play with that evidence along with you. . . .

Wrong connection, Todd [Ph.D.]. You can't mean that you studied this work "as a consequence" of what you've said before, or concluded that it is good "as a consequence" of their neglect. Find the right word.

Where, in such days, is there time for reflection on my aims, or for thoughtful review of the needs of each of my fifty or sixty charges? Above my desk is a playful photograph of my Earlham colleague Arthur Little, sitting on one end of a log, like Mark Hopkins, talking with a student at the other end. One student!

OBSTACLE 4: TEMPERAMENT

Why do I build for myself a hectic calendar, week by week? My university—unlike many—does not *require* such a pace. I choose it. Obviously the *chief* obstacle to my teaching well must be my own temperament, my character.

Among my character flaws—perhaps shared with many teachers (it led us into teaching?)—is an absurd insecurity, an obsessive need to be loved and approved by all. This leads to wasted energy, wasted emotion, unwise acceptance of tasks for which I am unsuited. And it often leads to grotesque errors of judgment, some of which can sear my memory for decades.

1958, a memory

    3:00 p.m.: A course at Earlham College in the History of Philosophy.

    A student yawns audibly.

    WB: Mel, are you bored?

    MEL: Yes, as a matter of fact I am.

How many times I have played over the appropriate responses I might have made. But what did I actually do? I *pled* with Mel for attention, apologized for my inability to make things interesting in dealing with Jeremy Bentham—in short, abased myself, as I had done five years earlier with Marchand, and made Mel feel even more superior than he had when he yawned. It makes me miserable to think about it, almost thirty years later!

June 10, 1972

With the detested task of handing in grades now completed, I am allowed to go to the College office and have a look at the student evaluations. I always debate with myself about whether to bother: Isn't it time, now, to stop attending to those always unreliable, always ambiguous scribbled notes? (Usually the tired and distracted students do them in the last fifteen minutes of the term, at the request of the College dean and a student committee that collates the results). But I almost always surrender to the hope that for once every comment will be enthusiastic. So today I have looked them up, with the usual result: I'm more exasperated by the three lukewarm comments and the one nasty dig than pleased by the seventeen praisepoems. "Course seriously flawed by failure to include more female writers." "Would have preferred more lecturing, fewer discussions." And the one that really burns: "Liked the approach of Mr. Simperson last year better." Simperson! That blowhard? How can that be? He's a terrible teacher, a menace to the students, a . . . But let's see what his students have to say about him this year? Feeling sneaky, I pull Simperson's folder. It is a mistake: his evaluations appear to be more favorable than mine. They all just love him. "His classes are just plain FUN." "His classes are the most exciting I ever took." "His course made me decide to major in English." I am miserable for an hour afterward: who wants to be admired by students who admire a fraud like Simperson so much?

Well, the fact remains that I do. A part of me wants unqualified praise from every student, even as I acknowledge that any teacher who tries to please every student will probably not teach any student very much. Perhaps I should just swear off looking at those evaluations? Or better, change my character?

Fear of rejection and desire to be loved can plague one's life—can torture one's dreams.

September 21, 1976 (returning from a year's leave, a week before classes begin):
Another teaching-anxiety dream last night.

I have been invited to return to Haverford College [where I taught for only two years, 1950–52], as a "Distinguished Professor of Humanities." I am sure that my new distinction will now at last convince the doubters. But I cannot find my assigned living quarters. Have they failed to assign me a room? Nor can I find where I am to teach. I wander the halls, looking for a catalogue or schedule. When I finally find one, my name does not seem to be listed. Oh, yes, here it is, with the course I am to teach: "Booth. Humanities (Latin)." Sheer terror—my true ignorance will be exposed at last.

I cannot see that kind of worry about negative responses as a sign of anything but weakness—a lifetime obstacle to my best teaching. One can of course put a favorable gloss on it, something like this:

Some "good teachers" succeed with only a special range of students: the very best or the weakest. But surely the teacher with a vocation to teach will want to teach every student who drifts into sight. He (I'm thinking of me, so it's not "she" for the nonce) will try to respond to *this* class *this* year with *these* texts and problems; every year or so he will burn all of his previously useful syllabi, class notes, assignment sheets, and exams. To get through to each class, he must teach *to* each class, not *from* his preconceptions.

What's more, within this unique batch, with its shocking differences from last year's batches, he will see each student as "promising," regardless of how unpromising the "material" looks: here's one (at Earlham in the early fifties) with manure on his shoes; a generation later, here's one (taking time out from the sit-in) with "fuck the life of the mind" penned like a tattoo on his upper arm; a generation later still, here's one with purple hair, apache style, wearing something that may at one time have been a tutu. "I'll probe behind that surface if it kills me," he tells himself, "and uncover the teachableness that I *know* is in there."

He'll teach 'em in small classes, if he can wangle small classes, or he'll teach 'em in large, if that is his lot. And he'll try to make every class for each one of them a memorable experience—the high point of each day. When he can't get to them in class, he'll insist on private conferences. He'll be willing to sacrifice everything else—content, "coverage," reputation, even "truth itself"—to ensure that no one of them practices the kind of passive reception or daydreaming indifference that he practiced in nine out of ten of his own undergraduate classes. He knows that they are all teachable, by somebody, and circumstances—the admissions office, the accidents of registration time—have elected him to carry the ball.

Well, maybe. But such an ideal goes sour when it becomes, not fear of the students' remaining untouched, but fear of being disliked or ignored. To love students in the sense of wanting to teach them is a virtue; to want to be loved or admired is usually a mistake and often a vice. It leads to talking too much. It can lead to imposing the teacher's one right view on material that should be seen as manifold and controversial. The effort to penetrate the student's surface can become a kind of self-serving seduction or even violation: Who *is* this "he" who has a right to insist that these charges take on his ways rather than continuing on their own? When the desire to be loved takes over, it can lead the teacher, as it leads political candidates, into grotesque oscillations from displays of benevolence to excessive gestures designed to prove toughness.

1955, a memory
    About ten minutes into the hour: "Nobody seems to be able to say much about Mill today [the text is *On Liberty*]. Ah, er, how many have

read the assignment? Only one? [Long pause. The kindly, patient teacher is at the end of his rope. He feels like weeping, or maybe stalking out, as Hutchins is reported to have done when a class failed him in this way. Suddenly he loses his temper.] All right. I've been patient long enough. Tomorrow we're going to have an examination on *everything we've read to date*. I told you earlier that you all looked so good that you'd make B's or better. Well, now I have to go back on that; there'll be some F's, you can be very very sure." He then lectures for the rest of the hour, stern, "dignified." But as he leaves the class at the end of the hour he catches himself thinking, "Perhaps if I had them to the house for another party, they would. . . ."

I have had colleagues whose main protection from such fears was to struggle for total mastery over a given specialty—as if to say, "I may not get them all to love me, but by God they'll respect or even fear me." I have indeed had fantasies of that kind; after all, if I had really known a great deal about Jeremy Bentham, I could have wiped Mel out with one stroke, and if I were an internationally famous expert on Mill they wouldn't dare etc. etc. But I have long since decided to go on taking crazy risks as a "generalist," pretending to know something about such unmanageable subjects as rhetoric, irony, the whole history of criticism, the entire history of fiction, and the relation of these already monstrous "fields" to just about everything there is. Never mind why. The result is that I make myself vulnerable in ways that contribute to the other obstacles I have described.

1980, a memory

A graduate course, The Novella. As a kind of specialist, I'm supposed to know about fiction and about literary criticism and about theories of interpretation. But I've never before taught a course in the novella; I have become interested in it, partly through the book *Forms of the Modern Novella* by my friend Mary Springer. And so, according to my principle of trying never to teach the same course with the same reading list more than twice, I am teaching what is perhaps my fiftieth new course. What's more, I am teaching Thomas Mann's *Tonio Kröger* for the first time, in translation, from Paulson's anthology. ("I never use textbooks." Except, of course, when I do use textbooks.)

The class has been having a lively discussion of the form of this work. What really holds it together, how is it unified, if it is? Things seem to be going quite well. I am almost pleased with our growing illustration of Mann's quest for beauty of form, so much more clearly illustrated in this novella than in those long, loose, baggy novels we all love for such mysterious reasons.

I call on a student who has raised his hand for the first time.

"Mr. Booth, do you think it would make a difference to our discussion if we had a text that wasn't mutilated? I've checked with the original and there are several paragraphs missing, just after the second page."

Well, it does make some difference indeed; it makes a lot of difference. For a sixty-one-year-old "formal" critic it makes more than just an intellectual difference: it makes him feel humiliated. He should have found time, according to his own usual practice, to read the story in the original, even if his German is so sluggish that he must always have a dictionary open as he reads. That's what any good scholar-teacher would have done—not just a specialist but even a good generalist.

I was able to laugh even then—at myself, at the pretentiousness of an aesthetic quest without the aesthetic object as a proper base. I am able to laugh a bit more wholeheartedly now. But I know that the same sort of thing might happen to me at any moment; it has happened so many times before.

I like your being honest Mariana (sophomore) *about not having read the poem carefully, but then one notch higher on the ladder of virtue would have been to . . .*

III · Ambiguous Successes, Unequivocal Rewards

How, after all this, can one hope to talk about the successes, the evidence that it is not all a mistake? (You have noticed, of course, that many of these failures could easily, with a little rhetorical juggling, be transferred to the column of successes. I could cite testimonials of gratitude, of which most of us receive more than we deserve—especially at examination time. The moments when praise from students seems totally disinterested and genuine are rare and treasured:

1978, a memory

The young man on 55th Street hails me from his car.

"Mr. Booth! You remember me? Hanford?"

"I sure do. You were in my freshman class." I don't mention my memory of how narrowly he escaped washing out in that freshman year.

"Gosh, it's good to see you, Mr. Booth. I've wanted to come in many times to thank you for that class. You know—"

Pause.

"What're you up to these days, Eric?"

"I'm in graduate school, I'm in the SSA [Social Service Administration]. I'll have my degree, I expect, in 1980. And you know, I *know* that I wouldn't have made it if it hadn't been for the way you worked on my writing in that freshman course. I've told lots of people about that, and I hope you're still doing it now."

He notices that I am pushing, not riding, my bicycle.

"You taking that someplace to get it fixed?"

"Yes."

"Well, why not let me haul it there in my car? I'd *love* to do even a little in exchange for that class."

By this time I am in such a glow of pleasure that I can hardly contain myself. Here he is, he's *making* it, his wife is teaching at a junior college to help put him through, and his little boy is one year old! And he is now working as research assistant at SSA, helping to revise reports.

It's hard, at such a moment, to remember that you didn't really do as much for the man as he now says and thinks. But it does feel like something real.

Some of the best times are the least predictable—completely unscheduled, completely unconnected with calendar or catalogue, and most important of all, not initiated by me. Once in a while students become so thoroughly warmed by an author or an idea or a line of work that they decide to take things into their own hands. Right now it is a seminar in Owen Barfield, organized *among* four faculty members *by* one student. Having had reading courses with each of us, this young man came to us one by one, saying something like, "Would you be interested in having an informal seminar with Saul Bellow?"—then approaching the others, "with Wayne Booth," or, "with Warner Wick?" Because we've had fun talking with him, because we like talking with each other, we agree to meet once a week, and here he is, an undergraduate, with the four of us enjoying ourselves—but I should say five, because he takes part actively himself.

Marvel of marvels, he takes that part without stammering—a young man whom I have seen stammer so badly that he could hardly be understood.

A cynic would argue that he has simply found a way to the ultimate self-flattery: "Get Saul Bellow, Warner Wick, Wayne Booth, and others to perform for *me*." But it's not like that at all: he has found a line of curiosity which we all share, and he has us sharing in a way we would not have done on our own. The conversation is not particularly scintillating, witty, profound. But it is serious: we are digging into the problems Barfield raises, and the inherent tension, in studying Barfield, between having a seminar of inquiry and a seminar that is merely an excuse for spiritual meditation seems to be under control: we are inquiring, and only peripherally risking a tone of meditation or worship.

Many years ago the initiator was Pete Klein, a philosophy student at Earlham (and now chairman of the Department of Philosophy at Rutgers), who organized a seminar on Toulmin's book *Reason in Ethics*. We met once a week at my home, with no course credit for the students and no pay for me—just for the joy of doing it.

I'm touched by your "Day After" paper, Chris [a freshman who has done an "extra," unsolicited response to the TV movie]. *Of course I can't promise you that your sense of despair is unjustified. But I can tell you that in 1948 (or was it '49?), when the Russians exploded their first bomb, most of us graduate students felt something like the anguish you feel now. One married couple I knew even decided not to have children, because "it is certain" that before they could grow up, "they will be incinerated." The threat was real then, it is real now, and you're right to think that nothing could be more important than trying to work against it. But meanwhile one should, I think, follow one's "pragmatic"* [we have been reading James's *Pragmatism*] *impulse to carry on with life—as indeed you did in deciding to work on your paper rather than simply giving up. We do not know that incineration lies ahead. The stand-off has worked, after a fashion, for nearly four decades—a fairly long period of a kind of peace, as human history goes. So many people have a stake in averting the ultimate disaster that it just may be averted.*

Not very strong comfort, that. I do appreciate your showing me the paper.

You need to look up—and think about—semicolons. (Wotta anticlimax!) Think about them as hard as about William James or the bomb? Well, that might be excessive. But just think about them for ten minutes, then return to James?

Chris hung on, did well. But moments of suspected success are rarer than the times when you can't be sure whether you have failed or succeeded. Most teaching moments are—I repeat—mixtures of intellectual and personal matters, of confusing signs of possible success, possible failure—mixtures that no analysis could properly sort out. They are like my encounter with John Lowarski:

November 23, 1973

8:10 a.m.: Each of my 23 freshmen could profit from an hour or so of private conference each week. Most of them get none, though I see them in groups of five each week; only the pushy ones, or the most desperate, search me out and get my entirely private attention.

When the desperate ones do come, you have to decide either to drive them away (to Student Health?) or to invite them further into your life than you can really afford to. Yesterday John came to my office hour. I had not seen him in several weeks, and had sent out invitations and warnings by the student grapevine: "Anybody see John around? Will somebody tell him I want to see him?"

And here he was, looking perhaps even gawkier than before: protuberant ears, thick neck, hair badly cropped, fixed smile with the upper teeth a touch too prominent: The Rube. But I have seen his essays, I know something of his mind: he is no rube but rather one of the most promising students I have.

I get down to business, with questions about his absences and about how far behind he is.

"Well, it's really been a kind of bad quarter for me. I mean, personal problems. I've just not been able to work up to par. I've been spending a lot of time just sleeping, goofing off."

Within a moment I see that I do have a choice: it's either at least an hour, talking of personal problems, followed by untold further hours, or five minutes, laying down the law about deadlines and referring him to a counselor. I don't have an hour. I am desperate with my own deadlines, including the promise to have the other half of the freshman papers read by noon tomorrow. It says something of how the "major research university" has changed me that I have any hesitation at all. At Earlham College it would never have occurred to me *not* to invite him to open up. Here I pause for ten seconds, go to shut the door, and ask, "Would you like to talk about the personal problems?"

Tears come to his eyes, and he pours out that old sad tale of the "crisis of meaning." What am I here for? What is the point of all this? All I see ahead are years and years of slogging away, working without purpose, just because my parents want me to. What is life for, anyway? His misery is absolutely authentic. The phrases are to my ears badly worn—but not to his. The first half hour (I feel pressed, even as I write this account next morning, pressed by those papers, which are still not read, and still promised for noon, and it is now 8:30 a.m.), we talk about the issues raised by the notion of dropping school for a year. Only after he has seen that I am not going to play the role of parent, pushing him either way, does he finally open up and confess to his real despair: for two years he's been feeling suicidal, and "I have nobody to talk to about it." I suggest a priest—on the hunch of his name. No good: he lost his faith two years ago, and doesn't feel he ever got much help from any priest.

The second half hour is spent talking about that, and about what kinds of talk might be helpful. Finally he agrees—and here I do insist—to try Student Health for counseling. I promise to write his parents about his problems, if he should decide to quit for a year and feels he needs some support with them—"It'd just kill 'em." We run quickly over his assignment deficiencies, which turn out to be almost nothing; he has managed, with all his misery, to get *all* the reading done—Aristotle's *Ethics* (three books of it), *Crime and Punishment*, Trotsky—and he even hands me his Trotsky paper before he leaves!

"Mr. Booth, I want to thank you. I didn't dare go to anyone else. I . . ."

He ducks his head awkwardly and leaves. And he survives the term, and the year. Did he survive the college years? I don't know. I feel the encounter, in retrospect, as a success, but I do not even know where John is now. He is not one of those who, like Hanford, have later said Thanks.

I remember, only now, that he had waited, before I saw him, for perhaps 30 minutes, while I completed a conference with David Zimmerman (a graduate student), ostensibly about Marxism, but initially about David's sense of failure in his seminar presentation last Monday evening.

"I was just terrible. I just never have developed any grace under pressure."

"Why did you feel so much pressure? Is there anyone in the group who seems to threaten you?"

"Well, frankly I was terrified, partly of you. With all your geniality, you are to me a very threatening figure. And then there is Doug . . ." (a bright but supercilious figure in the seminar).

Talking with David was not a hand-holding operation, as talking with John had to be. David is a man, a tough one—a union organizer before coming here. He audited my criticism class about three years ago, and I helped him a little in arranging to come to graduate school. Not a mistake, I am convinced, in spite of the awful job market. And yet here he is, confessing to terror, and to a failure that he has not in fact committed. After I have reassured him about that, we do have a good talk about the strengths and weaknesses of current Marxist criticism; I blushingly show him my one published political footnote, the one where I say something like "Capitalism has gotta go, but I don't know where." All in all, the kind of talk that I seldom seem to find time for with students these days: moments of genuine exchange, not simply moments when I give and they receive.

That's too simple: I mean moments when we are mutually grappling with ideas that I myself am still unsure about. Obviously I also received *something* from the talk with John, though the ostensible form was all helper-to-helped, not learner-to-learner.

Most of my conferences, like those I hear my colleagues talk about, and those I observe, glancingly, as I pass in the hall, seem to be of the pitcher-to-glass kind. Rarely are they even helper-to-helped (about personal problems). And the learner-to-learner kind is rare indeed. My scientist colleagues claim that they are always learning jointly with their advanced students, in laboratory projects. I half believe them, and I wish that I had more capacity to turn my encounters with my students into that. If I am not too tired, and if I keep my wits about me, I can almost always turn the request for passive help into an exchange. But often I *am* too tired; often I do not have my wits about me; often I feel flattered into showing off with "help."

Classroom successes are even harder to judge. About two times out of three I leave the classroom feeling disappointed in myself, or in my students, or in all of us. When I observe colleagues teach, I am usually aware of more faults than virtues. It shocks me to realize, as I write here, that I cannot think of a single flawless teaching job—not since my student days—by me or anyone else, no hour-long lecture or discussion that seemed as nearly flawless in its kind as an average musical performance by professionals. As an undergraduate I was of course often ravished. Even as a graduate student I can remember coming away from a discussion led by Elder Olson and thinking, "If only I can someday lead a class like that." But those days are long gone.

What does this say about the art itself? That it is so thoroughly subject to chance that nobody can claim to master it at all? Perhaps. If I am master of an art, why is it that I can remember so few moments—almost never full hours—when the room is what it should be, electric with thought, not *my* thought but *ours?* Why are there so few times like that fifty minutes dealing with the paragraph in Mill's *On Liberty* at Earlham, or that seventy minutes on *The Turn of the Screw* with Chicago freshmen, or that two-hour graduate seminar on Bellow's *Seize the Day?* I preserve from most courses a memory of only a half-period or two when all—or most—of the students were thinking, every one of them wanting to talk, but all attending to one another, listening, responding, struggling to figure out where all this might lead.

I cling to the belief that those moments are real: moments when all of us are engrossed not in our egos but in the problem, puzzling together, un-selfconsciously probing outward into an otherness too rich for any one of us to exhaust. How rare they are.

That beloved high school chemistry teacher I mentioned many pages back conducted classes only rarely. Luther Giddings just set us all to work in the laboratory and then talked with us about our work, one on one. Perhaps he had simply found that class instruction was for him too chancy. Indeed I remember his classes—dimly—as boring. Many a pedagogical theorist of the past twenty years has rediscovered his practice, recommending that all classrooms be "opened," the "dais" scrapped, the teacher working only with small groups or, at the extreme, only with individuals.

This breaking up of the lecture room is no doubt beneficial—up to a point. But it can lead to the formation of tight dyads that are for the student even more teacher-centered and essentially passive than the most authoritarian class. Students need to learn how to listen not just to authorities, whom they believe too easily, but to equals. Listening to an "authority," even one who disguises his or her power, and then responding as a subordinate, is a totally different art from engaging with an equal, really *listening*, and then working out together where the discussion ought to move: from disagreement and misunderstanding, through clarification, to further disagreement or even final agreement. It is not enough—though it is a lot—to learn to do this with another individual or in small congenial groups. We all need to learn how to do it in larger, heterogeneous, seemingly chaotic groups.

October 25, 1982

As I grow older, the task of goading the students into genuine discussion changes. They defer to me more than ever. They pretend to be discussing with one another, but they all have one eye on me—their very bodies lean toward me, even as their eyes flicker toward fellow students.

So I take measures. I write notes to myself warning that I must keep quiet. "Throw it back to them." "Pause for a long time." "Don't let them entice you into taking the ball away from them." But the troubles remain.

One highly effective measure is to stay out of the room entirely—when the time is ripe. Of late, I've taken to making sure that after a week or two of class I must be absent for one full period—without warning. Beforehand, I choose from the class the person most likely to lead the discussion well—it's a risky choice, because one can't know what will happen to the group when one disappears. This year, in Practical Discourse, I chose Kate Sparks, a marvelously articulate young woman who had been eager to discuss, but not too eager, willing to disagree with others, but not unduly assertive, open to criticism herself.

I took her to one side, after class, and asked her if she'd be willing to lead the discussion on Plato—the third that the class would have on him. She blushed, thought only a moment, and said, "Well, I guess I would, but it scares me silly." We then talked very briefly about what she might do, but I left her to choose what precise questions to discuss. I had asked the class to think hard about a short list of questions for next time, implying that I would be there to lead the discussion.

Everything I hear from the kids suggests that they had a wonderful time of it. Erwin said, "It was a fine, lively discussion. Everybody talked. And though some of us were frustrated because we didn't come to any conclusions, David Siegel gave a wonderful summary at the end."

Kate said, when I talked with her after class today, "Well, it *was* fun, but I don't think I could be a teacher. It's just too hard. And I had prepared reams of notes and didn't get through more than a small part. But everybody talked—and they all talked differently from when you are here. Somehow they talked more to each other, less formally, less as if doctoring their words for you."

The next step must be to have them talk, in my presence, about what we might do to ensure, even when I'm there, that they talk *to each other*. Of course there will always be a difference, if only because I must grade them—onerous, poisoning task. But I know from past experience that - with the right silent treatment I can get them to open up—on Thursday, when we begin on "Mr. Sludge the Medium."

Some of the best moves are made under pressure, when invention is forced by circumstance. Yesterday I had an "absolute" deadline with a manuscript that was due in NYC today—simply *had* to be mailed before 4 o'clock, in the new overnight-guaranteed system. By eleven or so it was clear that I couldn't make it, so I decided *not* to meet the deadline. By 2, with my class approaching at 2:30, the consequences of not meeting the deadline seemed very serious, yet I could not possibly meet my class and also get the manuscript finished and to the PO on time.

Why not, then, go to class, get them set up for discussion, put one of them in charge, while I went to the PO? That question answered, suddenly my mind was freed, and on the way to class I worked out the alternatives to write on the board, so that Rick Duerden could then conduct a discussion of *Their Eyes Were Watching God*. And that's what he did. When I got back to the class, about 40 minutes later, things were going swimmingly. Or so it seemed. Who knows what *they* thought about the experience, let alone what they got from it? Pete, who can be counted on to speak out, said, "That's really valuable, once or twice a quarter. But don't make a habit of it."

If you take as your goal getting everyone in a room to think and talk *together*, you can be sure to fail a good deal of the time. The difficulties are so great as almost to drive you back to straight lecturing, where providing general entertainment and the *illusion* of engagement with thought is—for someone like me who enjoys hamming—relatively easy. At such times of temptation, you can stave off the retreat by thinking about the next generation and what you hope that *they* will teach.

IV · Who's Next On Line? How should we try to train them? And how should we talk with them about the various "crises" that threaten their lives in the profession?

November 8, 1981

I am a sixty-year-old unsmiling public man, sitting in a fine big office, looking out through mullioned windows at the beautiful campus six floors below. I am looking out of the window in order not to have to look directly at the graduate student who has come to ask whether she should drop her work for the Ph.D. in English and apply to law schools. I have just written, this morning, ten letters of recommendation for students who are seeking jobs in English. I have been aware, as I write, that some of those ten students—I cannot be absolutely sure which ones, but I have some notions—will not get "decent" jobs teaching English. Most of them *will* get jobs of some kind; if they were graduate students at many a university, I could not be confident even of that. At the University of Chicago I can still hope to "place"—that is, to "market"—most of those who depend on me. Yet too many of those who are thus successful, in increasingly discouraging times, in times when everyone is suddenly cutting back, pulling in, hunkering down, will get jobs like the one described in a letter I received this morning.

> Dear Mr. Booth:
>
> I am desperate for two reasons. All the signs indicate that I won't ever get a tenure track here. They're happy to have me go on from year to year, for the next three years, and then I'll be dropped automatically, according to the rules governing "irregular" appointments. I just can't see the point in hanging around waiting for that.
>
> Especially when I think of the other reason: I'm simply going out of my mind with overwork. I have four sections of composition, with 30 to 35 students in each section. I've been really trying to give them the kind of education you and I believe in, but frankly the paper load is killing me, and I'm getting no time at all to work on the dissertation. Most of the kids seem to be responding, trying to do their best. I don't seem to have the troubles with mine that the other teachers talk about: indifference or hos-

tility, sheer laziness. I manage to get to them some way or other, but they need so much! Almost all of them really need regular individual help, or at least the kind of group-tutorial work that you do at Chicago. But I just don't have the time or energy. And frankly, I'm getting fed up and don't even *want* to see them privately. I'm getting so I feel hostile [like Butley? I wonder] when they come to the door, though at first I scheduled regular private conferences with every student.

I know you must have a lot of appeals like this, but I'll make it anyway: Don't you know of *any* decent kind of job for someone like me? I really do think of myself as someone who loves teaching English. And I'm good at it. This place is doing everything it can to kill me, to drive me from the profession. I'd like to stay in—and as they say, salary is no object.

Meanwhile the student sitting next to me is waiting for advice about whether to stay in the profession of teaching English, or to follow the thousands of would-be teachers into other professions that at least seem to offer something at the end of the line.

What does the professor say? What he would like to be able to say is that since teaching is, in his view, the noblest, the most important, the most rewarding profession in the world, she shouldn't consider for a moment subjecting herself to the miseries—and the probable debasement of character—entailed in getting a law degree.[9] What our society needs, more than any other single good thing, is a supply of devoted teachers who will . . . And on I would like to go, as indeed I do go on in some of the pieces in this book. I believe all that, but I did not know whether all that should be even hinted at in the hearing of this particular student. What would one have to know about her to give the right advice?

What I in fact said was equivocal, not to say weaseling. On the one hand, and on the other hand. If you are this kind, then so-and-so, and if you are that kind, then not. And only you can know, etc. etc.

9. The seeming arrogance of this remark (at least in the eyes of any lawyer chancing this way) should be read in the light of my earlier comments about the inroads on character threatened by the profession of English—and indeed by all specializations. Still, I may as well confess that the most startling debasements of character I have ever observed—oh, my language!—have taken place during the three years of law school. To explain what I mean, with convincing examples, would take twenty pages. But consider just the one basic matter of compassion. On average, when our English majors graduate, you can count on their feeling and expressing some response to human suffering, whether in literature or in what we call life. On average, three years later, those who transfer to law have had all that trained out of them. Of course they may be just putting on a show, at both ends of those three years—the show they think their superiors expect of them. But even as show, the change distresses me.

For a fine discussion of the way in which the habits of "talking like a lawyer" might, for young lawyers themselves, be enriched and modulated by reminders of other ways of talking, see James White's *The Legal Imagination* (Boston, 1973).

But there are two things I always want to say in 1981. If you think you could only be happy in this profession in one of the cushy jobs "at the top," one of the jobs that does not require you to teach composition (that's exactly how many people distinguish the good from the bad— whether or not one has to work at teaching how to write), then by golly, by gosh, don't hang on *here*. And secondly, if you do not see your gradu- ate work in English as some kind of end in itself, if it is not so rewarding in itself, at least a good deal of the time (despite ups and downs), if it is not the way you would most want to be spending your life if you were *not* having to plan, as we all must plan, for the future, then find another field. Or better, take the necessary steps to make these years rewarding.

November 5, 1985

Reading these words now, almost four years later, I am struck by how deceptively *easy* it is for me, in my secure position, to say all this to those who may be having to mortgage their futures with student loans, in the slim hope of getting a decent salary soon enough to avoid total bank- ruptcy. One of my graduate students will be $30,000 in debt when she receives the doctorate this spring. With the future pressing on her in that way, how can she avoid thinking of these years as some time of prepara- tion rather than as a time that is self-justifying? The notion of teaching as a liberal luxury is fine for those who have luxurious incomes, not so fine for those who are exploited by pusillanimous taxpayers and by ambitious and unimaginative administrators.

I suppose what I really would have liked to say to her, in 1981, is that this profession depends in part on a supply of profess-ors who would stick with it even if doing so meant taking a vow of poverty. To profess in that way carries its own kinds of risk. Such professions have always been ex- ploited by "the world," which is always happy to receive the services of devoted, impoverished flunkies. If "they" learn that you do this work from choice rather than as a mercantile bargain, they will envy you, fear you—and exploit you all the more.

So, then, whatever else I said to her, I should have added: If you do stay on here, feeling that finally you stay for the love of it, *don't let the outsiders exploit you for it.* Join the union, whatever "union" there is wher- ever you go, and make 'em pay for a service that money could never buy.

Teaching "English," under whatever title (I would go on), is not now, and for the foreseeable future will not be, a good way to make a handsome living. The hourly pay, if calculated for most beginners lacking the Ph.D., paid, say, from $475 to $3000 per course, would amount to between $1.75

and $10.50—figuring six twelve-hour days per week for thirty weeks (in fact one often works seven days a week). Even for those who get tenure-track positions after four to eight years on the doctorate—the average here is at least six—the starting salary will be far lower than what they would make as graduates of our three-year law school or two-year M.B.A. program. And the scholarship support for graduate study is lower, in the humanities generally, than in any other area. In short: don't become an English teacher *unless you have to*.

June 15, 1987

No matter what I had said to her, and to her twins who have come to me through these autumnal years, these years of hunkering down, I can see that what she really wanted to know was something like this: Is teaching English going to be worth it, in itself, after all?

It should be clear by now why, even though, as I have said again and again, my final answer would be an unequivocal yes, no simple short answer could possibly suffice. The right choice for me, in this time? Absolutely. The right choice for others I know? Sometimes yes and sometimes no. The same Karl Young who inspirited me in Freshman English later confessed that he wished he had "gone into" anthropology. I have one intelligent, sensitive friend who hates his teaching, especially the teaching of freshmen. I *had* another who can almost be said to have killed himself trying to become a really good teacher—against insufferable conditions in a college run by Dr. McChoakumfrosh. Two of my former graduate students have told me that they regret the choice of English teaching.

I cannot even say whether or not by mid-term next fall I'll be ready to quit. Every term, by about the eighth week, I feel like declaring intellectual bankruptcy—so that I could be held for only 10 percent of my debts: a glance at this dissertation, a spit-and-promise job on the freshman themes, a half-baked, mendacious committee report. That will no doubt happen again. But I'm writing this paragraph in late June, 1987, when the natural human capacity to remember only the good moments suppresses what the late November does to us ("sempiternal though sodden toward sundown"). The whole business looks like a genuine blessing, from here.

The journal entries that follow were written during the three-week "English Coalition" conference, summer 1987.

Wye Plantation, July 7, 1987

Nothing could have worked better to unite the 60 of us English teachers quickly than to have Chester Finn come from the Department of

Education to tell us just how we ought to think about teaching English. He gave a potted history of various educational fads in recent decades, using as whipping boy the "skills" movement—in his version it was sparked by knuckleheads who believed that it doesn't matter *what* literature or concepts you teach so long as students master abstract, formal skills. Relying on E. D. Hirsch, he reported "recent" research that proves, he said, that when we read we make steady use of a vast fund of background information. Nobody in the room doubts that banal claim, but some of us are aware of recent research that questions the whole notion of "background information" as something possessed in bits. He then spent most of his time running through the currently popular litany of the information our graduates don't possess [NB: *information*, not the intellectual know-how that I worried about on Occasion 4]. The tone was all "you teachers are to blame for this," and I could feel the temperature in the room dropping rapidly. Nobody at this conference has any illusions about what our graduates know; but all of us know that to talk of what they lack, and to recommend simply substituting *what* they lack into the present classrooms scarcely touches the real problems. All in all the talk was a prize example of failed public rhetoric: Finn hadn't a clue about who we are, and he gave us a speech that no doubt has wowed Rotary clubs and business conventions. But he should have known that you just don't get very far when you assemble scapegoats and spend your time accusing them of being responsible for becoming scapegoats.

When he told us that we should either buy Hirsch's list of about 5,000 terms, "what every American needs to know" (or as the new jacket has it, "The Thinking American's List,") or come up with a list of our own, he set the agenda for the conference in ways he could never have dreamed of. We now know that our task is to combat his way of working: we must try to *think* about how to *educate*. How are we to confront ourselves as we now are—a vast, complex, disorganized group of men and women with a vocation for "English teaching" but without a central, articulated notion of what that vocation requires of us and of our various publics? How can we turn our fellow citizens, who in some sense believe deeply in the importance of "English," into a nation of learners: a *learning* culture rather than an *information-processing* culture?

Wye Plantation, July 8, 1987
The mood today generally up. As we hear one another talk, we all seem to feel a bit surprised at the quality of all the others. Where are the power-grabbers, the ignoramuses, the nerds? I can't find them. Nobody fits the public stereotypes of a profession that has lost its way. There are of course some of us who are a bit *too* clear about the way we have been

travelling. KG, for example, seems to try too hard to portray himself as a bold revolutionary, teaching his students to be radicals:

> Just three weeks after I'd been fired on my first job, I was still teaching out the term and I was lecturing to my students about how language has real power, and I could see that they were not taking it in. [He mimed their boredom, very skillfully]. Just then in walks the principal, fuming, actually screaming, because of the letter I'd published in the local paper about him, and he interrupted the class, shouting at me: "I'm glad, glad, glad we fired you." He stalked out, slamming the door behind so hard that the glass partition broke. And I turned to my students and asked, "You have any more questions about whether language has power?" None of them did.

He did show power as he told the story, but I kept thinking about how he was leaving out the most important point, the goal I've heard some others struggling to express already: Our job is "to help students become responsible for their own meanings." His kids were learning to accept *his* meanings: None of them had "any more questions," and they could thus easily "empower" themselves into disasters that *he* has learned how to avoid. The trick is surely to empower oneself to become a self, and to exercise the power of self to change the world in ways that . . . But here I go, sounding almost like him: the trick is to impose *my* meanings, not his?

At lunch L., chairman of a high school department, explains that one of his problems in teaching writing is that his students don't have time even to read his comments on their papers. RD suggests the use of tape recordings. "Ha. My kids wouldn't even have time to listen to my comments. Many of them come in only for the morning; the average kid works 33 hours per week, encouraged by parents to see school as secondary to the job." The subject turns to public downgrading of teachers. M: "I gave up high school teaching and took a college job when they asked me to chaperone a Friday night party at a student's home, so that the parents could go out to *their* party. I knew I'd had it." A chorus of lamentations: there are a lot of good teachers out there, frustrated by bad schedules, overload, underpay, lack of support from parents and administrators, indifference and hostility of students who live in a world that "tells" them to get out as soon as possible. "Most of us came into teaching because we did have a vocation, but too many of us get destroyed by the conditions."

Wye Plantation, July 9, 1987
Larry Johannessen asks for a private talk with me about why he thinks this conference terribly important. A Ph.D. candidate at the University of Chicago, he teaches in a Chicago high school. We met in my room for two hours this evening:

What I worry about is that with all this public concern over preserving the classics we're going to forget about, and destroy, the average students, especially the "remedial" students. With them it makes no sense to begin by worrying about whether they will read Shakespeare. My 9th grade remedial group comes to me unable to read at all, and my job is to get them to see that education is something of their own. But you know, the "system" doesn't want that to happen. I took a group of remedial students at the 9th grade; their average scores were at 6th grade. By the end of the year, the average score had reached the 9th grade, while the two other remedial sections had advanced only one year, to 7th. So what did "they" do? They took me off that course, and I'm convinced it was because I had made the routine handling of "remedials" look bad.

Wye Plantation, July 13, 1987

I've been so deeply impressed by our discussions, and especially by the discussions among the secondary teachers I meet with each day, that I've agreed to do a small book on the whole affair. [By February 1988 I had come to see that most of what I had to say would be said by *this* book, and I have had to break my agreement.] The growing emphasis, deeply strengthened by the appearance of Shirley Bryce Heath, on teaching *persons*, on teaching them to take responsibility for their own meanings, on teaching to the end of building a nation of learners—this rising consensus seems so important that I find myself wanting to shout at "the nation": "Wake up. Stop squandering your heritage. Recover that noble dream of a universal democratic education. Stop inventing simplistic remedies and get down to the business of . . . ," well, of grappling, as we are doing here at this conference, with the manifold forces that now too often frustrate the efforts of even our best English teachers.

Of course we in the conference in many ways illustrate the very faults we deplore. Each of us tends to imply that what "I" do back home is just the right kind of thing, while what my colleagues do is deplorable—that our failures result only from our enemies' plots against us. And almost everyone exhibits a striking inconsistency in discussing our process here: everyone expresses frustration about "outcomes" for the conference, while inveighing against those who let anxiety about "outcomes" destroy the processes of genuine education. I myself have already partially corrupted my own path through these four weeks by beginning to worry about what I'll say in a book about it. The more profitable effect is that I've begun to think about how to improve my teaching in the fall—especially how to ensure a more active response from those freshmen who will be in my "Greek Thought and Literature" class. Herodotus will be formidable, for us all. I must, must revive my old practice of dividing them into teaching teams—provided, that is, they turn out, as *almost* all our students do, to be people who can work productively together.

Wye Plantation, July 16, 1987

Everyone seems today to feel the pace picking up; there's more confrontation with deep issues, less of the scapegoating of outsiders that we all needed for awhile. A very good day indeed: one excellent lecture (Richard ["Jix"] Lloyd-Jones), and two lively discussions: one with the secondary teachers, one with a mixture of all levels.

All of our discussions in this second week illustrate what we find ourselves saying about all genuine education: it is "recursive," or "spiral," not linear or strictly logical. We find ourselves using the word "messy"— about our discussions and about any really worthwhile education we can perform back home. Whatever words we use, we're obviously engaged in combatting the beloved simplifications that mar too much American educational tinkering. Today it was noticed that though the chair begins each session with a summary of what we've done so far, and with an announcement of our official topic, we are soon back on the topic of the previous day, or even of several days before; at one point someone said something important, to general applause, and George Shay rightly pointed out that he had not only said it a few days before but had written it into the minutes.

This afternoon, in a group drawn from all "levels," our new topic was to be writing. We began with a summary of the successes (generally but not universally agreed upon) of the "Bay Area Writing Project." Some expressed the hope that we might, as a conference, urge the adoption of their principles nationally. Others had reservations. Before we knew it, we were deep in a controversy about the subject from *yesterday*: "reading" and "literature." But this time we were facing the old issues in a new light, bringing in a perspective that had been obscured yesterday: that of the college teacher who, while teaching writing, feels that he or she must "cover" a given body of "material."

As Robert Denham said this morning, the process of observing ourselves educating ourselves here has been in itself educational about how we could do it better at home: we do it as we tell each other how our students should be led to learn: by first hearing an idea, fitting it into some previous scheme, translating it or trying it out on someone, hearing it again and hearing it better, trying it out on someone, hearing it again and hearing it better, trying again to say what it means, and then hearing it again, meanwhile circling about in swirling pools of other problems, sensations, emotions, and desires. Each of us has a given "agenda" (or, in Hirsch's terms, a given range of schemata), and we simply can't take anything in unless it joins with something we already have.

This is—as I don't trouble to point out to them—perhaps the deepest of all deep rhetorical principles: you succeed rhetorically to the degree that you can find a "topic," a place where you and your interlocutor can join, in order to rise together to places that at least one of you had not been willing to dwell in before; we learn new ideas only by joining them to old ideas, and the process is likely to be painful when that joining requires a breaking off of part of those old ideas from the total edifice.

Everyone here talks as if he or she were both "educated" and "open to further education." But in fact we all exemplify the plight of all students, including our youngest and oldest charges: we want to learn, but we are made in such a way that both to function at all and to function better we must to some degree cling to patterns that if clung to may prevent learning. Is this a real paradox? Should I play it up?

By now, at the end of the tenth day of conferring, I feel an overpowering desire to have the conference "succeed," and that feeling seems to be shared by most participants. The feeling accounts for the heightened tone in the discussions, and also for a new direction in the secondary group. Though we don't yet have any kind of formulated consensus, though many of us indeed doubt that a consensus will emerge, we spent some time this morning worrying—on the whole profitably—about how to disseminate views that in a sense we don't even have yet! We "brainstormed" (a good word; nothing else quite fits, though it is overused; at least it's better than "picked each others' brains") about how we could get the "word" out to various audiences: fellow teachers who are already active in professional "growth"; teachers who are indifferent, burnt out; administrators; parents; the broader public, including legislators. Some talked of powerful national groups—associations of principals and superintendents, for example—toward whom we might direct pamphlets or articles or speeches. "One telephone call to one parent each day will do more for your school than all the negative calls and letters of a whole year." People seem healthily aware that one primary aspect to the conference can never be transmitted: we have been rediscovering a vocation that can never be fully explained or defended in descriptions, statements of principle, or manifestoes.

Wye Plantation, July 23, 1987 (four days left to go)

Outside visitors have arrived, mostly journalists, and we silently close ranks against them. On the whole they behave well but they are all out of phase, and we have a hard time treating their mistimed interventions politely. Behind thier backs, Phyllis Franklin gave us a little lecture on the problem of getting journalists to *hear* what we have to say: "They are all looking for the one angle that will ensure the publication of their by-line, so try to be clear in advance about what *you* want them to hear." She was, perhaps unconsciously, summarizing what we find ourselves saying about the problems in *all* education: minds hear only what they can hear. One of the reporters, a former English teacher, seems especially troubled by our refusal to lay out, in a formal curriculum, precisely what all students should have covered by the end of each stage. He makes us see just how difficult will be our task in getting anyone "out there" to accept our refusal to recommend a "top down" demand for coverage of a given content. We have a vocation that sets other priorities: we want to educate a given kind of person, we hope for *people* who will take responsibility for their own meanings, and thus continue to read and write and think throughout their lives. We believe that the kind of people we would educate will on the whole finally "cover" what this reporter would demand of us, with his sense of speaking for Secretary Bennett [and all those I later listed in the Preface to this book]. We have—every single one of these hard-working and hard-pressed souls clearly has—a vocation that will always to some degree resist translation into the language of the unconverted: at some point in our lives each of us caught the bug of self-driven learning, and we want to spread it to the whole world. And we fear all those who would reduce the world of learning to a list of fixed possessions: something to be owned and clung to by the fortunate, something to be only envied by the unfortunate. A nation of learners—would that make a good title for my little book?

Chicago, December 2, 1987, 11:45 a.m.
I have just held the last class of the quarter, with twenty-one freshmen who have been grappling with the *Iliad* and Herodotus, not to mention Sappho, Archilochus, and Pindar. "Grappling" is the word: the ten weeks have been tough work for all of us, yet exciting for most of us. As I sit at my desk, calming down—it's almost more like catching my breath—I find myself thinking more about the two kids who weren't there today than of the nineteen who were.

Except for this final session, when I took full charge, the last six class periods have been taught by the students themselves, in teams of four. Each team has met in advance at least once with me or my extraordinarily able intern, Tim Child, and most of them have held additional sessions to plan their strategy (see my account on page 250 above). On the whole, the class sessions have gone "surprisingly" well—that is, the teams have themselves been surprised, both by how well the discussions have gone, after their worries in the preparation sessions, and by how many surprises they had to endure as they encountered unpredictable contributions from their classmates: "I don't see why you guys thought *that* was a good question about Book 8. Didn't you even notice . . . ?" My guess is that the top two-thirds of the class have a far better grasp of Herodotus— though nobody ever fully grasps that protean figure—than if I had fed them Booth's readings. I am even surer that they are more fully *engaged* with the stuff, more likely to re-read it, more likely to read more history, more likely to see college education as belonging to *them*, than if I had dished out *my* truths.

This paper is a pleasure to read, Paul (with exceptions noted below). You have taken on a serious, difficult thesis about Herodotus, and you have used quotations from the text effectively. But even though this is your third revision, it is very much still an "early draft," because you have failed to make clear to yourself, even at the end, just what the "conflict" is between the "Gods" as causes and the effects of human choice. At the end you seem to be saying that you have discovered a mystery, a contradiction that simply cannot be cleared up. But at the beginning, you talk as if your close reading had solved any problem there might be about it. You never make clear to me what you mean at points #3 and #10: what are the forces "acting collectively"? The claim that events result from multiple causes (one that you know I accept) requires a more precise analysis than the one you give it here (or the one that I gave in the final class!). As you perhaps know, the particular conflict that you describe here is the subject of many a full-length work—to say nothing of the debate about God's foreknowledge early in Paradise Lost. *I predict that you'll have fun with further thinking on this one, as you go on with "The Greeks" next quarter.*

Yet I am troubled by the lost, or partially lost, lambs: not just the two who were absent today, but Louise, who, though present, looked as she looked yesterday in my office—totally lost. Though I can't know just how lost any of them are—they seem all to have "read *at*" all the pages—it is clear that some of them would have dug in harder if I had been riding herd on them daily. The grant of freedom, through the "team" method, exacts a cost from those who are not ready for the freedom. In this last class hour I have connected that point about their freedom to Herodotus' own complex illustrations of the costs and benefits of freedom for the Greeks. But I sense that my connection may have come at the wrong time in the wrong form. Wouldn't it have been better to spend that last hour on a final effort to drag the sluggards into full engagement?

I know that my troubled postmortem will continue for several days, through the reading of the papers and examinations, and even as I move on to serious preparation for next term's seminar for advanced graduate students, Rhetorical Criticism. After the first three or four weeks, that seminar will be "taught" entirely by the students. But I must think harder than in the past about what that means, and about how to make it, for each of them, a kind of climax to their Ph.D. work so far.

December 4, 1987

I've read a few of their final papers by now, and chatted with a few, and the good signs are beginning to overwhelm my anxieties. "You know, Mr. Booth, I've been thinking, since my group ran that class, that maybe someday I could become a teacher." "Can you tell me about the English major here? Do all English teachers get to do what you do?" "I really liked the way you ran the class. I've got to know the other kids far better than in any of my other classes; we've studied together in the dorms, and we'll go on studying together." I of course discount some of this as possibly brown-nosing, yet the signs still look favorable: I've not entirely lost my touch. With only three more years to go, should I quit, as Norman Maclean put it when he retired, "while I'm winning?" Not on your life. What else could I ever do that would be as enspiriting as this?

February 15, 1988

Tonight for the first time in 5 weeks I can think of my graduate seminar without feeling anxious. They—9 advanced graduate students, not all from English—are now becoming a living, thinking body, not just the isolated, somewhat fearful individual competitors that they sometimes were in early January and that all students at this demanding stage threaten to become. Our previous 11 sessions were designed to introduce them to the range of promises and problems of "Rhetorical Criticism." We've had a superficial look at four ways of doing it—whatever "it" is: Aristotle's, Kenneth Burke's, Paul de Man's, my own. And we've thought about what happens when art works are viewed *as* rhetoric: a few poems, a story by Poe, *Othello* and Verdi's *Otello* (with Cynthio's novella). I've been running the show, though trying with only partial success to get them to see it as *their* performance, not mine. Meanwhile each of them has been preparing a draft of a "chapter" or "article" to be criticized in one of the remaining two-hour sessions of the term.

Today we had the first of these sessions, as Terry Martin led a discussion of his essay on the rhetoric of Donne's Devotional Sonnets: Donne's religious views present special problems to his art, and his sonnets reveal those problems when we consider his relation to various possible audiences—God, different parts of his own soul, 17th c. readers, and 20th c. readers. All 8 seemed to have read his essay with some care, and they

pushed Terry, courteously and firmly, on the needless sprawl of his poten-
tially powerful essay: its failure to focus its readers early on a clear question
or problem, and its various other weaknesses. I was at no point fully re-
laxed, feeling unsure whether we were hitting him too hard (everybody
objected to something or other) or not hard enough (he's so good that he
should be pushed to become really outstanding).

As we were drawing to the end, Lisa said, "I'd like to ask Terry whether he
found this session helpful or just destructive?" He looked surprised: "Oh,
I thought it was wonderful. I really learned a lot." And I felt that he had.

So I came home thinking. "At last. They're making it. It'll be one of
the better runs." We're sure to have sessions less successful than that one,
but I can hope that we'll have better ones too. And it seems likely that
each of the students will by mid-March be a good deal closer to a dissertation that she can respect (most of them *are* women) and that the world
will rightly value.

February 16, 1988

Did I relax too soon? Catherine comes to my office, looking desperate,
to say that she just cannot pull her essay on Elizabeth Bishop into shape.
"I have so many ideas, and they all seem superficial and undeveloped, and
they don't work together. I've felt really excited about the parallels I see
with the stuff we read by [Paul] de Man, and I think they're really *there*,
but when I try to write about them everything turns to mush. I've got all
the problems we found in Terry's paper . . . and then some."

So now I must wonder whether the session yesterday was more of a
worry to her than a help. It may have been "wonderful" for Terry, but it
wasn't wonderful for Catherine. If that kind of wide-ranging vigorous
criticism freezes her, what can I now do?

We talk for half an hour (that's all the time I have before Daniel, a
third-year student, arrives to discuss his plans for a "junior paper" on the
rhetoric of the debate out in California about Proposition 65). I probe and
probe for clues to the real problem. Is it a problem in the material, inherently elusive as "Bishop-and-deconstruction" is? She says so, though her
manner (and my memory of the high quality of her previous work) suggests to me that our true business is her acute fear of failure. With impossibly high standards, plagued with a sense that everything we said
about Terry's disorganization applies doubly to her unfinished paper, she
is almost immobilized.

Forced to send her away before either of us feels that it's time to quit, I
suggest another conference Thursday—"If you really need it by then."

February 18, 1988

Catherine shows up again, still full of self-denigration. Finally I persuade her to let me see what she has written already—and as I had suspected, the 10 single-spaced pages of printout she lets me speed-read turn out to be much closer to a finished paper than she herself believes; except for typos, the draft is better than many a student's final job. We talk a bit about what might be cut, what expanded, and about how some of the connections can be clarified (her initial sense of muddle was only partly justified). She seems fairly confident when she leaves—and I am exhausted. Such nursing of real talent takes as much energy as teaching a class of dullards—maybe more. Catherine is so bright that she can see the pitfalls in *every* path; any essay that she could possibly write is beneath her.

Still, after this second session I am not radically shaken from my earlier confidence about the seminar; much of what she said showed her thinking actively, and with some personal passion, about issues and procedures that would not have occurred to her six weeks ago. But who knows what disappointments may lie ahead? How many of this batch will teach? How many will teach well—and for how long?

PART V · *CEREMONIES*

And praise is comely.

Genevan Psalter

Sing ye praises with understanding.

Psalms 47 : 3

He who praises everybody praises nobody.

Samuel Johnson

And those who paint 'em truest praise 'em most.

Joseph Addison

INTRODUCTION · *The Occasions*

We American intellectuals are not usually good at celebration and eulogy. When asked to do a piece of what the Greeks called epideictic rhetoric, we are almost tongue-tied, as compared to our modern British or French counterparts, or to the ancient Greeks and Romans. Our after-dinner toasts are curt or slovenly, our words of praise for institutions—on the rare occasions when we praise institutions—are usually undercut by irony. Perhaps we are reacting against the daily flood of inflated praise-poems poured out by our advertisers and politicians. Or perhaps we are still reacting against an earlier time when prettying things up was a major business of life. For whatever reason, we seem to have taught ourselves that emotion-laden praise is sentimental, that to be sentimental is the same as to commit "sentimentality"—obviously one of the worst of vices, exceeded only by a few others that also threaten "personal integrity": insincerity, hypocrisy, dishonesty to oneself, inauthenticity. The best protection against those vices, we seem to feel, is a negative critical attention, a stance that will praise nothing that falls short of perfection.[1]

We teachers have compounded the inhibiting effects of this tough, no-nonsense pose by insisting that the only good prose style is a simple, clear style appropriate to "exposition and argument"—often reduced to a kind of "information transfer." Where earlier rhetoricians tried to teach eloquence, copiousness, the arts of amplification (e.g., Erasmus' *De Copia*), we too often teach only the useful but skimpy art of cutting back, of slimming down, of weeding out. According to many a textbook, the worst writing fault of all, next to lack of clarity, is redundancy. The way to write well is to follow Strunk and White's advice, in *The Elements of Style*, on how to avoid excess and confusion.[2]

If we are not allowed to express strongly favorable sentiment, and if we must remove all redundancies and vague generality from our prose, how are we to celebrate any life or institution? Celebration is the art of *amplifying* sentiments that are neither original nor precise nor unique to the given situation. It is the art of giving expansive and general thanks, in terms almost inevitably a bit hackneyed, for blessings that are shared only by the

1. See chapter 8 of *The Company We Keep* where I discuss the uses of that old-fashioned virtue, "hypocrisy upward."

2. See Terence Cave, *The Cornucopian Text: Problems of Writing in the French Renaissance* (Oxford, 1979).

few who have experienced some *cause* for celebration. All prayers of thanksgiving are alike, but every curse, like the curser, is unhappy in its own way.

Yet all of us sooner or later encounter many occasions when only eulogy, celebration, or thanksgiving will serve. For example, every teacher these days must spend many hours each term, writing letters of recommendation. In the fall, when the number of requests peaks, we produce surely far more pages in this strange literary genre, the vocational-encomium, than we write on our various current scholarly projects. We must all read those pages, too, great stacks of them, and we soon learn that our colleagues are not very convincing with their praise. Since all letters of recommendation must be favorable, the currency of praise suffers ever greater inflation, confirming our mistrust of all epideictic rhetoric.

Funerals, convocations, arts festivals, centenaries, retirement parties—we all enjoy or endure every year many occasions that require us to find good ways to talk about what's good in our profession. Only after many years of participation in such occasions, both as speaker and as listener, did I see the conflict between my instruction to freshmen—"Cut the deadwood"—and the requirements of public life. We desperately need a vocabulary of praise, an arsenal of topics and terms that might match in strength our powerful weapons for destructive critical work.

I cannot claim to manage celebrations especially well. My efforts, like those of my colleagues, seem timid and tongue-tied when compared with what the masters do when celebration is needed—Shakespeare's Henry V on his England,[3] Cicero on his friends, Winston Churchill on his beloved England, Jacques Barzun on Berlioz. But I am grateful for the occasions that have forced me to try my hand at unabashed praise.

We have a profession to celebrate. Why should we not work as hard to express its glories as we do to describe its weaknesses?

3. Can any other profession match, for sheer inconsistency, our simultaneous celebration (in plain style) of Strunkandwhite-ism and of Shakespeare as our greatest author? Reading almost any sustained speech taken from his works you might well find your red pencil flying—"Redundant!" "Clear?" "Wordy"—*if* you believed what most of our handbooks of good English say. And the "violations" are most flagrant—and most marvelous—when the copious bard turns to celebrations and eulogies.

OCCASION 14 · *Knowing in Ceremony*

The Meaning of Dedication

When I was in college I was sure of a lot of things, among them the notion that ceremonies like this were silly, too much like the funeral Huck Finn describes as all full of tears and flapdoodle. I stayed away from funerals and convocations with equal pleasure, knowing that my boycott expressed the battle of reason against the shoddy emotionalism of the booboisie. Taught in part by Robert Maynard Hutchins' epistles to the Philistines, I had come to believe that the proper business of a college was training the intellect to wrestle greatly with great ideas as found in the great books. From what I had seen of ceremonies, I knew that whatever else they did, they did *not* train the mind to wrestle with great ideas. Ceremonies in my experience uniformly bored me. Academic ceremonies were the worst kind of all, because they added hypocrisy to boredom, pomp and circumstance to the tears and flapdoodle. Everyone who thought about it knew that the true spirit of the academy was violated by these mindless, sentimental marchings in medieval dress, these handings out of sheepskin inscribed in gothic letters that many students could not even read and none could duplicate, these mumblings through malfunctioning loud-speakers, these cliché-laden speeches that said once again what everyone had heard dozens of times before.

Thirty years have of course produced exactly what that *young man I was* predicted would happen to everybody but himself: I have sold out. I now believe in ceremony, and to my *then* self it would be obvious that I have lost my intellectual ideals, have become tamed, institutionalized, reconciled to the sentiment and intellectual flaccidity that must inevitably mark ceremonial moments. From his point of view the worst thing of all is that, though I now enjoy ceremonies, I cannot, even now, claim that they are *interesting*. They are still inherently boring, just as he believed: as intellectually flat as a lecture on typing technique.

Some of you may not know about the new academic unit on campus, the Rhetorical Effectiveness Computations Center, established with a large grant from the National Endowment for the Humanities. The Fellows of RECC recently conducted a study of our convocations which proved that

Address at the University of Chicago Special Convocation rededicating new quarters for the College, October 26, 1973. Reprinted with permission from the University of Chicago Record.

99.77 percent of all who attended could not report afterward a single idea that the speaker had talked about; and this figure proved to be reliable at the .001 level! Seventeen percent of all *parents* fall asleep during the ceremony, on average, and four percent of all students (more of *them* stay awake, we hypothesize, because they are trying to remember which hand takes off the hat and which reaches for the diploma). For alumni over fifty, the figure is seventy-six percent. We could not get corresponding figures on faculty members, because they have cultivated the skill of falling asleep with their eyes open. All of which would seem to prove that my young self was right; ceremonies like this are anti-intellectual, and those who have today boycotted this one in order to read a good book are the true defenders of what the College stands for, while we are the Philistines who require quarterly doses of a kind of cheap emotional sweetening to go with our intellectual pills.

Not that the sweetening is all that sweet. Traditional cultures had ceremonies that *were* sweetened with words tested through time, words sifted by generation after generation of celebrants, who had come to know in their bones what good words were. We who are ashamed of the ritualized have all decided that only a new, individual, and essentially improvised word will be genuine, with the result that everyone today has the privilege of listening not—for example—to the words of the King James Bible or the Latin Vulgate or the Book of Common Prayer or something from Erasmus or Newman on liberal education, but to the undeathless prose of Oxnard and Booth.

This is perhaps hardly the occasion for my profound historical analysis of the invention of the concept of Boredom. You will not find it in the syntopicon of the world's great ideas, but its invention, sometime between Homer and Lord Byron, constitutes one of the great turning points in history. I give you only a fragment of what promises to become an extensive monograph.

Before the romantic individual was invented, people suffered from things like *tedium vitae*, melancholia, the spleen, or ennui, all of them internal conditions. The Copernican Revolution occurred when people began blaming everybody but themselves for their condition. The first Englishman recorded as using "bore" as a transitive verb was apparently Earl Carlisle, in 1768, and as you would expect, he and his contemporaries blamed it all on the French: it was "the French bore" and it was Frenchmen who bored. I perhaps should remind you that this was in the last stages of pre-romanticism, the period that I have now traced back to early Euripides. Within another fifty years the notion was fully developed that boredom was what the world threatened clever people with. As Lord Byron put it: "Society is now one polished horde,/Formed of two mighty tribes, the bores and bored."

Roughly paralleling this not-quite-finished history, I am writing two others, which unfortunately I also can only summarize here: histories of the word "interested" and of a group of ceremonial words. As the causes of tedium moved outward, so did the causes of its opposite, and people more and more asked the world to *interest* them by being novel, surprising, or relevant. The first really clear recorded use of "interesting" in our modern sense of something in the external world being interesting is again—as you might predict—just at the *true* beginning of the romantic period, by my old friend Laurence Sterne.

Meanwhile all external events which were not *interesting* were suffering a decline. From my monographs on words like ceremony, ritual, tradition, and authority, I mention only the word most pertinent to our inquiries today, *ceremony*, which began its decline at least as early as the Renaissance. I spare you, for example, most of my seventeen quotations from Shakespeare, all of them in some sense derogatory, as for example

> When love begins to sicken and decay,
> It useth an enforced ceremony—

and that other one, slightly paraphrased

> What have academics that laymen have not too,
> Save ceremony, save general ceremony.

It is scarcely surprising that people enjoying a newly discovered individualism, demanding of the world that it be *interesting*, discovering that in fact the world bored them—it is not surprising. I say, that such people should have labored to destroy all boring ceremonies. Why should we bright ones be periodically trapped among these impossibly dull people on this insufferable occasion, when we might be off learning something bright, shining, and new? A ceremony cannot, by definition, be bright, shining, and new.

It is thus only for those whose cultural habits lead them to seek other forms of engagement than simply being *interested* by something novel that ceremonies will not raise the question of boredom at all. Presumably I preach here to the converted—we who came this morning have made our choice, the choice of a boring ceremony. Our ceremonial engagement is opposed to boredom, not by being interesting, but by being active—not by startling us out of old errors but by reaffirming old truths. But of course old truths can become again interesting when they have been forgotten, and perhaps if I say them aggressively enough, we may manage a bit of interesting controversy even on this boring ground.

One modernist dogma teaches that there is only one kind of knowledge, the kind that can be clearly stated and precisely proved by logical or experimental processes. It is a dogma that has been attacked so often and so cogently in recent years that it should need no more attack from me here. (I say this, knowing that a good many of you have not taken these recent attacks seriously; but perhaps you will politely pretend with me that all of us here have recently reconsidered the empiricist and logistical dogmas that made our minds and our universities what they are—reconsidered them not in the sense of rejecting their usefulness for some kinds of inquiry, but in the sense of deciding that there are, after all, many logics and many languages; that we know, as Michael Polanyi says, far more than we can tell; and that no one of us in any field, however "hard" a science it may seem to be, could function without forms of knowing that we cannot prove by our standard tests.)

I invite you, then, to a few moments of communal testing of the knowledge we enact here: we *act out* here *what we know*, and what we know together as we act together is a curious fusion of fact and value, of theory and practice, of pure and applied, of knowing, doing, and making. It is, in short, a fusion that, once brought to light, should make our empiricist ancestors, from Hume to Bertrand Russell, turn in their graves.

What we know here, and cannot prove except on this kind of proving ground, I summarize under three fact-values, or valued-facts. Perhaps we can see these most clearly if we perform a little mental experiment. Imagine one of those little one-eyed green creatures that people have been seeing, some creature from outer space who knows nothing about us, accidentally dropping in this morning. Then imagine that by the end of this hour he— she? it?—somehow has been able to take in as much of this occasion as you yourself. What would he know, at the end, know in the sense of being unable to find good reasons for doubt about it. What would he know that he did not know at the beginning? He would have come to know the knowledge we enact here.

He would know first what we all know, that this College is a good thing to have. The word *college* dramatizes this knowledge of a valued-fact in its very meaning. The word connotes for everyone a place where various values meet: the value of cultivating minds and the value of doing that cultivating collegially. In anything that can be called a college, men and women do not pursue some abstraction called *ideas* or *the mind* in isolation from other people. Though much of the hard work must be done in privacy, we here pursue truth collegially, and in doing so we come to *know* the value of doing so. I remember in the time of our great student troubles, in 1969, that a student in Pierce Tower told me angrily that some of the professors had violated their principles by becoming just as passionate in defending the University as the students were in attacking it. There had been talk of burning the rare book room—now my new office—and some of us had become very angry about that talk. "You pretend to be men of reason," the student said, "but you just act blindly out of love for this place." But of course that is what he should have expected of us. Though we don't talk a lot about love of learning and love of the College, except on these mindless occasions, love is an integral part of our intellectual commitment. We know the value of the College in that love, and we celebrate it here.

Second, we know here the value of the past, of the facts of our tradition, of what other minds have done *for* us by thinking *before* us. In enacting this knowledge, we know our own total inability to begin everything new. As Edmund Burke argues eloquently in his *Reflections on the Revolution in France*, we think, at our best and at our worst, with minds that are inherited; we work together in a College we did not invent, in a University that would be nothing without its traditions. And we know that if any one of us were left on our own, to think and learn entirely in privacy, we would never come to think the bold, original, independent thoughts we now think, every hour on the hour. We know, in this ceremony, that we do not need any other reason for continuing these ceremonial trappings than that men and women we respect have found them valuable in the past. Tradition is for us here a good reason—now there's a truth that would really have shocked my younger self: "Tradition is a *good reason!*" When we have *better* reasons to change what our predecessors did and said, of course we will feel free to do so, but we will not change what they did and said for the sole reason that someone asks us to *prove* the worth of what they did and said. That they did it and said it—hard valued-facts in our experience—will carry more weight than any abstract principle about doubting everything that we cannot prove, or about the importance of change and novelty.

Third, in this experience we know that knowledge and experience are not sharply and finally separable. A college is a place where knowledge is pursued in concert, in the experience of trying it out on other people. This College is perhaps unique in the vigor with which it has sought ways of ensuring that every idea meets its clarifying and possibly destructive challenge as soon as it is conceived—or, as one sometimes feels, even sooner. It is no accident, comrades, that John Dewey lived and flourished here. Dewey's great polemic against fixed dichotomies of fact and value, theory and experience, action and passion, ends and means, truths and action, art and practicality, has by no means come to the end of its influence. But I challenge anyone to distinguish in Dewey's thought what is peculiarly his from what is George Herbert Mead's, and what is Mead's from what was in the air in Chicago at the time both men did their seminal work. This College in this University brings together the most thoughtful men and women it can attract, and it provides space where the business is visibly, inescapably, the experience of ideas, the testing of ideas not just for their abstract logical coherence but for their ability to persuade other inquiring minds and hearts. Here we shape our ideas in order to do justice, not simply to how they look on the page, not simply to where they lead in the ideal world, but to how they feel when tested by a qualified public in a proper public place.

We celebrate today the establishment of a new public place, a new forum for collegiate testing of our gropings for truth. We celebrate an ideal, but unlike the kind of idealism I deplored just now, ours is an idealism that never shrinks from an open testing. It is an ideal that is always under attack, often from those who look and act like friends of the academy and who think of themselves as scholars and teachers. The most serious attack recently has come, it seems to me, from a subtle, unspoken kind of pseudo-professionalism that seduces scholars into thinking that they do not have time for collegiality. How can I take time to teach Plato to freshmen when I am threatened by those three other people in the world who, like me, have specialized in the history of Singapore from 1910 to 1914—or the history of the word "boredom"? How can you ask me to work up a competence in Shakespeare or Dostoevsky when my book on the novels of Samuel Warren is still unfinished, and my tenure decision comes up next year? The new dean and the new masters will find, as did the old, that greater than any other single obstacle to a proper use of our new public space is a drive among scholars to escape that space to serve another and smaller, and often less critical, public, or to escape public testing entirely. I am not trying to assign moral blame. This is not a subject on which we can indulge in easy recriminations. As one who holds a much-valued private office in Regenstein and a very public office in Harper, I see a genuine and productive tension between those two spaces. But it is a tension that can be destructive as well.

It says a great deal about this University that we have this new space to dedicate to collegiality, that thousands of us, and particularly those faced with hard financial decisions, have felt it appropriate to spend our substance not only on magnificent resources for private study and for specialized testing of ideas but also on equally splendid resources for public testing in a space where specialists come together to make an undergraduate college.

Our creature from outer space knows all this, somehow, about this College and University, as he leaves this gathering. He has discovered a truth that he could not have learned in other forms of proving—a truth that might seem full of anomalies to anyone who thinks that truth and knowledge are limited to the deductively or quantitatively provable. The College is the beloved home of those who ask uncomfortable questions about love and homes; the emotional center of some who claim that emotions are or can be the enemy of the intellect; the source of communal norms for those who would argue that communal norms are essentially irrational, unprovable, and finally not subject to cognitive inquiry. But of course it is also the home of those who raise uncomfortable questions about uncomfortable questions. In a curious way, a ceremony of this kind, however emotional it may be for some, becomes for all, in its own way, a raising of questions. It is, if I am right, even a kind of thought: a *boring* kind, true enough, for those who seek novelty, because all of its questions and answers are old as the hills. But our creature from outer space knows, along with all these other discoveries tested here today, that being ceremonial together can be a way of knowing each other, of knowing that we all possess together these largely tacit kinds of knowing. To be bored is to wish that someone would say something new. But to be engaged in enacting old truths is to experience something beyond interest or boredom: it is to perform, with emotion, one more cognitive act in the great true drama of the College.

OCCASION 15 · *M. H. Abrams*

Madam President, I have the honor to present as a candidate for the honorary degree of Doctor of Humane Letters, Meyer Howard Abrams, the Class of 1916 Professor of English at Cornell University.

M. H. Abrams is one of those rare literary scholars whose name would appear on every humanist's list of the three or four most important figures of our time. Like all good humanists, he incites controversy—never more so than today, when he is in the thick of disputes about the proper way to study literature. What has never been disputed is the fundamental importance of every word he writes. He has transformed not simply the surface opinions people hold about books, authors, and events, but the more fundamental ways in which inquirers think. For literary historians, his great work *The Mirror and the Lamp* revolutionized the terms of debate about how romantic thought grew out of previous periods. For literary critics, it shattered simplistic oppositions between "mimetic" and "expressionist" theories and transformed the grounds for judgment about poetry. For theorists, it challenged, with its historical pluralism, the assumption that we should seek a single supreme paradigm of literature and criticism. What is more, that book, like his many essays and his equally great book *Natural Supernaturalism*, was not limited in its effects to the literary world. Probably no other professor of "English" of our time has influenced as many thinkers in as many different disciplines.

Nor have his contributions been only to scholars. A great teacher in the classroom, he has written and edited our most influential textbooks of literary study, showing the world that a textbook can be a major intellectual achievement.

In short, M. H. Abrams stands as a testimony to what humanistic study should be. Combining great gifts of originality and imagination with rigorous historical scholarship and a passion for education, he honors his profession, and he honors us here by accepting our praise.

It is my pleasure, Madam President, to present Professor Meyer Abrams for the honorary degree of Doctor of Humane Letters.

Honorary degree presentation, University of Chicago, May 27, 1982.

As soon as anyone dies, we all start touching up the portrait, turning the deceased into a paragon. If our eulogies simply substituted a better person for the real one, they might be harmless. But the trouble is, they substitute non-persons, polite caricatures that can easily corrupt our own efforts to live with the non-paragons who inhabit the real world. The rough edges get smoothed out, the marks of vivid individuality get reduced to a tiny list of conventional virtues, often enough covered by one supreme virtue, niceness. Such cleaning up is bad enough when applied to ordinary folks like you and me. But it can be vicious indeed when it is used to reduce a great, complex, and unmanageable figure like Richard McKeon to a size that we can easily accommodate.

Perhaps you have noticed the smoothing out going on during the past few days. Last week, whenever anyone talked of Dick—and we talked of him a good deal, just as we always did throughout his life—the portrait was a little bit like that of a dying tyrant: he *was* dying, and that was tragic, but behind his back we could still grumble about him. This week we are in danger of rounding off all the angles, and plastering over any part of the picture that doesn't quite accord with what a dead genius ought to be. I've been haunted, since the invitation to speak here, by the memory of just how scornful he could be when any of us got some historical point wrong—like the time when I innocently referred to the sixteenth-century logician Ramus as an Aristotelian! Dick's correction was long and detailed, and I don't want to invite, even in spirit, a similar correction here.

What can we say that he would not repudiate? Perhaps what he would want most would be an effort at accuracy, supplemented, of course, by some awareness of the *method* we have adopted for our eulogizing. Systematically, temperamentally self-reflexive, he would ask for hard thought here, thought about what we are up to, and about how we might have done it differently if we had thought hard enough. For me, our biggest loss is that he will not be able to tell us just how we got it all wrong.

After saying that Richard McKeon was a philosophical genius, a great thinker and teacher—I doubt that he would really object to that claim— perhaps the most important thing to be said about him is that he was not,

Remarks at Richard P. McKeon's memorial service, University of Chicago, April 4, 1985. Reprinted by permission of the University of Chicago.

for most of us, accommodatable, encompassable, manageable. He was not merely unpredictable, he was predictably disconcerting. I'm almost tempted to say—echoing an old campus joke about him—that he was, like the God of Augustine and Aquinas, incomprehensible. His thought was too large to be comprehended by any one of us, and his practice of that thought, as teacher, produced many moments of distress. He nagged us, he upset us, he undermined us. In short, Richard McKeon, philosophical genius, was on most occasions for most of us not a nice man. And we could not have profited from his genius if he *had* conformed to our standards of how nice boys should behave in company.

The first time he was mean to me was in 1943, when I found myself one of two students in a course on Plato's *Republic* taught by one Professor McKeon, about whom I knew absolutely nothing. Of course I saw myself as extremely well-informed about Plato. I had been reading Plato on my own for years. On the first day Professor McKeon simply told us to go away and read the *Republic* for the next period, one week later. I made the mistake of saying, "I've already read it several times." He looked at me, lit his pipe. I waited.

"Go READ it, this time," he snarled, and I shut up, went away, and tried to.

A week later he said, "What did you discover about it?"

"Well, it's really a great book," I said. "I like a lot of things in it. Of course it's full of bad logic, all those silly analogies that modern thought has taught us to reject. But I find the allegory of the cave just wonderful."

I'll never forget his scornful look. "Is THAT the way *you* read a book? You're reading it as if it were a novel. Has it never occurred to you that a philosophical work might be read philosophically?"

Not only had it never occurred to me, I didn't have a clue about what he meant by that. But the effect of his scorn and my shame and puzzlement was to make me dig in and *try to fight back*. For the first few weeks I labored to expose Plato's absurdities, while the Professor continued scornfully to show me that I had not yet really *read* that book. I grew increasingly frustrated as the weeks went by and finally I complained angrily to Napier Wilt, who had registered me for the course, that he had sent me to the most arrogant teacher I had ever known: "That dogmatic Platonist simply can't see *anything* wrong with Plato."

The result? I can even now remember more about that one class than about any other class I ever took—more about what the teacher said, more about the subject, and more about how to read a book.

My second example of just how un-nice he could be takes place two decades later. I have returned to *The* University as a professor, and the man I am by now calling Dick (though somewhat uneasily) has invited me to join the Committee on Ideas and Methods. And he has asked me to prepare an examination for a student whose "ideas" are being developed around the history of fiction. I send him a draft of the examination, and Dick summons me to his office. He clears his throat, taps his pipe. I feel cross to realize that I am already scared—a man of forty-two years feeling like a schoolboy about to be caned. And the caning comes.

"This whole examination assumes a strong distinction in fictional works between the didactic and mimetic. Why?" The cane has descended. I feel affronted—and still scared. I babble, as one tended to do in his presence.

"Well, ah, that's because, ah, well, after all, there just *is* a difference between the two kinds."

Long scary pause.

"Isn't there?"

He laughs.

"Ronald [Crane] and Elder [Olson] have always taught that distinction, but *I* don't know where they got it. It certainly isn't in Aristotle!"

I want to say that if he doesn't trust my way of examining he can just make up his own exam. But I don't. Instead I leave his office crushed, silent, and angry. But of course the first thing I do is go back and re-read the *Poetics* and start *thinking* about it once again. Neither I nor Aristotle, nor the didactic/mimetic distinction, have been quite the same ever since.

No, Richard McKeon was not, for most of us, a nice man. He was a holy terror, a stinging gadfly, a thorn in our flesh, an obstacle in the way of our thinking normally. We must not soften that picture by remembering only its favorable effects. He injured more than his fair share of mediocre and not-so-mediocre students. He drove some prospective philosophers and teachers into other professions. He infuriated many an audience, even as he transported many others. He taught us what we seem always to forget— that we cannot expect our geniuses to come cheap.

But here is where the reflexive turn is forced upon us, by our sense that Dick's critical spirit listens to us here. What do such anecdotes show if not the ultimate, unflagging generosity of a man who on all occasions was giving of himself, all stops pulled, no holds barred. Here was a man who, given a choice between being nice to you and teaching you a better way of thinking, would choose the troublesome way every time: a man with a genuine character, the unflagging philosopher.

When some people die our grief is compounded with pity for *them*— what a pity that their lives were so unfulfilled, so empty, so embittered. Facing the loss of Richard McKeon, I feel none of that; instead I feel something perhaps better described as worry about myself, and about us. How can we ever hope to replace the multiple stings of this gadfly, the generous blows from this giant of learning, the unflagging, invaluable underminings of this unremitting critic? How can we keep alive in ourselves the manifold, incomprehensible virtues of this arch-pluralist, this incarnation of the intellectual virtues? What will this University become, without the truculent, obstreperous, unpredictable, nagging, and finally inspiring presence of Richard McKeon?

OCCASION 17 · *Ronald Crane, Scholar and Humanist, 1886–1967*

Ronald S. Crane was, I am convinced, a great humanistic scholar. Scholarship is today on the defensive as it has not been in some decades. The air is full of attacks on research, seen as the natural enemy of teaching. And academic life in general is held in no high esteem. As portrayed in "academic novels," for example, our campuses house only phonies: comic pedants who, as Edward Rosenheim has pointed out, are never shown engaged in any activity that might reasonably attract a responsible human being with an IQ above 100. The reform pamphlets of the New Left have yet to describe, so far as I can discover, a single instance of scholarship worth pursuing; it is all a matter of "so-called scholarship," and of blind self-servers who, because they hate teaching and undergraduates, lock themselves up in "ivory towers" (I always find myself thinking of Harper West Tower, where I dwell), and count commas or invent abstract and irrelevant theories. In such a climate, to eulogize a man as a "great scholar" might very well be to damn him—as if one had called him a great nitpicker.

I suppose it is impossible to demonstrate to the unconvinced the difference between the great scholars and the feeble imitators or—what is the same thing—to show the value to "the world" of genuine scholarship. I read this summer an attack on our "knowledge factories," by a critic who cited, as his only example of what researchers do, a dissertation done at Michigan State, "An Evaluation of Thirteen Brands of Football Helmets on the Basis of Certain Impact Measures." No amount of argument is likely to show the author of the attack the total irrelevance of his example to what real scholars do. What perhaps I can do is assume that my readers already have some predisposition to honor the real thing when it appears, and try to explain why Ronald Crane, for so many of us, stood for what the university at its best can mean.

What he did was to set for us a model of what a scholar/teacher can do with a first-class mind, when that mind is backed by character. *Character* is almost as unfashionable a term as *scholarship*, but I know of no other word to describe the combination of moral force, intellectual integrity, and energetic persistence in inquiry that Crane exhibited.

Slightly revised from an article in *The Chicago Maroon*, September 29, 1967, p. 3.

The passion for truth is not so obvious a commitment as some other passions, but in Crane it was evident to everyone who was around him for more than a few moments. It was a commitment that, like any other, could sometimes trample on the feelings of others; Crane took it for granted that a student would want to find out the truth about a subject more than he would want to be loved by his teacher. He assumed that his deepest service to any student was to teach him how to find the truth, and he was sometimes surprised to discover that his rigorous criticism had been taken personally and interpreted as hostility. Students, on the other hand, were often surprised to discover that the man who had appeared to be a brutal enemy was in fact one who loved them.

His passion for truth took many forms. Most obviously, it expressed itself in searing criticism of other scholars' generalizations. I shall never forget the seminar period which left me, one day, in despair; a paper which I had thought might serve as a chapter in my dissertation had been annihilated before my eyes, and I felt that in the process I had learned my own unfitness for scholarship. To find the truth in such matters was just too difficult. Should I not just take a job somewhere as a teacher, which is what, after all, I had gone into this business to do in the first place? But then, of course, the question arose of what exactly I was going to teach *about*, if I couldn't say something that would stand up to the criticism of Ronald S. Crane. Because, you see, unfortunately his criticism had been convincing; I did not see how to answer it. So I decided to work the thing through—and as I did so I began to discover why Crane himself published so little: he applied to his own work the same rigorous standards he applied to us, and few of his drafts could escape the wastebasket.

"What's your evidence?" "Most people believe this, but is it true?" "This is clever, but does it satisfy you?" "This adroit juggling of abstract ideas is no doubt pleasurable in itself, but what does it have to do with the actual works of Fielding?" "The evidence you choose does seem to support your conclusion that the Twentieth Century is a 'rhetorical age.' But have you considered the amount of *pure* science, *pure* music, *pure* mathematics, *pure* philosophy, and *pure* history in our time? Can any earlier time exhibit so much that is *non*-rhetorical?" Such comments on my own work drove me back, again and again, to specific and laborious re-reading and thinking—facing the hard and irreducible facts that alone justified my professional commitment and tested my conclusions.

Crane's critical habit of mind continued until his death. Even in the hospital, when from many points of view he was "no longer himself," he maintained his determination not to be self-deceived. "Ronald, you're looking better today." "What's your evidence?" One day he told me that the chief indignity of dying in the hospital was for him the sense of being at the mercy of "a bunch of damned *a priorists.*" "I've led a life of scholarship, trying to be honest to the evidence, and I find myself surrounded by a bunch of white-uniformed graduate-student types, *poor* ones who have learned a few pat diagnoses and who haven't the slightest interest in testing their conclusions by observation or critical analysis."

In a time when, as Yeats says, "The best lack all conviction / While the worst are full of passionate intensity," Ronald Crane did not lose his conviction that it matters whether one respects or cooks the evidence, whether one reasons or rationalizes, whether one manipulates truth to serve self or schools the self to serve truth.

Such people are rare in any age. It may be that they are especially rare in ours. At least we have been told, throughout this century, that heroes of any kind are no longer possible, that honor is dead, or so close to it that the man of implacable integrity must be on the defensive:

> Now all the truth is out,
> Be secret and take defeat
> From any brazen throat,
> For how can you compete,
> Being honour bred, with one
> Who, were it proved he lies,
> Were neither shamed in his own
> Nor in his neighbours' eyes?[1]

I remember his shock when a critic misquoted him in print, and then apologized for the "*inadvertent* error." "Any scholar worth the name," he said, "will recognize his own natural inclination to reduce his opponent to terms that can be refuted. And he will check the original again, and again, and then one further time, to make sure that he has been accurate and fair."

When such values are held by a naturally combative and aggressive scholar—and Ronald Crane was never merely "tolerant" or "permissive" or "amiable" in his intellectual dealings—they are especially impressive. Ronald Crane had strong views, and he wanted them to prevail in the world of criticism and scholarship. But if Satan had come to him to offer all success and all honor, in exchange for one minor misprint, one slight bit of fudging, just a touch of deliberate distortion, the Master of Fudgers would have left the seminar room, like the rest of us, with his tail between his legs.

---

1. W. B. Yeats, "To a Friend Whose Work Has Come to Nothing," lines 1–8. Reprinted with permission of Macmillan Publishing Company, and of A. P. Watt Ltd. on behalf of Michael B. Yeats and Macmillan London Ltd., from *The Poems: A New Edition* by W. B. Yeats, edited by Richard J. Finneran, copyright 1916 by Macmillan Publishing Company, renewed 1944 by Bertha Georgie Yeats.

In a time when every kind of cheating on the evidence is defended in the service of reform or reaction, it is no mean thing to be a man who would rather fail than cheat. If, as seems possible, future historians characterize the twentieth century as a time of corruption and moral decay,[2] I hope that one or another of them will know of Ronald S. Crane and the few others like him. There are not many of them in any age, but each of them deserves at least a footnote—an honest one, carefully checked against the evidence and finally proofread as if the historian's life depended on it: "Ronald S. Crane (1886–1967), unlike his contemporaries, believed in many things: in the value of critical inquiry; in teaching as a natural twin of scholarship; in personal honor as inseparable from scholarly integrity; in 'the humanities' as the study of mankind's possibilities and achievements. In pursuing his beliefs he demonstrated that even in the twentieth century a man could give himself nobly to an ideal."

2. In 1987, re-reading this piece after almost twenty years, I hear Crane raising questions about this generalization: "Everybody says so, but is it true? What's your evidence?"

The Good Teacher as Threat

I don't have to tell you that I'm in a tight spot. You know as well as I do that you are an impossible audience. If Dean Charles Oxnard had set out to find the two hundred men and women in the world most likely to recognize, criticize, and reject any conceivable rhetorical ploy I might use, he couldn't have done better. On my one flank—let's call it the left flank, for convenience—I feel breathing down my back, or reading over my shoulder, or perched in the catbird seat, a pack of learned folk daring me to say anything new about that very old topic, teaching. I suspect that Norman Maclean, who a couple of years ago gave the best talk on teaching I've ever heard, is privately daring me, not only to say something *new*—he knows *that's* impossible—but to say something that he can't find at least seven sources for. If you think it is easy to say anything new about teaching, or even anything worth remembering, I invite you to look in any book of quotations under "Teach," "Teachers," and "Teaching." The desperation of the anthology makers can be seen in such precious items as these:

"A teacher affects eternity; he can never tell where his influence stops." Who wrote that bromide? Henry Adams.

"Nine-tenths of our university teachers are more competent to discuss the literature of England than the literature of America." That profundity comes from Stuart Pratt Sherman.

And as for originality, try these:

"We loved the doctrine for the teacher's sake." Daniel Defoe.

"We love the precepts for the teacher's sake." George Farquhar.

"We love the precepts for the teacher's sake." Oliver Wendell Holmes.

On my right flank, champing at the bit, knitting their high brows, turning their deaf ears, ready to cavil, and making bold to differ, equipped with a vast apparatus of modern equivalents of that old-fashioned grain of salt, computers at the ready, minds honed to a fine point with dozens of techniques for analysis—mathematical, propositional, statistical, and linguistical—on my right flank, I say, are those hard-liners who will judge anything I say as unreplicable, a muddle, indemonstrable, or statistically insignificant because

Address at a reunion of all those who had won the Quantrell Prize (the annual University of Chicago prize for "excellence in undergraduate teaching"), spring 1977.

I have confused my curvilinear prediction functions with my chi-square tests of association, and can't tell a Kruskal-Wallis analysis of variance from a hole in the ground.

I shall make only one other preliminary move to unite this diverse and highly critical body of listeners into a roaring, shouting mob of enthusiasts, and that is to reject the one speech you all expected to hear. "Part one: Teaching is in a bad way, especially everywhere else but at Chicago. Part two: There is a great tradition of teaching here. You in this hall tonight visibly embody that tradition. Part three: to the surprise of those of you who have left us, it is still alive here, though threatened by national trends and by certain villainous folk on campus—the *non*-Quantrell winners. Part four: Therefore do not worry, the task of revitalizing our traditions is in good hands, namely the Quantrell winners here tonight."

"Five minutes at most for my 'but seriously' ethos."

No, sorry that was a note to myself.

But seriously: anyone who embraces teaching as a vocation takes on considerable power with that embrace. And it could be said that the question from then on is the same as the one Yeats asks about Leda, after portraying that other embrace: Did she put on Jove's knowledge with his power? The power that a good teacher exercises, whether explicitly sought or even consciously repudiated, is the power to transform souls, the power to turn psyches away from or toward the light, what we might call, using a term Charles Wegener has adapted from Plato, "the power of psychogogics." (Or perhaps we should call it "psychopoetics"? Or "animafacture"?)

When college teachers are fully successful, they are successful beyond any of their conscious intentions about particular subjects: they make converts, they make souls that have been turned around to face a given way of being and moving in the world. We may deplore this effect or seek it passionately, but in either case it will be there, *if* the teacher is technically any good.

For all I know, the high school chemistry teacher who turned my soul toward what I called "chemical engineering" (though I knew nothing about it except that *Luther Giddings* thought it good)—that teacher did not set out to convert me to anything but doing a good job in high-school chemistry. But his incidental lessons ran much deeper. Working in conjunction with my one good English teacher (a beautiful, nay, even sexy young woman just out of college, eager to make converts to *her* brand of radical modernism), he managed to transform in one year—I have the diary entries to prove this—a more or less unquestioning young Mormon believer into—well, it's hard to summarize the beliefs of the new flaming youth who emerged from that year, but one good way would be to say that he had taken on most of the beliefs he had found expressed in the novels of Sinclair Lewis. It would oversimplify to say that Luther Giddings and Gene Clark surgically extracted the prophet Joseph Smith from my soul and transplanted the prophet Arrowsmith, that miserably isolated and in fact knuckleheaded prophet of objective science, but that's about what had happened.

I have no doubt that it was *not* Luther Giddings' intention to do missionary work for modernism. He spent most of his time trying to make me a good and honest inquirer into the regularities discoverable in that chem lab, where I came to work more and more hours each day, and which I still feel nostalgic about. But almost in passing he was inculcating a very special and quite misleading world view. I can remember, for example, that he told me one day, as a matter of established fact, that according to the laws of statistical thermodynamics, sooner or later when you put a teakettle on the bunsen burner the water will freeze instead of boiling. In the discussion that followed he reminded me, as of an accepted fact, that if you turned a dozen monkeys loose on typewriters and allowed them to peck away long enough, they would finally produce, somewhere in the great piles of nonsense, the complete works of Shakespeare. Marvelous revelation! I went home and announced it to my mother! Since the conversion process he had thus begun was reinforced by much of my new reading—for example, I found those monkeys again in Bertrand Russell—it was a long time before I came to question the specific attitudes or beliefs Giddings had encouraged. Three years later when I changed my major to English, fulfilling that other influence begun by marvelous Gene Clark, I by no means threw off all that Giddings had done. And of course I have still not done so. Why do I now read, or read *at, Scientific American?* Because of Luther Giddings. Just a few years ago I suddenly caught myself using that monkey example as if it were gospel truth; then, after a little reading about it, I concluded that the example, reinforced on the world by many prophets of what claimed to be a scientific world view, was really quite zany. In case you're interested, a physicist has finally taken the trouble to calculate the odds against those monkeys. In a piece called "The Meaning of Never,"[1] Charles Kittel shows that if you collected not the original dozen monkeys but three times as many monkeys as there are now people on earth, that is, about ten billion of them, allowed them to hit ten keys per second—faster than most of us can type—and let them type away for the entire age of the universe to date, which in seconds is about ten to the 18th power (last I heard), the odds against their typing out just one book, *Hamlet*—not all of Shakespeare's

1. Charles Kittel and H. Kroemer, "The Meaning of Never," Problem 4 in *Thermal Physics* (San Francisco, 1980).

works but one only—come out to $10^{164,345}$ to one, which, as Kittel says, leads to a pretty good definition of never, "for operational purposes." Why did I not question the non-fact sooner? Because an excellent teacher taught me *not* to, that's why.

I don't suppose anyone here will question the reality of this dangerous power I am talking about, as something that operates on some students at some times. But we are likely to underplay it for two reasons. First, we know that many students seem to resist all change; we have so many *visible* failures in our efforts to produce *any* desired change that we think very little is happening. Secondly, the changes we *do* see are almost all in directions that we desire. We call up these new spirits from the vasty deep, and when on rare occasions they do speak what we hoped they'd speak, we pronounce ourselves successes.

Yet we all know that what we have taught in one decade will often look false or even pernicious in the next. My student from twenty years ago visits me to thank me for making him what he is today. I look at him, and wonder why. I listen to him, and—if it is a day when I am capable of honesty—I am forced to deplore what I have, according to his testimony, wrought. Did I, as he seems to say, set him on the course of becoming the driest kind of unimaginative eighteenth-century scholar? Did I accomplish *that* just by repeating endlessly the formula that I had admiringly caught from Ronald Crane, "What's your evidence?"

None of you sharpies will have missed the fact that so far I have simply been underlining the obvious point expressed in Henry Adams's statement—"a teacher . . . can never tell where his influence stops"—though with a strong emphasis on the dangers implicit in the teacher's power. From here on in, things become less obvious, but by the same token somewhat more problematic. What are the consequences for a teacher—let us say, for the moment, Wilma Ebbitt, come back from the big world to her proper home—when she recognizes that the better she is the more dangerous she is?

It's a huge subject, that one, and I'll have time to touch on only two implications that every teacher knighted with a Quantrell award ought to think about. The first is that every effective teacher owes it to students to teach them the arts of reflecting on the personal and social meaning of what they are being taught. As a dean of the College once put it, it is simply not enough to stand to one side of the ladder of success, academic or other, and goose the students as they climb. Every teacher who wants to be not just effective but, in the Quantrell word, *excellent*, must become a philosopher, and must try to lead students into philosophical habits.

Now we all know that the word "philosophy" has been reduced by some philosophers to mean one technique among other techniques for solving such problems as can be—at least so the hope runs—*solved,* once and for all. No harm in that, except that it leaves us seeking a word to cover what we mean when we think of the skilled technician who wants to raise his sights and ask what his learning and teaching are *for,* what it is doing *to* or *for* his *students,* and what *they* will do *to* or for *society.* Whatever term you want to use for that process, I would argue that the world has always been short on teachers who sought the kind of wisdom about their teachings that cannot be demonstrated once and for all but that must be re-learned, in experience and hard thought, generation by generation. And I take it as obvious that philosophy in this sense, the pursuit of wisdom, is even more desperately needed in our generation than in most.

Since the situation in literature is what I know best, I'll illustrate my case from what I see happening in literary criticism at the moment. Put in over-simplified terms, we can say that Western literary culture has been passing through a period in which what I am calling *wisdom* has been by most influential critics deliberately repudiated as not the professional critic's business. Whole generations of students have been taught to recognize a set of fallacies that resulted if literature was joined to life: the intentional fallacy, the affective fallacy, the genetic fallacy, the didactic heresy, and what not—all of them having to do with efforts to argue about the relative value of different literary works in the service of souls and societies. Now we see everywhere a bursting out of new claims to free literature from those formalistic bonds imposed by the new critics or the Chicago critics or the Russian formalists, and to offer a view of life, or culture, or truth, or history, that will provide the wisdom necessary to innoculate students against a simply passive submission to the poet's will. In the older terms, this explosion is from the *intrinsic* to the *extrinsic,* but most of the newer criticisms would reject that distinction, substituting something like this: Each literary work implicates within itself a set of norms about what questions are appropriate to ask of it. Hemingway, to choose a favorite example of the new feminist critics, does not demand of us that we ask of his works, "Is it good for men or women to accept uncritically my machismo bravado?" Indeed, he seems to work quite hard to prevent our asking such a question. But surely, the feminist critics say, and I think they are right, surely *any* teacher who teaches *A Farewell to Arms* without inviting, somewhere along the line, a critical consideration of Hemingway's heroes as human ideals, and of his portraits of women as reflecting a peculiarly maimed creative vision, and of his vision of the good life as a singularly immature one—surely any such teacher is doing only half the job.

But, we have all said to ourselves in reply, who am *I* to take on such issues? *I* am not trained to judge the relative validity of visions of *life.* I am trained—let us say—to analyze a novel's structure, or to trace the history of a genre, or—to change the field—to conduct a rigorously designed controlled experiment on the learning abilities of pigeons. I am a literary critic, or a behavioral psychologist, not a professor of wisdom, not a guru, surely not a trained philosopher.

About thirty years ago a friend of mine went to a professor of English here to express his worries about what seemed the desiccated technicalities of his training. After some initial sparring, in which my friend tried to express what may have been a rather naive version of the point I am making here, the professor burst out:

"But, Mr. Mowrer, what is it that you would *prefer* to do over what we *are* doing?"

"Well," my friend stammered, "I chose to go into this profession because I wanted to teach my students how to *live.*"

There was a chilling pause. Then: "What the hell do *you* know about life?"

For years my friend would report that anecdote with embarrassment about his naive youth, because he had decided that the professor was entirely right. I can conclude my point about the first implication following from our dangerous powers by saying that the professor was only *half* right. He was right about my friend's incompetence at the time to relate literary studies to the making and shaping of souls and societies. He was right in defending technical mastery as a crucial part of graduate study. But he was wrong as could be in suggesting that Ed Mowrer should drop his concerns about life and stick to his last.

Still, we all know why the professor would talk that way. If we are all fallible in our specialties, are we not even more fallible in our claims to wisdom? The answer is yes, and here is where the second implication of our dangerous powers comes in: No teacher can work properly without a college, a real college. We all need the constant give-and-take of colleagues and students working on the same texts or the same experimental lines, all together engaged in a mutual philosophical critique of what we are doing. When instead we work "on our own," we become protected, frozen monosophists: in a word, either overt or secret dogmatists. Working with colleagues, we have a chance—perhaps a slim one—of improving our capacity to criticize what we do.

I have time for only one example of how that might work. Some years ago there was a shocking revolt in the Humanities staff when a black assistant professor Paul Moses, announced that he would never again teach

Huckleberry Finn because he had become convinced that that novel was bad for his students, both black and white, and because teaching it was too painful and difficult for him. You can imagine how we white liberals felt about that act of implicit censorship. I can remember few moments when an educational decision aroused so much anger and distress. I went on thinking about that objection many hours and many days, and partly as a result I have read and re-read *Huckleberry Finn* often since. Indeed, after some hours of conversation with Paul Moses and another black colleague, Charles Long, I finally began to get a glimmering of a truth about *Huckleberry Finn* that I could *never* have discovered for myself, not in ten seconds multiplied to the hundred-and-sixty-four-thousand-three-hundred-and-forty-fifth power. It is a book that invites and responds to a kind of criticism I had never dreamed of using since it had been drilled out of me at the beginning of graduate school. And my methods of teaching it—defending it not only as a wonderful book, which it is, but as a flawless one and a consistently mature one, which it is not—were subject to a criticism that I would never have conceived outside of a collegial situation of the kind this College has always striven for and often even achieved.[2]

I suppose my message tonight, then, neither new, to satisfy my left flank, nor demonstrated, to satisfy my right, is that we who have been dubbed knights of the glowing pedagogy are pretty dangerous, really, when left on our own. Even Socrates, I would say, would have taught better if, like Plato, he'd been surrounded by colleagues who were a bit less easily persuaded. We live in a time when it is becoming fashionable to breach disciplinary lines, as I have been advocating tonight. But those lines were invented because they did, after all, often prevent the abuses so easily committed by solipsistic prophets setting out to capture disciples. When departments knew (however naively) what the *discipline should be*, they exercised control over individual vagaries, and ensured by their examination and thesis requirements that students learned at least *something*. But I think we are now seeing a decline in a genuine intellectual collegiality. If we are not to leave our students floundering in a flood of confusing rival wisdoms, we must all not only prepare ourselves to answer that question, "What the hell do *you* know about life?" We must work with more energy than ever before to build *colleges* that will turn our so-called excellent individual teaching into what only *many* teachers working together can provide: an excellent undergraduate education.

2. I discuss this example at greater length in *The Company We Keep*, chapters 1 and 13.

EPILOGUE · *TO ALL WHO CARE ABOUT THE SURVIVAL OF INSTITUTIONS THAT PRESERVE TEACHING AND LEARNING*

INTRODUCTION · *The Occasion*

"We dare you to say something interesting about your frontline work, interesting to experts in your field yet intelligible to the entire University of Chicago community: faculty, administrators, trustees, students, wives, husbands." An invitation to that effect, though of course in less threatening language, is given once each year to a faculty member at the University of Chicago. The threat is only implicit; the scholar is expected to see "the Ryerson lecture" as both an honor and a challenge.

I took it as both, when I received the invitation in 1986, but I soon found my sense of the honor of the thing poisoned by my anxieties about how to meet an impossibly diverse audience. How could I hope to explain to physicists, biologists, historians, philosophers . . . , to say nothing of assorted non-academics, what it is that I struggle with each morning, most days of the year, when I sit alone trying to understand other authors' "texts" and "contexts," and trying to say something useful about them?

It was not that I had to wait long for my central idea. Obviously this occasion was ready-made for my purposes: a rhetorical occasion about rhetorical occasions. In a time when almost everybody seems to be saying that all texts are really "about their own writing," I was clearly presented with the ideally up-to-date "reflexive" moment. But to have a leading idea is not the same as to know how to pursue it, especially when that idea risks being exhausted in a paragraph: "I study rhetoric. This is a rhetorical occasion. I study what people do when they face occasions like this one. When they face occasions like this one, they talk like this. Thank you for listening to me." Many a piece of literary criticism these days, seeking to dramatize its own "reflexivity," seems finally almost as empty as that. So for a month or two I was increasingly anxious about not having anything to say.

But then, as frequently happens with me, the problem reversed itself: I found that the thing had already grown into a bloated monstrosity. Attempting to address what I increasingly thought of as the most critical audience I'd ever met, I had produced a draft that would have taken more than two hours to deliver. Yet with each effort to cut I seemed to be lopping off an essential bit, something required by some faction of my anticipated audience. Through draft after draft—perhaps a total of fifteen different versions—my anxiety increased. Of all the talks I have ever given, this one was thus most "labored"—with much of the labor going into removing the signs of labor.

The point is not to dramatize my courage and industry (though of course I take a not entirely secret pride in both). Nor is it to claim success. Nobody ever knows with any security whether a piece of rhetoric has been really as good as it should have been; even when nearly everyone says "bravo," you can't know whether you have found "all the means of persuasion" that the occasion implicitly provided. The point is thus to illustrate one extreme of the rhetorician's plight: while concern for audience and occasion can invigorate, it can also enervate. In the final weeks before delivering the forty-minute version, I found myself longing for the condition of a true philosopher, seeking nothing but *the truth* and disregarding the question of whether anyone will understand it when it is found. But the philosopher's rhetorical occasion—addressing God, or at most a tiny band of His representatives who are properly trained to look on truth bare—is not the rhetorician's occasion: *this* moment when *these* inquirers pursue together some elusive vision of a transitory truth. The rhetorician's truth, the teacher's truth, though as real as anything there is, cannot be separated from its history; it will always be embedded in this moment, this unique occasion.

OCCASION 19 · *The Idea of a University—
as Seen by a Rhetorician*

It is not often that a student of rhetoric faces an occasion that falls as neatly into his professional domain as this one falls into mine. The Ryerson lectures were designed as occasions for what the founders did *not* call "ecumenical rhetoric," discourse designed to bring together a community that is always tempted by modern forces to fall apart. I think I can claim, though with considerable anxiety, to be the first for whom this moment is a kind of setup: I am in effect invited to talk with you, a predetermined audience, about what the very existence of such a rhetorical occasion might mean. That is scarcely a comforting thought: it puts me on the spot in ways even more threatening than were faced by my threatened predecessors. As classical rhetoricians taught, the easiest way to guarantee failure with any perceptive audience is to be seen in advance as an expert in rhetoric. More is properly demanded where more is professed, and you can understand why I see troubles ahead.

My first problem lies of course in the very word "rhetoric." I was tempted, as I have often been in the past, to define that slippery term once and for all, but I have resisted, even though to grapple with its ambiguities would illustrate beautifully why Ryerson lecturers are notoriously nervous nellies. Just how much time should a lecturer spend claiming that, like Humpty Dumpty, he is to be the boss of definitions? Should I say, "Rhetoric on this occasion will *not* mean merely the art of winning, right or wrong, *nor* will it mean the clever use of bombast and trickery"? Should I insist that it will not even be the faculty, as Aristotle puts it, of "finding the available means of persuasion on any occasion"? Ted Schultz has recently advised me to abandon the sleazy term altogether and substitute something like "philosophy of discourse," or "theory of communication." But to abandon the term "rhetoric," with its long honorable history, just because it often suggests shoddy practices, would be like abandoning the term "philosophy," just because people talk about "the philosophy of tennis coaching," or abandoning the word "science" just because Mary Baker Eddy and the scientologists have each borrowed it for their purposes. Rather than defining it or abandoning it, suppose we just put a big question mark by what-

The Ryerson Lecture, University of Chicago, April 1987. Reprinted by permission of the University of Chicago.

ever your own definition would now be. You may or may not, by the end, want to apply the term "rhetorical study" to what we will have been doing.

I begin with a question that the very existence of these lectures forces upon us, no matter what our field: How is it that we can gather hopefully here, year after year, to listen to one another tell about our special work, when we know in advance that most of us, most of the time, have no real hope of understanding the special work of most of the rest of us? The trustees established the Ryerson series, with the special help of the Ranneys, on the assumption that it would be a good thing if specialists lectured "to an audience from the entire university on a significant aspect" of their research. They did not say, "Please talk down to that audience," or "Kindly choose some peripheral and general question of social, political, or ethical importance." No, we are asked to speak as specialists—and to make ourselves understood.

The trustees obviously assumed that we professors ought to be able to talk with our colleagues about what we do and why we do it. They must have assumed that everyone who *professes* a subject, any subject, no matter how esoteric, ought to be able to say something intelligible about it, or through it, or with it, to the non-specialist. Clearly they hoped for something more than a series of merely ceremonial occasions, pious gatherings of hypocrites only pretending to listen. They assumed that we could follow John Simpson, say, talking of extending "space science and exploration to the third dimension—that is, to travel out of the ecliptic plane"; or Karl Weintraub talking about an "empathetic and sympathetic understanding of the past," an understanding that "gives us the burden of relative and relativized knowledge"; or Stephen Toulmin talking about "the inwardness of mental life"; or Saunders Mac Lane talking about how a mathematician deals with "fuzzy sets"; or George Stigler talking about the disharmony between sound economic principles and unsound economic practice; or—but I need not go on. You already know that the list is threateningly diverse. If we face its diversity honestly, we must wonder just how much understanding can occur across our disciplinary borderlines. Our hosts assumed that we are, in *some* sense, at *some* level, a *uni*versity, a community of inquirers who have managed to maintain *some* kind of message center or telephone exchange.

I must now risk shocking those of you who do *not* know the academy from the inside, and risk boring those of you who do, by dwelling for a bit on some of the more obvious reasons for doubting these assumptions. I ask you who are professors whether we do not have overwhelming daily proof that no one of us can understand more than a fraction of the frontline work of the rest. We are all simply shut out of almost all front parlors but our own, permitted only to do a little polite begging at the back door: "Please, sir, please give a poor beggar just a slice of nuclear physics to keep me warm, just a tiny portion of paleontology to keep up my illusion of keeping up, just a touch of cosmology—the new anthropic principle, say—to help me survive the next cocktail party." We don't like to talk about it, but we know that even Ryerson lecturers fail, at least partially, with most of their auditors. One Ryerson lecturer who has come to all of these lectures told me that he has understood only about half of what has been said: "I grasped almost nothing in a couple of the lectures," he said, "about a third in half of them, two-thirds in a few of them, and all in only one—my own."

Shocking as such a fact might seem from some perspectives, no serious scholar is likely to be at all surprised by it. Centuries have passed since that fabled moment—was it in the eighteenth century or the late seventeenth?—when the last of the Leonardo da Vincis could hope to cover the cognitive map. Since that fatal moment, whenever it was, everyone, even that polymath down the hall who is said to "know everything," has been reduced to knowing only one or two countries on the intellectual globe, granting all the other countries only the most superficial of Cook's tours.

Perhaps some of you here once shared the naive ambition that my wife and I pursued, long before we met each other. As youngsters who wanted to know everything, we once set out to read every book in the closest available library. Though both of the libraries were fortunately very small, neither of us made it even to the *M*'s, let alone the *Z*'s. And our fate is an emblem for the condition we all live in. It isn't that we don't try. The academy attracts those who aspire to omniscience. We are the kind who would like others to say of us what young Christopher Tietjens' friend says of him, in Ford Madox Ford's *Parade's End*: "Confound you, Chrissie. You know everything!" [1] Tietjens is at the time making a list, *from memory*, of errors in the new edition of the *Encyclopaedia Britannica*. But not long afterward part of Tietjens' brain, and all of his hubris, are shattered by a bomb blast in the Great War, and he is reduced, in utter humiliation, to a pathetic attempt to memorize the very *Encyclopaedia* he had once scorned. Arriving at the *K*'s, he finds, under "Koran," the saying, "The strong man when smitten is smitten in his pride" (p. 170). It is precisely in our pride that we are smitten, when for one reason or another we discover just what a pitifully small corner of the cognitive world we live in. Though we can sympathize with Tietjens' impulse, we all know that even his original sense of universal mastery, as a young genius, was illusory. Not only can no one fully understand

1. Ford Madox Ford, *Parade's End* (four "Tietjens" novels: *Some Do Not . . .* [1924], *No More Parades* [1925], *A Man Could Stand Up*— [1926], and *The Last Post* [1928]), ed. Robie Macauley (New York, 1950), 19.

what any good encyclopedia contains, the encyclopedias themselves are almost uniformly inadequate and misleading; ask any expert in a given field
whether a reading of the encyclopedia entries in that field can educate even
the cleverest of readers to genuine competence. And if this is true of our
collective enterprises like encyclopedias, how much truer it is of each of us
as we try individually to figure out what on earth goes on in neighboring
subjects, across the hall or on the other side of the quad.

In short, the painful truth we voracious students discover, at twenty, or
forty, or sixty, is that what we sometimes call the "knowledge explosion"
has left us all ignorant of vast fields of knowledge that every educated man
and woman *ought* to have mastered. Is it any wonder that we tend to be
defensive in debate, sure that our next class or public lecture will reveal the
fatal truth: we are ignoramuses, and since we call ourselves professors,
scholars, even doctors, we risk exposure as frauds.

Perhaps I exaggerate. There may be in this room a few polyphilomathe-
matico wizards who can carry on a plausible conversation with experts in as
many as—shall we say, ten fields?—ten fields out of the hundreds listed in
the faculty directory. (I started counting them, but soon realized that I
didn't know enough in many areas even to tell what would constitute a
field. Take a look sometime at the listings under "Argonne National Labo-
ratories," or the "Department of Behavioral Sciences.") It is no doubt true
that many of us can give journalistic accounts of black holes, marginal utility, polymorphous perversities, ekphrastic poetry, and the oft-repeated rise,
over about twenty centuries, of the bourgeoisie. But for even the most
learned among us, the circle of what we might call *participatory* understanding does not extend very far.

During the past few months, I've been asking colleagues in various disciplines about just how much they understand of other people's work, using
the following test: Could you, given a week's warning, read an article or
book in a given field and then enter into a serious dialogue with the author,
at a level of understanding that the author would take as roughly comparable to his or her own? The answers varied widely in ambition and per-
suasiveness, not to say chutzpah, but you won't be surprised to learn that
no one claimed to be able to understand more than a fraction of what our
colleagues publish. Some were embarrassed by their confessions; most were
not. Some confidently blamed the bad writing in other fields. But all
confessed.

We would expect such confessions (or disguised accusations), when the
fields are obviously far apart: humanists don't usually claim to meet mathematicians where they live; botanists freely confess to bafflement about particle physics. But I was a bit surprised to find that hardly anyone claims to

understand all the work even within the home department. One philosopher told me that there is simply no one at this university, inside his department or out of it, who can understand his work; he is the lone inhabitant of
his tiny cognitive land. His circle of fellow-understanders consists of a tiny
band of similarly trained folk scattered around what we might call the
known world. Another philosopher tells me that he could understand, given
a week's lead time, perhaps 80 percent of what his fellow philosophers publish. He believes that perhaps even more than 80 percent of them could talk
with him about his work—"Not," he adds, "that they would have *really*
understood it, but at least we might be in the same ball park." A world-
famous mathematician tells me that he cannot follow the proofs offered by
most mathematicians; each sub-group of mathematicians has become so
specialized that the other sub-groups are unable to understand them, if by
"understanding" we mean being able to appraise, with full personal confidence, the validity of the proofs and thus the soundness of the conclusions.
The editor of a journal in biology says that he expects to understand about
fifty percent of the articles he publishes, and he adds, "I work harder at that
task than most of my colleagues." The editor of a chemistry journal understands 50 percent to 80 percent of the articles he chooses to publish, but he
"gets" hardly anything in most of the neighboring chemistry journals.

Obviously what my respondents have said depends on a relatively rigorous definition of "understanding." We surely ask more of ourselves than
simply being able to respond, after taking in the opinions of others, with a
plausible summary and an offer of our own plausible opinions. If we are to
do justice to the question I am raising, we should at least for a while adhere
to a more rigorous definition of "true understanding," something like this:
I have understood you if and only if I can say to you, "Yes, *but*," and say it
in a form that will lead you in turn to accept both my "yes" and my objections; not just my claim to have "got" your point, but my claim to have got
it so well that I can raise an objection to it that you in turn must take into
account. It is not enough for me to say to Professor Chandrasekhar, for example: "Oh, yes, I understand the theory of black holes. Black holes are
inconceivably dense concentrations of matter; they are so dense that their
gravitational force sucks in everything within range, including any photons
that happen to be around, so that no light, and indeed no particles or waves
of any kind, can ever emerge and therefore no information can come to us.
That's why they're called *black* holes. . . ." You and I could go on like that,
without even having to look anything up; that kind of understanding of
black holes, or cost-benefit analysis, or ethnomethodology, or thick descriptions, or the double helix, is in the air, like a lot of other half-baked opinions
we might pick up from reading the *New York Times* or *Scientific American.*

I might even think I had understood black holes well enough to look the professor boldly in the eye and add a clever reservation, like this: "*But* what I think you've got wrong, Professor, is that according to *my* notion of how scientific constructs work, black holes must be considered to be no more than plausible pictures, with no necessary connection with anything we might call the reality behind the pictures. . . ." And so on. Even if my earlier description, my "yes," were roughly on the right lines, which is unlikely, Professor Chandrasekhar cannot possibly respond either to my "yes," my report, or my reservations, with anything warmer than a friendly smile as a reward for trying. I could not possibly challenge him to the point of his saying, "Yes, you've taken the point of my most recent article; you have convinced me that you are a good judge of its quality, and I therefore must take your reservations into account. Let's inquire into your objection further." But if I cannot claim that kind of understanding, in what sense do I live in the same university that honors Professor Chandrasekhar's achievements?

Lest you think I am indicting others on my behalf, I here present myself as an extreme but by no means unrepresentative example of the ignorant professor. I now serve as third reader on a dissertation being written by a young man in South Asian Studies. He is writing about a group of Indian poets, translating their poems and doing a critical poetics of their kind of poetry. Of course I cannot read the poems in the original, and I have not yet read all of his translations. What's worse, I have never read a single critical work by the non-Western critics he deals with. What on earth, then, am I doing on that committee?

Is it any wonder that when one eavesdrops on a group of experts in a given field, talking about experts in other fields, one hears a lot of contemptuous dismissal? Just listen to the chemists talking about the biologists, the biologists talking about the clinical M.D.'s, the surgeons and internists complaining about one another, the humanists talking about the social scientists, and the economists talking about everybody.

Roger Hildebrand provides what is for me the climax to my survey as he talks about his switch a few years ago from particle physics to astrophysics. To us outsiders, that might look like a small leap, really a shift within the same general field, as compared with the distance, say, between art history and chemistry. But Roger says that he had to spend the equivalent of about three full years "becoming a graduate student again" before he could feel some confidence in dialogue with frontliners in his new field—before he could judge the importance of a new article in that field. Just think how much work would be required if he decided once again to shift to microbiology, say, or constitutional law.

It is no doubt true that as we move across campus to the "softer" social sciences, through history, and on to the even floppier software occupying the brainpans of us humanists, we find a somewhat enlarged circle of those who at least claim to understand one another. The non-quantitative historians have told me that they can understand *all* of the *good* work of other non-quantitative historians. Most computer-armed prosopographers claim to understand the work of other cliometricians, and of course they claim to understand all the "easy" work of narrative historians—at least well enough to be suspicious of their inherently soft results. Lawyers all tell me that they can understand the legal arguments of all *good* lawyers. The cultural anthropologists say that they can understand everything worth reading in the social sciences. But when I press these various representatives, asking the lawyers whether they really understand the so-called critical realists, asking the cultural anthropologists whether they understand the quantitative sociologists, and so on, they often fall back on invective: "Those people are not doing true law or true anthropology." Or: "That gang have been badly trained."

Perhaps the largest circle of those who claim to understand one another would be found in English and other modern language studies. Hundreds of thousands of us profess to understand just about anything that falls into our hands. But when we look more closely at humanists' claims to membership in large circles of understanding, they appear pretty feeble. After all, in the quantitative and mathematical sciences, people tend to recognize when they have not understood one another. But we students of the human tend to think we have understood when we have not.

Here, for example, is the opening of a chapter by Jacques Derrida, the philosopher perhaps now most influential on literary studies:

> What about the voice within the logic of the supplement? within that which should perhaps be called the "graphic" of the supplement?
> Within the chain of supplements, it was difficult to separate writing from onanism. Those two supplements have in common at least the fact that they are dangerous. They transgress a prohibition and are experienced within culpability. But, by the economy of differance [deliberately spelled with an "a," as a special term], they confirm the interdict they transgress, get around a danger, and reserve an expenditure.[2]

Now I have worked for about a decade to become comfortable with the recondite language in which that passage is written, and I think I sort of understand it. Unlike some of my more traditional colleagues, I am utterly convinced that it is *not* nonsense, though it is opaque somewhat—more so

2. Jacques Derrida, "Genesis and Structure of the Essay 'On the Origin of Languages,'" in *Of Grammatology*, trans. Gayatri Chakravorty Spivak (Baltimore, 1976), 165.

than in the original French. Still, if I were to study the chapter that follows it carefully and then write a summary, the chances are about ninety-nine to one that Derrida would *not* say of it, "Bravo: you have understood." Just ask yourself how you have felt about the typical review or reader's report on your own carefully-wrought opus. My own response to reviews is often, "How could anyone but a moron misunderstand me so badly?"

Let me offer now a true story that summarizes our plight. Each year a committee is appointed in the Social Sciences Division to decide on the award of the annual Galler prize for the best dissertation done during that year. A couple of years ago an economist on the committee, after reading the submissions from other fields, announced that a dissertation from economics that he would now submit was superior to all the others, and should get the prize. The other committee members insisted that before granting his case they should have a chance to read it and compare it with the others. "No," he said, "that's impossible. You could not possibly understand it." "But how can we judge," they insisted, "if we are not allowed even to see the work?" He remained adamant, and when they refused to award the prize to a dissertation that they were not even allowed to see, he withdrew himself, and the dissertation, from the competition. He tells me now that the Department of Economics no longer even considers submitting dissertations for the prize, because they are sure that the non-quantitative "literary" types—the historians and anthropologists—simply could not recognize high quality in economics if they saw it.

Though that is clearly an extreme case, it helps make the point that even if we could create a university inhabited solely by geniuses, geniuses who, unlike most actual geniuses, were full of an infinite good will toward, and determination to understand, one another's disciplines, geniuses who would accept the assignment to work on our problem, we would find that under modern conditions of inquiry, conditions that we have no hope of changing fundamentally, none of them could come to an understanding of more than a fraction of what the others would take to be real knowledge.

Must we not admit, then, in all honesty, that we are indeed a pack of ignoramuses, inhabitants of some ancient unmapped archipelago, each of us an island—let John Donne preach as he will—living at a time before anyone had invented boats or any other form of inter-island communication?

II

I assume that many of you have long since wanted to protest against my picture. We all know that the islands are not in fact totally isolated, that somehow we have managed to invent communication systems. Though it may be true that on each island we speak a language not fully intelligible on any other, and though it may be true that some of the islands conduct active warfare against some of the others, and though some islands are in a state of civil war, the fact is that somehow we do manage to talk with one another and come to judgments that we are convinced are not *entirely* capricious. We write interdepartmental and even interdivisional memos, we indite letters of recommendation at breakneck speed and in appalling numbers, purporting to appraise the quality of colleagues whose work we don't know beans about. We appraise other scholars according to what we take to be high standards, even when we ourselves cannot state literally what the standards are. We pass judgment upon students in "related fields" and one another whenever promotion is at stake, and we seem not to suffer intolerable anxiety about our decisions. Even more shocking, in view of the plight I have described, we ask our deans and provosts and presidents to approve our judgments, and even grant the right to reverse them, implying that somehow *somebody* can be competent to judge work in *all* fields. Finally, we busy ourselves with a great deal of what we call "interdisciplinary work": degree-granting committees like Ideas and Methods, imperialistic fields like geography, anthropology, English, and rhetoric, conferences and workshops galore. None of us really thinks that *all* of these operations are totally fraudulent. We act *as if* our discussions and conferences and tenure decisions make *real* sense. Do they?

How do we actually work, as we run those of our affairs that depend on some kind of understanding different from the one I have applied so far? Do we work, as some say, only according to blind trust of friends and mistrust of enemies? Do we work according to guesses only? Are we, as some would claim, simply servants of money and power? In what sense, if any, do we employ a kind of reasoning and proof—knowledge and genuine understanding under any definition—that we might point to without shame?

After my informants of the past months have confessed their ignorance, I have asked them to tell me how they in fact operate when judging colleagues whose work they do not understand. All of them have said something like this—though never in this precise language: "We are by no means fraudulent, because we have available certain rational resources that your definition of understanding leaves out. We have learned to make use of our knowledge [one professor even called it "wisdom"] about character and how to appraise character witnesses; we have learned how to read the signs of quality even in the fields where we cannot follow the proofs. We have learned how to determine whether a referee is trustworthy, and we have learned something about how to judge the quality of a candidate's thinking, just by the way he or she writes and speaks." They have not gone on to say, though I wish we could have shared this language: "You see, what all this means is that we are experienced both as practitioners and students of—rhetoric."

When I press them further with the question, "Do you make mistakes with this kind of thinking?" the answer is always "Yes, sometimes." But nobody I've talked with has claimed that the process depends on a trust that is utterly blind, totally a matter of non-rational power-grabs or log-rolling or back-scratching or money-grubbing. Everyone, absolutely everyone, has played into this rhetorician's hands by claiming to employ a kind of thought that is not identical with what we do when proving conclusions in our front-line inquiry—and yet a kind that is still genuine thought.

Of course nobody has claimed that we offer our rhetorical proofs to each other and test them as well as we ought; indeed my main point today is that we could all employ them better, and thus improve our quality as a *university*, *if* we all studied how such peculiar yet rational persuasion works. But even in our fallen condition, even as we in our imperfection now operate, we do not perform our personal and administrative judgments on indefensible, non-scholarly grounds; we perform those judgments on grounds that are considered non-scholarly only by those who think that all knowledge is of the kind yielded by front-line specialties, only by those who embrace un-critically the criterion for understanding, and thus of knowledge, with which I began. If knowledge is confined to what experts discover at the frontline, and if understanding is confined to participation in full dialogue at the frontline, then we operate ourselves without *knowing* what we do and without *understanding* each other. If we know and understand only what we can *prove*—with empirical observation, or with statistics, or with rigor-ous logical deduction—we will never *know* whether a colleague is worth listening to or promoting, unless we ourselves can follow his or her proofs, in detail, and then replicate them. All else is dubious, all else is guesswork, all else is blind faith.

But one thing we all know is that we know more than that criterion im-plies. Though unable to tell for ourselves whether the new mathematical proof is indeed new and indeed a proof, we learn how to consider, with the eye of non-specialists, both the rhetoric of scholarship that we cannot hope fully to understand, and the rhetoric offered us *about* the scholar, the argu-ments offered by those who give us some reason to trust or mistrust their judgment as specialists.

We all thus implicitly aspire to mastery in three kinds of rhetoric, leading to three kinds of understanding, not just one. There are, first, the many and diverse rhetorics peculiar to each of our various frontlines. Here each small group of experts relies on what Aristotle calls *special topics* of persuasion, the often tacit convictions that are shared by all within a discipline and that are therefore available in constructing arguments within the field: the assumption, say, that photographs of bubble chambers and their interpretations can somehow be relied on; or the conventional agreements about how to deal with normal curves and chi squares, about the proper use of graphs, about what makes a sound equation, or about how to do a sensitive report of poetic scansion or a convincing analysis of sonata form in a symphony. Though these assumptions shift over time, we can at any given time rely on them without argument in their support, as we construct our arguments to our peers. I'll risk offending some of you by dubbing this frontline stuff and its workings "rhetoric-1." If calling it "hard proof" will make you happier, feel free, but I know that few specialists will want to claim that they or their successors will find themselves fifty years from now relying on the same tacit assumptions, leading to the same conclusions, that they share today.[3]

A second kind that I call "general rhetoric," or "rhetoric-2," is what we share with members of every functioning organization or society—businesses, governments, clubs, families: the whole range of plausible or probable beliefs and modes of proof that make the world go round. Think of it as what even the most rigorous of scientists must rely on when testifying before a government committee. Here we rely on the *common,* or general topics: "More of any good thing is better than less of it—usually"; "It's wrong to lie, at least to friends and colleagues"; "Loyalty matters"; "Actions that usually produce bad consequences should be avoided." Obviously many of these are included in everyone's notion of "common sense": what *makes* sense in any argument.

Though the common topics are indispensable in every domain, they are especially prominent in our running of the university whenever we must appraise character. We all have a little storehouse of beliefs about character that we have to rely on, more or less efficiently, whenever we read a letter of recommendation, or predict the future behavior of a colleague in order to grant or deny tenure. Such common topics, "commonplaces," crop up in all public debate. "It is probable that someone who failed to carry through on her previous research plan will fail in this one; turn her down." "Ah, yes, but she was deep in the anguish of a divorce then, and she's changed a lot. I say give her the grant." "Well, but her strongest supporter is Professor Smiler, who has usually been wrong in his predictions that young col-

---

3. Note that the "area" classification into three rhetorics that I am building here cuts across the "quality" classification into sub-rhetoric, "mere" rhetoric, rhetoric-B and rhetoric-A that I found essential on Occasion 6. Rhetoric-1 and rhetoric-A overlap, but they are by no means identical.

leagues are late bloomers. Why should we believe him in this case?" Or: "The truth is that Louise and Harry used to live together, and they had an angry breakup. I think—though we must say nothing of it in public—that we cannot trust his negative judgment on her scholarly ability."

Rhetoric-2 is thus the set of resources available in the functioning of all organizations, not just of universities. Arbitragers and government officers function or fail to function, depending on whether the trust they yield to their CEO's and Marine sergeants and colonels is justified. We in the university similarly succeed to the degree that our trust is granted when it should be, withheld when it should not be. The ease with which rhetoric-2 can be abused accounts largely for why rhetoric has always had, and probably always *will* have, a bad press. Philosophers and moralists have often wished that it would just go away—but of course they express the wish for a purer world in the only language available to any of us when we press our wishes on the world: rhetorical argument.

There is, thirdly, a kind of rhetoric that is neither as special as the first nor as general as the second, a rhetoric relying on shared topics that are proper or special only to those within a university, but to all within that university, not to any one special group. We have no name for this peculiar stuff that we all to some degree share, but call it "the rhetoric of inquiry," or of "intellectual engagement": "academy-rhetoric," or "rhetoric-3." We learn how to judge whether the arguments in fields beyond our full competence *somehow* track, whether the style of presentation *somehow* accords with standards we recognize. We learn to sense whether a colleague, even in a quite remote field, *seems* to have mastered the tricks of the trade—not just the trade of this or that kind of economist or philosopher, but the tricks of this whole trade, the trade of learning and teaching for the sake of learning and teaching. One often hears, in the Quadrangle Club, not just the contemptuous comments I have mentioned about fools and knaves but comments like this: "What a mind that man has." "What a pleasure to argue with that woman—she never misses a stroke." "He always seems to have just the right analogy to make his point." "Have you noticed how you always come away from a conversation with him having to think through the problem in a different way?"

All three of these rhetorics are of course highly fallible. Even our many versions of rhetoric-1 are notoriously unstable, as I have already implied, shifting in threatening ways from decade to decade and field to field. But the second and third rhetorics are much more obviously fallible, indeed staggeringly so. Tough-minded appraisal of characters and witnesses through close reading of letters of recommendation and reader's reports, close listening during telephone calls and hallway conversations, careful appraisal of past records of performance—these are all dangerously unreliable, partly because charlatans can so easily mimic the proper use of the topics. If this were not so, we would not have so many successful frauds in every field. The Piltdown hoaxers, the Cyril Burts, the Darseys, the unqualified but practicing surgeons, the undiploma-ed lawyers—all the hoaxers of our world succeed as they do because they have mastered the surface conventions of all three rhetorics and through that mastery have collected or forged references testifying to high quality. We read about so many successes in this burgeoning field of pseudo-scientific conning that we are in danger of forgetting the solid and indispensable base of merely probable inferences on which it rests. The breakdowns in the system result from, and depend on, a process—the practice of producing sound conclusions from rhetorical proofs—that by its very necessities opens the door to frauds. But this is not to say that we, their dupes, could not protect ourselves better if we would study rhetoric as hard as we study lab techniques, say, or formal logic.

Again and again I have been told by my informants that "it's not really very hard to tell competent work from incompetent, even if you know nothing about the details and cannot replicate the argument or experiment." And when I then ask, "How do you *do* that?" I am told—never in this language—that "I do it using rhetorics-2 and -3—not the appraisal of frontline proofs but the careful judgment of both "general rhetoric" and "academy rhetoric." One editor told me, "Even when I know little or nothing about a special field, I can tell just by the opening paragraphs whether a would-be contributor is at least competent." What does that mean, if not that he claims to judge the author's skill in rhetorical conventions shared with other fields: skill in saying what needs saying and in not saying what should not be said; skill in implying a scholarly ethos appropriate to the subject; skill in avoiding moves that give away the novice; and so on. Though the practice and appraisal of such skills is chancy, if we ruled them out we could not operate for a day without disaster. Most of our journals would have to be scrapped, most of our grants and awards would have to be eliminated, and the university would have to surrender to total balkanization or even tribal warfare, becoming not a *uni*versity at all but a multiversity, a mere collection of research institutes warring for funds.

We can see how rhetorics-2 and -3 work, in a genuine university, by probing the grounds for our belief about the quality of any one of our more distinguished colleagues. I believe, for example, that George Stigler is really a very good economist. I would bet my next month's salary on my belief that when Stigler does economics, he is working at the highest levels of competence in his field (at least on his good days), and that in doing so he is not simply playing an esoteric power game but is actually pursuing one genuine kind of knowledge. But what's my evidence? Every bit of it, when taken by itself, is extremely chancy rhetorical inference, some of it of the second kind, some of the third, none of the first. I cannot really understand his frontline work, but when I dip into it I find enough similarities with work I do understand to give me some slight confidence. Still, my views of it are scandalously shallow. But then I start adding other bits. I've had some private conversations with George about the assumptions of economics as a field—highly general conversations, those, with me trying to put him on the defensive but always ending on the ropes, and thus increasingly impressed. Similarly, our talks about literature and about campus politics have impressed me considerably with the general quality of his reasoning, even though in themselves they tell me nothing directly about his work as an economist. I find myself admiring his more popular stuff, as in *The Economist as Preacher*;[4] not only is he a master of English style, but he offers dozens of signs that he belongs to a community of economists who respect him. Still, such reading in itself cannot tell me very much about his work as an economist. I can add to these his Nobel prize, but the fact is that it doesn't impress me much more than it probably impresses him; we all know that Nobel committees can make grotesque mistakes. The seemingly uniform esteem of his local colleagues counts most for me, but it could not in itself settle the issue; obviously whole departments and whole fields can misjudge quality. Finally, the fact of his election by his colleagues to various important university committees can again carry only slight weight, in itself.

But note that all of these weak clues point in the same direction, and they all come to a head when I hear other economists who are said to be good— note well that phrase—say that George Stigler is good and *is said to be good*. Each reason for trust is in itself slight. My confidence could be shaken quite easily by counter-testimony from someone I trust as much as I trust these witnesses, if I could find someone. It could be shaken if I discovered some obviously incompetent logic in his Ryerson lecture—his foray into the non-specialized academic rhetoric I am calling rhetoric-3. But after I have added together all the weak-but-still-pertinent reasons, it would take a good deal of contrary evidence to make me doubt his competence. What may be even more important, the half-comprehension that I gain by all of this peripheral activity adds to my own intellectual life. I take part, at a great distance, in Stigler's reasoning about economics, and I even dare from time to time to quarrel with him, ineffectually, about that weird first principle of his, the belief that people's behavior can be fully explained as the rational calculation of individual costs and benefits.

4. George Stigler, *The Economist as Preacher and Other Essays* (Chicago, 1982).

The relative weight of the three rhetorics varies from field to field, committee to committee, occasion to occasion. I once served on the Board of University Publications, and in the early spring we faced that annual ordeal, the decision about which of our colleagues should receive the Laing prize for a distinguished book. We had all read the major reviews of each eligible book, and we had all been urged to read all of the books, though I doubt that anyone had done so. Then, after preliminary balloting (based mainly, you see, on the rhetoric-3 of the reviews we had read), we were asked to read with special care those books that seemed prime contenders. In the preliminary balloting that followed, several books came out ahead of Sewall Wright's collected essays. I can remember that I had read at—I think that's the right expression—*read at* several of the essays in that monumental collection, working away dutifully because the reviews had uniformly described Wright and his book as of major importance. The essays seemed authoritative to me—that fairly small portion of them that I could understand at all. The logic, where I could follow it, made sense. The language carried authority. I found, after reading *at* four or five of the essays, that I was admiring the character who emerged from the various projects; to me it seemed obvious that this man was a serious, responsible, highly intelligent scientist. But I simply had no way of detecting for myself whether his results were original or sound or worthy to be influential, let alone worthy of the Laing prize. So, like most of the members of that board, I did not on the first round vote for Wright as number one, though he was among the highest. Rather, I voted for authors about whom I felt much more sure, because I could follow their frontline arguments.

Then in our final meeting a curious thing happened. Our late colleague Arnold Ravin spoke at some length about the true importance of Wright's work. As I remember his eloquent appeal, it went like this: "You must believe me, when I tell you that this is a major collection by a major figure, a genius who has transformed his field again and again. Believe me, though you yourselves cannot be expected to see the quality in these essays, this book is head-and-shoulders above the others on our list." Now here is where this anecdote diverges from my story of the economist and the Galler prize. *We argued back, and Ravin attempted to meet our arguments.* He gave another speech, longer and with different examples, with more testimonial quoted from other biologists, and with a repeated claim that since none of the rest of us were biologists, we were just not qualified to grasp the full cumulative importance of this record of a life's work. Finally, after an hour or so of debate, we voted decisively to give the prize to Sewall Wright, an author whose work only one person in the room could fully understand. And we had no positive evidence even of that: we had only Ravin's words as evidence that even he had understood Wright.

323

We voted, you see, mainly on the basis of powerful rhetoric of kinds two and three. We trusted the rhetorician because his arguments made sense to us, because they harmonized with what the other experts had told us, because they were not contradicted by what little we could infer from our own efforts at reading the essays themselves, and because we had reason to trust the judgment and integrity of Arnold Ravin.[5] Some of his arguments would have worked equally well in an insurance company's board room (rhetoric-2). His passion, for example, was not mere passion: it became hard evidence, because we felt that Ravin was not the kind of man who would fake passion like that, and passion like that could not be aroused except by an exceptional case. (So much, by the way, for the still-fashionable inclination to contrast reason and emotion; a powerful emotion, carefully appraised, can often be the hardest of evidence in this kind of reasoning.) But some of his arguments were special to this special kind of place. For example, he argued that Wright had been mainly responsible for the creation of a new discipline—a claim that would seem out of place in a business context, say, or in a psychotherapist's office. And I remember his saying that if someone a hundred years from now wanted to know both the state of that discipline and the special problems and methods it encountered at the time the book was written, the book would still live. So we all came to a choice that in retrospect still seems to me eminently sound, though I would not be shattered if some other work, neglected by us in those final moments, turned out later to be more important than Wright's.

Would we have done better to tell Arnold Ravin, "All that is *mere* rhetoric. We must vote only on and for those books that we ourselves can understand?" To say no to that route requires us to believe that there is a real difference between sound and unsound rhetorical appeals, that there is a whole domain of knowledge—uncertain, chancy, elusive knowledge but knowledge nonetheless—that is important not only in the awarding of prizes and promotions but in the day-by-day intellectual life of the university. Not only does every hiring and firing, every promotion, every establishment of a new department or elimination of an old one, every choice of a dean or president, depend on such topical reasoning. Our very survival depends on our control of that kind of knowledge—that is to say, on our repertory of rhetorical practices and norms. We depend on appraising the testimony and authority and general ethos of other people, as they appraise the testimony

5. After the Ryerson lecture a biologist friend said, "You know, Arnold Ravin could not have *really* understood Wright's work; it was beyond him." "Do you mean," I asked, "that we were wrong in listening to him?" "Oh, no; you were right, because *he* was right. But he was himself depending more on rhetorics-2 and -3 than you realized."

and authority of still others, who in turn depend on others . . . and no one can say where these circles of mutual trust end, except of course when societies and universities destroy themselves by losing the arts of determining when trust is justified.

Philosophers of science like Michael Polanyi[6] and Rom Harré[7] have argued that even the "hardest" sciences, even physics and chemistry and mathematics, do *not* depend mainly on the application by each individual of so-called scientific method to all beliefs, doubting every proposition until it has been shown to be falsifiable and yet not falsified. Instead, they say, each individual scientist survives as scientist by virtue of indeterminately large networks of critical trust, based largely on assumptions shared by many or most disciplines, (rhetoric-3). Each of them must rely, as you and I do, on broad ranges of belief that no one of us could ever hope to demonstrate independently. As Polanyi puts it, we are all inherently "con-vivial," dependent for our intellectual bases, as we are in our physical lives, on living *together*. Even as specialists, he says, we live in "fiduciary" structures that we have not constructed and could never construct on our own.[8]

III

What we have arrived at here is a picture radically different from that of the archipelago of islands forced to remain incommunicado. We need another picture of how we relate as specialists. Those who worry about those lonely islands too often take as an ideal the impossible notion of getting more people to add more and more specialties, as if there were some hope of making each island self-sufficient. Attacking this "Leonardesque aspiration," psychologist Donald T. Campbell, in a splendid essay precisely on our subject today, suggested that the best way to combat the "ethnocentrism of disciplines," the "tribalism" and "nationalism" of specialties, would be to

6. Michael Polanyi, *Personal Knowledge: Towards a Post-Critical Philosophy* (Chicago, 1958; rev. ed., New York, 1962).

7. Rom Harré, "Science as a Communal Practice," in *Varieties of Realism: A Rationale for the Natural Sciences* (Oxford, 1986).

8. "[W]hat earlier philosophers have alluded to by speaking of coherence as the criterion of truth is only a criterion of *stability*. It may equally stabilize an erroneous or a true view of the universe. The attribution of truth to any particular stable alternative is a fiduciary act which cannot be analysed in non-committal terms [that is, it depends on prior commitment to some enterprise shared with others]. . . . [T]here exists no principle of doubt the operation of which will discover for us which of two systems of implicit beliefs is true—except in the sense that we will admit decisive evidence against the one we do not believe to be true, and not against the other. Once more, the admission of doubt proves here to be as clearly an act of belief as does the non-admission of doubt" (Polanyi, *Personal Knowledge*, 294).

pursue the "fish-scale model of omniscience."[9] Picture each group of specialists as one scale in a total fish-scale, both overlapping and overlapped by
the interests and competencies of adjacent specialties. The total network, or
fish-scale, "knows" whatever is in fact known; though no one unit knows
very much, each unit is connected to all the others, through the unbroken
overlappings.[10]

Campbell hoped with this model both to relieve each of us from the
anxiety to know more than anyone can possibly know, and to encourage
more productive specialization in the areas where the scales overlap. The
new specialties thus developed would be in one sense as narrow as the
others; like everyone else in the university the new specialists would still
be ignoramuses when addressing most fields. But by concentrating on
hitherto-neglected connections, they would improve the efficiency of the
entire fish-scale. The *university* of his model would in a sense know itself
and know what it knows, while no one individual would have to feel guilty
about not pursuing the impossible project of learning what the network as a
whole has learned.

Campbell's model takes us in the right direction, but it may still be misleading, as a picture both of how we work at our best, and as a practice to
aspire to. Unfortunately, I can't find quite as neat an image for my own
notion of how we work. But suppose we imagine a fish-scale in which each
separate scale is not a scale at all but some kind of organism, perhaps like an
octopus, with many tentacles, some of them reaching only to one or two
adjacent scales, some leaping across to the opposite sides of the whole fish, as
it were. The tentacles often intertwine, and they are somehow able to send
half-intelligible, scrambled, but still not worthless messages to scales in unpredictable parts of the whole—well, of course the picture becomes visually
absurd. But the inadequacy of pictures shouldn't surprise us, since the uni-

9. Donald T. Campbell, "Ethnocentrism of Disciplines and the Fish-Scale Model of Omniscience," in *Interdisciplinary Relationships in the Social Sciences*, ed. Muzafer Sherif and
Carolyn W. Sherif (Chicago, 1969), 328–48. I thank Marvin Mikesell for this reference.

10. Anxiety about the ethnocentrism of experts was not invented in recent decades. As
early as 1902, Alexander R. Hohfield, summarizing a central session of the annual meeting of
the Modern Language Association, lamented "the increasing specialization of the papers"
and claimed that it was "rapidly decreasing the number of occasions when a considerable
proportion of those present are capable of joining in a discussion." Many a scholar has been
hard-pressed to find proper analogies for our plight. Just after World War II John Erskine,
describing how scholars claim to "cover" jointly fields that no one of them has mastered, re-
called an ancient Irish legend: "[T]here was a tower so high that it took two persons to see to
the top of it. One would begin at the bottom and look up as far as sight could reach, the other
would begin where the first left off, and see the rest of the way." I owe these quotations to
Gerald Graff, *Professing Literature: An Institutional History* (Chicago, 1987), 111.

versity is not really *much* like anything else in the universe. In my garbled image, a given physicist will not only occupy a given scale of expertise, as it overlaps adjacent fields, say mathematics and chemistry, but will also project "tentacles" across the entire network to the poets or musicians or art historians, as Professor Chandrasekhar did in his Ryerson lecture. Occupants of a given scale, a given specialty, do not hope to earn full occupancy of more than two or three further scales in a lifetime, but they not only hope for, but can achieve, a partial understanding of many. Remember: I am not yet pursuing an ideal university, only the best notion of how we ignoramuses actually work at our best. You might want to think here of professors who both occupy a single scale with high competence and extend themselves effectively into the larger network. (In one draft I began to list them by name; but the list not only risked offending by its omissions but also quickly grew too long. I wonder whether any other university can offer as many professors of the kind I have in mind).

IV

So much is, I would argue, a roughly accurate description of why we are not *as* fraudulent as my first picture suggested. You will have noticed, however, that my description, like all descriptions of human activity, is not what the social scientists call "value-free." Even the most neutral description of any human endeavor will reveal, to the careful listener, implied judgments and exhortations, and mine is no exception. Most obviously, I have implied throughout that for people to understand one another is not only a good thing in itself, it is the sine qua non of a genuine university. It follows from that, I think, that one of our main tasks is to improve our chances for genuine understanding—understanding, of course, of all three kinds. We need to expand the size, as it were, of each fish-scale and the area of overlap among the scales. We need to encourage ourselves in the growth of tentacles reaching from scale to scale. But, even more pressingly, we need to increase our understanding of how it is that we do in fact communicate by means of those tentacles, and how we might do it better.

The lines among the three kinds of improvement will always be blurred. Mastering the special topics of most fields will lead simultaneously to some improvement in the handling of the topics common to all rational discourse. Many fields, like my own, are built largely out of the topics that are shared by all scholarly and scientific fields. But though the lines are indistinct, we are all in effect custodians of all three kinds. The ideal university that is implied by all this would obviously be one in which we all worked even more steadily, aggressively, and effectively than we do now to increase the number of moments each day when genuine understanding takes place—with a consequent improvement both in the quality of learners and in the quality of judgments passed on the learners.

What would such a university look like? Well, as some of you know, it is getting easier and easier these days to move forward and backward in time, now that Shirley MacLaine and her multiplying siblings have taught us how to achieve out-of-body experiences. I happen to have just returned this week from a visit fifty years forward, and I have brought back a little history, published by the press of a university that occupies precisely our present site (not a single new building!). It calls itself, however, the University of Polytopia—not Utopia, no-place, but Polytopia, many places. The history, dated April 22, 2037, is signed by one Raphael Hythloday, Emeritus Professor of Education. Here is a painfully shortened version of Hythloday's report.

Having decided, just fifty years ago, to become a *uni*versity and not an archipelago of mutually incomprehensible, self-congratulating isolates, our governing committees turned to a serious study of those arts that we thought had been essential to our surviving with some quality, even as late as 1987. Our first decision, arrived at not without bloodshed, was to postpone all attempts to rise one more point in the reputation polls of the *multi*versities. Deciding to be a great *uni*versity down the road a decade or two, we abandoned the attempt to cover every topic that our rivals chose to cover. We stopped adding whatever new departments or subjects our rivals added, and we stopped wooing academic stars according to their present luminosity, recognizing that any multiversity like Berkeley could beat us at both those games.[11] Instead we began to operate according to a principle that came to be known as Booth's Law: 'Maximum luminosity of professors and departments is exactly like maximum luminosity in the heavenly spheres: it reaches the target millions of years after the star has burnt itself out.'" [Incidentally, Booth's Law applies locally as well as nationally. It means that Ryerson lecturers are chosen roughly 10.57 years too late.]

Attention to Booth's law led us to turn to an unprecedented search, far outshining that of the MacArthur Foundation, for men and women who

---

11. According to Graff (*Professing Literature*, 40–41), the first professor who was solicited by a rival institution on the basis of his publication list was Francis James Child, in 1876. He resisted the temptation, offered by the Johns Hopkins University, when Harvard agreed to release him from his teaching of—what else?—composition! A century later, we find ourselves spending a major part of our time on that kind of wasteful luring and responding.

had managed to preserve, even as late as their thirties or early forties, some vestige of the curiosity and enthusiasm for learning that they had shown when younger. We sought out and hired the most vigorously *curious* minds we could find, regardless of their degrees and publication lists. We then turned them loose in the university as it was. We attempted no master plan, and we imposed only two revisions of current procedures. First, all faculty members were required to teach at least half of their courses to non-specialists, graduate or undergraduate, with at least one course each year concentrating on the question of what kinds of argument are defensible, in one or more of the three rhetorics. Secondly, at tenure and promotion times the primary decision was to be made, not by a department alone, but by departmental representatives joined by a larger group from outside the department, all charged to apply one test only: Is this candidate *still curious*, still inquiring into one or more of the three rhetorics, and is it thus probable that at the age of forty, fifty, or sixty-six, he or she will still be vigorously inquiring?

The result was that we were all soon seeking, regardless of our specialties, to become masters of three rhetorics, not just one; we began to educate ourselves about where our topics, our locations, our always unpredictable problems, fit into the polytopicality that we no longer even desired to escape. Thus we did not give up on the quest for a common understanding, but the understanding we sought, as our one central value, was the one by which we still live, the one that is inherent in any attempt to live with our heterodoxies, our polytopicality: the quest for an understanding of how we understand, and why we so frequently fail to.

Many predicted that with departments no longer quite such bastions of autonomy as they had been, we would soon just fall off the national charts. But no one today will be surprised to learn that after a year or two of uncertain reputation, we quickly became famous as the national center for the study of the three rhetorics. The various publics who are always desperate for guidance in those rhetorics came to our support in such numbers that we were almost overwhelmed. Business executives and government officials came to realize that the *inter*translation of rhetorics—what we now feel comfortable in calling not "rhetoric-4" but "rhetorology"—was their own primary labor. Every scientist seeking a grant soon came to see that rhetorology was the primary resource when facing government officials and specialists in other fields. In short, The University of Polytopia found itself serving *public* needs in new and surprising ways. Money for professorships and fellowships flowed in, as our graduates became famous for the way they performed, and as our new kind of professor, recruited when young, became famous for teaching the world how to perform responsibly and effectively in its rhetorical exchanges.

No one now will be surprised by another development, but it surprised almost everyone at the time: I mean the sudden new importance of our undergraduate College, which quickly became honored as a national center for the study, not only of the three primary rhetorics, but of rhetorology. Unlike the colleges in multiversities, ours was no longer considered as somehow in conflict or competition with advanced research and instruction. Rather it was viewed as the facilitator of the most original, least imitative thinking and research. Faculty members, now required to pursue problems that arise when disciplines must make decisions together about what is worth learning and what should be taught, soon found themselves deepening their specialties as they thought about how their rhetoric-1 was or was not valuable to non-specialist undergraduates. As they considered what they knew that everybody *ought* to know, and pressed themselves about precisely where they belonged in the new Polytopia, and as they encountered solid practical problems raised by their curiosity about developing new major fields, they inescapably met with colleagues from hitherto unlikely locations. Soon it became clear that one of the most profitable challenges to the advanced expert was the planning of a staff-taught undergraduate course. Many who had thought of college teaching as a costly rival to graduate research and teaching discovered in such meetings new problems, and new disciplines for dealing with them.

The College was of course not the only center to become flushed with new importance. All of the committees and programs that had traditionally located themselves where the fish-scales overlap, and thus inevitably pursued rhetorology, found themselves with strengthened support— but also with a new and threatening pressure to probe deeper. No longer could anyone get any credit just for putting together a superficial non-understanding of two disciplines and calling the result "interdisciplinary."

Naturally enough, we soon found that every student in every program, from the freshman year to the Ph.D., was studying the question of how to improve argument, under the different requirements of the three rhetorical domains. Every field, already steeped in the frontline problems of rhetoric-1, soon included some systematic inquiry into those problems, together with inquiry into how that field could better relate itself to other fields and to the world.

No longer could anyone be forgiven for ignorantly pursuing in one field problems that had long since been solved in others. Fortunately it has now been two full decades since the following groups discovered, through rhetorology, that they were in fact studying the three rhetorics and rhetorology under other names, and that they had wasted effort in duplicating inquiry already performed elsewhere.

[I must apologize for the heavy detail that follows here. Hythloday becomes a bit cryptic, apparently feeling that he must make a little ingratiating bow, however perfunctory, toward almost every field. I have cut some of his examples and all of his tedious footnoting, and I have changed his order: with characteristic arrogance, he risked ranking fields according to his idea of their importance; with characteristic prudence, I have re-ranked them in simple alphabetical order.]

—anthropologists studying how root metaphors constitute societies;
—art historians quarreling about the validity of Gombrich's views of representation;
—business school professors founding centers for "decision research" and "cognition and communication," with the purpose of discovering just how minds are changed;
—classicists studying the history of the goddess Peitho, the goddess of persuasion;
—cognitive psychologists repudiating behavior modification models and studying ways in which the mind performs "constructionist" operations that escape full formalization;
—composition specialists organizing writing courses and composing books on discourse theory;
—cosmologists studying the kind of "chaos" that is actually organized;
—cultural anthropologists reducing the territory of nomothetic social science and pursuing instead what came to be called "local knowledge" and "thick descriptions";
—Divinity School professors organizing workshops in practical reason;
—economists writing entire books on the "rhetoric of economics";
—educationists protesting the reduction of pedagogy to computer models;
—Graduate Library School professors organizing seminars in communication theory;
—historians arguing for the cognitive force of narrative, or debating the "objectivity question," or urging the study of historiography;
—lawyers dealing with the appraisal of witnesses, or debating about critical realism;
—linguists pursuing, after decades of pure syntactics and semantics, a new pragmatics;
—literary critics studying the same problem under words like "irony" and "disambiguation";
—mathematicians studying fuzzy sets;

—philosophers of science studying how adherents of conflicting paradigms do actually sometimes manage to communicate across seemingly impenetrable border lines;

—professors of French studying the sources and consequences for Montaigne's kind of argument of Montaigne's kind of skepticism;

—professors of Italian rediscovering Vico's powerful new science;

—psychoanalysts and philosophers inventing a new term, "ethogenics," for the study of behavior as *generated* by persons who inescapably exhibit a character, an ethos;

—sociologists studying how people get together or fall apart through ambiguous convention;

—statisticians studying how we deal with uncertainties that escape simple numeration;

—students of "informal logic" rehabilitating many of the so-called "fallacies," such as the *argumentum ad hominem*;

—theologians and professors of Far-Eastern languages studying hermeneutics;

—urbanologists studying conflict resolution in the ghetto;

[But I must here cut another page of Hythloday's account, on down through increasingly imperialistic claims that his field covers not only urologists, Western European Studies, and the Writing Tutors program, but even the zoologists and their study of communication among our siblings, the chimpanzees.]

It was as late as 1997 [Hythloday continues] before we instituted the present requirement that every dean and provost, on taking office, enroll in a training course in the three rhetorics necessarily exercised in such offices. The course includes a study of how to appraise witnesses, with readings both from that part of legal training that deals with the subject and from that part of the classical tradition that teaches appraisal of ethos. When are we, in fact, justified in trusting a testimonial? What are the marks of a reliable letter of recommendation? Just what kinds of departmental rhetoric should a provost attend to? What are the true qualities of character that qualify a man or woman to become a citizen of the University of Polytopia? Soon we found that the bibliographies of rhetorical study, formerly consulted by few, were in universal demand. The library could not meet the demand for Aristotle's *Rhetoric*; photocopiers were kept busy duplicating the works of Cicero and Quintilian, now sold out.

Finally, we found ourselves organizing, as the major annual university-wide, College-sponsored event, the Liberal Arts Conference that has for nearly five decades now dragged departments, sometimes still kicking and screaming, into confrontation with each other about the rhetoric of the so-called disciplines and the rhetoric of the so-called interdisciplines. A key moment in that conference has come to be the annual Ryerson lecture, sponsored by the board of trustees and delivered by a faculty member who has been required, since an early date that we have not been able to discover, to address either the rhetoric of his or her discipline, as it relates to rhetorics-2 and -3, or as it relates to the rhetoric-1 of other disciplines.

A recent visitor asked us why the University of Polytopia has never followed Berkeley and Davis (in the California system), Virginia, Carnegie Mellon, Iowa, and others, in establishing a Department of Rhetoric. But is not the answer obvious? A *university* run by a faculty whose members, while cultivating their own gardens, insist on looking over the garden fence and even visiting with the neighbors—such a university has no need for a department of rhetoric. With most faculty members now pursuing new specialties, discovered where previous disciplines had overlapped without their defenders' quite knowing it, just about everyone practices rhetorology in order to teach the rhetorics better.

Everyone reading this report today will know that we have not discovered, in all this innovation, any easy, cheerful harmony. New and seemingly irreconcilable differences have turned up as we have faced hitherto-unsuspected problems. And it is easy for us now, though it was hard for scholars back in 1987, to see the grand difference between our polytopian achievement and their utopian dreams. First, we have not called for or depended on any fundamental changes in human nature; we look for no great and unlikely upsurge of benevolence. Some increase in the exercise of benevolence and mutual trust does seem to have *resulted* from our changes, but the changes did not depend on them, and the kind of critical trust we exercise with one another does not depend now on loving-kindness or even everyday courtesy. Secondly, nothing we have done has required any imposition of radical structures by some powerful philosopher-president. We have always left the departmental structures intact, except where disciplinary discoveries have produced natural reshapings. In short, everything we have done is based on observing what we already did, in 1987, in coping with our pandemic polytopicality and the universal ignorance that sprang from it. We simply urged all scholars to observe how they worked when they felt best about their work—and then to pursue that best, in the service of their own deepest interests. Incidentally, one of the main intellectual rewards of all this was the abandonment, once and for all, of that old shibboleth, a Unified Language of All the Sciences. Our *university* does not now exhibit, nor does it ever hope to exhibit, a single language applicable to all worthwhile inquiries. Instead, we proliferate, we multiply, we rejoice in variety. We have not, it is true, discarded Occam's razor entirely; it still does some service in the rhetoric-1 of most fields. But the law we most celebrate is no longer the law of parsimony; it is instead the law of fructification: "Never pursue a problem without at least two hypotheses—and don't despair when two or more of them survive your tests. And never forget that all human problems resist reduction to any one formulation or method of inquiry."

Well, that ends my selection from Hythloday's report from the University of Polytopia. I confess that what he has to say makes me even more uneasy than I was when I began: I am not at all clear where I might personally come out, if judged by his norms of vigorous intellectual curiosity sustained into the later years of life.

But I must also confess, abandoning now all ironies, that I do dream of living in a university somewhat more like the one he describes than the present University of Chicago. I love the life in this university as it is, but I see us as increasingly engaged in the futile pursuit of top prize as a *multiversity*. Surely it is not unrealistic, not the least bit utopian, to hope that we might resist the various temptations thrust on us by international competition, and instead set our own course, as we have often—quite miraculously, when you come to think about it—set our own course in the past.

Index

335

Index

Cosmology, 331
Cost-benefit analysis, 313
Council for Basic Education, 30
Courage, 70, 206, 232, 308; as scholarly ideal, 66; as threat, 270
Courses, staff taught, 330
Coverage: desired by public, 272 (*see also* "Cultural literacy"); as dispensable, 253; as mistaken goal, 82
Crane, Ronald S., v, 17, 291, 293, 300
Creativity, 178–79. *See also* Novelty
Credulity, as effect of journalism, 141–50
Crews, Frederick, 76
Crick, Bernard, 38–39
Crises, proclaimed, 129–32
Crisis of confidence, as unnecessary, 21, 90–100
Critical reader, training of, as ideal goal of journalism, 141–50
Critical realism (in legal studies), 315, 331
Critical theory. *See* Theory, critical
Critical thinking, as goal of "English," xii, 7–9, 31, 78, 199, 237. *See also* Thought, critical
Critical understanding, 21–23, 25, 128; defined, 21; as goal of "English," 78, 93 (*see also* Critical thinking); as self-defense, 33–35; as unpredictable, 27
Critical Understanding (Booth), 242, 249
Criticism, 8; of circumstances, 203–5; as destructive of eloquence, 279; as freezing, 275–76; history of, 254; of metaphors, 203–4
Criticism, literary, 5–6, 17, 44, 47, 59, 301, 331; as pursuit of wisdom, 301; specialized language in, 315
Culler, Jonathan, 6
Cultural anthropology, 315, 331
"Cultural literacy," 31, 43n, 88, 267; dangerous current simplification of, 212
Cultural Literacy (Hirsch), xii, 212
Cummings, E. E., 206
Curiosity, xvii, 64, 170, 256, 329; as center of education, 62–64; about what is worth knowing, 170
Curricula: deficiencies of, 9–10; designing of, 107–8; by democratic vote, 158; graduate, 76, 89; graduate, tied to undergraduate teaching, 89; reform of, 105; systematic, 92

Daedalus, 143
Dalby, Max, 16

Dartmouth international conference on "English," 92
Darwin, Charles, 146
"Decision research," 331
Deconstruction, xii, 79, 82, 86, 107, 275; as rhetorical, xv, 36n
de Man, Paul, 81, 84, 274
Democracy, 12, 118, 166
—education in principles of: as task of journalism, 149; as goal of "English," 42, 115, 117, 267, 269, 272
Democratic education, noble dream of, 269
Democratic equality, as possible threat to education, 166
Denham, Robert, 270
Derrida, Jacques, 6, 9, 36n, 81, 84, 315
Descartes, 245
Description, not value-free, 327
Despair, as error, 99
Desperation of young teachers, 263–64
De Vries, Peter, 210
Dewey, John, 58, 92, 94, 178
Dialectic, xv, 8, 10, 83
"Dialogics," 9
Dichotomies questioned: action/passion, 285; aesthetic/didactic, 22; altruism/selfishness, 188; art/practicality, 285; avant-garde/traditional, 26; critical/historical, 26; didactic/mimetic, 291; elementary/advanced, 21; ends/means, 285; fact/value, 67n, 93, 146–48, 284, 285; faith/reason, 93, 94, 146; head/heart, 146–48; human arts / practical or technical arts, 129; ideological/objective, 26; intrinsic/extrinsic, 301; knowing/doing, 284; knowing/making, 284; knowledge/experience, 285; language of truth / language of power, 129; literature/rhetoric, 25; mimetic/expressionist, 288; objective/subjective, 22, 36, 69, 93, 147; private pleasures / public goods, 22; professional/intellectual, 162, 163; publish/perish, 240; pure/applied, 284; reason/emotion, 324; reason/faith, 93, 94, 146; research/teaching, 162–64, 240; rhetoric/reality, 22, 32–43; rhetorical/aesthetic, 26; scholar/society, 50; science/religion, 148; social utility / personal fulfillment, 194; theory/experience, 285; theory/practice, 21–22, 284; thought/feeling, 94; truth/commitment, 149; truth/action, 285; whole man / subject matter, 161